COPING WITH UNCERTAINTY

Coping with Uncertainty

Youth in the Middle East and North Africa

Edited by Jörg Gertel and Ralf Hexel

SAQI

Published by Saqi Books 2018

ISBN 978-0-86356-960-9
eISBN 978-0-86356-970-8

First published in Great Britain in 2018 by

Saqi Books
26 Westbourne Grove
London W2 5RH
www.saqibooks.com

A full CIP record for this book is available from the British Library.

Typeset by Charles Peyton (charlespeyton@gmail.com)

Printed in Lebanon

Published in partnership with

Contents

PART IV: COMPARING YOUTH

APPENDICES

Preface

Ralf Hexel

Coping with Uncertainty: Youth in the Middle East and North Africa, a project of the Friedrich-Ebert-Stiftung, was produced in partnership with the University of Leipzig, Kantar Public (formerly TNS Infratest Politik-forschung), TNS Morocco, and research centres and polling institutes in the respective countries of the Middle East and North Africa (MENA).[1] A scientific advisory board of renowned researchers from the MENA region and Germany developed the scientific concept for the study and the questionnaire used.[2] The University of Leipzig drafted the comprehensive questionnaire of approximately 200 questions in close cooperation with the scientific advisory board and the other project partners.

The study is oriented towards two overarching questions: What does the situation look like for the youth six years after the so-called Arab Spring?[3] How do young people deal with the new insecurities and uncertainties of their everyday lives? An attempt is made to close knowledge gaps with a wide range of questions, because the everyday situation of young people in the MENA region has never been thoroughly investigated transnationally and systematically, and, to date, only limited findings have been available.

---

1. The study has also been published in Arabic – مأزق الشباب في الشرق الأوسط وشمال أفريقيا (Beirut, Dar al-Saqi, 2018) – and in German – *Zwischen Ungewissheit und Zuversicht. Jugend im Nahen Osten und in Nordafrika* (Bonn, Verlag J.H.W. Dietz, 2017).

2. The members of the scientific advisory board were Prof. Dr Mathias Albert (University of Bielefeld), Prof. Dr Asef Bayat (University of Illinois), Professor Emeritus Dr Hajo Funke (Free University of Berlin), Prof. Dr Jörg Gertel (University of Leipzig), Dr Sonja Hegasy (Leibniz-Zentrum Moderner Orient, Berlin), Dr Ghassan Khatib (Birzeit University, Ramallah), Prof. Dr Rachid Ouaissa (University of Marburg), Prof. Dr Hassan Rachik (Université Hassan II, Casablanca), Junior Professor Dr Nadine Sika (American University of Cairo), and Dr Isabelle Werenfels (Stiftung Wissenschaft und Politik, Berlin).

3. The term 'Arab Spring' is controversial, both in the region as well as in international scholarly debate, because the seasonal connotation of spring as the beginning of an imminent positive time or development. The authors of the study are aware of this but have decided to use the term despite this ambivalence.

For the survey, interviews were conducted with some 9,000 young people aged 16–30 in eight countries in the MENA region: Bahrain, Egypt, Jordan, Lebanon, Morocco, Palestine, Tunisia, and Yemen, as well as Syrian refugees living in Lebanon. Thus some 1,000 young people from each country, including Syrian refugees, consented to be interviewed in summer 2016 for sixty minutes. In addition, qualitative interviews were conducted in winter 2016/17, because not all aspects of everyday life, values, and social orientation can be assessed in purely quantitative terms. The names of these respondents have been changed for publication.

The MENA region is in a state of fundamental crisis and upheaval characterised by military conflicts, terrorist attacks, state collapse, and long-running socio-economic problems. This affects young people in unique ways. The authors of the study therefore chose 'insecurity' and 'uncertainty' as key terms for capturing and describing their situation. Insecurity applies to living conditions and the availability of resources, while uncertainty concerns how they deal with the future as regards their hopes and dreams.

Young people in the MENA region often face the challenge of dealing with fear-filled insecurities in their everyday lives, but at the same time they have hopeful visions of the future. This publication presents examples of how they function in increasingly difficult and conflict-laden circumstances and find solutions to the problems they face. It is noteworthy that the majority of these young adults remain confident about the future despite economic disadvantage, lack of political participation, and the pervasive sense of insecurity that varies from country to country. This is particularly surprising given the disappointed hopes of the Arab Spring uprisings of 2010–11, in which young people in particular were involved. Although their economic situation and social participation have since declined, they are often optimistic about life. Fewer than 10 percent of young people are firmly intent on emigration. Due to their difficult situations, however, they are torn between constantly recurring thoughts of emigration and their strong bonds to their families and their homeland.

Young people are the key players in shaping the future of the MENA region. Those aged 15–29 now account for 30 percent of the population, their highest percentage ever. Their attitudes, values, and visions are clear indicators of possible future developments in the societies in which they live. While the political and economic situations in the MENA countries currently offer little room for optimism, the results of the study paint a picture of young people who are better educated than ever, who are strongly attached to their homeland, who have a positive approach to life, and who are ready to take responsibility and engage socially. The prevailing authoritarian power structures in the majority of their countries, however, prevent them from effectively contributing their talents, knowledge, and commitment in shaping their own lives and their societies. The region will experience stability and development only if young people are able to participate politically and economically in shaping the future. For this to occur requires success in establishing more inclusive societal models.

The present study provides an empirically based contribution to the debate on young people in the MENA region, helping frame it by presenting a broader set of information. The results of the study represent an invitation to further discussion and comparisons of current insights in light of the new findings presented here.

On behalf of the Friedrich-Ebert-Stiftung, I would like to thank all of the institutions and individuals that contributed to the preparation of the study. Under sometimes very difficult conditions, they found a way to conduct interviews and otherwise communicate with thousands of young people in the MENA region, to record and evaluate relevant data, and to analyse these data scientifically. Through admirable teamwork and coordination, contributors from eleven countries produced an assessment that represents a major contribution to the study of young people in the MENA region.

I would like to thank the following people in particular: the members of the scientific advisory board, whose knowledge and expertise laid the foundation for the scientific quality of the study; the study co-editor Prof. Dr Jörg Gertel from the University of Leipzig, whose conceptual and substantive contributions significantly shaped the study; my colleague Dr Friederike Stolleis, who coordinated the study's editorial work and also made important contributions to its content; and Helmut Dietrich, who coordinated the surveys in the participating countries under difficult conditions.

The survey results underlying this study, which have been summarised in tables and graphics, are available at http://www.fes.de/lnk/youth-study.

INTRODUCTION

1

Youth in the MENA Region, 2016–17

Jörg Gertel

Coping with Uncertainty: Youth in the Middle East and North Africa addresses two questions: What does the situation look like for youth six years after the so-called Arab Spring? How do young people deal with the new insecurities and uncertainties of their everyday lives? In recent years, terrorism, armed conflicts, and wars have become more prevalent in the Middle East and North Africa (MENA), while economic conditions and labour markets have deteriorated in many Arab states, often hitting young people the hardest. The actual situation of youth, however, is largely unknown inside as well as outside the MENA region. In the wake of the social and political upheavals of 2011, renewed interest emerged about the region's young people, often regarded as the protagonists of the Arab Spring uprisings. Numerous studies, national surveys, and small-scale analyses have been published, but systematic, transnational research on the MENA youth, based on intensive and comparable individual interviews, has not, however, been conducted – until now.

The empirical findings of this study reveal the various uncertainties faced by young people in the MENA region. Two structural dynamics coincide in their lives. On the one hand, adolescence, a sensitive period in life, is characterised by the insecurity of finding one's own position and role in society. The transition to adulthood is uncertain at many stages even under the best of circumstances. On the other hand is the more recent situation of precariousness and unstable social conditions that has rendered the period of youth in the region even more difficult. Insecurity manifests itself as exposure to violence and a lack of resources, hindering one's capability to act. Therefore, while insecurity affects these youths' everyday lives, uncertainty relates to the future. What kind of tactics and strategies help young people cope with angst-producing uncertainty and permit them to live confident lives?

This publication provides answers to this question and presents the key results of some 9,000 interviews of young people in the Arab world aged 16–30.[1] The aim of the study is to open up space to analyse the situation of youth in the Arab world more comprehensively than previously possible. The focus is on eight countries, which allows for examining a wide range of daily life in the MENA region: Bahrain, Egypt, Jordan, Lebanon, Morocco, Palestine, Tunisia, and Yemen. In addition, young Syrian refugees living in Lebanon were included to discern issues and problems concerning migration and flight in the region.

This chapter introduces the surveyed countries and target groups, followed by discussing the study's design, including the context of current youth research. The individual chapters of the present volume and findings are then summarised.

The MENA Region

Any multi-country study must address the question of whether individual states can be meaningfully compared at all. The development discourse offers insight into juxtaposing national developments. Identifying, measuring, and comparing the so-called development status of countries, as in Table 1.1 for the MENA countries, has been controversial for decades. One position assumes incommensurability, arguing that non-comparable entities and often un-measurable properties are forcibly and incorrectly related to one another by an arbitrary application of numerical indicators (Crush 1995; Escobar 1995). In contrast, another position emphasises that only through aggregated statistical statements can non-observable phenomena be identified, categorised, and investigated (Simon 2006). Finally, there are considerations that topics and topologies, regardless of the methodology by which they are examined, are shaped discursively. They are coined, for instance, by power asymmetries, political desires, or economic interest (Pieterse 2001). In post-colonial situations, like in the Arab world, this may result in the establishment and perpetuation of a supposed inferiority of countries through improper comparisons (Sachs 1992). These arguments should be kept in mind when countries under consideration are classified on the basis of statistical criteria.

For several years, levels of development have been measured according to the Human Development Index (HDI), which examines income in addition to life expectancy and education (see Table 1.1). According to HDI

---

1. Additional empirical findings by country are available online, http://www.fes.de/lnk/youth-study.

Table 1.1 **Development Indicators of Arab Countries**

	Bah-rain	Leba-non	Jordan	Tuni-sia	Pales-tine	Egypt	Mo-rocco	Ye-men	Syria
Human development	**Very high**	**High**			**Medium**			**Low**	
HDI Rank	44	65	77	90	107	110	129	154	118
HDI Index (2013)	0.82	0.77	0.75	0.72	0.69	0.68	0.62	0.50	0.66
GDP (2011–2013)	42,400	16,600	11,400	10,800	4,500	10,700	7,000	4,000	10,700
Population (2013)	1.3	4.8	7.3	11.0	4.3	82.1	33.0	24.4	21.9
Urban population	89	88	83	67	75	44	58	34	57
Literacy rate	95	90	98	80	96	74	67	66	85
Guest worker remittances (% GDP)	..	18	12	4	..	6	7	4	3
Youth unemployment	5	17	29	35	41	34	19	34	36
Internet users	88	61	41	41	..	44	55	17	24

Source Arab Human Development Report (UNDP 2016).

Note All figures are rounded | The table includes the countries investigated in the recent study; Syria was added in order to portray the situation before the armed conflicts in 2011. HDI Index = Human Development Index and is based on three indicators: life expectancy, education, and income. GDP = Gross Domestic Product (per capita in US dollars, calculated on the basis of purchasing power parity). Population is expressed in millions of people. The urban population is given as a percentage of the total population. The literacy rate is reported as a percentage of the total population that is 15 years of age and older. Remittances from guest workers are represented as a percentage of GDP. Youth unemployment is expressed as a percentage and refers to the age group of 15–24 (2008–2013). It should be noted here that it is difficult to measure unemployment, because hardly any formal, institutionalised vocational training exists in the MENA region; additionally, the line between work and non-work, as well as between paid work within and outside of the formal sector – with often changing activities, fluctuating work periods, and payments in the informal sector – is very difficult to draw (see Chapter 7). Internet users are displayed as a percentage of the total population for 2012.

categories, Bahrain has a very high level of development, in 2013 ranking forty-fourth worldwide. Lebanon, Jordan, and Tunisia have achieved a high level of development, while Palestine, Egypt, and Morocco are at a mid level. Yemen has a low level of development, ranked 154th globally. The countries in this study thus represent the spectrum from wealthy to poor and in this way frame various different conditions that affect young people.

National incomes in the MENA region are quite unequal. In Bahrain, which serves as an example of a prosperous country, citizens earn threefold the per capita income of the Lebanese and more than tenfold the average income of Yemenis. In terms of demographics, Egypt is the largest country, with more than 80 million inhabitants, and Bahrain, with 1.3 million, is the smallest. At the same time, Bahrain, like Lebanon and Jordan, is highly urbanised, while in Yemen, Morocco, Egypt, and Tunisia, rural areas and agriculture still play important roles. Moreover, the Arab countries vary in their dependence on remittances, tourism, and foreign investment. In recent years, however, the economic situation has worsened in the region overall, and youth unemployment rates are high.

Terrorist attacks, armed conflicts, and war continue to shape the everyday lives of many people. Yemen is affected on multiple fronts – by war, hunger, starvation, and the spread of infectious diseases. In summer 2017, some seven million people suffered from acute malnutrition, and more than 300,000 suspected cases of cholera were reported. Syria is crumbling into spheres of influence and conflict zones, and hundreds of thousands of people have been killed by acts of war. Another 12 million people have fled: Syrians have become internally displaced persons or refugees in neighbouring countries, including in Lebanon. Syrian refugees in Lebanon represent an extremely vulnerable group that has increasingly become part of everyday reality in the MENA region.[1] Meanwhile, Palestine continues to be shaped by Israeli occupation, and in many other places the security situation is tense.

The Study

In view of the political upheavals and problematic security situation in some MENA countries, simultaneously conducting thousands of face-to-face interviews lasting more than an hour each represents a conceptual as well as a logistical challenge. Nevertheless, within the framework of the present study, approximately 9,000 young people aged 16–30 were interviewed over the course of a few weeks in summer 2016 (see Appendix 1: Methodology) Three characteristics shape the sample: covering a variety of stages in young people's lives; the ability to make comparisons among and between countries; and the representative nature of the study including the weighting factors at work.

Given the wide age range of the sample, people at different phases of life and responsibility are covered. On the one hand are the group of young people who still live with their parents (69 percent), and on the other the group of young adults who live with their partners (29 percent).[2] The latter are mostly married and in some cases have children of their own. Those living with their

---

1. In 2014, 41 percent of forcibly displaced people worldwide were recorded as being in Arab countries, although they represent only 5 percent of the global population. In addition, for each person who dies in armed conflict, three to fifteen others die indirectly from illnesses, medical complications, and nutritional deficiencies (UNDP 2016: 39).
2. A small group, 2 percent, live in other configurations.

parents see themselves primarily as youth (95 percent), as do those with their own households (83 percent). Only a small group of them classify themselves as adults (17 percent). This suggests that about two-thirds of interviewees are tied closely to their parents: they live together, eat together, or support each other financially. In short, they still form a unit of reproduction. This economic, social, and emotional interdependence on their families of origin also holds for young adults with their own households. The structure of the sampling thus allows for the empirical investigation of the transitions from childhood to the adult world and the processes shaping this passage. The process includes, for example, transitioning from education and training to professional life, establishing a partnership or marriage, moving from the parents' home, and starting a family and having children. This alone makes it clear that 'youth' as a single group does not exist. As noted, even the majority of married people still consider themselves to be youth.

The structure of the sample – 1,000 respondents per country – allows for comparing and contrasting the findings between countries. All overarching information – for example, averages for the 9,000 respondents – relates to the nine target groups (i.e. eight countries and the group of Syrian refugees in Lebanon). This generates the effect of each country being equally important, independent of the aspect examined. For example, aspects of demographically tiny Bahrain are compared with populous Egypt, which has 63 times more inhabitants. Thus, while Bahrain and Egypt are vastly different in population size, in terms of economic activity, one can see that the citizens of Bahrain earn an average of four times as much income as Egyptians. However, the overarching findings should not be viewed as representative of the entire MENA region or of the Arab countries. Rather, they represent the study universe of the nine target groups, whereby each country and the Syrian refugees are attributed the same weight. Moreover, the sample size only allows limited analysis of internal differences within each country. In addition, one should keep in mind that spatially manifested differences within countries are more sensibly understood from settlement sizes than in relation to administrative distinctions between urban and rural areas, which are delineated differently from country to country (see Table 1.1).

Three weighting factors structured the sampling of respondents. The selection of respondents and the subsequent weighting ensured that gender ratio and age distribution correspond to each country's actual demographics, and the regional distribution of the sampling also corresponds, with a few exceptions, to the distribution of the population according to national administrative units (see Appendix). While gender relations and

Table 1.2 Characteristics of Surveyed Youths and Young Adults

	Bah-rain	Leba-non	Jordan	Tuni-sia	Pales-tine	Egypt	Mo-rocco	Ye-men	Syrian Refugees[d]
Human development	**Very high**		**High**			**Medium**		**Low**	
Men/Women	51/49	52/48	52/48	50/50	51/49	51/49	50/50	52/48	50/50
Age (Ø)	23	23	23	23	22	23	23	23	24
Arabic as native language	100	99	100	100	100	100	93	100	99
Knowledge of English	94	60	20	44	30	28	14	5	10
Describes self as youth	96	88	100[b]	95	95	85	93	92	83
Education[a]									
– Low	1	14	14	10	4	25	26	49	64
– Medium	20	21	46	28	27	30	35	15	26
– High	79	65	40	62	69	45	39	36	10
Marital Status									
– Single	73	80	72	87	68	72	87	55	43
– Married	26	19	27	13	31	27	13	43	55
– Other	1	1	1	0	1	1	0	2	2
Occupation									
– Pupil/student	56	41	30[c]	39	42	32	44	26	2
– Not working	21	25	57	44	35	49	42	61	54
– Paid work	23	34	13	17	23	19	14	13	44

Questions 1, 3, 4, 11, 14, 22, 23, 25, 27, 65, 66, 67.

Note n=9,000 · All figures are displayed as percentages (except for 'Age', here the average age is given; ø = average). Rounding errors may occur. | [a] Education: in order to compare different national educational systems, only the situation of the oldest group (26–30 Years; n=2,867) is considered here. 'Low' includes illiterates, those who are able to read and write, and everyone who has a primary school education; 'Middle' refers to everyone with an intermediate school education; and 'High' to everyone who gained at least high school education, including all those with a college degree. [b] In Jordan, only people who described themselves as 'Youth' participated in the survey. [c] For legal reasons, only people who were at least 18 years old participated in the survey in Jordan. Accordingly, the number of pupils is smaller. [d] Syrian Refugees in Lebanon.

age distribution are balanced and in accordance with national distributions, the empirical findings reveal considerable internal segmentations among young people (Table 1.2). For example, they are quite different in terms of family status and education. Depending on the country, 43 to 87 percent are single, while 13 to 55 percent are already married. As for education, in Bahrain, for example, 56 percent of respondents are students, while only 2 percent of the Syrian refugees are. Employment status also varies. In the majority of countries, 13 to 23 percent of young people work for pay, while in Lebanon 34 percent are employed; and 44 percent of the Syrian refugees living there also work. Thus, very different national contexts characterise the situation of young people in the MENA region.

Concerning methodology, the quantitative statistical findings have been supplemented by the results of more than 100 qualitative surveys. At least ten were conducted in each country. These in-depth interviews were carried out during December 2016 and January 2017 and involved people who had previously participated in the quantitative survey (see Appendix, 1: Methodology). The six-month gap between the quantitative and qualitative surveys permitted discussion of the first empirical findings with young people. Individual statements from the interviews contextualise the findings presented here.

The following personal positions on the question of what constitutes youth are presented by way of introduction to highlight the spectrum of thought on being a youth and young people's self-perceptions in the MENA region:

> I think that part of youth is doing sports, going to clubs, travelling, and enjoying life. As a young person, I have dreams and plans that I want to achieve. I think about the future, about my children, and what I will provide for them, for example, what education they receive.
>
> Mariam, 26, married, works as a teacher in Bahrain (BA-3)[1]

> In our time, to be young means to enjoy life, to continue with my studies, and at the same time to enjoy my life to the maximum. The time of youth is the most important in life. As young people, we are exposed to many events, and we gather many experiences from different people. This allows us to plan for our future lives.
>
> Hanna, 20, single, from Casablanca, Morocco (MA-10)

> There is no doubt that the circumstances that determine our lives today are harder than ever before. I believe the previous genera-

---

1. The following codes represent the number of the qualitative interview undertaken in the respective country (here: Bahrain; see also Appendix 1: Methodology)

tions had a more comfortable life compared to us. They lived their lifestyle in quieter and more stable times. Our lives are fundamentally different from the start, because we grew up with revolutions, unstable conditions in public spaces, the loss of security, the absence of the police, and the experience of several unexpected changes in government.

> Sara, 17, student, from Bani Suef, Egypt (EG-2)

Youth is the basis of society and the foundation on which it is built. I mean that the young man is the one who establishes the family. He becomes the spouse and father, the brother who has a position in his country. In order to become a member of society, we must first find a job that permits a standard of living to establish a family, to start a career, and to have aspirations that can grow. At present, I believe young people have no aspirations, because we can't find work. So how can we start a family, live, eat, or drink? We are not at all safe. Every day we hear of bombs. My sense of security has diminished because of many things. We are experiencing all kinds of violent acts, like explosions and gun battles. When I go out into the streets, I'm not sure I'll return home uninjured.

> Muataz, 29, married, works in Giza, Egypt (EG-3)

As a young man, I am forced to work hard, here or elsewhere. Youth is a time for hard work. The future is unclear and unstable, but I hope for better living and working conditions and also with regard to living standards.

> Samir, 26, Ramallah, Palestine (PS-4)

I regularly went to the internet cafe to meet people my age [online], from here and from abroad, for example the USA. I know I work hard and live 'hand to mouth'. I am not even able to improve my situation or to enhance my possibilities of buying an apartment. I do not mean that I feel like I'm worth less, but I do feel that they have better opportunities there than we have here. They work, and the state helps them, and their parents help them. I do not blame my father for it. It's not his fault, but we really struggle with the conditions. This is particularly true of the past five years – that is, the period after the revolution and the poor economic conditions that we have at the moment. I have only one vocational school certificate, so I am far from thinking about getting married. This has now become almost impossible. Marriage means having an apartment and that means half a million Egyptian pounds [about 25,000 euros]. I don't have that. It is hard enough to be well fed. I work just to be able to survive.

Ahmad, 20, works as an electrician in Egypt (EG-8)

These statements illustrate the dynamics of youth as a stage in life. For some, it is a time to enjoy life and fulfil dreams. For others, it means working hard and acting responsibly. For yet another group, what stands out is that being a youth today is not comparable to the experiences of earlier generations. Given the recent economic problems in the MENA region, young people face increasing difficulties in fulfilling their expected social roles, while at the same time their access to new media offers them the possibility of relating their individual situations to others' experiences globally. These different positions are also apparent and are being addressed in the current research on youth.

Youth Research
Young people in the MENA region have rarely been the subject of social science studies. It is only in the postcolonial era – since the second half of the twentieth century – that 'youth' as a social category was conferred social relevance. Until then, the agrarian societies in the Middle East and North Africa primarily distinguished between children and adults. 'Adolescence' consisted of the very moment of passing from one life stage to the other, which was marked by such rituals (i.e. rites of passage) as marriage and the birth of one's children. Two events – the al-Qaida attacks of 11 September 2001 and the Arab Spring of 2010–11 – altered this outlook; public attention scale-jumped, shining an international spotlight on the young people of the region.

In earlier times, the social significance of youth was only of a temporary or passing nature. It meant young men could be recruited for military service, and youth repeatedly became the object of rhetorical engagements, for example, during independence movements and nation-building processes (Ouaissa 2014b; Hecker 2012). They also stood out in the 1970s and 1980s during protest campaigns against state austerity measures (Walton and Seddon 1994), and they made their presence visible during the Palestinian uprising (first intifada) (Larzillière 2004). In short, positive and negative images about youths have alternated over the past few decades (Bayat 2010b), but only in the new millennium did Arab youth attract international attention.

From the beginning, examinations of young people have been concerned with encapsulating their experiences conceptually and empirically (Bourdieu 1980). Three questions are relevant here: What does the term *youth* represent? Is there a social category within society that can be meaningfully described as 'youth'? If this category or class exists, how is it defined?

The debate on youth in the MENA region has for a long time been concerned almost entirely with the so-called youth bulge – the growing demographic importance of young people – as a starting point for the formation of a new social class (Dhillon 2008). Indeed, the proportion of young people in MENA societies has never been as high as it is today: those aged 15–29 account for 30 percent of the Arab population (UNDP 2016: 22). Nevertheless, age classifications as social groups remain arbitrary; simply applying an age range hardly serves to adequately delineate social groups. Indeed, several developments intersect when examining the emergence of youth as a socially relevant group.

Among these developments, institutions of socialisation, such as schools and universities, have emerged to make formal education of young people a standardised and mass phenomenon. At the same time, a bundle of transformations are shaping a new labour pool: agricultural labour is declining in importance; wage labour is replacing subsistence activities; child labour is increasingly shunned; and access to remunerated work is increasingly standardised. Simultaneously, urbanisation is growing rapidly, and a new leisure and consumer culture has emerged, often out of the urban fabric. Parallel to these socio-institutional changes responsible for forging youths as a social group, biological developments (i.e. puberty) and social transitions – such as the conclusion of one's education, the start of professional life, entry into the military as well as moving out of the parental living space, marrying, and having children – play a role in delimiting and defining the phases of youth.

The extent to which young people as a social group play a role in the development of a specific youthful habitus, or lifestyle, remains questionable (Bayat 2010b), as the sheer number of young people, with a multitude of everyday practices and life plans, manifests as diversity rather than uniformity. Post-colonial studies reveal that social categories are not fixed per se, but are continuously negotiated based on divergent and converging interests. From this perspective, both youth identities and youth as a category represent bundles of narratives within a plurality of discursive fields. This corresponds to the reflections of Bennani-Chraïbi (1994), who in the 1990s labelled identity formation as *bricolage culturel* to describe the 'constructed identities' of Moroccan youth (see also Schaeffer Davis and Davis, 1989).

With biographical transitions towards adulthood, in particular marriage, increasingly being postponed, the conditions for identity formation have once again changed. More and more young people who leave school and remain unemployed, as well as university graduates, lack the resources to buy or rent an apartment, a precondition for marrying, as the interview with Ahmad from Egypt illustrates. Instead of entering the world of adulthood, young people remain in 'waithood' (Singerman 2007), a kind of precarious latency that greatly prolongs the duration of youth (Dhillon and Yousef 2009; Honwana 2013). This phase is characterised by ambivalence and uncertainty.

On the one hand, this phase is an expression of economic problems and involves forced dependencies on the family and an absence of self-determination. Due to lack of work, young people must continue living with their families, which entails much more than merely 'waiting'. These young people are unable to disentangle or separate themselves from their narrow socialisation unit and to develop standing of their own. They become an enclosed group or 'contained youth' (Gertel 2017). On the other hand, this period may also generate creative and transformative potential. Identities may become more complex; different attitudes toward life unfold; and youth cultures develop. In contention with Mannheim's (1928) classical generation concept, and implicitly in the continuation of Bennani-Chraïbi's reflections, Emma Murphy asserts,

> In the case of Arab youth, individuals may move in and out of this generational narrative fluidly – experiences like unemployment, delayed marriage or political frustration draw people in, but the patchwork composition of contemporary youth identities means that nothing is set in stone, different components of the narrative have greater or lesser significance for individuals and at different points in time, and opportunities or material fortune can render it

less immediately relevant. (2012: 16)

Amidst the advancing global dissolution of national borders in terms of cultural flows and economic articulations, studies on youth culture have come to focus on group formation, the importance of peer groups, and sub-cultures, such as music scenes (Hecker 2012; Swedenburg 2012). It should, therefore, be kept in mind that while youth takes shape as a social category in the MENA region, its internal differentiation is simultaneously increasing.

Parallel to the establishment of youth as a social group, both the societal role and influence of young people have recently changed. They are not only regarded as actors for shaping the future, but are more precisely considered – especially in the African context – as 'social shifters' (Durham 2000) and 'social breakers and makers' (Honwana and DeBoek 2005). Young peo-ple in the Arab world are better educated than ever and are more media savvy than all other social groups (Braune 2008; Richter 2011; Transfeld and Werenfels 2016). Because many have English as a common language, they are increasingly able to form cross-border social networks. They were, temporarily, the central protagonists of the Arab Spring, kicking off various protest movements (Alhassen and Shihab-Eldin 2012; Khalaf and Khalaf 2012; Bayat 2017). Yet, since the uprisings of 2011, little has improved for them. To the contrary, their economic situation has deteriorated. Insti-tutional permeability has decreased, and social participation seems more difficult than ever. Their position in the societies of the MENA region is thus currently in question.

In the past ten years, the research landscape dealing with young peo-ple in the MENA region has become more diverse, more multilingual, and in some aspects more complex. German-, French-, and English-language works, in addition to Arabic and other languages, have been published. At the same time, the production of knowledge about youth has increasingly become a political arena shaped by a struggle for interpretation, which is often reduced to two perspectives: 'youth as a problem and danger' or 'the problems and dangers of youth'. Statistical data, especially those making transnational connections, remain rare. Detailed, aggregated, empirical findings explicitly about young people are thus difficult to access. Such studies are usually produced by government agencies within individual Arab countries and by market and opinion research. Yet civil society and international agencies are also interested in empirical surveys, as are private research institutes and public universities. This has resulted in a competitive field of knowledge production, which, to simplify, can be divided into two groups.

On the one hand, there are studies conducted by international organisations, national government authorities, semi-public organisations, market research companies, and public relations firms. These actors tend to take quantitative approaches (Lamloum and Ali Ben Zina 2015; Burson-Marsteller 2015). They use different survey methodologies, such as telephone inquiries, online surveys, and standardised questionnaires. Frequently, such studies focus on just one country, so coverage of the region is not comprehensive. When they adopt an interregional scale, their research often remains descriptive, with little analytical depth, and frequently relies on secondary data. Education, labour markets, and employment are favoured topics, along with labour migration and consumer behaviour. One crucial example of youth research is the *Arab Human Development Report 2016: Youth and the Prospects for Human Development in a Changing Reality* (UNDP 2016). No quantitative surveys were conducted for its compilation. Instead, its authors evaluated existing secondary data, such as that stemming from the World Value Survey, market and opinion research outfits like Gallup, and the World Bank. In many cases, information from national statistical institutes was also essential. Here, however, knowledge production is tied to institutional interests, which leaves its integrity open to doubt. In the case of the 2016 *Arab Human Development Report,* opaque editorial processes have been made public. In particular, it was shown that individual content was politically negotiated – for example, by submitting it to ambassadors for comment – and content subsequently censored (Al-Ali et al. 2016).

On the other hand are studies carried out by university and academic research institutions (Bonnefoy and Catusse 2013; Gertel and Ouaissa 2014; Hegasy and Kaschl 2007; Herrera and Bayat 2010). Here, different knowledge systems come together at an international level. As there are different national experiences with youth studies, as well as corresponding linguistic misunderstandings and lack of awareness of others' work resulting from insufficient language skills, however, the exchange remains limited. Qualitative approaches are usually preferred, using such methodologies as field research, qualitative surveys, target group discussions, and media analysis. Often, the choice of methodology is constrained, because the financial resources of academic research are limited, or elaborate approval procedures cannot be fulfilled.

Investigations in the MENA region have focused, for example, on questions of identity negotiation, youth cultures, and media use, as well as on political mobilisation, resistance, and protest. In the wake of the Arab Spring, the Sahwa Project (2014–17) and Power2Youth (2015–17), both consisting of international scholars funded by European resources, significantly broadened the research on youth in the region, generating new insights and identifying important research perspectives. This materialised in dozens of working papers, interviews documented on film, personal portraits, and conferences. The Sahwa Project, composed of Arab and European partners, examined transitions, transformation processes, and future perspectives in Morocco, Algeria, Tunisia, Egypt, and Lebanon. The work of Power2Youth, which analysed the causes and dynamics leading to the exclusion or inclusion of Arab young people in the labour market and civilian life, was largely based on existing quantitative data and addressed the transformational effects of individual and collective youth action. Its focus was on Morocco, Tunisia, Egypt, Lebanon, Palestine, and Turkey. In these cases, scholars have been quite critical of the policy goals associated with both these programmes. In a paper scrutinising the governability of youth, Catusse and Destremau contend,

> From a bird's eye view, the public policy discourse on youth and the 'youth problem' is abundant and sometimes excessive. Despite the institutions founded at the establishment of the regimes and dedicated to Youth [and] the installation of the youth problem as a major concern, a closer look brings to light the fact that concrete data and information about youth are often sparse and not always reliable. These institutions and concrete mechanisms for implementing policies are, in reality, not very significant. More often than not, they are empty shells, heavily politicised but with little means. (2016: 14)

Challenged by such considerations, the present study aims to make a contribution to situate the debate about young people in the MENA region on a more comprehensive, information and data basis. The following results thus represent an invitation to complementary reading – in other words, to reconcile familiar insights with the new findings presented here.

Study Focuses and Findings

Uncertainty

Jörg Gertel explores the meaning of uncertainty from conceptual and empirical perspectives. Uncertainty refers to what the future might hold; most, if not all of it, is unknown to us. The future cannot truly be foreseen. We know only to a certain extent how things will unfold. Nevertheless, individuals as well as societies are continually trying to hedge against uncertainty, orienting everyday life towards the future in trying to plan it. While uncertainty thus relates to the future, insecurity concerns the present and the capability to act. Respective tactics and strategies largely depend on access to resources. It is young people with poor resources who are particularly affected by insecurity. The analytical focus is therefore on the question of how securities are produced and for whom corresponding strategies tackling uncertainties are most successful.

Values

Jörg Gertel and David Kreuer investigate the values of young people in North Africa and the Middle East. Values are understood as orientation patterns and as reference points for individual and collective goals. The great multitude of values and scripts for life are subject to change; they are by no means stable or fixed. While fundamental institutions of socialisation – such as family and school – instil and transfer predominantly country-specific characteristics, three general aims stand out as a consequence of growing uncertainty. Resting on a foundation of respondents' almost uncontested and hopeful trust in God, these consist of a desire for justice, order, and security; a desire for an appropriate standard of living, which is often connected to obtaining an adequate job; and a desire for a trusting partner and good family relations. The authors reveal that four bundles of values – sense of community, orientation towards success, quest for freedom, and desire for decency – are important for today's youth in the region. Individual values and the realities of life, however, are complex, and given the disturbing experiences of war and violence, biographical disruptions become more common. Unconditional trust in God, however, a very personal matter, provides many with confidence, even in times of crises.

Religion

Rachid Ouaissa examines whether the increase in young people's religiousness, which has been observed for several years, reflects a rise in or return to religion or whether it represents individual strategies aimed at establishing one's own identity in an environment of tension brought about by pressures of globalisation and the longing for local culture. The empirical data at a glance paint a picture of MENA youths as rather pious. Women feel more religious than men. In general, heightened religiousness often starts after youths finish school and is found mainly in large towns and among the wealthy, especially when the father has a high level of education. In contrast, less religious youth hail from families with lower educational capital, that is, from society's lower middle and poor classes. In general, young people, as noted, consider religion first of all to be a private matter. Religiousness is a source of hope and optimism. Religion for the MENA youth today no longer serves political or ideological purposes, but instead centres on individual well-being and self-discipline, making it more of a channel for spirituality. Where one finds high degrees of piousness, it is primarily felt at the individual level, no longer in terms of a collective social utopia. Ouaissa interprets this as a decline in political religiousness and as an increase in social religiousness. This leads him to consider whether the Arab world is thus experiencing the beginning of a new secular age.

Gender

Ines Braune addresses the changing gender roles among young people in the MENA region. She argues that inequalities in Arab societies are often framed primarily as gender-specific, an approach that does not take into account other decisive factors and instead often obscures them. Focusing on four themes – marriage, education, future aspirations, and sexual harassment – she draws a picture that reveals both the interrelationship of different spheres of life and the shifts and further deterioration of intersectional inequalities. Here, armed conflicts, such as in Syria and Yemen, play a structuring role, as do certain attitudes shared by men and women. For example, while at first glance women appear to marry early, a more detailed analysis reveals that it is young people from the lower classes, men and women alike, who have taken this step. With regard to sexual harassment, the author shows that many more women are affected. That said, it also appears that young men and women hold equally misogynist attitudes, regardless of their level of education. Gender issues are thus always embedded in society and need to be addressed within social configurations.

Family

Christoph Schwarz analyses the role of the family and shows that it continues to play a role, indeed a key role, for young people in Arab countries. Especially in the case of financial need, the family and networks of relatives constitute the most important contacts. Young people themselves are interested in strong family ties, consider having their own children to be important, and would change little about their upbringing. At the same time, they are also pursuing autonomous goals in this regard, for example, wanting to select their own marriage partner. On the other hand, the question of marriage does not determine their self-perception as youth or adult, as is often assumed. Schwarz concludes that although economic and social opportunities for the youths' and parents' generations are different – the parents perhaps having had more opportunities due to the political and social realities of their youth – young people today generally do not hold this against the older generation or respond to it with misgivings, demands, or hostility.

Economics

Jörg Gertel investigates how young people – in the face of three decades of neo-liberal politics, including massive privatisation and the dismantling of the welfare state – are assessing their economic situation. With respect to their parents, the younger generation is affected by three dynamics: lack of job security, growing economic polarisation, and the failure of educational promise. Even with significantly improved education, social upward mobility has moved beyond the reach of many. Indeed, the abolition of the welfare state has been accompanied by a massive decline in reliable public employment. Today, only one-third of young people (pupils and students excluded) work in any capacity; all others are temporarily or even permanently without work. Even then, nearly one-half of this labour force is precariously employed. Thus the importance of the family as a social and economic security net continues and increases. Breaking with one's family is almost unthinkable for the current generation of contained youth, because few other institutions can cushion their economic insecurity. Insecurity hence becomes a chronic condition, with precariousness omnipresent. Today, young families starting out as well-educated, dual earners should have optimistic outlooks for the future, but instead they are constrained by massive economic problems. About half of the young men who are already head of a household judge the economic situation of their families to be 'rather bad' or 'very bad'. Thus, new social ruptures are evident. Exacerbating this situation, those young people still living with their parents are in a situation of 'borrowed security'; the dramatic impact of uncertainty hits the moment they leave their parents' household.

Middle class

Jörg Gertel and Rachid Ouaissa reveal that the Arab middle class, an important factor for social stability in past decades, is disintegrating. Young people are still able to identify their family's class, largely based on the education and occupation of their parents, but society has been polarised by a series of ruptures driven by two intertwined dynamics: over the last generation, shifts in employment structures have led to significant declines in economic security. More recently, this situation has been compounded by wars, armed conflicts, revolutions, and internal unrest, further shattering human security. In the process, the middle class has crumbled into various segments exhibiting differing degrees of instability and precariousness. As a result, the young generation finds itself involved in two ambivalent processes. First, with the dwindling stability of class positions, the young generation is losing an aspect of their social identity that once provided certainty. When social structures collapse, identifying with the state is no longer easy or a given, especially as regards its political practices. Second, political mobilisation – defined as the struggle for participation – is most pronounced among groups that have recently experienced social downward mobility. These experiences are ultimately reflected in the preferences of young people for specific political systems. Those amongst the economic winners – that is, the upper middle class – represent the largest group of those who desire a 'strong man' at the top of their country's leadership, while a religious system based on Islamic law is most often favoured by the lower middle classes and the poor. Although the majority, primarily embodied by the core of the middle class, still prefer a democratic system, this middle class is increasingly falling apart.

Hunger and Violence

Jörg Gertel and Tamara Wyrtki emphasise that in the context of growing uncertainty, two forms of security are decisive: securing basic needs and the absence of direct and structural violence. The latter includes malnutrition and hunger. The findings reveal the varying characteristics of food insecurity and violence affecting some young people. In Egypt and other import-dependent countries, for example, they often lack the purchasing power to acquire the food available. In Palestine, on the other hand, Israel's policies fuel poverty and food insecurity, amongst other things. Meanwhile in Yemen and Syria, millions of young people, including children, are threatened by war and hunger. They have experienced collapsed economies, breakdowns in social relations, and the death of family members. Often, even family members are no longer in a position to help each other. Thus, many young people are traumatised, feeling themselves hopeless, without prospects. According to the authors, long chains of transactions causally link spaces of hunger and violence (such as those within the MENA region) with spaces of profit (such as stock market trading floors), although territorially far apart. Insecurity is thus characterised by the disintegration of social responsibilities, while liabilities – concerning speculation and business deals contributing to war and hunger – have, until now, rarely been pinpointed.

Migration
Jörg Gertel and Ann-Christin Wagner scrutinise young people's mobility in the Arab world, an aspect of society often misjudged. The empirical findings reveal that only a small group, less than 10 percent of youth, is firmly committed to migration. Moreover, labour migration among them is usually to other Arab countries, and while the desire to work abroad is linked to historical, colonial, and linguistic connections to Europe; it remains limited. The opportunities made possible by virtual mobility, the fortification of many countries' external borders, and the high cost of migration have all contributed to this dynamic. Those affected by precarious situations are, however, torn between thoughts of migration and deep, emotional connections with their home countries and families. Emigration is thus by no means understood as a simple 'way out'. The authors reveal that mobility among young people is generally shaped by three mechanisms: readiness to change one's life plan, with single men exhibiting the greatest flexibility; previous migration experiences within the family network, which further increases the probability of individual mobility; and as a consequence of armed conflicts, with forced migration, including escape and asylum, being an everyday reality for many Arab youth. In countries hosting refugees, enforced immobility often constitutes additional uncertainties, exacerbating insecurities in everyday life.

Communication
Carola Richter explores the role new media plays in the everyday lives of young people in the MENA region. The coining of the terms 'Facebook

revolution', 'Twitter protest', and 'Al Jazeera effect' points to the seemingly immense political significance of new media. The author argues, however, that while media usage is converging globally – the same technologies and formats are available around the world – an internal shift in media use has appeared. Due to long-standing distrust of the media, and the recent withdrawal of the MENA youth from day-to-day politics, new media are increasingly solely used for private communications, in particular to maintain social networks. Smartphones, like no other devices, enable easy access to the internet and allow young people to keep in touch with friends and relatives as well as share music and pictures digitally. At the same time, traditional mass media, often state-controlled, remain present and continue to play a role for young people with limited access to digital media, such as in Yemen and with the Syrian refugees in Lebanon. Richter concludes that for young people, media-based communication works in two directions, as triggering and as coping mechanisms in dealing with the uncertainties of everyday life.

Politics

Mathias Albert and Sonja Hegazy deal with the importance of politics for youths, looking at how close to or far from politics they have positioned themselves six years after the events of the Arab Spring. Three findings are crucial. First, the 2011 uprisings show the potential for politicising young people in Arab countries, which in many cases allow only limited political participation. Second, a large majority of young people have distanced themselves from politics after the region's recent experiences, emphasising that they are no longer interested in politics. In doing so, however, they are often referring to party politics, because at the same time, they also express interest and commitments related to the arena of everyday politics. Third, in a seeming contradiction, a large proportion of young people want a greater state presence. This primarily concerns improved social security, which they think the state should provide in the face of growing uncertainty. Hence, the authors conclude that young people embody significant potential for constructive changes to the political order in the future.

Mobilisation

Nadine Sika and Isabelle Werenfels highlight political mobilisation among young adults. They conclude that the events of 2010–11 represent the climax of their political mobilisation geared towards changing state–society relations. In the aftermath of this, the question in many cases now concerns the extent to which youths are actors of change. Despite the disillusion of many with formal political processes in recent years, young people remain ready to become politically active. The areas in which they might act, however, have shifted. They are now more interested in standing up for socio-economic objectives than for political change. The findings reveal that young men aged 22–25 mobilise most frequently. This includes those who have experienced violence in their lives and those more pessimistic than others of their generation. Mobilised youth also show higher confidence in non-governmental organisations than non-activists do. Moreover, young people living in republics who experienced a regime change in 2011 appear to be more likely to mobilise than those from monarchies. The authors contend that in general, the politically active as well as the non-engaged are equally less interested in political freedom and civil rights – including minority rights – than in the security of basic needs and the absence of violence.

Civic Engagement

Friederike Stolleis analyses the civic engagement of young people in the MENA region. Based on the empirical findings, she underscores that they are generally willing to work for the interest of others as well as for social objectives and specific topics. Rarely, however, do they engage through formal civil society organisations (CSOs), such as school or student groups, youth groups, associations, religious institutions, political parties, and trade unions. Only one-third of those engaged become members in CSOs. While wealthier young people are more likely to be more active than poorer ones, they are rarely members of CSOs. Young people of the lower and middle classes are more strongly committed within the framework of such organisations. The latter are also more likely to be pessimistic and to have experienced uncertainty than their peers. According to the author, the motivations of today's young people differ from those of earlier generations. For the latter, civic engagement often occurred in the context of anti-colonial liberation movements or in relation to struggles for an independent state. With the change in young people's values and goals, and the firm grip with which the authoritarian states of the region control and co-opt civil society institutions, the institutions have obviously lost their appeal today.

Comparison with the German Shell Youth Study

Mathias Albert and Jörg Gertel compare the findings of the present study with the outcomes of the long-running German Shell Youth Study. The purpose of the comparison is to situate the empirical results of the MENA study within a broader societal context and to establish a reflective means for estimating the range of analytical explication. This is possible because some key concepts and fields of content in both studies not only overlap, but also explicitly relate to each other. The authors emphasise that while country-specific differences are crucial, they are in some ways greater within the MENA region than between individual Arab countries and Germany. In terms of commonalities between MENA and German youths (aged 16–25), the issue of security is first in almost all areas of daily life. This applies, for example, to labour market access and to personal security in general. It becomes obvious, however, that Arab youths often find themselves at structural disadvantages; they are often forced into greater dependences restraining, for example, the possibility of being successful in globalising labour markets.

§

In conclusion, the present study is predominantly empirical in nature. It enables, first of all, young people from the Arab world to 'speak', transmitting their voices to the general public. It is thus driven only to a limited extent by theoretical principles. The empirical findings, however, have not been generated in a theory-free environment, and their representation does not unfold in an unbiased or neutral political space. Hence, later discussions should examine the ambivalence of theoretical coining, problem orientation, and description on a case-by-case basis. It should be kept in mind that this is the first study of its kind on the MENA region. It will thus yield even more value as an instrument when it is repeated in later years, as in the case of the Shell Youth Study.

2

Uncertainty

Jörg Gertel

THIS CHAPTER INTRODUCES the conceptual dimension of uncertainty and illustrates, based on empirical findings, how uncertainties affect the everyday lives of young people in the Middle East and North Africa (MENA) and how the youth cope with them. The primary aim is to scrutinise their vulnerability within the context of growing insecurity within the MENA region in relation to group and country specificities. I argue that establishing security in its various forms serves as a means to hedge against uncertainties. But the strategies deployed to construct security are not only limited, they also vary in scope, depending on the structure of exposure and the resources available to one. Moreover, given the accelerated transformation of social conditions, previously successful strategies increasingly no longer work. Uncertainty and insecurity continue to expand, particularly affecting young people in the MENA region.

Generally speaking, uncertainty is part of everyday life. It relates to what the future holds. A great deal, if not everything in this regard, is unknown to us. It cannot be predicted. On the one hand, incidents to come are situated outside the realm of human influence. On the other hand, even if future events can be influenced, individual and societal actions will always entail uncertainties. Human action constantly generates unintended consequences, whereas reflexivity, the permanent coupling of action with the current state of knowledge, remains limited. Hence, we can know only to a certain extent how matters will develop. Regardless, individuals and societies constantly try to hedge against uncertainties, orienting certain aspects of everyday life towards the future in developing tactics and strategies in planning ahead.

Uncertainty is unequally distributed across space and time. It is not a constant, unchanging property of the future, but instead varies, depending on how it is perceived, experienced, and handled. The spectrum of uncertainty may encompass situations in which even the most basic of certainties involving knowledge about the immediate future is lacking. Take for example the context of war, when in specific situations it may be entirely unclear if one will survive for the next few seconds or minutes. Uncertainty is also part of long-term developments. For instance, one's future can be constrained by structural predispositions (e.g. access to education or property rights) that perpetuate or foster insecurities (e.g. hindrance to social mobility). This can even occur over the course of generations. Individual consequences, however, remain unclear.

There is one uncertainty to which young people in particular are exposed: they are required to emancipate themselves from sheltered family relationships to begin mastering the challenges of a globalised world. Adolescence represents the phase in life when ties to parents and the immediate socialisation context are gradually loosened. New roles are tried out, while personality and identity are formed. This is repeatedly linked to personal insecurities and uncertainties, which converge with general social constraints, and in the MENA region have recently been exacerbated by political instability, economic problems, and violent developments. Three questions are therefore addressed at the start of this chapter: How is uncertainty contained and security obtained? Which social transformations influence the way in which security is configured? What happens if previous strategies for coping with insecurities no longer work?

Hedging Uncertainty: The Production of Security
To ascertain how uncertainty can be contained, three arenas of human action are distinguished: the individual, the household, and the polity levels. Here, tactics and strategies are developed and materialise to generate various forms of securities within the realm of uncertainties. These arenas of action can often only be analytically delineated and separated from each other while in everyday life, they intersect and overlap and assume different meanings to particular individuals and groups. Neither the simple causality of the interrelations depicted here nor the spectrum of practices addressed in the following offer a complete picture of all the tasks that may be undertaken to contain uncertainties. They rather serve as examples to shed light on a number of conceptual starting points that offer insights into the possibility of producing security. These reflections draw on remarks by Giddens (1992) on the structuring of society and on Bourdieu's (1983) concept of capital.

The individual

At the level of the individual, biologically driven sensitivities, emotional and discursive processes combine and are deposited in various layers of consciousness or acted upon. It is from here that identities are negotiated. Structural forms of socialisation mesh in this process with the subjective production of experiences. Ontological security is of crucial importance in this regard. It offers confidence and trust that nature and the social world are as they appear, including the existential foundations of the Self and of social identity. The continuing search for ontological security aims to stabilise the capacity to act over the course of time. It is an attempt to counter uncertainty.

The repertoire of individuals' responses to uncertainty is articulated with different levels of action and in many ways dependent on them. The making of experiences and human action hence dovetail with respective societal contexts (Scott 1991). Given the limits to consciously reflexive action, much of ontological security is produced through routines that permeate daily life. Structured and pre-determined by routines, the implicit criteria for action are often only rendered explicit in the discursive consciousness during particular situations, above all in crises (Reckwitz 1999: 319). Such a situation unfolds, for example, when agents lose control, and their autonomy of action is stymied, when instability penetrates deep into the construction of the Self, for instance when violence is threatened or used, generating traumatic experiences.

Giddens (1992: 112) captures these 'critical situations' as events characterised by a radical, unpredictable caesura that affect many people simultaneously and threaten or destroy the certainties of routines. As a consequence, general unpredictability occurs. In such cases, when events or developments cannot be explained or mastered by oneself, or more generally, when ontological security is threatened, the question arises of when responsibility is delegated to expert systems or forces of faith. Calkins (2016) draws on situations of severe poverty and marginalisation in Sudan to identify delegation to the religious realm, that is, placing trust in God. In the chapters in this volume on values, religion, and hunger (Chapters 3, 4, and 9, respectively), interrelations between knowledge and faith are scrutinised in more detail with reference to young people in the MENA region to shed light on these dynamics.

The household

Solidarity-based relationships between individuals are, generally speaking, most strongly developed within kinship structures, often conceptually assessed as 'households'. In this arena, needs, such as material insecurities, are routinely counterbalanced, and its members engage in the redistribution of risks; those able to work provide for household members unable to work, and in many cases healthy family members care for sick relatives. The large arena of uncertainties, which these strategies strive to contain, pertains inter alia to the production of material security, to the 'economy of survival' (Elwert et al. 1983; Evers et al. 1983) or 'livelihood security' (Chambers and Conway 1987; Ellis 2000; Scoones 2015).

These approaches emphasise access to resources, as they constitute a fundamental pre-requisite for the capacity to take action. Basic needs and livelihood security are thus directly linked to being able to have command over resources. Giddens' notion of structure as a recursively organised set of rules and resources reveals the connection between (individual) actions and (social) structures. This perspective allows one to grasp the processes that by generating the conditions and possibilities for action by the individual within a given social context also subsequently enable the production of material and social securities. In reference to Bourdieu's work (1982, 1983), the empirical analysis here involves four forms of resources (Gertel 2007, 2010): incorporated resources, related to the body (e.g. education, nutritional status); institutionalised resources, tied to specific individuals (e.g. social networks); allocative resources, connected to property rights (e.g. ownership of land, machinery, livestock); and monetary resources, likewise based on property rights, but easy to exchange (e.g. money).

This approach to resources provides a conceptual basis for capturing complex social and economic processes empirically. It offers a means to quantitatively and qualitatively comprehend the mechanisms determining the handling of resources, for example at the household level, including the accumulation of resources, their convertibleness, and utilisation by third parties. Moreover, the consequences of actions – in the sense of habitual or institutional feedback that structure the conditions of livelihood security – can be traced back to the bodies of those affected. Societal developments are assumed to imprint individual bodies and shape incorporated resources. In this sense, as regards the first arena of action – the individual – the body should be comprehended as the ultimate entity of social space.

The polity

The third arena of action relates to the polity. This refers to groups, communities, and concerns overarching social forms. These range from the construction and the discursive power of language (topologies, categories, texts) to reproduced social practices and their materialisation in social institutions and formal organisations. This arena entails first and foremost the involvement of the state, which holds responsibility for generating institutionalised forms of security – for example, implementing its monopoly on the use of force within its territory, guaranteeing citizens' physical security, ensuring legal certainty, and fulfilling its welfare role and safeguarding citizens' basic needs.

The most comprehensive provision of social protection for citizens is associated with the welfare state (see Offe 1984). The state formulating and implementing social policy developed during the era of industrialisation in nineteenth-century Europe with the formation of nation-states and democratic decision-making processes. At the time, wage labourers were increasingly exposed to new risks and conditions, including accidents in the workplace and related disability and unemployment. Other conditions, such as illness and old age, were not new, but traditional systems of assistance, such as the extended family, were in decline. The founding of trade unions was the most important precondition for developing new state-regulated forms of welfare provision. Initially, social insurance schemes – pensions and health and accident insurance – exclusively covered factory workers. Additional groups were only gradually incorporated into social security systems, and not until the late 1960s did fully developed welfare states became firmly established in Western Europe. By the 1980s, however, benefits portfolios were being subjected to deep cuts in the wake of an international debt crisis and the growing power of neo-liberalism. During this time, two processes coincided in the post-colonial countries of the MENA region. The first was the establishment of independent states, which faced the subsequent challenges of breaking free from colonial dependencies and overcoming feudal social structures. The second was integrating external interventions, initially legitimised as 'development aid', into local societies' national planning and welfare provisioning.

To explain the failures of shaping the future through large-scale project interventions or schemes, Scott (1998) applies insights about the establishment of European (welfare) statehood to post-colonial societies in the Global South. This is crucial for comprehending the inadequate provisioning of social security. Scott emphasises how four mechanisms contributed to the failure 'to improve the human condition'. First, he notes that simplification and standardisation of complex realities are crucial for the administrative ordering of nature and society. In this context, certain elements perceived as illegible and irrational – such as traditional structures – are transformed into legible and administratively appropriate forms. In this undertaking, portions of reality are re-designed. The instruments of standardisation, of central importance as specifications of appropriation procedures, include for example land registers, concession maps, population statistics, as well as plans and blueprints for modern settlements. Second, Scott highlights that the administrative toolkit of rationalisation combines with an ideology that he calls 'high modernism', involving unwavering faith in science, technology, and progress, which gives rise to certain forms of planning and social organisation. Third, Scott contends that interventionist potential becomes 'lethal' if the first two mechanisms – standardisation and faith in modernity – are conjoined with the power of the state or international organisations. These actors are capable of implementing far-reaching plans and can give material expression to them on a large scale. Fourth, Scott cites a weak civil society, which lacks the capacity to resist the aforementioned plans, due for example to war or economic weakness. According to Scott's line of argument, people in post-colonial situations have only a limited capacity to respond to the complexities that threaten their livelihood security. The groups affected should not, however, be seen merely as victims of modern planning, but as capable of subverting official plans and developing alternative strategies. At the same time, it is apparent that institutional and social securities are increasingly negotiated within post-national spaces, beyond the reach of national influence.

In sum, uncertainties are omnipresent. People strive continually to hedge against them by creating various forms of security. This often occurs simultaneously in different arenas of action, whereby physical integrity and the absence of violence are essential requirements. Ontological security plays a crucial role at the individual level. Developing daily routines is an essential strategy in this context. On the spectrum between knowledge and belief, individuals make decisions as to what they themselves can handle and when to delegate responsibility to expert systems or religious institutions. Strategies to produce material security come together at the household level, aimed above all at livelihood security. The interaction between rules and resources lies at the heart of empirical analysis, as this is what structures options for actions that can produce various forms of security. The polity arena above all generates institutionalised human security in a wide range of forms. In the globalising world, characterised by profound upheavals, the question arises however whether established strategies can continue to be successful.

Growing uncertainty: poverty and inequality as drivers

Uncertainties are constantly reconfigured due to social transformations, such as political unrest, economic cutbacks, and personal losses. In the MENA region, these developments particularly affect young people. Here, three dynamics will be discussed that give rise to new social situations that restrict and devalue established strategies for coping with insecurity and hedging against uncertainties in the three arenas of action: precarisation of working and living conditions, dissolution of institutional securities, and growing global inequality. These dynamics further social fragmentation and have led to changes in living conditions in the broader Mediterranean area.

1. The realm of European labour comprises a sensible starting point for comprehending the first dynamic, the discursive field of the precarity debate. Given the MENA region's problematic economic situation and the severe changes in employment relationships (see Chapter 7), this approach offers a new take on aspects of uncertainty and insecurity in the region. In contrast to pure micro-level poverty and resource analyses, the emphasis here is on meso- and macro-level developments. Drawing on Castel's (2009) observation on the return of social insecurity to the sheltered societies of the Global North, Dörre (2009) argues that social insecurity became a mass experience in Europe even before the financial collapse that began in 2007. To him, it unfolded as a generic consequence of functioning financial capitalism. He argues that financial capitalism's *Landnahme* – the commodification of non-capitalistic forms, including the commons – has produced a new form of precarity.

Castel and Dörre (2009) take a multi-dimensional view of precarity and precarisation, stressing, '[A]longside] the labour force perspective (e.g. income and employment security), the professional activity perspective (e.g. identification with the tasks and the quality of social relationships) and, along with it, status, social recognition and individual planning capability, are important' (p. 17). In this regard, four aspects characterise precarity: in the first instance, the employment situation is crucial. If employees' circumstances fall below a certain level of income, protection, and social integration, they are described as being precarious. There is in addition a subjective side to precarity. Living in precarity involves a general loss of meaning, a shortfall in social recognition and extended planning insecurity. Furthermore, precarity is thus considered to be a relational category. It depends on how the 'standard of normality' is defined within a particular society, which varies and may shift over time. The precariat is thus not a homogeneous class (Standing 2011). Finally, the erosion of standards of normality gives rise to conceptually distinct zones of social integration, precarity, and complete decoupling (see Marchart 2013a, who talks more comprehensively about a 'society of precarisation'). Lorey (2012) takes this argument further, pointing out that certain modes of governance have come into being with the emergence of wage labour and industrial capitalism. Under the neo-liberal regime of flexibilisation, deregulation, and reduced protections, precarisation as a mode of governance undergoes a normalisation that makes it possible to 'govern through insecurity'. Simultaneously, precarisation is '"democratised' under neoliberalism as it moves into the mainstream' (ibid., 25).

2. The dissolution of institutional securities, the second dynamic, unfolds in the context of expanding uncertainty in globalising societies. Bauman (2007), in his oeuvre about liquidity, identifies five societal challenges of the modern age that also affect the MENA region. First, he emphasises that today's social forms (structures, institutions, patterns) will not be able to preserve their shape and expression much longer, as they fragment and disintegrate more rapidly than they can be created. In particular, forms that are just starting to take shape are not given sufficient time to solidify and become established. Due to their shortened life expectancy, they cannot therefore serve as orientation for human action or for long-term life strategies. Their life expectancy is actually shorter than the time required to develop a cohesive and consistent strategy, and it is shorter again in terms of putting an individual life project into effect.

Bauman further considers the separation between power and politics in nation-state structures to be problematic. Much of the power that should be available in the modern state to allow it to work effectively is now moving towards the politically uncontrolled global space, which in many cases is extra-territorial. The absence of political control turns the new power structures into sources of profound and essentially untamed uncertainty. Political institutions are becoming increasingly disconnected from citizens' daily problems, to which the state pays less and less attention. Cast off by the state, through subsidiarity principles or outsourcing of contracts, these functions become the playthings of unpredictable market forces. They are abandoned to private initiatives and individual acumen.

The gradual but on-going withdrawal of communal and state-supported welfare provisioning moreover undermines the fundamentals of social solidarity. The notion of 'community' rings increasingly hollow. Interpersonal ties, once woven into a safety net thanks to lengthy, continuous investments of time and effort, have grown increasingly fragile and exist only on a temporary and inconsistent basis. Society is increasingly viewed and treated as a 'network'. It is perceived as a matrix of random connections and disconnections and as a multitude of seemingly endless combinations.

The collapse of long-term thinking, planning and action, as well as the increasing erosion and disappearance of social structures within which thought, planning, and action could be inscribed in long-term future frameworks, above all, means that political history and individual life intersect as a series of shorter projects and episodes. While in principle these appear endless, they do not combine into the type of sequences in which concepts like personal development, becoming adult, or career planning can be applied meaningfully. Finally, Bauman takes the view that past success does not necessarily increase the probability of future accomplishments. Rapidly and thoroughly discarding out-dated information and quickly aging habits could be more important for future success than recollecting past actions and developing strategies based on lessons previously learned.

Bauman concludes that responsibility for solving the dilemmas that arise from permanently changing circumstances is ultimately on the shoulders of individuals, who supposedly have 'free choice' and should therefore bear the consequences of their actions. Thus, while external forces generate threats, the potential costs are outsourced to the individual. Consequently, the mechanism that best serves individual interests is no longer conforming to rules, but rather 'flexibility', which is characterised by a readiness to alter one's style and tactics at short notice, unhesitatingly abandon commitments and loyalties, and pursue opportunities as they become temporarily available rather than pursuing one's own established preferences (Bauman 2007: 1–4).

3. The third dynamic of growing uncertainty concerns the expanding global inequality. Material insecurity appears to be increasing everywhere in Europe as well as in the MENA region. Extending earlier debates about marginalisation and poverty in so-called developing countries, the current discourse refers to 'global inequalities', which have increased on a worldwide

Table 2.1 **Operationalisation of Uncertainty**

Arenas of security	Chapters of the study (1–15)	Empirical indicators (exemplar)
1. Absence of violence	Hunger and violence	Experiences with violence
2. Social security	Civic engagement	Participation
– State	Politics, Mobilisation	Institutions
– Household	Family, Gender	Trust
3. Livelihood security	Economy	Income, Debts
– Resources	Middle class, Migration	Mobility, Migration
– Rules	Values, Shell-Study comparison	Preferences
4. Ontological security	Uncertainty	Anxiety about future
– Knowledge	Communication	Media use
– Faith	Religion	Religiosity

scale. Today, 72 percent of the world's population owns just 2.4 percent of global wealth, and economic polarisation is further growing: while between 2000 and 2015, the poorer half of the world's population only received a 1 percent share of the increase in global wealth, 50 percent of this increase went to the richest 1 percent of humanity (Credit Suisse 2016). Theoretical considerations, addressing global inequalities, often implicitly equate one end of the spectrum, i.e. the poorest, with insecurity, and the other end, the wealthiest, with security. By analysing data over long periods, the processes of social redistribution become visible, revealing alternating periods of development, either towards greater equality or heightened inequality (Piketty 2013; Milanovic 2016; Atkinson 2015).

Beyond diagnoses, competing approaches are put forward to explain the causes of poverty and inequality. One approach, crucial for the following argument, addresses the polycentric and post-national dynamics of financial capitalism (Harvey 2005; MacKenzie 2014; Beckert 2016). The technology-driven acceleration of trading and information exchange does more than enable algorithm-based transactions worth billions of dollars or euros. Being faster than 'real time', some technological activities are only indirectly or partially controllable by humans. They give rise to unintended consequences that may only materialise with a delayed, highly potent impact, for example, price hikes for basic foods arising from stratified financial products like derivatives, which contribute to generating new spaces of hunger (Gertel 2015).

For the study of insecurity and uncertainty, these dynamics trigger the following questions: Which conversion processes of new insecurities are emerging in the broader Mediterranean area? How is the MENA region situated within the framework of global inequalities? What conclusions can be drawn for the region based on the debates about the collapse of the welfare state and growing precarity?

The analytical focus of this study concentrates on the situation of young people after severe societal disruptions, including the financial crisis (2007–8), the Arab Spring (2010–11), and the more recent migratory and refugee movements triggered by armed conflicts in Syria, Libya, and Yemen. These developments emphasise the meshing of global dynamics anew. Contingent, uncertain, and risky working and living conditions no longer affect only post-colonial societies and people on the 'periphery' of the Global North. Instead, they affect our global society, including in the MENA region, although they take shape under different circumstances. The consequences of the spatial and social conjoining of insecurities are precisely what the empirical findings of this study reveal (Table 2.1). It identifies the three arenas noted above in which securities are established and strategies to hedge against uncertainties unfold: on the individual level, where ontological security is crucial and in many cases is based on routines; the household, where livelihood security is fundamental and predominately structured through available resources; and the polity, where the community or the state provide human security, for example through transfers of public benefits. Obviously, freedom from violence lies at the heart of all endeavours to attain security.

Empirical Analysis of Insercurity and Vulnerability

The following analysis seeks to identity group- and country-specific vulnerabilities among young people in the MENA region given that security is unequally distributed. This involves first examining the manifestations of insecurity, then identifying the vulnerable groups, and finally addressing the internal structure of their vulnerability. To shed light on manifestations of insecurity, three analytical levels are distinguished: perceived and structural insecurities and vulnerability.

Perceived insecurity

Correspondingly the analysis starts with acknowledging young people's personal appraisal about the importance of security or insecurity in their lives. Subjective perception is thus the central focus here. Respondents were asked two related questions: a general question relating to their overall appraisal and a subsequent query about individual aspects of insecurity

Table 2.2 Young People's Self-Assessment: 'Secure' or 'Insecure'

	All	Bah-rain	Tuni-sia	Jor-dan	Mo-rocco	Egypt	Leba-non	Pales-tine	Ye-men	Syrian Ref.[a]
Ø	**6.5**	**7.6**	**7.4**	**7.1**	**6.7**	**6.7**	**6.6**	**6.5**	**5.2**	**4.5**
Insecure (1) ↑										
– War	5.4	7.0	6.5	6.3	6.1	6.1	4.9	6.3	**3.3**	3.9
– Economy	5.6	6.7	5.9	6.4	6.5	6.6	5.4	5.5	4.4	**3.3**
– Career	5.7	7.2	6.3	6.5	6.4	6.5	5.3	6.5	3.9	**3.4**
– Family	6.7	7.8	8.0	7.5	7.0	7.0	6.7	7.5	5.2	**3.8**
– Violence	6.8	8.2	7.8	6.8	6.2	6.7	7.1	6.8	5.8	**5.6**
– Emotions	6.8	7.3	7.6	7.1	6.8	6.7	7.1	7.1	6.6	**5.2**
– Food	7.3	8.8	8.8	8.0	7.1	7.3	7.8	8.0	5.8	**4.9**
– Health	7.5	7.7	8.4	8.1	7.4	7.2	7.7	8.1	6.9	**6.3**
Secure (10) ↓										

Question *'If you consider your personal situation in all its parts and aspects today (school / job, family, economic situation, political transformations, future developments, etc.), all in all, do you feel rather secure or rather insecure?'*
Question *'Can you specify the area of security? Please rate your situation on a scale from 1 (not at all secure) to 10 (totally secure) – I feel secure / insecure in the following fields: …'*
Questions 1, 9, 10.

Note n=9,000 • The figures represent arithmetic means. Rounding errors can occur. | The lowest value per row (representing 'insecurity') is shown in bold. ø = average. The complete options to answer Question 10 read as follows: *'I feel secure / insecure in the following fields'*: 'My economic situation; My health status; My emotions; My exposure to violence; My access to food; The future of my family; The probability of armed conflict; My future professional career.' | [a] Syrian Refugees in Lebanon.

(Table 2.2). In which areas do young people feel particularly insecure? They point to the 'probability of armed conflicts' as of crucial importance, followed by 'my economic situation' and 'my future professional career'. Next in the ranking, but by a large margin, are 'the future of my family'; 'my emotions'; 'my exposure to violence'. The highest overall level of security appears to concern 'my access to food' and 'my health situation'. These findings on insecurities correspond with respondents' value orientations (see Chapter 3), where it becomes apparent that three guiding principles are of primary importance: the desire for general security, as well as for law and order; the desire for an adequate standard of living, including suitable jobs; and the desire for trusting partner- and family relationships.

In terms of national patterns of perceived insecurity, young people in Bahrain, Tunisia, and Jordan clearly feel the most secure. There are hardly any differences in the aggregated values for young people in Morocco, Egypt, Lebanon, and Palestine; all are situated in the mid-range of the rankings. Youth in Yemen and among Syrian refugees in Lebanon feel

Figure 2.1 **Self-Assessment: Security by Country**

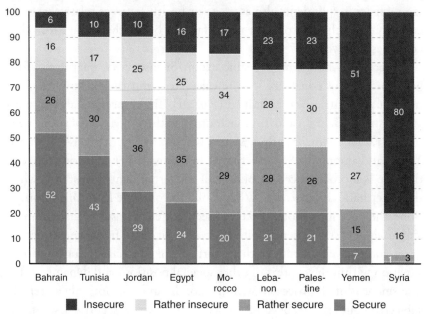

Figure 2.1 **Self-Assessment: Security by Country**

Questions 1, 10.

Note Figures are given in percentages. Rounding errors can occur. | The quartiles, four groups ideally of the same size, were derived from the sample's distribution of scores, resulting from the averages calculated for the eight aspects (Items) under investigation (see Table 2.2). Basically, the spectrum of scores stretches from 1 point = 'Not at all secure' to 10 points = 'Totally secure'. The group limits were drawn as follows: those who scored 5.38 points or less were designated as 'Insecure'; those who scored between 5.39 and 6.63 were designated as 'Rather insecure'; those who scored between 6.64 and 7.75 were designated as 'Rather secure', and those who received average scores of 7.76 or more were designated as 'Secure'.

the greatest insecurities. They are affected by violent conflicts that impact many areas of their everyday lives and that are also shaping their futures. Obviously, the differences between countries are sometimes pronounced. Upon close inspection, this affects a variety of issues, such as assessments concerning the 'future of my family'. Here young people in Tunisia ('rather secure') and Syrian refugees in Lebanon ('rather insecure') constitute the two poles. There are also marked gaps in respect to 'future professional careers' and concerning 'access to food'; here the Bahrainis and the Syrian refugees form the two poles of the spectrum. Different insecurities not only exist between countries, but also within them. In Tunisia and Lebanon, respondents view, for example, their health situation as rather secure, but perceive their economic situation and the probability of armed conflict as potentially creating much greater insecurity. In Yemen and among the Syrian refugees, respondents also assess their health status as relatively secure compared to other factors, but it still falls far below the average for other countries surveyed.

To capture the country-specific extent of insecurity, quartiles – four groups ideally of equal size – were calculated, and their distribution for individual countries was examined (Fig. 2.1). The respective target groups vary in size. In Bahrain and Tunisia, more than three-quarters of young people feel rather secure or entirely secure, whereas a minority feels this way in Yemen and among the Syrian refugees. In the five other countries, the relationship is more balanced. Around half the respondents feel secure, while the other half feels insecure. What is one to conclude from this information? The questions about 'perceived security' elicit answers that combine appraisals of past experiences with an assessment about future consequences of on-going developments. Both are further linked to classifying one's own situation within the context of other societal positions and dynamics. This assessment is often processed within seconds, and it is not only extremely subjective, but extends beyond the scope of a narrow security assessment, which would be based exclusively on the availability of resources.

Structural insecurity

Another level of analysis addressing insecurity stems from more objective, i.e. reconstructable, indicators, which extend beyond subjective assessments. A strata index proved most viable for this approach and was calculated from several variables, including fathers' educational status, property ownership, other indicators of wealth, and the family's current economic situation (Fig. 2.2; Appendix III). These four variables cover several properties and represent the resource portfolio of households. The level of education attained by a respondent's father reflects the family's educational resources and correlates with the employment and income situation in the families of origin (see Chapter 7). Property ownership is a central indicator of allocative resources. Home ownership is often the area in which families have invested the bulk of their available capital over many years. It is also the vehicle for inter-generational transfers of accumulated income (i.e. inheritance). The wealth ranking consists of three indicators and forms the interface between accumulated and available income. The indicators selected here also represent mobility aspects (along with owning a vehicle, having internet access, etc.) that are unequally distributed in society (Table 2.6). Appraisal of respondents families' economic situation primarily takes into

Figure 2.2 Strata Index by Country

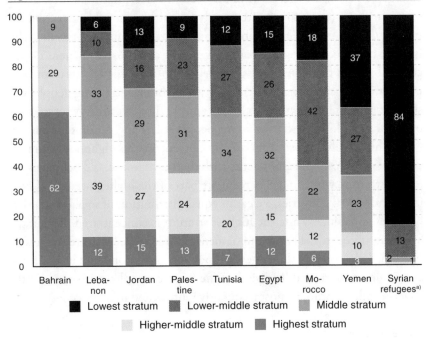

Questions 1, Strata Index.

Note Figures are given in percentages. Rounding errors can occur. | Portrayed are quintiles derived from the Strata Index, representing five groups, ideally of the same size. It should be noted that they display relational and not absolute statements about the strata, referring to the universe of the sample. Based on the distribution of the requested indicators (cf. Appendix), between 3 and 14 points can be achieved: the lowest stratum scores 5 points or less, the lower-middle stratum between 6 and 7 points, the middle stratum between 8 and 9 points, the higher-middle stratum between 10 and 11 points, and the highest stratum scores 12 points or more. | [*)] Syrian Refugees in Lebanon.

account the availability of monetary resources, but implicitly also refers to medium-term development of the national economic situation and situates the assessment within known societal structures. It is therefore well suited for relative positioning within a resource-dependent strata evaluation. When constructing the strata index, points were allocated to each of the indicators (see Appendix III). Overall, each of the 9,000 cases accumulated between three and fourteen points. Based on the distribution of the total values for the individual cases, five groups of equal size (quintiles) were created and designated accordingly: lowest stratum, lower-middle stratum, middle stratum, higher-middle stratum, and highest stratum (Fig. 2.2).

The first striking point about the empirical findings is that scarcely any difference in the distribution between men and women in different strata emerges. In terms of age, however, it becomes clear that the oldest group of respondents (aged 26–30) frequently fall within the lowest stratum (28 percent), while only a few belong to the highest stratum (11 percent). This is more balanced among the youngest group (aged 16–20), where 18 percent fall within the lowest and 18 percent within the highest stratum. This polarisation emerges even more clearly when comparing young people who still live with their parents with young adults who have already set up their own household. In the case of young people still living at home, 15 percent fall within the lowest stratum and 17 percent in the highest stratum. In contrast, 35 percent of respondents with their own household belong to the lowest stratum, while only 8 percent are part of the highest stratum. Looking at individual countries, a clear unequal distribution of social strata thus becomes apparent. While the highest stratum is concentrated in Bahrain, Syrian refugees in Lebanon and Yemenis frequently constitute the lowest stratum. Lebanon has the largest proportion of respondents in the higher-middle stratum, and Tunisia has the largest middle stratum while the lower-middle stratum is most frequently represented in Morocco.

Vulnerability

The next level of analysis links the perceived and structural perspectives on insecurity in order to identify groups ranging from the most vulnerable to the most resilient. To that end, the strata index (five fields) was combined with the security index (four fields). The resulting possibilities (twenty fields) were amalgamated to aggregate areas around the two extreme positions (lowest stratum and highest perceived insecurity versus highest stratum and highest perceived security) (Table 2.3). This produced five groups: (A) lower strata, with an insecure life assessment; (B) lower strata, with a secure life assessment; (C) the middle stratum, comprising all fields of security; (D) higher strata, with an insecure life assessment; and (E) higher strata, with a secure life assessment.

Group A

Lower strata and insecure life assessment (29 percent): This is the largest group. It contains people who live in insecure circumstances in terms of both the availability of resources (strata index) and their own perception (security index). This group shows an almost equal division between men (52 percent) and women (48 percent). In contrast to the two younger age groups (aged 16–20 and 21–25), the oldest age group (aged 26–30) constitutes the largest bloc (40 percent). Moreover, 41 percent describe

Table 2.3 **Groups of Uncertainty and Vulnerability**

	Insecure	Rather insecure	Rather secure	Secure
Lowest stratum	A 14	4	B 2	1
Lower-middle stratum	6	6	5	4
Middle stratum	C 4	7	7	6
Higher-middle stratum	2	5	6	6
Highest stratum	D 1	2	E 4	7

Question 10 (Quartiles), Strata Index (Appendix)

Note n=9,000 • Rounding errors can occur. | The table displays the building of five groups (A–E) of different vulnerabilities; they emerge by linking four groups (quartiles) of Security (Figure 2.1) to five groups (quintiles) of the Strata Index (Figure 2.2). They embody different features of Security/Insecurity. Bold black lines mark the group limits. All information is given in percentages (adding up to a total of 100 per cent).

themselves as refugees, by far the highest number of refugees among the five groups (Table 2.4). In terms of respondents' education and employment situation (see Chapter 7), those in school and university are in the minority (9 percent school pupils, 5 percent university students), while the segment of labouring young people accounts for 27 percent. Those temporarily not working stand at 29 percent, and those permanently without remunerated work constitute the largest segment at 30 percent, almost all of them women. Concerning the outlook for the future of their society, more than half of this group is rather pessimistic. Meanwhile, slightly more than half feel confident about their own future prospects (Table 2.13). Group A is thus categorised as the most vulnerable.

Group B
Lower strata, but secure life assessment (13 percent): The findings for this group are ambivalent. In terms of availability of resources and objective criteria concerning living standards, they belong to the lower strata, but in terms of their attitude towards life and their self-perception, they classify as secure. The ratio of women to men is balanced; there are also scarcely any differences across age groups. Analogous to the first group, it contains a very small number of students and the lowest number of people with employment, while the number of those temporarily and permanently without remunerated work stands above average. This group appears, however, as the most religious (7.6 out of 10 points). Overall, 80 percent are optimistic about the future of their society

(Table 2.13). In this respect, group B is the most confident and, along with the middle stratum, also clearly holds the most positive view of their own lives and the future.

Group C
Middle strata, secure and insecure life assessment (24 percent): This group corresponds with the entire middle group from the strata index. The ratio of men to women is also almost balanced. The middle age group (aged 21–25) is represented to a somewhat greater extent (36 percent compared to 33 percent for the youngest and 31 percent for the oldest group). Employment status is almost balanced within this group, with school pupils, the employed, and those temporarily without remunerated work forming the largest groups (Table 2.4). Overall, three-quarters are optimistic and confident about their own future and that of their society (Table 2.13).

Group D
Higher strata with insecure life assessment (11 percent): This is the smallest group. It is also characterised by ambivalence, but represents the inverse of the scenario of group B. In terms of resource availability and objective criteria pertaining to living standards, this group belongs to the higher stratum, but they rank as insecure in terms of their attitude towards life and their own perception. Men dominate in this group, at 55 percent, compared to 45 percent women. In addition, this group consists of rather younger individuals. It is also the category into which the largest number of Christians fall (12 percent). With regard to education and employment status, university students stand out as the largest group. The smallest employment segment is composed of those who never work for monetary income. The group also contains the largest proportion of people (23 percent) who are very interested in politics. Overall, two-thirds of group D are optimistic about the future of their society (Table 2.13).

Group E
Higher strata and secure life assessment (24 percent): This group contains people who live in secure circumstances in terms of both available resources and according to their own perception. The ratio of men to women is almost equal. The youngest age group is dominant. When it comes to education and employment status, school pupils and university students are most frequently represented. As in group D, roughly half of

Figure 2.3 Vulnerable Groups by Country

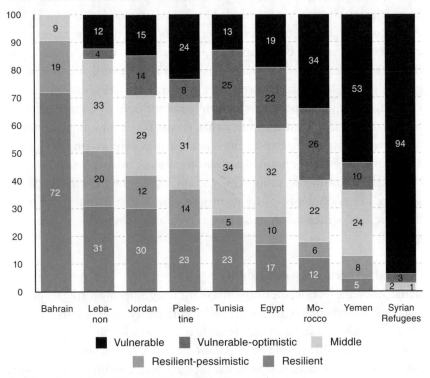

Question Security Index (Figure 2.1) & Strata Index (Figure 2.2).

Note Figures are given in percentages. Rounding errors can occur. | Portrayed are quintiles, representing five groups of different vulnerabilities. For calculation see Table 2.3. It should be noted that the various groups display relational and not absolute statements about the vulnerabilities, referring to the universe of the sample.

the respondents have health insurance. A good three-quarters hold an optimistic view of the future of their society. When it comes to their own future, two-thirds feel confident, but the largest group with mixed feelings (almost one-third) is found here as well (Table 2.13). Overall, group E is the most resilient, allowing its members to cope with threats.

How are these five groups distributed across the countries examined? The vulnerability–resilient spectrum ranges from young people in Bahrain, who frequently appear secure and resilient, to the Syrian refugees in Lebanon, who are almost entirely insecure and vulnerable (Fig. 2.3). The dichotomy could scarcely be greater. Young people in five countries – Lebanon, Jordan, Palestine, Tunisia, and Egypt – can predominantly be considered secure, representing considerably more than 50 percent of resilient members if the middle stratum is included in this calculation (groups C, D, and E). In contrast, in Morocco and Yemen, the majority must be categorised as insecure. A second observation is possible when only considering the distribution of the two ambivalent groups, B and D, while excluding the middle group, which is relatively evenly distributed across the countries studied, with the exception of the peripheral positions of Bahrain and the Syrian refugees. It then transpires that group B – containing the lower strata with a secure life assessment – is most prevalent in Tunisia, Egypt, and Morocco, which combined account for almost two-thirds, 65 percent, of group B. Meanwhile, group D – comprising the higher strata with an insecure life assessment – is frequently represented in Bahrain, Lebanon, and Palestine, which combined account for more than half, 56 percent, of group D.

Internal Structure of Vulnerability

In the following section, the properties of the five groups are further explored to reveal the structure of insecurity and vulnerability on group-specific levels. Four analytical steps are involved: first, an introduction to general living conditions is provided (i.e. social profile, work-life balance, household infrastructure); second, past personal experiences are scrutinised (stability, ruptures in everyday life, experiences of violence); third, social integration is examined (trust in institutions, access to social networks); and fourth, perceptions and thoughts about the future are investigated (fears, appraisals of future developments). This section thus offers a first glimpse of the situation of young people in the MENA region. The findings are further explored in more depth in the subsequent chapters.

Living conditions

Analysing the social profile of the five groups reveals notable variations in education and employment situations (Table 2.4). Whereas among the rather secure, groups D and E, more than half of respondents are still pursuing educations as school pupils and university students, this is only the case for one-seventh of the most vulnerable, group A. The converse applies as regards current and structural unemployment. Many people, both women and men, are engaged in some form of labour, but if they are not paid for it, they are categorised as temporarily or permanently out of work, or 'unemployed'. This applies to well more than half of the most vulnerable, groups A and B, but to only one-quarter of the most secure, group E. Generally,

Table 2.4 Social Profiles of the Groups

	All	A Vulner-able	B Vulnerable-optimistic	C Middle	D Resilient-pessimistic	E Resil-ient
	100	29	13	24	11	24
Employment status						
– Pupils (school)	18	9	17	21	20	**26**
– Student (university)	17	5	10	16	**32**	28
– Permanently without work	18	**30**	22	16	9	8
– Temporarily without work	25	29	**34**	25	20	17
– Working	22	**27**	18	22	19	20
Own household	29	**42**	28	26	18	19
Refugee (Yes)	17	**41**	7	9	8	4
Health insurance (Yes)	30	14	29	36	41	**42**
Religiosity (Points: 1–10 Ø)	7.3	7.2	**7.6**	7.1	7.1	7.5

Questions 15, 24, 25, 65, 66, 67, 68, 95, 121, 169.

Note n=9,000 • Figures are given in percentages (except the last row, concerning Religiosity; this row shows arithmetic means between 1 = 'not religious' and 10 = 'very religious'); ø = average. Rounding errors can occur. | 'Own household' indicates that the young adults are no longer living with their parents, but with their partner or with their own family. Bold figures represent the highest scores per row.

almost one-fifth of respondents are engaged in paid employment relations. People who work for wages are however concentrated in the most vulnerable group. Thus, remunerated work cannot be simply equated with 'security'. Group A as noted above, contains by far the highest proportion of refugees and has a high share of young adults who have already established their own household. Their exposure is further compounded by asymmetric access to formal provisions against illness. The vulnerable are hence the least secure.

When the self-assessment of young people's work-life balance is considered, between one-quarter and one-third emphasise that they strike a good balance between work and leisure (Table 2.5). On the one hand, however, around half of the young people are not using their full potential; they are under-challenged. They do not exploit all the possibilities in their daily lives, education, or work, and in some cases this is considered to be an enduring situation. Along with some school pupils, individuals who are temporarily or permanently out of work are particularly affected by this phenomenon. On the other hand, a good 10 percent of young people feel stressed. Here too the permanently unemployed are most frequently affected. Moreover, the most vulnerable group most frequently displays pathological findings.

Table 2.5 'Work–Life–Balance'

	All	A	B	C	D	E
I am consistently not using my full potential and I am ill	7	**9**	**9**	7	5	4
I am consistently not using my full potential	20	21	**23**	22	18	16
I am not using my full potential	28	27	27	26	27	**29**
I live a good balance between work and leisure	31	25	28	**35**	34	34
I feel stressed	9	9	9	7	9	**11**
I am permanently stressed	4	**5**	3	2	4	5
I am permanently stressed and I am ill	3	**5**	2	2	3	1

Question *'Are you already at the maximum of your performance concerning your studies, your work, or your daily affairs? What describes your situation best?'*

Question 84.

Note n=9,000 • Figures are given in percentages. Rounding errors can occur. | Bold figures represent the highest score per row.

In groups A and B, up to 9 percent stated that they consistently do not exploit their potential to the fullest and that they feel sick. A further 5 percent in group A report that they are permanently stressed and feel ill. In contrast, those from the middle group most frequently consider their personal situation to be balanced. The most resilient, group E, is characterised by a concentration of people with close to a good work–life balance, while also exhibiting the highest frequencies of both low-level stressful situations and feelings of not maximising their potential.

Allocative resources include, for example, ownership of housing as well as household hardware and amenities (Table 2.6). Housing, in the form of an apartment or house, is the realm in which private individuals invest the most money over the course of their lives. This is where money acquired through work, and interest on capital, is frequently saved. Two-thirds of respondents or their parents own their apartment or house. There are, however, pronounced differences among the five groups in terms of accommodation. While not even half of the respondents (42 percent) among the most vulnerable, group A, own their home, roughly twice as many people in groups C, D, and E, the three most secure, do so. When it comes to basic household infrastructure, fundamental amenities – water, electricity, television – and a separate kitchen are almost universally available. Specific household hardware and appliances are rather unequally distributed, allowing for a stratified wealth ranking. The most insecure, those in group A, have a lower level of access to satellite reception and refrigerators, with

Table 2.6 Household Resources: Available Infrastructure

	All	A	B	C	D	E
Owner of the place you live in = Yes	68	42	59	80	**86**	83
How many years have you been living in this housing situation? (Ø)	13	10	14	**15**	**15**	14
Tap water	92	82	92	95	97	**99**
Separate kitchen	92	85	89	95	**98**	**98**
Electricity	90	86	92	91	**93**	**93**
Television	86	82	86	87	**92**	90
Satellite antenna	80	67	79	83	**89**	88
Refrigerator	80	55	84	89	94	**96**
Computer/Laptop	53	14	34	62	82	**90**
Internet access [a]	47	12	19	54	76	**86**
Car/pick-up/lorry [a]	39	1	1	42	80	**85**
Air conditioning [a]	32	2	4	30	61	**73**

Question *'Which of the following items do you have available in your household?'*

Questions 51, 52, 55.

Note n=9,000 · Figures are given in percentages. Rounding errors can occur. Bold figures represent the highest score per row. ø = average. | [a] These items have been applied for the strata ranking. Accordingly, their distribution in the table is predetermined.

Table 2.7 Stability in Life

	All	A	B	C	D	E
Political situation	33	**45**	25	31	31	23
My economic situation	18	**38**	10	11	14	5
Prospects to live a fulfilled live	9	**17**	6	6	8	5
Trust in my friends	5	**7**	4	4	6	4
Personal belief in my skills	3	**5**	1	1	3	1
Personal faith in my religion	1	**2**	1	1	**2**	1
Relations with my family	1	**2**	1	1	**2**	1

Question *'In life, some things continuously change; others rather remain as they are. To what extent is there stability in the different areas of your life?'* Here: 'Unstable'.

Questions 167.

Note n=9,000 · Figures are given in percentages. Rounding errors can occur. Bold figures represent the highest score per row. | Five options to answer this question were given: 'Unstable', 'Rather unstable', 'So-so', 'Rather stable', 'Stable'.

even greater polarisation evidenced by ownership of computers, cars, and air conditioners.

Personal experiences

Investigating experiences of personal changes, ruptures in everyday life, and experiences of violence scrutinises past personal experiences and reveals levels of individual instability. Above all, young people frequently consider their political situation and to a lesser degree their economic situation to be unstable (Table 2.7). Apart from group A, only small sections, in single-digit percentages, of the other groups indicate instability as regards their 'prospects to live a fulfilled life' or 'trust in my friends'. Almost none of the respondents characterised their own faith, religious convictions, and relationships with their families as unstable (see Chapter 3). As might be expected, respondents from the most vulnerable, group A, are frequently exposed to political and economic instability while for the most resilient, group E, only about one-quarter of respondents consider the political situation to be unstable; all other areas are identified as being rather stable.

These insights about personal changes correspond to the findings about ruptures in everyday life during the last five years (reference point: summer 2016; Table 2.8). Five situations generate similar results and are considered 'very important' by between one-fifth and one-quarter of young people: personal cutbacks due to growing violence, food shortages, job loss, changes in the family, and social instability. Growing violence, like the other situations, affects the most vulnerable, group A, in particular. One-third consider growing violence to be 'very important', and a further one-third deem it 'important'. In groups B and C, however, a quarter of respondents view growing violence as 'very important' and a further third consider it 'important'. The most pronounced differences among the five groups are found when it comes to food shortages. Here, quite obviously, the lack or poor availability of resources combines with overall conditions of armed conflicts in Syria and Yemen – respondents from these two countries constitute more than half (56 percent) of group A – and thus set the stage for food shortages (see Chapter 10). On the other hand, Bahrain and Lebanon, in one case (group E) together with Jordan and in one case (group D) with Palestine, make up more than half the members of the two most resilient groups. Food shortages did not play a major role in these countries over the five years. The selective impact of developments after the Arab Spring also becomes apparent in statements on general insecurity (item: 'social instability') and economic distress (item: 'job losses'). 'Changes within the family' are however largely not group-dependent. A lower frequency, however, is found within group D.

Table 2.8 Changes in Life

	All	A	B	C	D	E
Growing violence	26	**33**	26	24	19	20
Food shortage	25	**35**	27	22	15	17
Job losses	24	**32**	24	20	17	19
Changes within the family	22	**24**	21	20	15	23
Social instability	21	**30**	22	19	13	15
Sectarian divisions	16	**24**	16	14	10	12
Increasing separation from the outside world	15	**22**	16	13	9	11
Climate change	15	17	**19**	15	10	14

Question *'What about changes in your life during the last 5 years. How important are they?'* Here: 'Very important'.

Question 141.

Note n=9,000 • Figures are given in percentages. Rounding errors can occur. Bold figures represent the highest score per row. | Five options to answer this question were given: 'Very important', 'Important', 'So-so', 'Unimportant', 'Very unimportant'.

Table 2.9 Experiences with Violence

	All	A	B	C	D	E
Have you ever ...?						
1. Witnessed violence	32	**43**	32	32	26	23
2. Experienced psychological violence	14	**24**	9	13	11	7
3. Experienced expulsion or displacement	12	**32**	4	5	7	2
4. Experienced your house being destroyed	11	**28**	4	5	6	2
5. Suffered from hunger	10	**27**	4	4	4	1
6. Experienced any form of violence	8	**11**	5	8	7	5
7. Experienced violence within the family	7	**12**	5	7	6	3
8. Experienced sexual harassment	6	6	6	**7**	6	4
9. Been beaten up several times	5	**8**	4	6	5	2
10. Needed to see a doctor as you have been beaten up	5	**8**	3	4	4	2
11. Suffered from torture	4	**9**	2	2	2	1
12. Joined a demonstration that turned violent	4	**4**	**4**	**4**	**4**	3
13. Been injured in an armed conflict	3	**6**	2	2	3	1
14. Been in jail	3	**5**	2	3	2	1
No experience of violence (1–14)	57	37	61	59	66	**72**
One experience of violence (1–14)	17	14	**24**	20	15	17
Multiple experiences of violence (more than one)	26	**49**	15	21	19	11

Question 168.

Note n=9,000 • Figures are given in percentages. Rounding errors can occur. Bold figures represent the highest score per row. | Two options to answer this question were given: 'Yes' and 'No'. The table displays the 'Yes' answers.

The following explanations pick up on the findings above in examining personal experiences with violence within the context of increasing political instability and spreading conflict (Table 2.9). Asked about various violent experiences, the respondents' two most frequent answers were having 'witnessed violence' and having 'experienced psychological violence'. Two findings are particularly striking: experience of violence is concentrated in group A, while sexual harassment (verbally and physically) was experienced in all groups at almost the same level (see Chapter 5). The aggregated data reveal an underlying pattern: almost three-quarters of the most resilient, group E, have had no personal experience of violence to date. In contrast, half of the most vulnerable, group A, have had multiple experiences of violence. Subsequently, the spectrum of insecurities is unequally distributed among young people.

Social integration

In contrast to violent experiences and destabilising developments, trust in institutions and social networks represent positive experiences. Statements about trust in organisations and institutions provide insight into respondents' perceptions of the stability and credibility they grant the state and its organs. Table 2.10 reveals, however, that young people mostly trust, above all, in their families as a social institution, as indicated by 80 percent of respondents. The military ranks second (54 percent), followed by the educational system, the police, the government, and the public healthcare system, which are each trusted by one-third of respondents. By far the lowest level of trust is accorded to parliaments and political parties (14 and 9 percent, respectively; see Chapter 12).

When the five groups are comparatively analysed, the following pattern emerges. First, all groups trust the family to an almost equal degree. The most resilient, group E, expresses trust most frequently, comparatively speaking, in four additional institutions – educational establishments, the police, the government, and the public health system – which receive high approval rating across all groups. The most vulnerable, group A, in contrast, expresses comparatively greater trust than other groups in institutions that generally have average to low trust values. These include tribal structures, religious organisations, the United Nations, human rights organisations, and parliament. This result may be related to the group's regional composition, given that a large part of this group, as noted, consists of Syrian refugees in Lebanon and of Yemenis, who on the one hand are highly influenced by ethnic groups and tribes, and on the other hand, due to war and

Table 2.10 Trust

	All	A	B	C	D	E
Family	80	79	78	80	78	**83**
Military	54	52	**68**	59	46	48
Educational system	42	35	36	38	45	**57**
Police	40	30	33	34	39	**52**
Government	34	25	30	31	35	**49**
Public health system	33	26	30	26	36	**50**
Legal system and courts	26	25	**37**	30	19	22
Tribe	25	**34**	24	26	21	16
United Nations	24	**28**	24	23	19	24
Religious organisations	23	**26**	**26**	24	18	18
Media	20	17	**23**	21	15	22
Human rights NGOs	19	**26**	18	18	13	14
Trade unions	18	18	**19**	**19**	16	18
Militias (armed groups)	17	10	**22**	19	16	19
Neighbourhood associations	16	**20**	17	18	11	10
Parliament	14	**17**	15	14	9	11
Political parties	9	8	8	**11**	9	8

Question *'What about your trust in different institutions?'* Here: 'Trust'.

Question 114.

Note n=9,000 • Figures are given in percentages. Rounding errors can occur. Bold figures represent the highest score per row. | Three options to answer this question were given: 'No trust', 'Limited trust', and 'Trust'.

ensuing flight and migration, have already had relevant experiences with the United Nations and human rights organisations. The second most vulnerable, group B, by contrast gives the highest approval rating to the military, trusted by two-thirds of the group. Comparatively high trust values are also accorded the legal system, religious organisations, the media, and trade unions. The middle, group C, gives trade unions and political parties top ranking. This corresponds to the finding on the middle stratum that the central segments of this stratum are most frequently linked to democratic structures (see Chapter 8).

Access to social networks includes the possibility of social integration, the opportunity to locate oneself within society, and access to a social safety net that can be mobilised in emergencies. This contributes to ontological security. Establishing and maintaining social networks require, however, time and commitment, while the networks are to a certain degree subject to the principle of reciprocity; that is, exchanges and transactions, including information, are based on mutuality. In this context, the calculation of

Table 2.11 Social Networks

	All	A	B	C	D	E
Are you part of a fixed group of friends – a clique? = Yes	58	44	54	64	**66**	**66**
Do you use the internet? = Yes	75	51	65	83	92	**96**
– Hours/day (Ø)	5.2	3.7	4.3	5.0	6.1	**6.4**
How do you use social networks?[a]						
– Keep in contact with friends and family	38	38	30	34	36	**44**
– Share music / videos	21	12	16	19	22	**31**
– Organise meetings with my friends	19	10	13	16	23	**28**
– Look for work opportunities	11	6	11	9	12	**16**
Neither clique nor internet	14	**31**	20	8	3	2
Security: Whom do you approach…						
… in case you need money?						
– Family	80	70	82	82	84	**88**
– My partner[b]	57	52	57	60	61	**68**
– Friends	20	**24**	21	22	19	14
– Nobody	2	**3**	2	2	0	1
… in case you are looking for work?						
– Family	42	39	39	40	45	**47**
– Friends	32	**35**	30	33	31	27
– My partner[b]	27	25	24	27	25	**33**
– Internet	20	6	16	23	24	**34**
– Public institutions	20	12	23	24	20	**25**
– Private initiatives	7	4	7	**8**	7	**8**
– Neighbours	6	**7**	6	6	4	3
– People of same origin	6	**8**	7	7	4	3
– Nobody	6	**9**	6	5	5	2
… in case you are sick?						
– Family	79	74	76	79	84	**86**
– My partner[b]	62	60	57	62	69	**73**
– Friends	11	12	11	11	**13**	11
– Public institutions	6	5	**14**	8	3	4
… in case of personal problems?						
– Family	66	66	66	66	**67**	66
– My partner[b]	58	54	57	60	58	**69**
– Friends	31	23	26	34	36	**37**
– Nobody	5	5	**6**	4	4	4

Questions 129, 132, 149, 153, 155.

Note n=9,000 • Figures are given in percentages (except the third row, showing the duration of Internet sessions in hours per day). Rounding errors can occur. Bold figures represent the highest score per row. ø = average. | [a]*'How do you use social networks like Facebook, blogs, or WhatsApp?'* = 'Frequently'. The question was addressed to Internet users only. The following options scored 5 per cent or less: 'Look for a possible partner'; 'Discuss politics'; 'Discuss religious affairs'; 'Mobilise friends and other people for politics'; 'Actively oppose specific political positions'; 'Mobilise friends and other people for religious affairs'; 'Actively oppose specific religious positions'. With the question *'Whom do you approach …?'*, only answers scoring more than 2 per cent were considered. [b]Percentages were calculated for married respondents only.

Table 2.12 Anxieties Concerning the Future

	All	A	B	C	D	E
Increasing insecurity	34	**46**	36	32	26	22
Becoming seriously sick	33	**40**	36	30	28	27
Becoming poor	32	**46**	32	27	26	23
Losing my work[a]	30	**39**	31	27	26	23
Becoming a victim of a terror attack	29	**38**	31	28	23	19
Armed conflicts threatening your family	28	**39**	29	27	19	17
Not being as successful in life as you wish	26	29	**30**	26	22	23
Falling out seriously with your parents	22	21	**27**	24	18	21
Being forced to leave your country for economic reasons	22	**33**	20	20	16	13
Being forced to leave your country for political reasons	20	**28**	19	18	16	15
Staying unmarried and single	17	**20**	19	16	14	14
Becoming dependent on drugs	16	18	**22**	17	11	13
Not having friends	16	**19**	17	14	15	13

Question '*Let us now talk about your anxieties concerning the future. Are you anxious about …?*' Here: 'Very much'.

Question 140.

Note n=9,000 • Figures are given in percentages. Rounding errors can occur. Bold figures represent the highest score per row. | Five options to answer the question about anxieties concerning the future were given: 'Very much', 'Fairly', 'A little', 'Not at all', 'Cannot happen'. [a] This question was answered by all interviewees, not only those who are employed.

values concerning gift and reciprocity could span long time periods. How are young people integrated into online and offline networks? Overall, a good 60 percent are part of an established group of friends, or a clique, i.e. a circle of friends of the same age (Table 2.11). The frequency of this, however, is unequally distributed. Among the most vulnerable, group A, not even half belong to a clique, while among the secure, groups C, D, and E, two-thirds of respondents have a circle of friends. This pattern is repeated as regards internet use, although here the differences are even more distinct, in terms of the proportion of users and the duration of use. The most prevalent use of virtual social networks is to stay in touch with family and friends; this is almost the same for all user groups. Conversely, around one-seventh of respondents have neither internet access nor an established group of friends. The two most vulnerable groups clearly stand out here. A good one-third and one-fifth, respectively, appear socially isolated in this respect. In this instance, perceived insecurities and resource insecurities combine in weak social networks.

Whom do young people turn to if they experience minor difficulties or major predicaments, such as if they need money, fall ill, have personal problems, or are looking for work? The answers to this question reveal the relative importance of social networks and the strategic options at hand. The most striking finding is that in all four instances cited, the family is again by far the most frequent choice. In the case of illness and in money-related matters, more than three-quarters of young people turn to their families. When it comes to personal problems and to the search for work, the family still ranks number one for most respondents, but friends and one's partner emerge as important in these instances. The most important differences between the groups relate to the need for money. Between 70 percent in the most insecure, group A and 88 percent in the most secure, group E would turn to their parents. In contrast, in the case of personal problems, there are almost no differences between the groups in terms of whom they would turn to for help. The field appears broadly homogenous here. A considerable number of people, often cutting across the five groups, say that they have no one to turn to if they run into personal difficulties. This predominately concerns the search for work, but also personal problems and money-related issues.

Future expectations

Against the above backdrop, what anxieties do young people have about the future (Tables 2.12 and 2.13)? Generally speaking, uncertain and unstable conditions are most likely to produce fear. This includes fear over growing insecurity, fear of impoverishment, possible job losses, fear of falling victim to a terrorist attack, and fear of armed conflicts threatening the family. About one-third are 'very anxious' of the first six scenarios represented in Table 2.12, and a further one-fifth selected 'fairly anxious'. Together, this encompasses about half of all respondents. When the five groups are analysed comparatively, the members of group A, the most vulnerable, feel most frequently exposed to different fears concerning their future. This applies to group B, otherwise among the most confident, also in three regards: being less successful than they would like, falling out with their parents, and becoming addicted to drugs. Despite the great optimism this group expresses, its members face heavy pressure to avoid or escape from poverty.

Conclusion

This chapter addresses the importance of uncertainty in the lives of young people in the MENA region. I argue that establishing security in its various

Table 2.13 Perception of the Future

	All	A	B	C	D	E
Personal life and future						
– Rather pessimistically	13	**27**	8	9	11	6
– Rather optimistically	65	54	72	**74**	62	65
– Mixed, both ways	22	19	20	18	27	**29**
Society's future						
– Rather pessimistically	30	**41**	20	25	32	27
– Rather optimistically	70	59	**80**	75	68	73

Question *'How do you perceive your own future and personal life?'*
Question *'And what about the future of our society? Do you perceive it … ?'*

Questions 165, 166.

Note n=9,000 • Figures are given in percentages. Rounding errors can occur. Bold figures represent the highest score per row.

forms serves as a means to hedge against uncertainties. Conceptually speaking, securities are constructed within three interlinked arenas: ontological security on the individual level; livelihood security at the household level; and welfare provision at the level of the polity, generally embodied by the community and the state. The absence of violence is of fundamental importance in these contexts. While the production of securities serves to contain uncertainties, the young people in the MENA region face major challenges. In recent years, societal conditions and everyday life in the region were fundamentally altered due to political upheavals, escalations in violence, and economic difficulties as well as the dynamics of globalisation. Today, previous coping strategies to mitigate insecurities are only successful to a limited degree or not at all. Young people, not being a homogenous group, are hence confronted with differing degrees of exposure and vulnerability. At first glance this is revealed empirically if the most vulnerable group is compared with the most resilient group; these two groups together make up more than half of all respondents. The most resilient group, which lives in secure circumstances in terms of resources (stratum index) and its own perception (security index), consists primarily of school pupils and university students. Three-quarters have no personal experiences of violence; they have strong networks in the form of an established group of friends or via the internet; and their trust in family, educational institutions, police, and government is largely undisturbed. Only a small proportion emphasise that they have major fears about the future. Uncertainty appears manageable, and many of them are confident. In contrast, the most vulnerable group – which lives in insecure circumstances in terms of resources and their own perception – consists above all of young adults who have already established their own household. Two-thirds, however, are temporarily or permanently out of work. Well over one-third describe themselves as refugees. They have experienced dramatic upheavals in recent years, and around half have already experienced multiple episodes of violence. One-third is largely isolated socially; these young people lack an established group of friends and have no internet access. This group also sees itself as facing several major fears. Around half view their personal future as gloomy or mixed. The uncertainties are correspondingly dramatic and also have somatic consequences. For some, stress or the sense of not using their potential is so pronounced that they feel ill. Overall, the situation of young people in the MENA region thus oscillates between uncertainty and confidence.

PART I

HABITS & VALUES

3

Values

Jörg Gertel & David Kreuer

VALUES ARE POINTS of reference for human behaviour. In this chapter, we examine the importance of the values and aspirations of young people in the MENA region. We explore how stable their values are, given the multiple crises and on-going disruptions in Middle Eastern societies. In the 1990s, Bennani-Chraïbi (1994) first described identity formation among Arab youth as *bricolage culturel* (cultural assemblage). The term captures the combination of identity fragments resulting partly from values and beliefs considered 'traditional', and partly from 'modern' cultural references including creative strategies for coping with recent social and economic problems and challenges. Since then, the requirements of society have further increased for them. Current prerequisites include a greater readiness for mobility, spontaneity, assertiveness, and independence, but above all flexibility, creativity, velocity, and problem-solving skills. Entering the world of paid employment now demands such key competencies as loyalty, reliability, discipline, and thoroughness. In some instances, the actors may also need special linguistic or social skills as well as the ability to navigate religious and regional configurations. Many young Arabs have thus become flexible crafters of their own identities and biographies in these multifaceted worlds.

Today, new normative points of reference have emerged in biographical narratives in Arab countries. This is due to accelerated globalisation, omnipresent communication networks, and disturbing experiences of visual and physical violence. In the context of increasing uncertainty and widespread insecurity following the Arab Spring, a central question is how the loss of opportunities and reliable institutional anchors might affect young people's values. We consider values to be suppliers of socially and personally desirable choices and patterns for self-orientation (Fritzsche 2000):

> [Values] are not concrete prescriptions for action, not norms, and they are neither binding nor compulsory. Values are individual

concepts of what is worth aspiring to. As such, they are rather general points of reference by which human behaviour *can* be oriented; but [it] does not necessarily *have to* . . . While norms are primarily effective *between* people and structure our behaviour . . . values are 'in' people. (Ibid.: 97, our translation, emphasis in the original)

Our exploration of values is presented in four sections. We start by introducing the young people interviewed. We then explore and discuss their value sets. Next we discuss correlations and clusters of values that connect groups of youth beyond national borders, and then we focus on the impact of societal ruptures and young people's anxieties, shedding light on individual discontinuities and the transformation of values.

Characteristics of Arab Youth

Arab youth and young adults were interviewed across eight countries in the summer of 2016. They are aged 16–30, and the majority still live with their parents. Just under a third of them, however, have already established a household of their own. This is particularly the case for women, who tend to marry at a younger age than the men of their generation. Despite this, almost all of them self-identified as 'youth' (91 percent of females, 93 percent of males) rather than 'adults.' Almost all of them have a very strong connection to their parents: they live with their parents, and often also eat together; two-thirds still belong to the same unit of reproduction, meaning that they can have their own spending money, but a large share of household members' income is pooled in a common budget. Even in the case of young adults with their own household, they retain numerous connections to their parents (see Chapter 7). The key characteristics used in the following to describe the youth are their level of education, language skills, class status, involvement in social networking, life goals, and views on the importance of family, children, and intergenerational relationships as well as their sense of belonging. These characteristics are closely tied, we argue, to shaping young people's values.

Education

Investigating education is not particularly easy. For one, some respondents are still in the midst of their training and education. Moreover, school enrolment rates have sometimes changed dramatically (often increasing) within just a few years, rendering comparisons across groups somewhat

Table 3.1 Youth and Education

Highest degree achieved	All Average	Gender Male	Gender Female	Age 16–20	Age 21–25	Age 26–30	Household Parents	Household Own
Illiterate	4	2	5	2	3	5	2	8
Read and write	2	2	3	2	2	4	2	4
Primary school	15	16	15	17	13	16	13	20
Secondary / Intermediate school	41	44	39	61	34	27	47	29
Baccalaureate / A-levels	16	17	16	13	22	14	17	14
Technical / Vocational diploma	5	6	4	2	6	6	5	4
University degree (BA / MA)	16	14	18	2	20	28	14	21
PhD	(7)	(5)	(2)			(7)	(4)	(3)
Total (percent)	**100**	**100**	**100**	**100**	**100**	**100**	**100**	**100**

Questions 3, 4, 15, 26.

Note n=9,000 • Figures are given in percentages. Rounding errors can occur. | 'Household Parents' = Interviewee lives with parents in the same household; 'Household Own' = Interviewee has established own household. Figures in brackets represent single cases.

problematic, particularly when an entire region, not just a single country, is considered. What is the general and overall educational status of the interviewees? When three groups with the lowest formal education are clustered together – namely, the illiterate, people who can read and write but have no formal education, as well as those who have no more than a primary school education – one finds that as much as one-fifth of respondents have only a minimal formal education (Table 3.1). The large majority, however, have had secondary school educations. Corresponding to their age, one segment of interviewees is still in (vocational) training, while the older ones might have already graduated and are working, either unpaid (e.g. work as housewife) or in paid employment. Therefore, age is important in assessing educational levels.

When age is applied, the youngest group (aged 16–20) has by far the highest proportion of secondary and intermediate-level students, and only a small number has more than a high school diploma. The middle group (aged 21–25) shows a much broader distribution of educational degrees. In the oldest group (aged 26–30), among which many have completed their education and training, we find the greatest polarity: one-quarter have no or only minimal formal education, while three-quarters have completed higher education (more than one-quarter holding university degrees). This polarity is even more pronounced among those who have established their own households. Overall, a pattern emerges that is known from other studies: enrolment rates and education levels have generally improved over time. The difference between countries, however, is considerable. A comparison of the average number of school years completed shows Bahrain, Tunisia, Palestine, and Lebanon in the lead, with an average of twelve or thirteen years of school, followed by Jordan, Morocco, and Egypt, with an average of ten to eleven years of education. The lowest averages are eight years of schooling in Yemen and seven years for Syrian refugees in Lebanon.

Language skills

Almost all surveyed youth (99 percent) cite Arabic as their native language. Of note, spoken Arabic dialects differ greatly from one another in terms of vocabulary, pronunciation, and even grammar. It is only the written language, namely Modern Standard Arabic, which is taught in schools, that guarantees a speaker the ability to communicate across national borders. Second native languages, following far behind Arabic, are English (2 percent, mainly in Lebanon), Amazigh (only in Morocco), and French (primarily in Morocco). As regards a second language that young people master, English comes in first place (34 percent), clearly ahead of French (18 percent). This situation is reversed in Morocco and Tunisia (combined, 55 percent French, 29 percent English), as both countries historically have strong ties to France.

Class status

Social stratification is distinct from country to country. To understand the different access to resources, we calculated a 'social strata index', based on four criteria: educational status of the father, wealth ranking of the household, housing situation, and economic self-assessment (see Chapter 2). The higher a respondent's and his or her family's score in these areas, the higher their social status. Our analysis reveals some pronounced differences: the higher the social stratum, for instance, the greater the proportion of younger and single rather than older and married persons. Members of the lower strata tend to feel less secure and have less optimism for the future.

Social networks

Three-quarters of those surveyed use the internet, and almost half of them have an internet connection in their home. Such social networks as Facebook and WhatsApp are used primarily to connect with family and friends

(75 percent of users) and only rarely for political (9 percent) or religious mobilisation (*ta'bi'a*) (13 percent). Three-quarters of those interviewed own a smartphone. At the same time, more than half are part of a fixed circle of friends, and almost all are satisfied or very satisfied with those friends. One in seven respondents, however, is not part of a group of friends and does not have access to the internet. This situation is most common among Syrian refugees in Lebanon and young people in Yemen and Morocco. Generally, the strongest feelings of attachment are to 'offline institutions', that is, their family (average ranking of 8.2 on a scale 1–10), home region (average of 7.1), and religious community (average of 7.0). Young people without internet access tend to have higher scores here. On the other hand, it is the internet users who feel a greater connection to young people in the rest of the world, in particular through common interests in fashion (35 percent), football (34 percent), and music (32 percent). This can be further broken down by gender. Males dominate as regards interest in football (49 percent of males compared to 18 percent of females) and computer games (34 percent to 24 percent), while the connection through fashion is more markedly female (39 percent to 30 percent).

Life goals

Asked to choose one individual goal from a list of four possible choices, almost half of respondents opted for 'a good job', almost one-third for 'a good marriage', and just under one-fifth for 'good family relationships' (Table 3.2). This points to the central importance of work and the hope of a fulfilling future associated with employment. The differences between men and women are, however, remarkable for the first two goals. Almost two-thirds of men opted for a good job compared to one-third of women. This corresponds with the current labour market situation in which men continue to be the main earners, and women engage in paid work primarily as a temporary activity. Those women often seek employment during the period between graduation and the onset of new demands with the establishment of an independent household (see Chapter 7). In particular, women often switch back to unpaid work in the home after having children. Subsequently, a majority of young women, though no longer an overwhelming majority, see a good marriage as their most important goal in life. This desire increases with age. A good marriage occupies the number one spot for the group of young adults who have already established their own households.

Table 3.2 **Characteristics of Young People in the MENA Region**

	All
	Average
Religion: *'How religious are you?'* (10 points = 'very religious'; here: 8–10 points)	52
– 'Religion is a private matter and nobody should interfere' = 'Yes'	83
Individual goals: *'What is more important for your personal future?'* (Select one option)	
– 'A good job'	48
– 'A good marriage'	30
– 'Good family relations'	19
– 'Good friends'	4
Social relations:	
– 'Family: One needs a family to live a happy life' = 'Yes'	92
– 'Children: One needs children to live a happy life' = 'Yes'	85
– 'Raising children the same way your parents raised you'[a]	71
– 'Generations: Relations between younger and older generations'[b] = 'In tension'	44
– 'Older generation should reduce their demands'[c] = 'Yes'	34
Self and society:	
– 'I feel excluded from society' (10 points = Agree completely; here: 8–10 points)	17
– 'I am part of a minority' (10 points = Agree completely; here: 8–10 points)	10
– 'I perceive myself as a citizen with the same rights as all other citizens' (1 point = Completely disagree; here: 1–3 points)	10
Future: *'How do you perceive your own future and personal life?'*	
– 'Rather pessimistic'	13
– 'Rather optimistic'	65
– 'Mixed, either way'	22
– 'And what about the future of society?'	
– 'Rather pessimistic'	30
– 'Rather optimistic'	70

Questions 120, 121, 124, 127, 133, 138, 139, 144, 165, 166.

Note n=9,000 • Figures are given in percentages. Rounding errors can occur. | The options to answer questions are as follows: 'Religion': (Scale 1–10) 1 = 'Not religious at all' / 10 = 'Very religious': 'Exclusion', 'Minority', and 'Citizenship': (Scale 1–10) 1 = 'Completely disagree' / 10 = 'Completely agree'.

Importance of family

A related question concerns the importance of family, children, and intergenerational relations (Table 3.2). The large majority of young people believe one needs family if one is to lead a happy life. Differences between the genders, age groups, and those with different marital statuses are small. The family is firmly seen as the most important point of reference. A similar pattern emerges when it comes to children. For many, the desire to have children of their own is very much evident. This desire increases with age and peaks among those who have established their own households. Of note, more than two-thirds

Gender		Age			Household	
Male	Female	16–20	21–25	25–26	Parents	Own
47	57	51	53	52	51	56
82	85	81	84	84	82	85
62	34	52	50	41	54	33
19	41	22	31	37	24	45
16	22	20	16	20	18	21
4	4	7	3	2	5	2
90	93	90	92	93	91	94
84	86	81	86	89	83	91
70	71	70	69	73	69	73
44	44	45	44	42	44	42
37	32	34	36	34	36	32
19	16	18	17	18	16	21
11	10	10	10	9	10	11
11	8	9	9	11	9	10
16	11	12	13	16	12	17
62	67	67	64	63	66	63
22	22	22	23	22	23	20
33	27	29	30	32	29	33
67	73	71	70	68	71	67

a The full question reads as follows: 'Would you (or do you) raise your children the same way as your parents raised you?' Answers here = 'In exactly the same way' and 'About the same'. **b** The full question reads as follows: 'How would you describe the relations between the younger and older generations in your country?' = 'In tension'. **c** The full question is as follows: 'The older generation should reduce their demands in favour of the younger generation.'

would raise their children in the same or similar manner as their parents raised them. This indicates that despite societal ruptures, social norms and values are being transferred to the next generation with a certain consistency.

Society
How secure, supported, and socially connected do young people feel when measured in terms of their perceived exclusion from society, belonging to a minority, or feeling like a second-class citizen? There is a small group (between 10 and 20 percent) who feel completely excluded from society.

They are more likely to be men than women, and, above all, have already established their own households.

In summary, young people are receiving more formal education than ever. Arabic combined with English skills is by far the most significant linguistic point of reference. Three-quarters use the internet or own a smartphone. A job is crucial to their ambitions in life, which is strongly devoted to the values of family and children.

Value Sets of Young People

The central reference point for our further analysis of values is a question posed to the respondents regarding what they see as worth aspiring to in life. The following question was asked: 'As individuals, we have ideas and visions about our personal life, our attitudes, and behaviour. If you reflect about possible achievements in your life, how important are the following points for you?' The interviewees were then presented with twenty-eight options to evaluate on a scale ranging from one ('absolutely unimportant') to ten ('absolutely important') (see Table 3.3).

On an initial look at the results, the top score for 'believing in God' and the lowest score for 'being politically active' jump out. Belief in God is seen by most as a private matter, and as such is an area in which nobody should interfere (see Table 3.2). Religious faith does not, therefore, imply that the respondent is socially or politically active or mobilised in a religious context. Rather, it is a personal decision to trust in God. This leads, as evidenced in the qualitative interviews, to a kind of optimism that is remarkable in the face of the insecure living conditions, armed conflicts, and uncertain prospects for the future. When asked why Arab youth are so optimistic despite their often-precarious situations – two-thirds indicated that they view their own future and that of their country in an optimistic light – the response from Buraq, a 19-year-old from Yemen, is emblematic. He emphasised,

> I share the same positive outlook, because we believe in God and believe he will help us and provide all good things. (YE-2)

Afrah, a 28-year-old unmarried university graduate who works in Sana'a in a workshop for the disabled, replied,

> Even though I live in hard times with psychological, economic, and social problems, I trust in God that such crises will come to an end, and we will defeat corruption and have a better future. (YE-4)

Table 3.3 Importance of Possible Achievements in Life

	Total	Male	Female
Believing in God	9.1	9.1	9.2
Respecting law and order	8.9	8.9	8.9
Achieving a high standard of living	8.8	8.8	8.8
Having a partner whom I can trust	8.8	8.7	8.8
Engaging in a good family life	8.7	8.7	8.7
Aiming for more security	8.7	8.7	8.7
Living a consciously healthy life	8.6	8.6	8.6
Having good friends, who appreciate & accept	8.5	8.5	8.4
Acting always in an environmentally conscious way	8.4	8.5	8.4
Being able to select my partner	8.4	8.5	8.4
Being proud of the history of my country	8.4	8.4	8.4
Being diligent, hardworking, and ambitious	8.4	8.4	8.3
Enjoying life as much as possible	8.3	8.3	8.3
Being financially independent from others	8.3	8.4	8.2
Being connected to others	8.3	8.3	8.2
Paying attention to the codes of honour and shame	8.2	8.2	8.2
Safeguarding the traditions of my home country	8.0	8.0	7.9
Developing my imagination and creativity	7.9	8.0	7.9
Spreading the message of Islam	7.9	7.8	8.0
Tolerating opinions that I do not agree with	7.7	7.7	7.7
Acting independently of the advice of others	7.5	7.6	7.5
Avoiding Westernisation	7.1	7.2	7.1
Supporting socially excluded and marginalised people	7.0	7.0	7.0
Allowing my decisions to be guided by my emotions	6.7	6.6	6.8
Doing what others are doing	5.9	6.0	5.8
Having power and exerting influence	5.8	6.0	5.6
Pursuing my own agenda, even if against the interest of others	5.2	5.3	5.1
Being politically active	4.7	4.9	4.5

Questions 3, 131.

Note Answers are represented in scores (arithmetic mean), ranging between one point ('Absolutely unimportant') to ten points ('Absolutely important'). The dashed lines distinguish four ranges of closely clustered values.

Equally, 26-year-old Esraa from Gaza in Palestine, is optimistic despite the challenging living conditions there, asserting:

> Yes, I am optimistic, and I am a true believer in God, and I am sure that God will help us. (PS-5)

Nawal, a Syrian refugee in Lebanon, underlined,

Table 3.4 Importance of Possible Achievements in Life: By Country

	Total	Bahrain
Believing in God	9.1	9.5
Respecting law and order	8.9	**9.8**
Achieving a high standard of living	8.8	**9.8**
Having a partner whom I can trust	8.8	**9.5**
Engaging in a good family life	8.7	**9.4**
Aiming for more security	8.7	**9.6**
Living a consciously healthy life	8.6	**9.7**
Acting always in an environmentally conscious way	8.4	**9.7**
Being financially independent from others	8.3	**9.6**
Paying attention to the codes of honour and shame	8.2	4.6
Spreading the message of Islam	7.9	5.8
Avoiding Westernisation	7.1	4.9
Supporting socially excluded and marginalised people	7.0	3.1
Allowing my decisions to be guided by my emotions	6.7	**9.3**
Doing what others are doing	5.9	5.4
Having power and exerting influence	5.8	3.3
Pursuing my own agenda, even if against the interest of others	5.2	2.3
Being politically active	4.7	3.1

Questions 1, 131.

Answers are represented as score (arithmetic mean) 1 = 'Absolutely unimportant' ⇔ 10 = 'Absolutely important'.

> I am optimistic that life will be better, and we pray to God for an improved situation so we can go back to our country and live a better life. We depend on God. (LB/SY-6)

Politics, by contrast, is seen as untrustworthy, driven by special interests and cronyism. According to Mohammad, a 26-year-old from Lebanon,

> [Being] a politician means to be a liar. During the elections, they run after people and pay them money so they will elect them.' He added, 'The politicians are responsible for the fighting. [They] are a mafia, which means that the state has become a mafia.' (LB-7)

Buraq, a 19-year-old from Abyan, Yemen, stated emphatically,

> We get nothing but a headache from politics. It is only about how

Yemen	Syrian Ref.[a]	Tunisia	Leba-non	Mo-rocco	Egypt	Jordan	Pales-tine
9.8	9.3	9.4	9.2	8.2	8.5	n. a.	9.1
9.1	9.5	9.1	9.1	7.7	8.5	8.6	8.5
9.0	9.0	9.5	9.1	7.8	8.2	8.3	8.8
9.2	9.0	9.1	9.0	7.8	8.1	8.4	8.9
9.1	8.9	9.1	8.9	7.7	7.9	8.4	8.7
9.0	8.8	9.2	8.7	7.8	8.0	8.4	8.6
8.7	8.7	9.0	8.8	7.8	7.9	8.3	8.6
8.6	8.8	8.5	8.8	7.8	7.5	8.1	8.0
7.5	8.7	8.6	8.6	7.7	7.6	8.2	7.9
9.4	9.0	9.3	8.6	7.6	8.3	8.6	8.7
9.2	7.5	8.7	6.6	8.0	7.6	n. a.	8.1
8.0	**8.4**	7.5	7.6	7.3	7.0	6.5	7.1
7.4	7.9	**8.3**	7.9	7.6	6.9	7.2	6.9
5.8	6.6	6.1	6.7	7.4	6.6	6.3	5.5
4.9	6.7	5.5	5.6	**6.8**	6.4	6.0	5.9
5.3	5.9	5.9	**6.6**	6.4	5.9	6.4	6.3
4.2	5.3	5.4	5.5	**7.0**	5.6	6.3	5.7
4.5	3.9	4.1	5.3	**6.3**	6.1	4.6	4.5

Note Only the five most important and the five least important items, ranked per country, are represented in the table. All other items were omitted. Bold figures represent the highest score per row. | n. a. = no answer. [a] Syrian Refugees in Lebanon.

to lie and lie. The political language in Yemen is the language of arms. (YE-2)

Said, 30-year-old from Morocco, similarly asserted,

Politics in Morocco is basically rigged. Parties can change nothing. All the parties' programmes are identical. (MA-1)

The questions about achievements in life further reveal a clustered group of fifteen items that obtained almost equally high approval ratings, ranging from 'respecting law and order' (8.9 points) to 'paying attention to the codes of honour and shame' (8.2 points). Another, smaller cluster fell in the middle to upper range of approval. These include 'safeguarding the traditions of my home country' (8.0 points) and 'acting independently of the advice of others' (7.5 points). A fourth bloc, including 'avoiding Westernisation' to 'having power and exerting influence', follows before the two elements with the lowest scores: 'pursuing my own agenda, even against the interest of others' and 'being politically active'. The results are almost identical when looked at through a gender-specific lens. Slight differences appear only in the areas of political involvement, asserting one's own goals, power and influence, and the importance of financial independence, but these are generally lower-ranked categories. There are also hardly any distinctions across age groups. The most remarkable differences appear among individual countries (Table 3.4). In general, there are four crucial findings.

First, 'believing in God' is a clear first in only three countries: Morocco, Palestine, and Yemen. In Bahrain and among Syrian refugees in Lebanon, 'respect for law and order' comes in first place, and in Tunisia, 'achieving a high standard of living' is the main concern. In Egypt and Lebanon, the gap between 'believing in God' and other values is extremely small.

Second, the most important values tend not to differ much across countries. Thus, in a majority of the countries with the exception of Morocco, 'believing in God' is followed in varying orders by five other values espoused: 'respecting law and order', 'achieving a high standard of living', 'aiming for greater security', 'engaging in a good family life', and 'having a partner whom I can trust'. Three aspects thus stand out among these responses and provide a good summary of the societal condition of young people in the Arab world in 2016. Many of them are primarily concerned about security, achieving or re-establishing law and order; obtaining an adequate standard of living; and having a trustworthy relationship and good family life.

Third, 'paying attention to the rules of honour and shame' also received high scores. These are traditional values that derive less from Islam and more from popular traditions and tribal structures. They have repercussions for notions of social reciprocity, the status of individual families, and relationships between the sexes. These traditional rules are not only important in Yemen, but also in Tunisia, among Syrian refugees in Lebanon, in Palestine, Jordan, and Lebanon. Almost fully urbanised Bahrain is the only country where these rules no longer appear to play a role. In Egypt and Morocco, they seem to be of secondary importance.

Fourth, the least important aspects for individuals' ideas and visions in the various countries are, some outliers notwithstanding, closely grouped with low ratings (Table 3.4): 'being politically active', 'pursuing my own agenda, even if against the interest of others', 'having power and exerting influence', 'doing what others are doing' or 'allowing my decisions to be guided by my emotions'.

Cross-Regional Value Dimensions

To identify connections between the answers given by the surveyed youth across national borders, we used a common statistical procedure – dimension reduction via principal component analysis. This resulted in isolating four factors that describe correlations among the twenty-five[1] aspects rated. These factors can be interpreted as value dimensions. They explain about half of the variance (i.e. the dispersion around the arithmetic mean). We assigned illustrative labels to these value dimensions:

1. Focus on community: relationships and consciousness
   * Having good friends who appreciate and accept me
   * Having a partner whom I can trust
   * Engaging in a good family life
   * Living a consciously healthy life
   * Acting always in an environmentally conscious way
   * Being connected to others

These statements emphasise the social embeddedness of individuals and their responsibility for themselves and for the environment.

2. Focus on success: conformity and power
   * Doing what others are doing
   * Being politically active
   * Pursuing my own agenda, even if against the interests of others
   * Having power and exerting influence
   * Allowing my decisions to be guided by my emotions

Personal success takes centre stage here. Both social conformity and asserting one's own interests without regard to the sensitivities of others are seen as appropriate means to the desired end. Often, this stance is coupled with political involvement.

3. Focus on freedom: creativity and independence
   * Acting independently of the advice of others
   * Developing my own imagination and creativity

---

1. For this analysis, we excluded three items from the list – 'Believing in God', 'Spreading the message of Islam', and 'Being able to select a partner by myself' – as they generated a high number of non-responses. The first two questions were not asked in Jordan, and the third did not apply to those who were already married.

- Being diligent, hardworking, and ambitious
- Tolerating opinions that I do not agree with
- Enjoying life as much as possible

The focus here is on forms of self-realisation in which creativity, enjoyment, and tolerance play significant roles, as does hard work for being able to stand on one's own feet.

4. Focus on decency: security and tradition
- Paying attention to the codes of honour and shame
- Supporting socially excluded and marginalised people
- Avoiding Westernisation
- Aiming for more security
- Respecting law and order

Here, the desire for security and reliable moral frameworks in uncertain times is crucial, including care and support for more vulnerable social groups.

Each person can carry, embody, and live parts of all four dimensions. Accordingly, the four value dimensions – community, success, freedom, and decency – are present in various combinations in each individual subject, constituting complex identities. Are there, however, similarities between different individuals? To answer this question we identified closely aligned cases via cluster analysis. In this process, an increasing number of individual cases were gradually clustered according to their relative similarity, until (in our case) five groups coalesced.

We will now describe these five groups of youth who share similar values. For this purpose, the frequency of occurrence and the connection to the four value dimensions is important (Table 3.5). The labels are our interpretations of the statistical results and illustrate trends rather than clear-cut divisions. With regard to the subsequent analysis, it is important not to assume that young people in the Arab world would necessarily fall into one of the five types identified. The description simply clusters cases and shows trends that can be extrapolated from the 9,000 interviews by using statistical procedures. These findings should therefore be seen as an invitation for further discussion and not as a directly applicable recipe for political, economic, or social intervention. The five types should be read in combination with Table 3.5 and the preceding description of the value

Table 3.5 **Group Clusters and Value Dimensions**

Type	Com-munity	Suc-cess	Free-dom	De-cency
1. Decent but inflexible (48 %)		−		+
2. Educated and confident (17 %)	+	−	+	−
3. Insecure and with few prospects (16 %)			−	
4. Self-involved and looking for success (13 %)	−	+		
5. Individualized and flexible (6 %)		+		−

+ above-average importance, • − below-average importance

dimensions. The findings reveal that the set of values applies independently of age, educational level, and economic status.

Type 1 – Decent but inflexible: This group, by far the largest, encompasses almost half of the sample (48 percent of respondents). Their shared characteristics can be summarised as attributing a high degree of importance to decency and a low degree of importance to success. The individuals in this group respect rules of honour and shame, support the socially marginalised and excluded, avoid Westernisation, strive for greater security, and respect law and order. They are not at all focused on success. This implies that they are not keen on doing what others are doing, are not interested in politics, do not pursue their own agenda against the interests of others, and do not wish to exercise power or influence.

Based on other aspects of the questionnaire, a comparison of respondents' answers allowed the construction of a picture of the everyday lives of this group of young people. It appears that many in this group either do not work, or they live off transfer income (i.e. income not based on their own work, but received predominantly from their parents). They are more likely to live in small towns or refugee camps and consider themselves as belonging to the lower-middle or lower class, assessing their own economic position as poor. They often have debts. The respondent's father is more likely to work as a day labourer and the mother as a housewife when compared to other types. It is important to them that their food is halal. The members of this group spend more time than others surfing the internet and frequently visit friends and relatives. Their fixed group of friends is often very significant to them. This type considers all fundamental rights to be important and believes that the older generation should make sacrifices beneficial to the younger generation. They are quite inflexible, however, in terms of their life planning. For example, they are not ready to marry into a different religion or class; to leave the family to obtain better qualifications; or to accept work under unfavourable conditions. This group often prefers a religion-based political system.

Type 2 – Educated and confident: Members of the type 2 group consider community and freedom to be important, while success and decency are not (17 percent of respondents). Many of them are students who live exclusively from transfer incomes, belong to the highest social stratum, and predominantly live in large cities. Their parents are more likely to be retired with a pension compared to the parents of other types. The educational level of their fathers and their own foreign-language skills are above average. They use the internet intensively and see themselves as more religious than average. They do not consider children as necessarily crucial for personal happiness, and they would raise their children differently from the way their parents raised them. The individuals in this group are more satisfied than others with the distribution of wealth between the older and younger generations. Their leisure activities often include listening to music, watching movies, reading, cinema and theatre, dancing and parties, shopping, playing music, or acting. These young people tend to be apolitical and are more loosely tied to offline institutions, such as family, tribe, or faith community, than other young Arabs. They feel safe, perceive their economic situation to be very good, and look with confidence towards their own professional future. Their political system of choice often has a 'strong man' at its head.

Type 3 – Insecure and with few prospects: The type 3 group (16 percent of respondents), which accords relatively little importance to freedom-related values, is more likely to include married people (both men and women) who have generally left their parental home. They often self-identify as belonging to the lowest class and tend to live in rural areas. Their parents often work in agriculture and have low levels of formal education. These young people are more likely than the average to live without internet access and to lack foreign-language skills. In their free time, they listen to prayers, sermons, and religious recitations. They perceive their own situation to be insecure, their economic position as poor, and their future prospects as holding little promise.

Type 4 – Self-involved and looking for success: This group (13 percent of respondents) scores low on community values and high on success-related items (e.g. doing what others are doing, having power and exerting influence, being politically active, pursuing their own agenda). An above-average number of young people in this group are without work and do not have control over an independent budget. They consider themselves a part

Figure 3.1 Values among Young People in Arab Countries

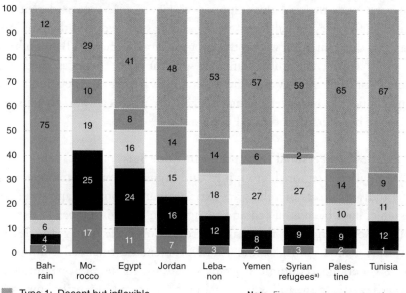

Type 1: Decent but inflexible
Type 2: Educated and confident
Type 3: Insecure and with few prospects
Type 4: Self-involved and looking for success
Type 5: Individualised and flexible

Note Figures are given in percentages. Rounding errors can occur. a) Syrian Refugees in Lebanon.

of the lower-middle class and are more likely to live alone than other young people. They spend their leisure time more frequently in cafes or youth clubs than their age-group peers. Politically, they often favour a combined socialist-Islamic system.

Type 5 – Individualised and flexible: Success-related values are important for type 5 individuals (6 percent of respondents), while decency plays a minor role for them. There are more men than women in this group, and they are overwhelmingly city dwellers. They are often not part of a set social group or clique, perceive fundamental rights as rather unimportant, and see themselves as less religious than those in the other groupings (and indeed as less religious now than five years earlier). Nevertheless, they ranked 'believing in God' the highest (as did the other four types). They are involved in civil-society projects more often than the average respondents and are flexible in terms of life planning.

The distribution of these groups in the individual countries of the survey reveals their relative importance (Figure 3.1). Type 1 (decent but inflexible) makes up half of all young people surveyed, and therefore the internal differentiation within this group is large. Generally, Bahrain has a completely different profile compared with the other countries: the indigenous youth of the city-state are predominantly part of type 2 (educated and confident). However, country-specific differences are also obvious, for instance between Morocco and Tunisia.

Anxieties and Personal Disruptions in Value Sets

Beyond these regional groupings and trans-national commonalities, the individual sets of values are extraordinarily complex and, one can assume, have been adjusted and realigned in some instances as a result of the social frictions that have increased over the past years. Terror attacks, armed conflicts, wars, and problematic financial conditions have generated economic insecurity and added new uncertainties to everyday life. In the following paragraphs, we aim to identify how individual visions, as a consequence of these experiences, have changed and affected value sets.

The collapse of institutional anchors due to the dismantling of welfare states and to increased civil strife is reflected in a deep-seated mistrust of the political system. Almost no one among the young generation is willing to engage in politics. These young people have significant reservations about political parties and parliaments, and only one-third are prepared to declare trust in their government, least of all the most vulnerable groups (see Chapters 2 and 13). Apart from their own families – which enjoy high levels of trust across all categories regardless of gender, age, or marital status – only the military appears to have high credibility for more than half of those surveyed. The sense of uncertainty and fear in connection with institutional failure is seen primarily in the increase in physical violence associated with terrorist attacks and armed conflicts and in the difficulties of securing a livelihood (Table 3.6; see also Chapter 2). On the one side, this includes the fear of falling into poverty, losing one's job, not being as successful as one would wish, and even having a serious falling out with one's parents, which for many would mean losing their most important buffer and fall-back option for coping with increasing uncertainty. On the other side, the direct physical dimension of insecurity – exposure to violence – is also important. There is frequent fear of becoming a victim of a terror attack and of armed

Table 3.6 Anxieties Concerning the Future: 'Are you anxious about ...' – 'Very much'

	All	Bah-rain	Mo-rocco	Egypt	Jor-dan	Pales-tine	Leba-non	Tuni-sia	Yem-en	Syrian Ref.
Increasing insecurity	34	2	19	23	14	21	32	65	**73**	51
Becoming seriously sick	33	14	26	29	20	25	30	**61**	42	46
Becoming poor	32	15	20	23	23	26	26	**54**	53	51
Losing your work[a]	30	16	28	17	17	26	26	**59**	39	45
Becoming a victim of a terror attack	29	6	20	26	12	13	22	57	**58**	44
Armed conflicts threatening your family	28	1	17	16	10	12	23	57	**59**	50
Not being as successful in life as you wish	26	12	20	19	14	17	19	**61**	46	30
Falling out seriously with your parents	22	16	18	13	11	12	12	**59**	39	17
Being forced to leave your country for economic reasons	22	2	15	13	14	9	22	33	41	**44**
Being forced to leave your country for political reasons	20	10	12	8	16	11	17	33	32	**43**
Staying unmarried and single	17	13	14	14	8	10	8	**38**	34	15
Becoming dependent on drugs	16	1	17	17	7	5	8	**45**	32	14
Not having friends	16	10	9	11	7	8	12	**36**	23	24

Questions 3, 140.

Note Figures are given in percentages. Rounding errors can occur. The bold figures represent the highest score per row. | (Question 140) 'Let us now talk about your anxieties concerning the future. Are you anxious about ...?' [a] Everyone was asked this question, not only those working.

conflict threatening the family. Fear of falling seriously ill also haunts a large group.

When young people in the individual countries are compared, it is striking that Tunisians give high scores overall with regard to possible areas of insecurity. In Yemen, Tunisia, and Lebanon, the sense of growing insecurity ranks first among anxieties, while for Syrian refugees, Palestinians, and Jordanians, the fear of falling into poverty takes first place. Moroccans fear losing jobs most of all. For Egyptians, the dominant fear is of falling seriously ill, while Bahrainis have the most anxiety over falling out with their parents. Overall, although the order of the rankings varies, the top seven categories are of almost similar importance (Table 3.6), indicating increasing uncertainty in everyday life.

Table 3.7 Violence: Experiences and Attitudes

	Total n= 9,00
'Do you rather agree or rather disagree with the following statements?' Five option to answer: here = 'Strongly agree'	
If I consider all the violence presented in the media, I get sad and depressed	44
I hate violence. I cannot stand when people suffer from it	40
In the public space, the situation is becoming increasingly tense	38
I believe that the use of violence will only cause further violence	34
In order to defend myself, or my family, the use of violence is legitimate	23
Women dressing inappropriately should not complain about sexual harassment	20
I am afraid that armed conflicts will threaten my livelihood and my family	16
In case of severe conflicts, we have to demonstrate strength, even with violence[a]	15
In order to be able to defend myself, I practice a self-defense sport (karate, etc.).	6
Others continuously threaten me	5
'Have you ever ...?' ('Yes')	
Witnessed violence	32
Experienced psychological violence	14
Experienced expulsion or displacement	12
Your house / your means of production being destroyed[b]	11
Suffered from hunger	10
Experienced any form of violence	7
Experienced violence within the family	7
Experienced sexual harassment (verbally, physically)	6
Been beaten up several times	5
Needed to see a doctor as you have been beaten up[c]	5
Suffered from torture	4
Joined a demonstration that turned violent	4
Been injured in an armed conflict	3
Been in jail	3
Overall experience 1–14	
Experience of violence = never	57
Experience of violence = one time	18
Experience of violence = multiple times (minimum 2 experiences from the list of 14)	26

Questions 3, 168, 170.

Note n=9,000 · Figures are given in percentages. Rounding errors can occur. The bold figures represent the high score per row. | Since these are sensitive questions, the response also depends on the interview situation. One sho therefore be very cautious in interpreting these findings.

This uncertainty is compounded by de facto experiences of violence (Table 3.7). Men are more often exposed to violence than women are, and the older cohorts more often than the younger ones. Country-specific differences are even more pronounced. In some cases, well more than a half of respondents – as in Morocco, Jordan, Egypt, Lebanon, and Bahrain – said they have had no experience of violence at all, including having witnessed

yrian Ref.	Yemen	Palestine	Tunisia	Morocco	Jordan	Egypt	Lebanon	Bahrain
57	54	40	45	16	31	31	39	**84**
52	52	41	44	21	30	25	36	**61**
57	41	31	41	17	26	18	38	**73**
49	46	41	42	18	23	25	37	20
20	23	10	23	9	16	11	16	**75**
22	35	**30**	29	10	21	14	13	2
35	34	5	22	9	7	10	15	5
18	17	9	**25**	7	15	9	16	20
5	8	3	**16**	7	6	6	4	1
8	6	2	**9**	7	4	6	1	1
55	38	42	53	29	29	22	16	1
31	28	16	18	8	11	9	4	1
71	14	6	3	4	5	3	2	1
61	4	9	4	5	6	3	4	1
45	19	6	2	6	6	5	1	1
11	**15**	12	12	3	6	5	2	1
8	**18**	8	8	7	5	5	2	1
3	8	2	10	**12**	4	9	1	1
5	**10**	6	9	4	5	5	2	1
7	**8**	5	5	6	4	5	3	1
16	4	3	2	4	2	2	1	1
2	3	3	**9**	4	2	6	2	1
6	5	2	2	4	2	3	1	1
4	**4**	**4**	2	**4**	**4**	2	2	1
15	42	50	40	57	61	69	80	**97**
7	17	23	**35**	25	22	15	13	1
77	42	27	25	19	17	17	8	2

ull questions read: **a** *'In case of severe conflicts, there is no other solution: we have to demonstrate strength, even violence.'* **b** *'Have you ever experienced your house or your means of production being deliberately destroyed?'* **c** *'Have you ever needed to see a doctor because you have been beaten up several times?'*

violent acts. For young people from Syria and Yemen, where armed conflicts and war are omnipresent, the situation is completely different. Similarly, more than half of the youth in Palestine and in Tunisia emphasised that they had encountered violence. Most frequently, they had been witnesses to violent acts or perceive themselves as victims of psychological violence.

For some individuals, these experiences have caused disruptions to their value sets. Mahmoud, a 27-year-old Palestinian from Birzeit, pointed out:

> My father was imprisoned nine times, and they demolished our home last year. We have nothing now. [I] had a problem. I was shot and injured and remained in hospital for more than one month, and I submitted a complaint to the police. [Nothing] happened, because those who shot at me are influential and have connections. I trust no one. There is no one to trust in this country. (PS-7)

Fatima, a single 27-year-old from the besieged city of Taiz, Yemen, underlined:

> I don't trust anybody, because these days, everyone behaves badly . . . I used to have this positive outlook, and I was optimistic. But everything turned for the worse, and every day the deterioration increases. So I am not optimistic anymore, and I became pessimistic. (YE-7)

For Fatima, the grinding attrition of war has left its mark. Sara, a single 17-year-old student from Bani Suef, Egypt, emphasised:

> Concerning my inner feeling of security, I do not know. A long time ago, my mom used to tell me, 'If you see anybody lifting anything heavy, help him,' but now she is telling me, 'Do not talk to anybody.' (EG-2)

Iman, a 23-year-old Bahraini who has not been able to complete her studies or find a long-term job, described the experience of social isolation following the Arab Spring:

> Before the revolutions, people were better off. They were happy with small things. Now they have all the luxuries, and they aren't happy. People have become more complicated and confused. They have many issues. No one feels good or comfortable. At family gatherings, we used to feel happy, unlike nowadays. People don't like gatherings. They prefer to stay alone, away from people and noise. I used to meet my friends, [but] now we don't meet a lot. We make plans, but we cancel them. (BH-10)

Public space in the Middle East and North Africa is increasingly experienced as unsafe, political order as arbitrary, while acts of violence go unpunished. As a consequence, social structures and institutions are falling apart, and new ones have not had enough time to take hold. Uncertainty translates into ontological insecurity, challenging the routines and commitments taken for granted in everyday life.

Conclusion

Arab youth and young adults have a diverse range of values and life plans; these are not fixed, but subject to change. The fundamental institutional settings for passing on values are country-specific. The interaction of family, school, and social networks establishes historical narratives and local configurations that shape socialisation in each place. Throughout the region, three general value patterns can be discerned: desire for law and order and safety; desire for an appropriate standard of living, which often goes hand in hand with the demand for adequate jobs; and the desire for a trustworthy partner and good family relations. Regional conformities determine identity formation parallel to national characteristics: the most important value sets characterising Arab youth today are, according to our analysis, a sense of community, focus on success, striving for freedom, and emphasis on decency. Young people position themselves at different points within the matrix of these value dimensions. However, individual expressions of value sets and the realities of life are complex. They may be shaped by biographical disruptions as experienced in situations of flight, war, or violence. Often, belief in God – a personal matter in which no one should interfere – provides young people with the power to cope with misery and distress.

4

Religion

Rachid Ouaissa

DOES AN OBSERVABLE INCREASE in religiosity among young people in the Middle East and North Africa (MENA) signal the rise of or a return to religion, or does it constitute a series of individual postures, the creation of personal identities amidst the conflicting pressures of globalisation and a longing for local culture? An attempt is made here to comprehend and define this connection, between religiosity on the one hand and individual attitudes and behaviours based on religious conceptions on the other.

Religion in the MENA region has been strikingly reconfigured since the mid-1980s and certainly since the so-called Arab Spring that began in 2010–11. The failure of post-colonial development models, and their associated pan-Arab and nationalist narratives, allowed an Islamic discourse to gain a foothold among broad sections of Arab societies. Islamic movements have increasingly become gathering points for frustrated and marginalised sections of society, as well as growing, pious Arab middle classes (Kepel 2000: 9). These movements have become parallel rentier systems par excellence, especially against the backdrop of the state's burgeoning withdrawal from the provision of social welfare (Müller 2002: 126-129). Indeed, in many Arab countries, the adoption of structural adjustment programmes dictated by the International Monetary Fund and the World Bank has allowed Islamic movements to assume control of social welfare functions (Ouaissa 2012). Similarly, the gradual opening of political systems since the early 1990s has led to the emergence of Islamic political parties, many of which participate in the political process and have won seats in national parliaments. There has also been an appreciably enhanced public visibility of Islamist groups, which have been buttressed by the return home of so-called Afghanistan veterans and fighters from the 1991 Gulf War. Furthermore, global Salafism and Wahhabism have gained in appeal.

In socio-economic terms, worsening objective (real) and subjective (perceived) inequalities in the MENA region have been accompanied by increased economic liberalisation, which has stimulated new patterns of consumption among youth in the Arab world. In short, global consumerism has reached large sections of the Middle Eastern middle classes (Mitchell 1999). The ensuing balancing act between forms of globalised consumption and local forms of Islam is becoming increasingly apparent, with Islam itself being subject to a kind of concurrent economisation and de-ideologisation (Haenni 2005), producing new manifestations of religious faith that have been referred to as 'Cool Islam' (Boubekeur and Olivier 2009). Halal products, such as Mecca-Cola, and fashionably veiled women are indicative of these 'hybrid' forms of consumption. In essence, globalisation is being Islamised. Indeed, in the case of Jordan, Tobin (2016) has spoken of a 'neo-liberal Islamic piety'.

This is a turbulent phase, one characterised by state withdrawal from society, a legitimacy crisis among the ruling elite, the globalisation of consumption patterns, increased influence of new media, and a sense of humiliation resulting from the massive Western presence in the region, especially in the aftermath of the Gulf War. In response to all of this, everyday religiosity in the region seems to have grown, with Islamic symbols becoming more visible in daily life, in the aesthetic make-up of cities and urban centres, universities and schools, and other public places. Esposito has described this revival of religiosity in the following terms:

> The indices of Islamic reawakening in personal life are many: increased attention to religious observances (mosque attendance, prayer, fasting), proliferation of religious programming and publications, more emphasis on Islamic dress and values, the revitalization of Sufism (mysticism). This broader-based renewal has also been signified by Islam's reassertion in public life: an increase in Islamic oriented governments, organizations, laws, banks, social welfare services, and educational institutions. (Esposito 1999: 10)

For Dekmejian (1988), this reversion to religious values (especially among younger generations) has been generated by an ideological vacuum left by the failure of nationalist ideologies: it also serves as a protective shield against 'westernisation'. Growing economic uncertainty and the intensification of social inequality since the mid-1990s are also important factors in this resurgence of religion, which has provided many with hope and social sustenance.

El Ayadi et al. (2013: 286), in their comprehensive study of everyday religious practice in Morocco, distance themselves from the thesis of a 'return' to religion and speak instead of a 'renewal' of religion. The elite's ideological instrumentalisation of religion, as well as an increasingly educated population, play important roles here. Ideological emphasis on religion is especially observable among young people aged 18–24. The following question thus arises: Does all of this actually constitute the rise of or a return to organised religion and religious values, or is it in fact a series of individual postures designed to create personal identities in the matrix between globalisation and the longing for local culture?

Among the young people surveyed for this study, 94 percent belong to the Islamic faith and 6 percent to the Christian faith. In Egypt, 8 percent of those surveyed are Christian, and 92 percent Muslim, while in Lebanon, 58 percent are Muslim and 38 percent Christian. In terms of age, those surveyed were aged 16–30, thus belonging to the generation born between the late 1980s and the early 2000s. Beginning in the 1980s, a decline in oil prices on the world market underpinned a persistent economic crisis throughout the region, while economic restructuring and enormous national debts curtailed opportunities for social advancement in the state sector. Though members of the younger generation are generally better educated than their parents, they are caught in an on-going employment crisis that afflicts almost all the Arab states.

Conversely, their parents – the generation of the 1960s – benefited from the state development models of that decade. This generation was the bearer of the nationalist and pan-Arab 'grand narratives' at a time when the oil industry was booming, benefiting both oil and non-oil Arab states. Between 1973 and 1983, some countries in the region achieved annual growth rates of up to 11 percent of gross domestic product, fuelled by oil export revenues, regional labour migration, and financial support from large exporters to semi-rentier states. Until the 1980s, unemployment stood around 5 percent in Egypt and 1.6 percent in Jordan (see Winckler 2005: 88), with the state assuming the role of principal employer and service provider, as well as offering careers and opportunities for social advancement. The social contract between the states and societies of the Arab world was thus closely tied to policies of official wealth redistribution.

The empirical findings show that in more than half of cases, the degree of education among respondents' fathers is medium or high, and that in all Arab countries, with the exception of Lebanon, the principal employer of respondents' fathers is the state. With the exception of respondents from

Figure 4.1 Religiosity 2016 and 2011

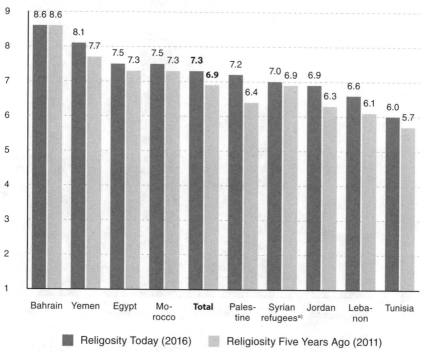

Legend:
- **Religiosity Today (2016)** (dark bars)
- **Religiosity Five Years Ago (2011)** (light bars)

Bahrain: 8.6 / 8.6
Yemen: 8.1 / 7.7
Egypt: 7.5 / 7.3
Morocco: 7.5 / 7.3
Total: 7.3 / 6.9
Palestine: 7.2 / 6.4
Syrian refugees[a]: 7.0 / 6.9
Jordan: 6.9 / 6.3
Lebanon: 6.6 / 6.1
Tunisia: 6.0 / 5.7

Questions 1, 121.

Note Scores represent averages (arithmetic mean) ranging on a scale from 1 ('Not religious') to 10 ('Very religious'). Rounding errors can occur. [a] Syrian Refugees in Lebanon.

Syria and Yemen, more than 70 percent of those surveyed (97 percent in Bahrain) rate the economic situation of their family as good or very good, while 62 percent rate their personal economic situation as good or very good. In total, some 30 percent of interviewees categorised themselves as members of the upper class, and 50 percent as belonging to the lower middle class. More than 90 percent of respondents (apart from those in Morocco and Egypt) live in condominiums or houses, but often as tenants and not as owners (see Appendix II: Questionnaire, questions 50, 52). Yet the basic view of the future among the young people surveyed appears to be shaped primarily by fear.

In response to the question 'How religious are you today?', on a scale of 1 (not religious) to 10 (very religious), the average for respondents was 7.3. Young people in Bahrain proved most religious (at 8.6), while those in Tunisia were the least religious (at 6) (Figure 4.1). Overall, there has been a

Figure 4.2 **Religiosity Today – Religiosity Five Years Ago**

Figure 4.2 **Religiosity Today – Religiosity Five Years Ago**

■ Religosity Today (2016)　　■ Religiosity Five Years Ago (2011)

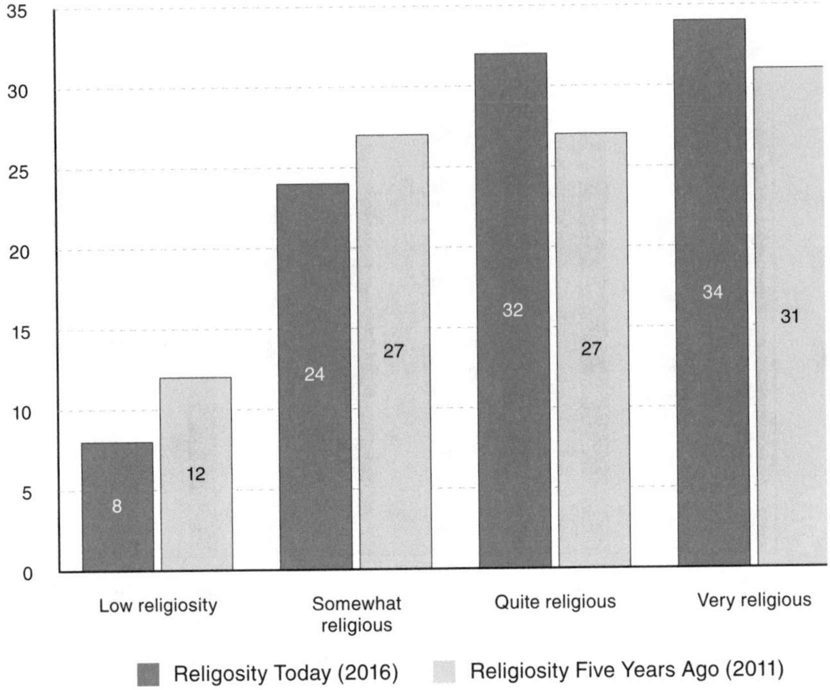

Questions 1, 121.

Note Figures are given in percentages (3 % no answer). Rounding errors can occur.

slight increase in religiosity among respondents as compared with five years prior (i.e. before the Arab Spring, or roughly 2010–11, when the degree of religiosity scored a mean average of 6.9. Incidentally, at this time, young people in Bahrain also scored highest (averaging 8.6), while those in Tunisia scored the lowest (averaging 5.7).

In general, then, it seems that young people in the Arab world today evince a higher degree of religiosity compared with their elders, but this is not particularly surprising. After all, the older generation believed in state-driven utopias and profited from economic prosperity, whereas the rise of today's younger generation appears to have been stymied. Consequently, the current popularity of religion and religious values among young people in the Arab world appears to serve as a kind of substitute for a lack of social and professional opportunity. This argument is laid out in the following steps: The religious attitudes of the young people surveyed are identified, whereupon connections between this attitude and deeper societal conditions are

Table 4.1 Religiosity by Age

Age	Low religiosity	Somewhat religious	Quite religious	Very religious	Total
16–20	9	24	33	34	100
21–25	8	25	32	35	100
26–30	8	25	32	35	100

Questions 3, 121.

Note Figures are given in percentages. Rounding errors can occur. | Referring to Question 121, the group 'Low religiosity' scored 1–4 points, 'Somewhat religious' 5–6, 'Quite religious' 7–8, and the group 'Very religious' scored 9–10 points.

examined. The responses to being asked how religious they are today and how religious they were five years prior are progressively analysed according to the respondents' most fundamental characteristics, such as class membership, father's level of education, as well as residence. This data are also used to determine which groups have changed in terms of their self-assessed religiosity, and political attitudes regarding the degree of religiosity are discussed.

Current State of Youths' Religiosity in the Arab World

The answers provided here are grouped to obtain a differentiated picture of the degree of religiosity among the young people of the eight Arab states surveyed, as well as among Syrian refugees in Lebanon. The self-rankings on a scale of 1 (not religious) to 10 (very religious) were divided into four groups, based on the questions 'How religious are you today?' and 'How religious were you five years ago?': group 1, low religiosity (1–4); group 2, somewhat religious (5–6); group 3, quite religious (7–8); group 4, very religious (9–10).

Based on these groupings, across all countries, 34 percent of the surveyed young people rated as very religious and 32 percent as quite religious. About 24 percent of respondents are somewhat religious, and only 8 percent rated as low religiosity (Figure 4.2). Comparing these figures with those for the respondents' degree of religiosity five years prior, an increase is noted for the quite religious (from 27 to 32 percent) and the very religious (from 31 to 34 percent). On the other hand, the numbers decreased for respondents expressing low religiosity (from 12 to 8 percent) or rating as somewhat religious (from 27 to 24 percent). This indicates an overall increase in religiosity, and possibly of religious radicalism, over the last half decade. Today, a total of two-thirds of the respondents classify as quite religious or very religious compared to 58 percent five years ago. Similarly, only 32 percent

Figure 4.3 **Religiosity by Gender**

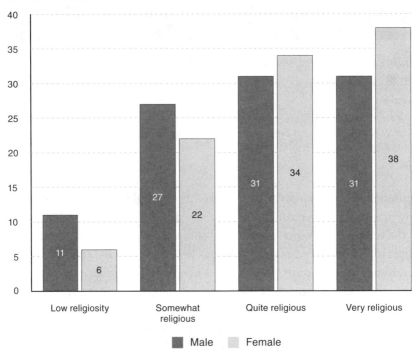

Questions 3, 121.

Note Figures are given in percentages. Rounding errors can occur.

of respondents rate currently as of low religiosity or as somewhat religious, compared to 39 percent five years ago.

If one differentiates the degree of religiosity according to age, there are hardly any differences in degree. Generally, it seems that young people do not become more religious as they age (Table 4.1). A comparison between the respective religiosity of men and women shows that of those interviewed, women are more likely to be quite or very religious (Figure 4.3). Of the two-thirds of young people who ranked as very or quite, 72 percent were women, and 62 percent were men. On the other hand, the proportion of those who are of low religiosity or are somewhat religious – a total of one-third – is higher among young men (38 percent) than among young women (28 percent).

That women exhibit a higher religiosity than men is not surprising. Though progress has been made in this area, opportunities for women's social advancement remain much less than for men across the MENA region.

Table 4.2 Religiosity Today and Five Years Ago, by Country

	Low religiosity		Somewhat religious		Quite religious		Very religious	
	Today	Five years ago	Today	Five years ago	Today	Five years ago	Today	Five years ago
Egypt	6	8	20	27	**43**	35	32	30
Bahrain	6	6	2	2	5	5	87	87
Yemen	6	10	14	20	26	24	**54**	46
Jordan	**8**	21	31	29	39	28	22	22
Lebanon	**13**	21	32	34	31	25	24	19
Morocco	8	3	**18**	30	43	43	31	25
Palestine	**7**	18	27	34	39	30	27	19
Syrian refugees	6	8	36	35	34	32	24	25
Tunisia	**15**	21	43	41	33	29	9	9

Questions 1, 121.

Note Figures are given in percentages. Rounding errors can occur. Figures in bold represent the maximum difference between 'Today' and 'Five years ago' (minimum difference of 5 per cent).

The economic changes of the last few years have taken a particular toll on female adolescents, but in addition to the crisis in the labour market, it could be that reversion to a patriarchal order in times of social, political, and economic turmoil has played a key role in the increase in female religiosity. The United Nations Development Programme suggests that 'the labour markets in Arab countries, either implicitly or explicitly, condone gender segregation in the workforce and encourage females to focus on child-bearing and child-rearing' (UNDP 2009, 46).

A comparison by country (Figure 4.1) reveals that young people in Bahrain are particularly religious, with a score of 8.6. As noted above, regional religiosity averages 7.3. Youths in Yemen (8.1), Morocco (7.5), and Egypt (7.5) also ranked above average for religiosity. Those surveyed in Jordan (6.9), Lebanon (6.6), Palestine (7.2), and Tunisia (6.0), as well as the Syrian refugees in Lebanon (7.0) are largely in keeping with the overall average. The detailed view of the degree of religiosity as revealed by the groupings shows that 87 percent of respondents in Bahrain and 54 percent in Yemen are very religious, while the majority of young people in Morocco (43 percent), Egypt (43 percent), Jordan (39 percent), and Palestine (39 percent) ranked as quite religious. Respondents in Tunisia (43 percent), Lebanon (32 percent), and the Syrian refugees in Lebanon (36 percent) rate as somewhat religious. Those of low religiosity are to be found especially in Tunisia

Table 4.3 Religiosity by Milieu of Residence

	Large city 100,001+	Mid-sized city 1,001–100,000	Rural up to 20,000	Refugee camp
Low religiosity	8	10	8	5
Somewhat religious	21	34	21	25
Quite religious	31	34	31	40
Very religious	40	22	40	30
	100	100	100	100

Questions 5, 121 .

Note Figures are given in percentages. Rounding errors can occur.

(15 percent) and Lebanon (13 percent) (Table 4.2). Thus one can divide the countries into three groups: countries with very high religiosity (Bahrain and Yemen), countries with a high religiosity (Egypt, Morocco, Jordan, and Palestine), and countries whose young people are classified as of low religiosity: Tunisia, the Syrian refugees and Lebanon.

These results are not surprising. The Gulf states are considered more religious and conservative than the rest of the MENA region, while religion remains central as a source of official legitimacy to the monarchies in the Gulf and to those of Jordan and Morocco. In Egypt and Palestine, meanwhile, religious movements have been gaining in influence since the mid-1980s, as foundations for resistance, such as in Palestine, or as providers of social advantage, as in Egypt. Such movements have frequently taken the places of secular regimes and offered alternative social models. Tunisia, however, still appears to be influenced by the secular politics of Habib Bourguiba and Zine al-Abidine Ben Ali. This secularism continues to exert a hold over the everyday practices of the population. Similarly, the relatively low religiosity of respondents in Lebanon could be explained by the country's religious plurality. Of the surveyed young Lebanese, 58 percent are Muslim (60 percent Shiʻi, 40 percent Sunni) and 38 percent Christian.

Young people exhibit different patterns of change across the MENA region in terms of their religiosity at the time of the survey compared to before the Arab Spring. Based on the percentages in Table 4.2, young people in Bahrain have evinced no significant change in religiosity, whereas in Egypt one observes a marked trend from low religiosity and somewhat religious towards increasing religiosity. In Jordan, the decline of somewhat religious in favour of quite religious is notable, while increasing religiosity is also observable in Lebanon, Palestine, Yemen, and Morocco. Indeed, in Morocco, whereas the low religiosity group expanded, from 3 percent five years prior to 8 percent at the time of the survey, the very religious group also expanded similarly, increasing by 6 percent. Stability is more evident among Syrian refugees in Lebanon, while in Tunisia, Palestine, and Lebanon, a decline of 'low religiosity' and an accompanying increase of 'quite religious' from 29 percent to 33 percent is perceptible.

Ultimately, then, there has been a marked increase in religiosity in all the countries surveyed. Political events as well as economic conditions and crises are decisive factors in determining the religiosity of the young people surveyed (see Chapter 7). Also of importance is the status of religion in the respective political systems and the type of legitimation upon which the systems rely. It is interesting to note, however, that in Morocco – a country governed since the parliamentary elections of 2011 by the Islamic PJD Party (Parti pour la Justice et le Développement) – the number of youth who identify as non-religious has increased over the last five years.

Structural Conditions and Youth Religiosity

Analysis by residential milieu reveals that all four groups – from low religiosity to very religious – have a notable presence in large cities (Table 4.3). In this respect, large cities (pop. 100,001-plus) are heterogeneous and inhabited by young people who reported a low degree of religiosity (8 percent) as well as those who ranked themselves as somewhat religious (21 percent) and quite religious (31 percent). The city, then, accommodates those who consider themselves very religious as well as those who consider themselves not or not very religious. The very religious have a significant presence in large cities (40 percent), whereas rural areas (pop. up to 20,000) are their second most common habitat (40 percent). Beyond the large cities, those youth rated as being of low religiosity (10 percent) and somewhat religious (34 percent) are especially present in mid-sized cities (pop. 1,000 to 100,000). One might surmise, then, that such environments are inhabited above all by young people of low religiosity and those somewhat religious.

In 1969, Ernest Gellner argued in his study of Morocco that urban Islam is more tolerant than rural Islam. The social transformations and different mobility patterns of recent years, however, as well as a massive tendency towards urbanisation, seem to have partly altered the forms and intensities of religiosity in Arab countries. As Table 4.3 suggests, a conservative form of Islam seems to have established itself in the large cities of the MENA region. Such places are inhabited above all by highly religious young people, some 71 percent of those very religious and quite religious. This quota is comparable with those young people surveyed in rural areas,

Table 4.4 Religiosity and Father's Level of Education

Level of education	Low religiosity	Somewhat religious	Quite religious	Very religious	Total
Illiterate	7	23	34	36	100
Read and write	8	21	32	39	100
Primary school	8	31	34	27	100
Secondary / Intermediate school	9	25	34	32	100
Baccalaureate	10	28	35	27	100
Technical / Vocational diploma	7	25	36	32	100
University degree (BA, MA)	8	17	26	49	100
Ph.D.	9	13	15	63	100

Questions 30, 121.

Note Figures are given in percentages. Rounding errors can occur.

where 71 percent ranked as quite religious or very religious. In urban centres increasingly inhabited by economic migrants from rural regions, it would appear that religious communities serve to compensate for the less close-knit character of city life. Of particular interest here are the small and medium-sized towns, which seem to harbour the least intensely religious groups. In recent years, the Arab bourgeoisie has increasingly withdrawn to exactly this kind of setting. In fact, most young people identify with 'low religiosity' and 'somewhat religious' (together 44 percent) live in small and medium-sized towns.

The empirical findings also show that the father's level of education is medium to high among more than half of respondents, and that in all countries surveyed with the exception of Lebanon, the state is the principal employer of the respondents' fathers. As shown in other sections of this study (see Chapter 7), the father plays an important role as a guarantor of the status of the family and in the socialisation of young people. His influence on the religious orientation of Arab youth is thus obvious.

What is the relationship between the social status of the interviewees and their degree of religiosity? This question relates to the connection between the religiosity of respondents and the father's degree of education and to the relationship between a respondent's self-described social class and their religiosity. As Table 4.4 shows, those respondents whose fathers have higher levels of education usually rated as very religious, whereas those whose fathers had little education tend to be somewhat religious or quite religious. Sixty-three percent of those whose fathers hold a PhD are very religious, as

Table 4.5 Religiosity and Self-described Class Membership

Class	Low religiosity	Somewhat religious	Quite religious	Very religious	Total
Wealthy	9	18	15	58	100
Upper-middle class	10	23	34	33	100
Lower-middle class	8	25	32	35	100
Poor	7	28	33	32	100
Destitute	13	18	34	35	100

Questions 47, 121.

Note Figures are given in percentages. Rounding errors can occur.

are 49 percent of those whose fathers graduated from university. It is also notable that whereas 16 percent of those surveyed (1,386 respondents) had fathers with a PhD or university degree, 15 percent described their fathers as illiterate. These are proportionally similar groups, and yet only 36 percent of those with illiterate fathers ranked as very religious.

Furthermore, the data on the social background of the four groups indicate a link between self-described class membership and religiosity (Table 4.5). Among those respondents who classified their families as wealthy, 58 percent considered themselves to be very religious, while only 9 percent rated themselves as being of low religiosity. One can also see a clear correlation between those ranked as quite religious and being upper-middle class, at 34 percent. That said, many of the very religious also described their family as poor and destitute, while those interviewees considered somewhat religious are to be found predominantly in the lower-middle class (25 percent) or the poorer classes (28 percent). Also notable is that the largest percentage of those characterised as low religiosity (13 percent) also considered their family to be among the most destitute members of society. This was despite only 3 percent of those questioned describing their family as destitute, whereas 30 percent positioned it in the ranks of the upper classes, describing their family as wealthy. This study thus contravenes the link often drawn between high religiosity and poverty or a low level of education. In fact, the very religious seem to be drawn predominantly from the ranks of the financially secure and well educated, whereas the less religious seem to belong, above all, to the poorer social classes.

The interviewees are, on average, much better educated than their parents, but their opportunities for social advancement are less and their fears for the

Table 4.6 Religiosity and Feelings of Security

	Low religiosity	Somewhat religious	Quite religious	Very religious
Insecure	38	31	24	23
Rather insecure	21	26	27	21
Rather secure	19	24	28	24
Secure	22	19	21	32
	100	100	100	100

Question 121, Security Index (see Figure 2.1).

Note Figures are given in percentages. Rounding errors can occur.

Table 4.7 Religiosity and Outlook on Society's Future

	Low religiosity	Somewhat religious	Quite religious	Very religious
Rather pessimistic	37	34	30	26
Rather optimistic	63	66	70	74
	100	100	100	100

Questions 121, 166.

Note Figures are given in percentages. Rounding errors can occur.

future greater. Prior to the implementation of structural adjustment programmes in Arab countries, the huge public sector offered bountiful opportunities for social advancement, while the number of university graduates
increased dramatically with the massive investment in education that began at
the end of the 1970s. This coincided, however, with a deterioration in employment opportunities on the labour market, especially in the public sector.

This situation is reflected in the data from this survey insofar as the
young people surveyed placed particular emphasis on economic uncertainty and job-related concerns, as well as the risk of an outbreak of armed
conflict. It is no longer possible for university graduates – especially those
with technical qualifications – to be absorbed by a crisis-ridden public sector. Overall, it could be that religiosity serves as a kind of capital to compensate for the reduced social and professional opportunities enjoyed by an
older generation equipped with educational capital (Table 4.6). Religion
provides security and optimism, imbuing gloomy economic prospects with
a degree of hope.

As Table 4.6 shows, young people of low religiosity also feel the most insecure (38 percent), whereas the very religious feel the most secure (32 percent). It can be observed that the sense of security increases as the degree of religiosity increases, whereby 'security' is taken to mean confidence in one's personal and professional future. Experiences and levels of security in the areas of health, food, emotion, family, economy, career, violence, and war are summarised in Table 2.2. Religion thus appears to compensate for a certain lack of prospects, by providing a degree of security that allows the very religious respondents to feel more optimistic about their and their society's futures (Table 4.7).

Overall, then, religiously inclined young people seem much more optimistic than those who self-described as non-religious or low religiosity, with religion apparently providing a sense of hope to many frustrated young people, such as Muhammad, a married 30-year-old from Yemen, who explicitly stated, 'We are optimistic because we follow the Islamic religion.' As Table 4.7 indicates, 74 percent of very religious young people are optimistic about the society's future, whereas the degree of pessimism is greater among those of low religiosity (37 percent). Religion, it seems, offers not only security, but optimism as well in times of crisis, upheaval, and change.

Religion is no longer understood as an overall social or political project or as the basis for a collective Islamic social utopia. Rather, it is a prop in the realisation of an individual utopia that also serves as an asset in times of uncertainty. This is illustrated by the fact that though the interviewees largely considered themselves religiously minded, their trust in religious institutions was not very high. Though such confidence was expressed by 23 percent of respondents in answering the question 'What about your trust in different institutions?', this paled in comparison to trust in the family (80 percent), the military (54 percent), the educational system (40 percent), and the police (40 percent). Confidence in religious institutions was highest amongst those young people surveyed in Bahrain (89 percent) and lowest in Tunisia (42 percent) (see Table 2.10). Traditional religious institutions, such as the Zawiya, also enjoy great respect among the youth of Morocco and Egypt. Respondents in Jordan have the highest levels of trust in religious institutions (49 percent) and those in Bahrain had the lowest (4 percent).

Young people in the Arab world, it seems, increasingly view religion as a private matter. Indeed, 83 percent defined it as such when asked 'What do you think? "Religion is a private matter and nobody should interfere".' This view is particularly pronounced among young Tunisians (93 percent) and Syrian refugees (92 percent). Similarly, 60 percent of interviewees want Islam to play a more important role in everyday life. Only 13 percent of the

Table 4.8 Religiosity and Preferred Political System

	Low religiosity	Somewhat religious	Quite religious	Very religious
Strong man who governs the country	31	23	21	32
Religious state based on sharia	6	9	12	12
Democratic system	37	43	40	33
Combined democratic and Islamic system	10	12	12	10

Questions 113, 121.

Note Figures are given in percentages. Rounding errors can occur.

young people surveyed, however, claimed to be engaged in religious institutions when asked 'Where and how do you engage?', with Egyptians the most frequently engaged, at 17 percent.

Overall, the empirical findings suggest that a large majority of the very religious youth are not politically active or are only politically active to a limited extent. In addition, the mobilised youth are generally less religious than the non-mobilised youth. The percentage of political activists who claimed a low religiosity stands at 38 percent, which is greater than the equivalent figure among non-activists (see Chapter 13).

To assess attitudes in respect to the role of religion within political systems, young people were asked, 'If you look around the world, what kind of political system would you prefer?'. Eleven percent of respondents were in favour of a sharia-based system of government (18 percent in Jordan, 33 percent in Palestine, and 17 percent in Yemen). A further 11 percent endorsed a political system based on both democratic and Islamic principles. This rate is higher in Jordan (22 percent), Yemen (18 percent), and Morocco and Palestine (15 percent each). Conversely, more than 38 percent of those surveyed were in favour of a democratic political system, while 26 percent wanted a 'strong man' government (see Figure 12.3).

Young people of low religiosity as well as the more religious tended to favour a democratic political system (Table 4.8). That said, a majority of respondents reported a desire for a 'strong man who governs the country' as their second preference. It is striking that this desire for a strong, though just, leader associated with the political tradition of the region was common to both the least and most religious respondents. It would be interesting to deepen the study here to establish whether both the highly and less religious respondents identify a similar kind of strong man as desirable.

Could it be that those of less religiosity might favour personalities such as Gamal Abdel Nasser or Bourguiba, while the very religious might endorse religious leaders, for example a righteous caliph? Either way, the desire for political change and a longing for justice seem considerable amongst both demographics and, as briefly noted, all four groups endorse a democratic system. This desire is clearly stronger among the somewhat religious (43 percent) and quite religious (40 percent), while amongst these same groups, the desire for a strong man is slightly weaker (23 percent and 21 percent, respectively) than it is among those of low and high religiosity. One might suggest, then, that the most and least religious tend to prefer strong leaders, while the moderately religious lean towards a democratic system.

As expected, only a minority of respondents endorsed a sharia-based religious state. This wish emanated above all from those quite religious (12 percent) and very religious (12 percent). A political system combining democratic and Islamic elements was desired to a much lesser extent overall, and then primarily among those young people ranked somewhat religious (12 percent) and quite religious (12 percent).

Conclusion

The empirical evidence presented here suggests that religion plays an increasingly important role in the everyday lives of the young people of the MENA region. The data do suggest national differences, but overall they paint a picture of relatively pious youth. Women are more religious than men, while there is no significant difference in religiosity across age groups.

The study also indicates that the very religious and quite religious are more likely to be found in large cities and rural areas, whereas those in mid-sized and smaller urban centres tended to be somewhat religious or with little religiosity. Viewed according to the father's level of education as well as self-reported social class, it appears that the very religious tend to come from families that can be described as wealthy and in which the father holds a university degree. Furthermore, those young people exhibiting a less pronounced religiosity tend to come from families with reduced educational capital and from the ranks of the lower-middle classes, including the poor. It also seems clear that religiosity serves as a source of hope and optimism. It is less as a basis for political and ideological attitudes than for personal well-being and self-discipline. Religion, it appears, functions more as a channel for spirituality rather than a vehicle for a political ideology.

One can draw on the ideas of Taylor (2009) to suggest that the young people surveyed here seem to have arrived in the age of 'expressive individualism'. Taylor uses this term to describe the state of Western religiosity in the 1960s, invoking Émile Durkheim's 'social place of the sacred' to distinguish paleo-, neo-, and post-Durkheimian periods. In the first period, the social order was heavily hierarchical and structured by religion. In the neo-Durkheimian period, religious affiliation was strongly politicised, and religion was a force for political and social mobilisation (much like nationalism). In the post-Durkheimian period, however, religion becomes a matter for the individual, with piety a way of life and expression of one's own personality. Taylor speaks here of the search for spirituality as something that lends harmony and balance (Taylor 2009). Indeed, under this rubric, even mass religious events and spectacles are to be understood as expressive of the search for new forms of individual spirituality.

Religiosity seems to aid the young of the Arab world in their search for perspective, serving as a refuge and source of hope in a world that seems to have become culturally, politically, economically, and socially unmoored and in which the predominant political systems are not highly trusted. Economically, this phase seems to be characterised by a crisis of the developmental state, the failure of older developmental models, and the implementation of structural adjustment programmes – a period underpinned, perhaps, by a neoliberal agenda. The 2010–11 revolts that shook the Arab world have ushered in a new cycle, one coloured by ideological fatigue and an on-going attempt by non-organised movements to bring about individual utopias, frequently in opposition to the social order. This background explains the new logic of pragmatism that appears endemic to today's actors. In the light of the data, then, one might conclude that religion in the Arab world has become a personal matter. Piety is increasing, but primarily at the level of the individual, rather than in the form of a collective striving for a social utopia, as was the case with Arab nationalism or political Islam.

Overall, then, religion has become a means for realising particular, individual ways of life, even though it frequently retains the trappings of a collective experience. Indeed, Schulze (2012) has spoken of the liberation of individual lifestyles from the state paternalism that ensued from the failure of state-directed social models and a concomitant gain in the legitimacy of individual visions of utopia. This could be taken as the beginning of what Taylor calls a post-Durkheimian order, in which values and norms are separated (Schulze 2012: 45ff). The responses of those interviewed seem to indicate a decline in political religiosity and an advance in social religiosity. Is this the dawn of a secular age in the Arab world?

5

Gender

Ines Braune

WOMEN'S VOICES AND BODIES were at the centre of the Arab uprisings. Although women and men demonstrated side by side to claim freedom and dignity – standing up for everybody's rights in patriarchal societies – it was the female body that drew the greater share of violent physical attacks and sexual harassment. The countless assaults by authorities as well as private individuals against women confirmed the vulnerability of women and their families in Arab societies. At the same time, public discussions about labour migration and refugee flows tend to focus on young men and questions of masculinity. What do these discourses reveal about gendered inequality and about gender roles in Arab countries today?

This chapter argues that due to the pronounced public relevance of gender in the MENA region, inequality is often approached through a gendered perspective (AHDR 2005, 2016; El Feki et al. 2017). A gendered analysis of the whole survey is therefore not offered nor is the focus exclusively on women-related issues. Instead, the intersections of gender, education, nationality, and social background of relevant issues are analysed. Inquiries are made into marital status, education, job and family, and sexual harassment to present a nuanced picture of gender in the MENA region.

Youth or Married? Youthful and Married!

Who in the MENA region has been considered as youth from a historical perspective, particularly in relation to gender? In a 1969 study about young people in rural Morocco, for example, women were excluded, as they were viewed as either children or mothers, but not youth. A transitional life stage for women coming of age did not exist (Pascon and Bentahar 1969: 11–12). Youth, at the time, was not yet seen as a self-evident concept marked by certain aspirations, but rather as a short phase between the end of childhood and the onset of adulthood.

Figure 5.1 Who Is Married? National Perspective

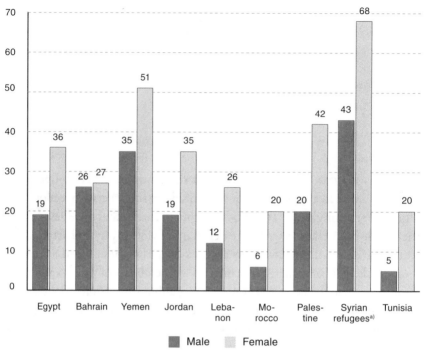

Questions 1, 3, 14.

Note Figures are given in percentages. Rounding errors can occur. **a)** Syrian Refugees in Lebanon.

Indeed, youth as a life stage is quite a recent phenomenon in the Arab world, emerging over the last fifty to sixty years. In a Harvard University project on adolescence covering the twenty years from the mid-1960s to the mid-1980s, Davis and Davis (1989) remark on the difficulty of even finding a term in Arabic to define the period between childhood and adulthood. In their view, the introduction of public education first and foremost demarcated and even institutionalised recognition of such a life stage. '[S]chool has created the concept as well as the expectation of behaviour associated with it,' as they put it (Davis and Davis 1989: 59). Because of formalised, school-based education, both boys and girls now experience a transitional period just after childhood but before becoming full-fledged adults.

Youth as a concept is now well established in the MENA region, and the age range associated with it has been significantly extended. Bayat introduced the concept of 'youthfulness', associated with a specific habitus and mind-set of being young, to debates about young people in the Arab world. He claimed that cities in particular are central in turning young people into youths (Bayat and Herrera 2010: 7).

The present study found that the vast majority of young people consider themselves to be youths (92 percent) independent of gender, residence, and level of education. Nevertheless, a much higher proportion of women than men surveyed are engaged or married, divorced, or widowed. This finding reflects the expectation in Arab societies that girls enter earlier into marriage, thereby living in a prescribed, 'regulated' context and assume responsibilities and motherhood within their own household. At the same time, this difference suggests that young men are older by the time they are financially able to marry (see Chapter 6).

Who is married: a national perspective

Among youth in the MENA region who are married, one-fifth (21 percent) are men, and a bit more than one-quarter (28 percent) are women. There are, of course, national differences, as shown in Figure 5.1.

In Morocco and Tunisia, the proportion of married young people is very low, 13 percent in the two countries combined. Interestingly, in these two countries, the gap between the percentage of married young men and married young women is the highest. In Morocco, young women account for 77 percent of married young people while in Tunisia they account for 79 percent. Together, these findings reveal that in these countries young people generally marry at an older age, particularly men, who rarely marry before the age of thirty. At the other end of the spectrum, young Syrian refugees are the most likely to be married among the populations surveyed, at 55 percent, followed by young Yemenis at 43 percent. The prevalence of marriage among this group is by far the highest. The high degree of uncertainty they experience seems to lead them to seek security through social bonding. In the other countries, the proportion of young people who are married ranges from 13 to 31 percent. While the difference in numbers between married women and men is very high in Morocco and Tunisia, it is very low in Bahrain. The favourable financial position of many young men as potential husbands and providers might be one reason for this level of relative parity. In contrast to Bahrain's affluent society, the proportion of young married women and men is also relatively balanced among the indigent in Yemen as well as Syrian refugees. It can be argued that in times of extensive insecurity and poor prospects, where an improved situation does not appear to be on the horizon, marriage becomes a security concern.

Figure 5.2 Who Is Married? Social Strata Perspective

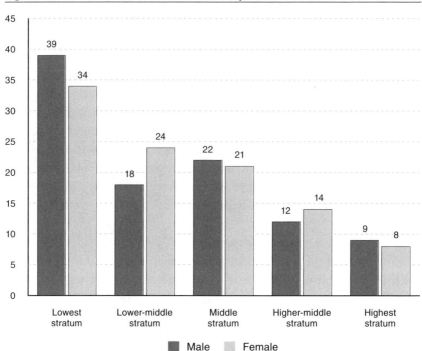

Questions 3, 14, Strata Index (see Appendix).

Note Figures are given in percentages. Rounding errors can occur.

In such situations, extending social networks via marriage and founding a family becomes more important than the financial capacity of a future husband.

In a nutshell, more women than men are married in all the survey countries, but of course with differences across nations. The most equal numbers of married women and men are found in Bahrain and Yemen, but for different and sometimes opposite reasons.

Who is married: a social stratum perspective

Looking at those young people who are married through the lens of social background, it is striking that the majority of those married in the sample belong to the lowest social stratum or the lower middle stratum (see Chapter 2; Appendix III). This is true for men and women alike (Figure 5.2).

This is especially revealing, as the middle, upper middle, and highest strata constitute a much larger group of people. To get a clearer picture, it is necessary to take massive national disparities into account (see Chapter 2, Figure 2.2). Most of the young people who are married are Syrian refugees living in Lebanon. The refugees belong almost entirely to the lowest stratum (84 percent), and a small percentage to the lower-middle stratum (13 percent). Almost no one is considered part of the upper-middle or the highest stratum. In Bahrain, quite the opposite is the case. Almost all young Bahrainis belong to the upper-middle (29 percent) or the highest stratum (62 percent).

Despite these national differences, however, the majority of married young people are part of the lower classes throughout the Arab countries. Indeed, the poorer the socio-economic background, the higher the proportion of married young women and men. While 34 percent of young women from the lowest stratum, 24 percent from the lower middle stratum, and 8 percent from the highest stratum are married, the proportion of married men across all the strata is similar. They amount to 39, 18, and 9 percent of respondents, respectively, from the lowest, lower middle, and highest strata. Both men and women from the lower classes are more often married than men and women from the higher classes. This is of importance when it comes to the question of whether single or married people consider themselves as belonging in the category of youth or adult. Young singles see themselves predominantly as youth (96 percent), but a large majority of married people also consider themselves as youth (83 percent). More in-depth analysis, however, reveals that a combination of social stratum, educational level, and class assessment determines whether married young people consider themselves as youth. Both men and women (married and unmarried) who come from a lower social background (and assess themselves as poor), and have only a primary school education, more often perceive themselves as adults than do married young people from the upper-middle and upper classes who have greater levels of education. The latter more frequently consider themselves to be youth and have social and economic backgrounds along with a specific youthful habitus reflective of their perception in this regard.

As discussed earlier, girls did not traditionally experience a transitional period between childhood and adulthood, that is, 'youth', until the growth of cities and institutionalised education allowed for the emergence of youth as a general life stage for both genders. Now, an even greater convergence is underway in terms of how young men and women perceive themselves. For example, place of residence – rural or urban – does not predict whether respondents consider themselves as youths or adults.

Figure 5.3 School Attendance

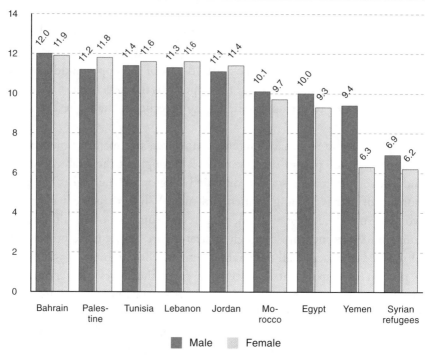

Male   Female

Questions 1, 3, 26.

Note Averages (arithmetic mean) are given in years. | Information about the school attendance was limited to 13 years – even if respondents spent 14 or more years at school – in order to make the numerical comparison between different school systems more meaningful.

Furthermore, it is striking that marriage is no longer an exclusive indicator of whether young people perceive themselves as adults. Rather, this self-assessment depends much more on education and socio-economic background. For young people of the middle and upper classes, it appears socially acceptable to maintain a 'youth' lifestyle for longer periods, independent of marital status.

Education Matters

Achieving equal access to education is a primary concern in terms of promoting gender equality in the MENA region. In considering educational disparities, it is important to examine where gender is the main factor and where other intersectionalities are relevant. As a basis for discussion, it must first be emphasised that the recent generation of young people, men and women alike, is better educated than any prior generation.

Table 5.1 Highest Educational Level Achieved, by Country and Gender

			Male	Female
Morocco		Up to and including primary school	15	18
		Secondary / Intermediate school	41	44
		Higher than secondary school	45	38
Tunisia		Up to and including primary school	16	14
		Secondary / Intermediate school	42	39
		Higher than secondary school	41	47
Egypt		Up to and including primary school	14	21
		Secondary / Intermediate school	59	45
		Higher than secondary school	27	34
Jordan		Up to and including primary school	14	11
		Secondary / Intermediate school	66	60
		Higher than secondary school	21	29
Palestine		Up to and including primary school	5	2
		Secondary / Intermediate school	50	36
		Higher than secondary school	45	62
Lebanon		Up to and including primary school	11	8
		Secondary / Intermediate school	32	30
		Higher than secondary school	57	62
Yemen		Up to and including primary school	30	58
		Secondary / Intermediate school	29	21
		Higher than secondary school	41	21
Bahrain		Up to and including primary school	9	11
		Secondary / Intermediate school	48	44
		Higher than secondary school	43	45
Syrian Refugees		Up to and including primary school	59	63
		Secondary / Intermediate school	30	29
		Higher than secondary school	11	8

Questions 1, 3, 27.

Note Figures are given in percentages. Rounding errors can occur. | The educational qualifications were grouped into three categories: 'Up to and including primary school'; 'Secondary / intermediate school'; 'Higher than secondary school'.

In nearly all the surveyed countries, boys and girls attend school an average of at least ten years, although regional and gender gaps do exist (Figure 5.3). The duration of education is almost identical in Bahrain, Palestine, Tunisia, Lebanon, and Jordan. It is less in Morocco, Egypt, Yemen, and for the Syrian refugees. At the same time, when the length of education decreases, the gender ratio changes. For instance, among the refugees, the young Syrian men have attended school for only about seven years, with women having had on average an even shorter period of education. The difference between boys' and girls' levels of education is greatest in Yemen, where girls attend school for fewer than seven years, three years fewer than boys. It is also important to note that fewer Yemeni girls ever attend any school (although some girls attend as long as boys). In contrast, some surveyed countries have high enrolment rates, with boys and girls both attending school for eleven to twelve years. This is true for Bahrain, Jordan, Lebanon, Palestine, and Tunisia. In these countries, in fact, girls on average attend school slightly longer than boys.

Education: a gendered and national perspective

Examining the degrees obtained by women and men in the MENA region helps provide a clearer picture of existing educational gaps (Table 5.1). Whereas the survey identified no illiterate young persons at all in Bahrain, Lebanon, and Palestine, where nearly all children are enrolled in the institutionalised school systems, a high percentage of Syrian refugees identified themselves as illiterate (men 11 percent, women 18 percent). Illiteracy is also relevant in Yemen, with the greatest gap in literacy being between the genders. The percentage of illiterate women is eleven times higher than that of illiterate men, 25 percent versus 2 percent. Syrian refugees and Yemenis constitute the overall majority of surveyed young people unable to read or write. A small number are also found in Egypt and Morocco, again, with the larger segment being women. In most surveyed countries, young people who completed secondary school constitute the largest group overall. Notable is the relatively high number of university degrees; the percentage of women holding a university degree equals or slightly exceeds that of men in Egypt, Jordan, Palestine, and Tunisia. This is also true in Bahrain and Lebanon, where an especially high proportion of young people – more than half of respondents in each country – hold a university degree.

Clearly, the young generation on the whole is well educated. Syria and Yemen, countries experiencing armed conflict and a high degree of insecurity, are exceptions. Across all surveyed countries, women are much more likely than men to have a weak educational background. In contrast, the percentage of highly educated women, those holding a university degree, exceeds that of men. The central issue thus becomes how these young women can benefit from their education (see below, 'Future Aspirations: Jobs or Family').

Education: a generational perspective

The educational status of the younger generation overall stands in great contrast with their parents' generation. Illiteracy among mothers and fathers of the respondents is far more common than among the young generation.

Table 5.2 **Mother's Highest Level of Education**

	Mo-rocco	Tuni-sia	Egypt	Jor-dan	Pales-tine	Lebanon	Ye-men	Bah-rain	Syrian Ref.
Illiterate	43	22	18	18	6	6	82	5	56
Read and write	12	1	11	4	2	6	4	1	10
Primary school	23	41	10	22	17	23	5	6	24
Secondary school	15	19	26	36	38	31	4	48	7
Baccalaureate	5	6	10	7	24	19	2	1	1
Technical diploma	0	1	11	12	5	3	0	3	0
University degree	1	4	12	1	8	11	1	34	1
PhD	0	0	0	0	0	0	0	1	0
Don't know	2	7	3	1	0	1	1	2	2

Questions 1, 39.

Note Figures are given in percentages. Rounding errors can occur.

Fathers were identified as illiterate most frequently in Morocco and Yemen as well as among the Syrian refugee population. Among respondents' mothers, one-quarter are illiterate, with considerable variation across countries (Table 5.2). In Yemen, 82 percent of mothers are illiterate, while among Syrian refugees the figure stands at 56 percent and in Morocco 43 percent. Furthermore, in Egypt, Jordan, and Tunisia, one-fifth of mothers are unable to read or write, whereas this is true for only 6 percent or less in Bahrain, Lebanon, and Palestine.

The findings also reflect general standards among different national educational systems. In some countries (Morocco, Syria, and Yemen), the older generation generally shows a fairly high incidence of illiteracy among men and women alike, whereas in others (Bahrain, Egypt, Jordan, Lebanon, and Palestine), more members of the parental generation were able to gain a higher education degree. Nevertheless, women in the parents' generation are overall more poorly educated than men, and fathers are more likely to hold a degree from an institution of higher education, with the exception of Lebanon, where a greater percentage of mothers hold a higher education degree.

Leaving aside the case of Syrian refugees, who have an alarming illiteracy rate among young women, the survey, generally speaking, indicates that young women are better educated than their mothers and are considerably less likely to be illiterate. These findings, however, offer no information about quality of education, which is often criticised in the Arab world (see UNDP 2016), and does not indicate whether well-educated young women are able to translate their education into (high-value) jobs.

Future Aspirations: Jobs or Family

The aspiration of young people of both genders in terms of jobs and family are of special interest. In particular, what do young women aspire to depending on their educational background? This question can be addressed by examining the choice between job and family as a young person plans for the future. Survey respondents were asked what they consider most important for their future: a good marriage, a good job, good friends, or good family relations. They could select only one option. Roughly speaking, for young men a good job is the most important goal (62 percent), whereas for women it is a good marriage (41 percent). Women ranked finding a good job as second in importance (at 34 percent), close behind marriage, whereas 19 percent of men cited a good marriage as most important. The third option, maintaining good family relations, was cited as most important by 22 percent of women and 16 percent of men, whereas having good friends was deemed a low priority overall, cited as most important by only 4 percent of women and of men. This last finding underlines that the key point of reference for identity construction as well as for social and financial protection is one's own family, with networks of friends outside kinship circles being of lesser importance.

Clash of attitudes

The survey question about the importance of marriage or a job to one's future reveals significant differences and interests between young men and women, but also among women of different social backgrounds (Figure 5.4). Among young men, the importance of finding a good job declines as social stratum rises: 70 percent of young men from the lowest socio-economic stratum state that a good job is most important for their future, as compared with only 52 percent of young men from the highest social stratum. An interpretation is that those from a secure social position are sure to get what is perceived as a good job. At the same time, the importance of a good marriage is slightly more important among men of higher social strata. For these men, whose economic situation is assumed to be secure, the role of family networks may be a focus of more attention.

The perspectives of women in the survey revealed an opposing trend. It is a remarkable finding that women from the upper-middle and highest

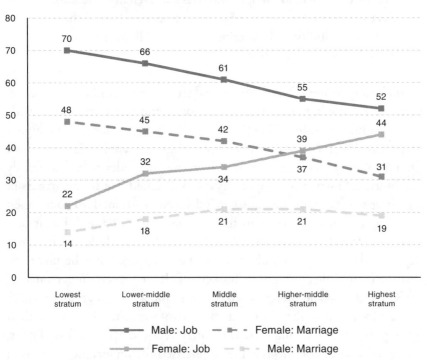

| | Male: Job | Female: Marriage |
| | Female: Job | Male: Marriage |

Questions 3, 127, Strata Index (see Appendix).

Note Figures are given in percentages. Rounding errors can occur.

economic strata stated that having a good marriage is less important than securing a good job. About 22 percent of women from the lowest social stratum want most to get a good job, whereas 44 percent of women from the highest stratum aim foremost to find a good job. Only 31 percent place greater importance on a good marriage. Sakha, a 30-year-old woman from Jordan, has a master's degree in international law and supports herself working in the media and education sector. She described her position as follows:

> I don't think about getting engaged to someone, especially when I see someone living in a house full of conflicts between their parents and problems around money issues. In general, I seek a partner who is ambitious, intelligent, and civilised, who is open-minded and accepts that I work at night and that I have male colleagues, someone who is cultured and keeps traditions. It isn't necessary

that he hold a university degree, but he has to accept the idea that I remove the hijab in foreign countries and even in Jordan, and he has to respect the opinions of others, someone who will share life and responsibility and suffering and who will accept being supported by my income (JO-7).

While young women from higher social strata are more likely to focus on getting a good job, to earn their own money and find fulfilment outside of or in addition to founding their own family, young men of the higher social classes stress the importance of marriage and family relations. These findings starkly challenge tradition in terms of gender roles and family and household structures, especially if it is assumed that both partners in a marriage come from the same general social position. Two young men reflecting on their expectations for marriage illustrate the different perspectives. Thirty-one-year-old Ahmad, from Bahrain, holds a university degree and works in the public sector. He is engaged, but he mentions that the commitment 'might be broken off'. 'I have a certain personality,' Hassan said. 'I would prefer her to be a wife and a mother at home. That's enough for her. A husband should take care of the rest. If he doesn't, then he may as well be sleeping' (BH-12). Thirty-year-old Muataz, from Egypt, also holds a university degree. He emphasised the importance of a good marriage, saying, 'Our prophet says that you should marry the woman for her beauty, family tree, and religion – which is the most important thing. Her education and satisfaction also are important. She must [also] bear me in any situation. I need a wife that could raise my children correctly' (EG-3).

Women from the lower socio-economic strata more frequently see their future as determined by a good marriage (48 percent) rather than a good job (22 percent). Good family relations (26 percent) are of secondary importance for them. Young men and women from the lower social strata appear to conform to traditional gender roles, whereby men prioritise their job and being responsible for family income, and women strive for a good marriage. A young Jordanian woman illustrates this perspective. Fatima is not yet married and currently is supported by her father's income.

My future husband? [He should be] someone who can help me get out of the financial situation I'm in and who'll help me fulfil my dreams, someone who fears God and can inspire me to be

Figure 5.5 Women Who Have Never Been Employed, by Social Stratum

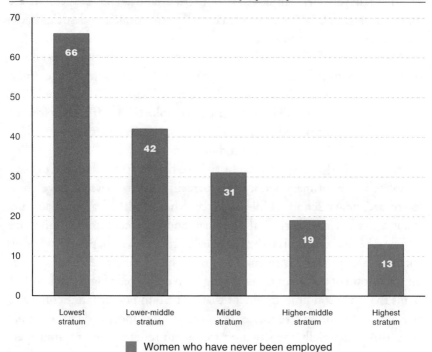

Women who have never been employed

Questions 3, 127, Strata Index (cf. Appendix).
Note Figures are given in percentages. Rounding errors can occur.

more devout, who has a good reputation in the community, and who is loving and not aggressive. I will be a housewife to my husband and will work to take care of our domestic needs (JO-6).

Who is working? The issue of women who have never been employed
For women in particular, the crucial point in their educational and occupational biographies seems to be entry into the labour market (see Chapter 7). Among the young people surveyed who are working, the overwhelming majority are men. Nevertheless, about one-quarter of those who work are women. Among respondents who are, for various reasons, temporarily without work, about 40 percent are women. Particularly striking, however, is the high percentage of women who never work, in the sense of not engaging in paid labour (96 percent). This group consists mainly of hard-working housewives. Almost three-quarters (72 percent) of women

who have never been employed are married, and about 26 percent are single or engaged. What kind of national, educational, and social backgrounds do these women have?

About one-half of those who have never worked are between 26 and 30 years old, and one-third are 21 to 25 years old. In the youngest age group (16 to 20), only 20 percent reported that they had never been employed. The group of women who have never been employed consists, therefore, of slightly older and married women who may have given birth to a child, so they are occupied with childcare and housework.

In terms of education, the majority have never attended school or have completed only primary school (44 percent). Thirty percent have completed secondary school, while 11 percent have finished a baccalaureate, about 4 percent hold technical diplomas, and 11 percent hold a university degree. Above all, it seems to be social background that shapes the working opportunities of these women. The lower the social stratum, the greater the likelihood of a woman never having been employed (Figure 5.5). It thus seems that the economic argument that women in poorer families have to be employed in order to contribute to the family's income does not apply here. This is especially the situation for Syrian refugees. Seventy-four percent of the female Syrian refugees belong to the group of women who have not been employed. Together with women not working temporarily and students, the total is 88 percent. Of note, as soon as Syrian refugees receive public assistance, they are not allowed to work.

The group of never-employed young people consists almost entirely of women, mainly those with lower social and educational backgrounds, and in case of the Syrian refugees, in a context of insecure structures. All these factors restrict women's options to shape their own future.

Sexual Harassment

As noted above, social power relations and state security issues are often negotiated through the female body in the public space. Especially in times of instability, the treatment of women, as well as the positioning of women-related issues, serves as an indicator of the extent to which justice and freedom are being safeguarded in a society. The same holds true for interaction in the public space. The pervasiveness of attacks against women in countries across the MENA region has shaken faith in the public order. In societies like those in the region – where according to traditional values, the family's honour and reputation are tied to the integrity of the women's body – such assaults affect the entire family of a victimised woman. Assaults

Figure 5.6 **Cases of Sexual Harassment**

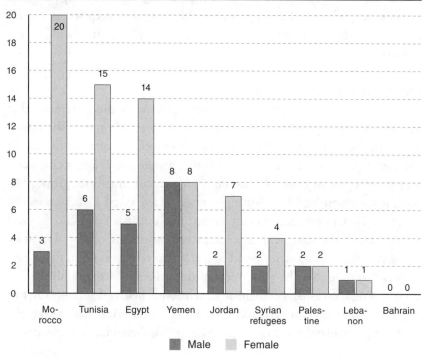

Questions 1, 3, 168.

Note Figures are given in percentages. Rounding errors can occur.

against women become de facto attacks against men, who experience social humiliation through their incapability to ensure protection for the women in their families.

Women as well as men reported having experienced verbal or physical forms of sexual harassment (Figure 5.6), most commonly in Egypt, Morocco, and Tunisia. Significantly, a remarkably high proportion of respondents in Morocco and Egypt refused to respond to the survey question on sexual harassment – 9 percent in Egypt and 6 percent in Morocco, compared to about 1 percent in other countries. The prevalence of acknowledged experience of such harassment is alarming in Jordan, among Syrian refugees, and in Yemen. Hardly any cases were reported in Bahrain, Lebanon, and Palestine. In addition, in these three countries, men reported being targeted approximately as often as women. In the other countries, the majority of those who have experienced sexual harassment are women.

The problem of sexual harassment is especially urgent in large cities. It becomes less relevant the less populous the area. The exception is Yemen, where sexual harassment of men is predominantly associated with a rural context.

Rising tensions in public space

Young people were asked whether they agree with the statement that personal safety in public space is becoming increasingly tense. The results underline the argument that the situation is especially urgent in the public space of larger cities. The majority of young people live in larger cities, and they perceive an increase of tensions, independent of gender. Almost 80 percent answered 'agree' or 'strongly agree' when asked if these tensions have increased, 14 percent were undecided, and only 8 percent said they did not agree with the statement. The increased tensions are observed most by young people in Bahrain, followed by the Syrian refugees and in Palestine.

It is revealing that the perception of the situation in the public sphere as becoming increasingly fraught with tension is first and foremost felt in larger cities in general but is perceived as more conflict-ridden in the refugee camps in particular. Sara, a 17-year-old Egyptian, shared her experiences:

> When I go down the street, I find people's ethics have totally changed. Seventy-five percent of the youth are completely unethical, and there is no safety. I feel afraid while walking, and when I wear a skirt and loose clothes, I keep getting harassed verbally. And people can rob me in the street, so I hold my bags really tight. No one helps at all. I saw a girl who was harassed, and she was screaming, and I was shocked by people's reaction. They even blamed her for having a loud voice and said she should have walked silently. In the past, men were afraid to do that [harass women], because other men might hurt them, but now if the victim shouts, people will blame her, not him (EG-2).

No clash of attitudes

Survey respondents were asked for their view on the statement 'Women dressing inappropriately should not complain about sexual harassment.' As shown in Figure 5.7, possible responses were strongly disagree, disagree, so-so, agree, or strongly agree. Remarkably, there was no general tendency to disagree with the statement. Overall, the proportion of those who agree

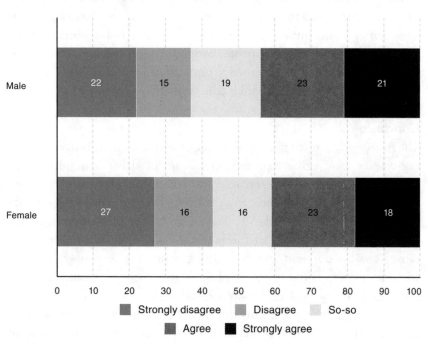

Male
| 22 | 15 | 19 | 23 | 21 |

Female
| 27 | 16 | 16 | 23 | 18 |

0 10 20 30 40 50 60 70 80 90 100

■ Strongly disagree ■ Disagree ■ So-so
■ Agree ■ Strongly agree

Questions 3, 170.

Note Figures are given in percentages. Rounding errors can occur.

with the statement is greater than the share of those who do not agree. A gendered analysis reveals that women respondents are slightly more likely than men to disagree with the statement. A greater percentage of men than women agree with the statement or have no clear opinion on it (answering 'so-so').

Bahrain represents a major exception, as almost all young Bahrainis (except for 2 percent) disagree with the statement, men and women alike. Putting aside the voices of Bahraini men who disagree with the statement, the overwhelming majority of young male respondents support the idea expressed in the statement. If the dissenting female Bahraini voices are put aside, the absolute number of women who disagree is lower than the number of those who condone the statement. Respondents' level of education does not affect the overall findings. There is no difference in attitude towards the statement whether the respondents are illiterate, have some education, or hold a bachelor's or master's degree (when Bahrain is excluded).

To sum up, many more women than men are affected by either verbal or physical harassment. This is of main concern in urban areas, where young people are convinced that the situation in public space is becoming increasingly tense. Concerning the dress code of women and assaults in public space, the majority of young people assign the responsibility for verbal or physical assault to women deemed to be dressed inappropriately. They do so independently of gender and their educational background.

Conclusion

The Arab world is often perceived through a gendered perspective. Depending on the issue, other aspects – including social background, national affiliation, and generation – are relevant to explaining inequality and insecurity for young people. Generally, the living conditions of young men and women have been equalised to a certain degree. Both men and women now experience a distinct phase of youth, in rural and urban areas alike. At the same time, the duration and durability of youth are very much linked to social background. Young people of the higher socio-economic classes are much more likely to identify as youth and enjoy a youthful lifestyle independent of marital status. This distinguishes them from the majority of the married young people surveyed, both men and women, from the lower social classes.

In terms of education, the level of education attained by the current generation of young people exceeds that of their parents' generation. This is particularly true for women. Nonetheless, women are disproportionately represented among those with a weak educational background. In contrast, women also represent a slight majority among those who hold a university degree. The crucial point here is the entry into the labour market and related life plans and expectations. At this juncture, lines of social conflict run between women with higher educational and social backgrounds and men's attitudes towards working women. In contrast, the mind-set of women from the lower social strata seems to see their role as conforming to the traditional expectations of men.

Examining the issue of sexual harassment, a norm of discrimination against women's bodies emerges. Men and women, independent of their educational and social background, equally share a misogynist mind-set. Apart from the different national settings and areas of armed conflict, social background above all intersects with gender with regard to insecurity and inequality.

6

Family and the Future

Christoph H. Schwarz

THIS CHAPTER EXAMINES the role of the family in the lives of young people in the Middle East and North Africa (MENA). It concerns not only the relevance young people attribute to their family of origin, but also the families that they formed or will form themselves, an undertaking considered the most important step in the transition to adulthood. That said, although family continues to be the central social institution for young people, marriage – in contrast to what one often reads – does not necessarily mark the end of youth, especially when one scrutinises the subjective perspective and self-assessment of these young people surveyed.

The first section of this examination – based on surveys of 9,000 people, aged 16–30 in eight MENA countries plus Syrian refugees in Lebanon – briefly summarises the scientific and policy discussion on the role of the family in the lives of the youth in the MENA region and also looks at the key issue of the impact of young people's prolonged economic dependency on their families and concomitantly stalled transitions to adulthood. The second section outlines the economic and affective dimensions of interviewees' current familial situations and the impact of their upbringing. The third section addresses young people's perception of intergenerational relations in the family and in broader society. The fourth section discusses how young people perceive future opportunities with regard their transition to adulthood, self-perception as youth or adults, and family formation and future prospects. The conclusion summarises the findings and questions for further debate.

The Role of the Family in the Middle East and North Africa

For the last two decades, the situation of youth in the MENA region has been discussed from a predominantly demographic perspective among policy makers and within international organisations working in the area. In these assessments, the 'youth bulge' has been a constant cause for concern.[1] Well before 2011, most prominently in the 2002 *Arab Human Development Report* (UNDP 2002), the Anglophone discourse on youth in the region focused on the unresolved issue of how to integrate the large cohort of young people into a largely saturated labour market, in particular against the backdrop of reductions in public sector jobs. The lack of capital – resulting from unemployment, underemployment, or falling real wages – had made it increasingly difficult for youth to become financially independent of their elders and form families of their own. Whereas international organisations in the decades before had campaigned for higher investments in education and delayed marriage to grant young people, in particular young women, the necessary time for further education, with the youth bulge it became evident that stalled transitions to adulthood had become a problem for almost an entire generation in the region.

Diane Singerman (2007), who coined the term *waithood* to describe this phenomenon, also pointed to a particular 'political economy of marriage': due to high youth unemployment, it was becoming increasingly difficult for young people to accumulate the resources regarded as necessary to enter into marriage, which, according to many observers, was culturally still considered the most important step in the transition to adulthood. The combination of the high social value attributed to marriage, the high cost of marriage, and youth unemployment in a shrinking labour market led to the massive social exclusion of young people, making full participation in society increasingly difficult for them. All this ultimately kept them dependent on their family of origin far longer than previous generations had experienced.

Against the above backdrop, many of the publications discussing the phenomenon implicitly assumed a tendency toward strong intergenerational conflicts, as older generations in many Arab countries had received support from state-centred economies during their own transitions to adulthood (Salehi-Isfahani 2008; Dhillon and Yousef 2009). The 2016 *Arab Human Development Report* (AHDR) (UNDP 2016) refers to these debates, examining how waithood is negotiated within the family. Since 2011, however, the concept of waithood has appeared increasingly problematic, since it was often used in the programmatic neo-liberal framework that seeks to

---

1. The term was coined by Fuller (1995), who used it in a publication for the CIA concerning debates on security and foreign policy. Against this backdrop, it is obvious that the term connotes an image of young people first and foremost as rather faceless, a quantitative mass constituting a potential threat to political stability.

'activate' young adults by educating them to become small-scale entrepreneurs, thus individualising and de-politicising the social risks of growing up within this context. Herrera (2017a) and Sukarieh (2017) criticise the AHDR accordingly. In this sense, it is worth noting that the reality of many youths and young adults can rather be understood as precariousness not so much characterised by passive waiting as by a hectic, increasing social acceleration and need for short-term planning in the informal sector (Schwarz 2017; Schwarz and Oettler 2017).[1]

Understanding the role of the family is key to understanding demographic developments and generational transitions in general. This holds especially true in MENA societies, where young people represent the demographic majority and in which the family tends to occupy a more pivotal socio-economic role than in Western contexts, where family has often been discussed from the perspective of reproduction. Some scholars, among them Halim Barakat, have considered the family in MENA societies the 'basic social unit of social organisation and of production' (1993), underlining the importance of primary group relations beyond the sphere of reproduction. According to Jörg Gertel (Gertel 2017; see also Chapter 7), this centrality of the family in almost every socio-economic and socio-psychological aspect of life results in the phenomenon of a 'contained youth,' one who is barely able to detach from the close ties of the family of origin. Other social scientists have highlighted the pivotal role of the family for the stability of patriarchal or 'neo-patriarchal' orders in MENA societies, be it with regard to gender relations or authoritarian political rule (Sharabi 1988).

Most of this scholarship is based on modernisation theory, according to which 'family' in the MENA region tends to be associated with 'tradition' and often represents an element of inertia and, due to its patriarchal character, an obstacle to 'development'. Several observers in recent decades have questioned the implicit assumption of a contradiction between patriarchy and modernity, pointing, on the one hand, to the functionality of certain patriarchal structures for modern forms of domination and, on the other hand, to the aspects of women's agency in MENA societies that are often overlooked. They paint a more dynamic picture and shed light on

---

1. The term *waithood* also seems problematic with regard to youths' political agency before 2011, as young people are in the end imagined as passive subjects. Such a perspective would not take into account public mobilisations like the protests by unemployed graduates for public sector jobs – a frequent phenomenon in Tunisia and Morocco (Emperador Badimón 2009; Schwarz 2017; Hamdi and Weipert-Fenner 2017) – as well as less visible forms of activism, or latent strategies, like the ones that Bayat (2007, 2010a) called 'youth non-movements'.

dramatic changes in familial structure and intergenerational relations with sometimes contradictory repercussions for socio-economic components, demographic development, and gender roles (Hopkins 2003; Stack 2003).

Despite the largely undisputed centrality of family in MENA societies, and its featuring in cultural production – e.g. 'escape from the family' is a recurrent theme in Arab literature (Rooke 2000; van Leeuwen 2000) – discussions on family as a subject on its own, i.e. on empirical changes in the role and structure of the contemporary family, have almost come to a halt, as Joseph (2008) asserted almost a decade ago. The events of 2011 have not led to further examination or reconsiderations in this area in Anglophone research.[1]

Living Situations and Family Life

The data of this survey allow for a snapshot of the familial situation of the 9,000 young people surveyed. Against the backdrop of often insecure and unpredictable developments in the MENA region since 2011, the data illustrate first and foremost that the role of the family in the lives of young people is difficult to overstate. The indispensable role of the family in the lives of the interviewees is made immediately obvious by their housing situation: the vast majority live in a family context, be it with their own parents in the same household (69 percent), in the same home as their parents but in a separate household (3 percent), or with their partner in a newly established household (24 percent). Slightly less than 4 percent live in other conditions, i.e. alone or in a shared apartment with friends or under other circumstances.

General economic situation

Those young people still living with their parents in the same home, live in households with an average of 5.6 people, including themselves. Almost two-thirds indicated that they have a room to themselves. When asked who presides over the household, the vast majority cited their father as the head of household (85 percent), whereas a minority of 13 percent identified their mother. Among those who said that their mother is the single head of household, the majority (60 percent) have fathers who are deceased. These

---

1. Exceptions include the edited volume by Alsharekh (2007), on the family in the Gulf states before 2011; by Hasso (2011), on the family crisis and the state in Egypt and the United Arab Emirates; and by Gebel and Heyne (2014), on patterns of family formation in women's transitions to adulthood across the region. Moreover, the situation of celibate women is receiving more attention now, for instance, by Labidi (2017).

responses at first sight appear to indicate a clear continuity in the patriarchal structure of families in MENA countries, but with regard to the question of who manages the everyday affairs for their household, 59 percent of those still living with their parents said their father, while 48 percent said their mother (multiple answers possible). That almost half of the interviewees see their mothers as active in 'managing affairs' in the household is reason to assume more complex negotiation patterns between the predominantly male 'heads of household' and the actual 'managers', who are often female. Such internal household decision processes in different family configurations are indeed complex and require further qualitative research.

Most of the interviewees are quite satisfied with their family's current economic situation, judging it 'rather good' (60 percent) and even 'very good' (11 percent). Looking back to 2010, the year before the Arab uprisings, among those aged 15 years and older at the time, 58 percent said their family's situation had been 'rather good', and 19 percent thought it was 'very good', indicating a slight perception of deterioration since 2011. Furthermore, it is noteworthy that an overwhelming majority (almost 80 percent) consider their family to belong to either the upper middle or the lower middle class.

Naturally, these assessments differ widely according to the regional context and the political situation in the respective country. For example, among Yemenis and Syrians who had to flee their country or currently face violent conflict, a much higher percentage perceive themselves as poor, whereas among Bahrainis, hardly anyone identified themselves in this category (see Table 8.1).

Economic dependency on the older generation

Only 46 percent of the young people responded that they manage their own budget. They do so mainly with salaries earned through their work (55 percent of those with a personal budget) or partial funding from their families (46 percent; multiple choices possible). Of those aged 25–30, around every tenth interviewee continues to entirely depend economically on their families. Among those whose only source of income is transfers from their families, other persons, or institutions, 65 percent are students, and 8 percent are long-term unemployed.

All of these results indicate the high economic dependency of young people on their families, which moreover remains the single most important socio-economic unit that young people approach in case of need. In the qualitative interviews, this dependency was described as emotionally hard to bear. Take for example Sameh, a 29-year-old Cairene, who commented, 'This feeling is very difficult for any youth. And parents spend huge amounts of money on their sons in order [for them] to graduate with qualifications. But unfortunately, salaries are very low, and there is a great disparity in salaries ... In these difficult living conditions, they ask for parents' help' (EG- 6). Others, like Mohamed, a 17-year-old from Jordan, point to social circumstances. He stated, 'The youth are not to blame. It is due to the decline in employment, which has forced young people to ask for money from their parents' (JO-9).

Affective aspects of family life and upbringing

The family is clearly the social group that young people in the MENA region feel the strongest attachment to when compared to their national, religious, and tribal communities and the 'Arab nation' (Figure 6.1). What is also telling is that they hardly feel any attachment to 'young people around the world', a result that can be read as having a rather low degree of generational identification, i.e. identification with young people in European or neighbouring Arab countries who, to name but one commonality, also witnessed large protest mobilisations in 2011.

This lack of identification with youth is important because it contradicts images in Western media at the time, which conveyed the impression that young people across the region were involved in a common struggle and that this struggle had strong transnational and intergenerational elements (see also below, 'Perspectives on Intergenerational Relations').

In the qualitative interviews, young people rarely articulated having conflicts with their parents or members of the older generation. Instead, they usually talked about their parents with respect and affection. Take the example of 16-year-old Celine from Lebanon, who said, 'I trust my mother because she is the closest person to me, and she knows how to distinguish between the good and bad, because she has enough experience in life, and she is capable of helping and directing me towards what is best' (LB-10). A statement like the following, by Moataz, a 21-year-old from Egypt, indicates how the family of origin is central to questions of migration and spatial mobility. He remarked, 'I would love to live here in Alexandria, near my parents, because I have lived here all my life. I would like to be near my work and my family ... I also want to travel abroad but I would be very distant from my family. I don't know if I would be emotionally loyal to that place as much I am to here' (EG-4).

Figure 6.1 **Attachments to Social Groups and Imagined Communities**

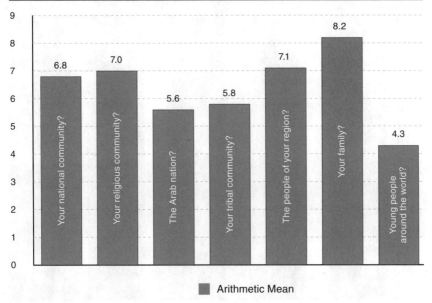

Figure 6.1 **Attachments to Social Groups and Imagined Communities**

Question 126 *'What about your attachments to different groups. Do you feel attached to … ?'*
Note Answers ranged from 1 ('Not at all') to 10 ('Totally').

Against this backdrop, it is noteworthy that parents in general do not seem to resort to physical violence with regard to the upbringing of their children or their everyday interactions with them. The overwhelming majority of respondents (91 percent) claimed that they have never experienced violence within their family, with only a slight discrepancy between men and women.[1]

Moreover, most young people perceive the social education they received from their parents as rather positive; they would hardly change anything. When asked 'Would you (or do you) raise your children the same way as your parents raised you?', the majority responded 'in exactly the same way' (37 percent) or 'about the same' (33 percent). Only 24 percent said they would raise their children differently or 'in a very different way' (6 percent). There are hardly any differences between male and female responses, but nationality and class seem to be important factors as regards the intergenerational transmission of educational styles with Syrians, Lebanese, and Moroccans being the most conservative in this regard, and Bahrainis,

---

1. Even if we assume that some of the data might be false – a taboo subject that interviewees prefer not to address with strangers – and taking into account that notions of 'violence' can vary, this is still a noteworthy result that deserves further research.

Figure 6.2 Social Education Styles in Different Social Strata

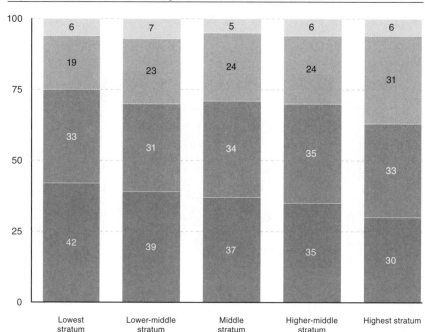

Question *'Would you (or do you) raise your children the same way as your parents raised you?'*

Question 139 Strata Index (see Chapter 2, Appendix)

Note Figures are given in percentages. Rounding errors can occur.

Egyptians, and Yemenis aiming to raise their children differently. The relevance of strata, as calculated in the index, is presented in Figure 6.2.

Many interviewees of the 'wealthy', or highest, social stratum would try to raise their children in a style different from their own experience, whereas those of the lowest and lower middle strata tend to a stronger degree to prefer to raise their children in ways similar to their upbringing. There is hardly a gender factor among the strata, except that women of the lower stratum seem to be slightly more conservative than the men. It is important to keep in mind that expressing a preference for change in social education in the context here does not necessarily suggest the possible adoption of a more liberal versus a less liberal style, or a more conservative versus a less conservative style, and so on. Rather, these results should mainly be read as

Figure 6.3 **Perception of Wealth Distribution between the Generations**

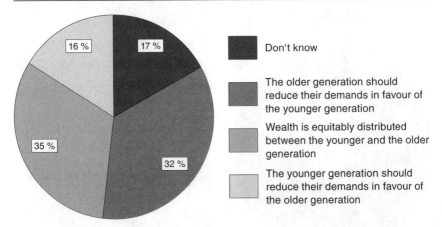

Figure 6.3 **Perception of Wealth Distribution between the Generations**

Don't know

The older generation should reduce their demands in favour of the younger generation

Wealth is equitably distributed between the younger and the older generation

The younger generation should reduce their demands in favour of the older generation

Question 144 *'What about the distribution of wealth between the generations? Which of the following statements corresponds most with your opinion?'*

an indicator of the degree of identification with the older generation, which in general tends to be rather high.

Perspectives on Intergenerational Relations

The survey data do not suggest intergenerational conflict or resentment among the younger generation towards the older generation. To the contrary, most young people have a positive outlook on the current state and future development of intergenerational relations in their immediate environment and society at large. Interviewees do, however, see intergenerational conflicts more frequently emerging beyond the realm of their own family, i.e. in their neighbourhood or the broader society: 76 percent described relations between the older and younger generations in their family as 'in harmony', while 58 percent said the same for their neighbourhood, and only 47 percent said the same for their country. In terms of their own country, 44 percent said such relations are 'in tension'. Only a minority of 11 percent, however, are afraid that intergenerational relations in their country will deteriorate in the future, whereas a majority of 46 percent thinks they will improve. Their projections for their neighbourhood and their own family are even more positive, with assumptions for improvement of 47 percent and 53 percent, respectively.

Regarding the economic dimension of intergenerational relations, around one-third of respondents feel that the 'older generation should reduce their demands in favour of the younger generation', whereas almost the same percentage think that the 'wealth between the younger and the

Figure 6.4 Relevance of Family for One's Own Life Planning

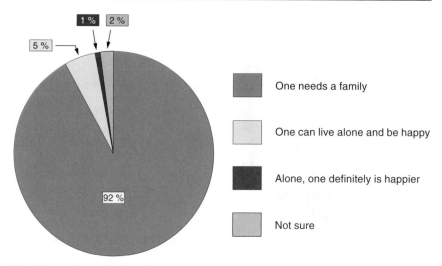

1 %   2 %

5 %

92 %

One needs a family

One can live alone and be happy

Alone, one definitely is happier

Not sure

Question 133 *'Do you believe that one needs a family to live a happy life, or can one be as happy or even happier living alone?'*

older generation is equitably distributed', and 16 percent even demand that the younger generation 'reduce their demands in favour of the older generation' (Figure 6.3).

Perspectives on Family and the Future

More than one-quarter of the interviewees are married, but there is a significant gender factor: 36 percent of the women are married compared to 21 percent of men, corroborating that women tend to marry at a younger age than men. The overwhelming majority (80 percent) of those who are married have left their parents' household. Among the small number of divorcees and widows/widowers in this survey (n = 84), most of them (60 percent) have moved back to or remain in the households of their family of origin. This once more highlights the relevance of marriage to living situations and independence from one's family of origin. In accordance with the general character of MENA societies, young people in the countries under examination are family oriented; their answers confirm the continuing relevance of family life. When asked if 'one needs a family to live a happy life', the overwhelming majority (92 percent) responded positively, while a small minority (5 percent) responded that 'one can live alone and be happy' (Figure 6.4).

Likewise, when asked how important 'engaging in a good family life' is for them on a scale of 1 ('absolutely unimportant') to 10 ('absolutely

Figure 6.5 **Attitudes and Priorities**

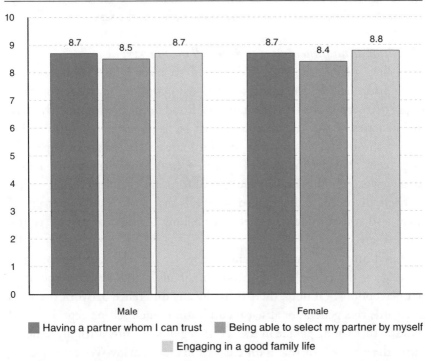

Question 131 'As individuals, we have imaginations and visions about our personal life, our attitudes, and behaviour. If you reflect about possible achievements in your life, how important are the following points for you, on a scale from 1 ('absolutely unimportant') to 10 ('absolutely important')?'

Note Rounding errors can occur.

important'), interviewee responses averaged 8.7, again highlighting the overwhelming importance of family (Figure 6.5). It is remarkable that there are hardly any differences in this regard when comparing marital status, i.e. whether single, married, engaged, or divorced. Likewise, there are hardly any differences among nationalities.

Nevertheless, despite the strong commitment to family life from young people in the MENA region, the data in Figure 6.5 equally illustrates that they want a high degree of autonomy in certain areas of decision-making, for example, when it comes to selecting their partner. When asked the importance of choosing a partner on their own on a scale of 1 ('absolutely unimportant') to 10 ('absolutely important'), the average was 8.4, one of the highest values among 28 items on personal life, attitudes, and behaviour (see Table 3.3). Moreover, the interviewees have clear expectations as regards their partners. 'Having a partner whom I can trust' is rated even higher (8.8), with insignificant differences between the sexes.

Transition to adulthood: is marriage still the marker?

At a first glance, the results discussed so far might corroborate the assumption held by the many scholars who consider marriage the most important step in the transition to adulthood in the predominantly Muslim societies of the MENA region. That is, it comes as no surprise that among those interviewees who are not married (i.e. single or engaged), 95 percent consider themselves 'youth'. A look, however, at their fellow interviewees who have taken the step of forming a family of their own – married, divorced, and widowed[1] – reveals that more than 80 percent of them also still consider themselves to belong to the category of 'youth' rather than 'adult'.

Based on these results, it seems fair to say that the social meaning of marriage as the critical social marker of an adult does not correspond to self-perceptions. Of note, there is hardly any difference between the sexes as regards this generational self-identification. Such self-perception could indicate that young people in the MENA region currently attribute a meaning to the label 'youth' that is different from that in many Western societies, where youth is generally associated with being economically dependent on one's parents while at the same time not assuming responsibility for others. Factors such as economic independence, biological age and the social meaning attributed to it, parenthood, and financial independence should be reconsidered in future research given that the data from this survey to a degree contradicts this predominant assumption of the centrality of marriage in self-perceptions of being an adult.

Future perspectives and priorities

The preferences young people expressed regarding their personal future were striking when asked to identify the most important issue regarding their personal future. The respondents highly value such family-related aspects as a 'good marriage' (30 percent) and 'good family relations' (19 percent), but nevertheless, a 'good job' is the single most important goal to the majority (48 percent; only one answer possible). Age, gender, and employment seem to be the most important factors influencing these orientations. Those who

---

1. Jordan was excluded from this tabulation because only individuals over age 18 were interviewed there.

Figure 6.6 Future Orientation: Female Respondents

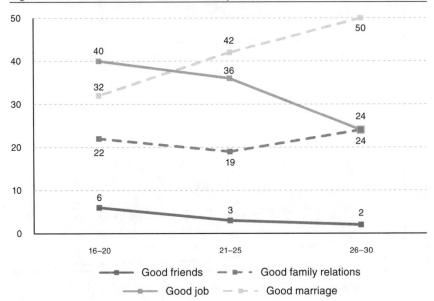

Question 127 'What is most important for your personal future?'

Questions 3, 4, 127.

Note Figures are given in percentages per age group. Rounding errors can occur.

already work tend to attribute less importance to a job and more importance to a good marriage. Dividing the sample according to age groups
and gender revealed that female interviewees' priorities change decisively
according to age group (Figure 6.6), while in comparison, the priorities of
male respondents tend to remain relatively stable throughout age groups
(Figure 6.7).

What is most remarkable is that 40 percent of women in the youngest
age group (16–20) see 'a good job' as their most important goal. In comparison, in the intermediate age group (21–25) and the oldest group (26–30),
the importance of their job dropped to 24 percent. Among the latter, 50
percent said a 'good marriage' is most important. If one interprets these
graphs as indicators of shifts in aspirations during young women's lives, and
how girls and women imagine their gender role at a certain age, one could
say that younger females still have high aspirations for self-realisation by
assuming an active economic role through their labour, whereas in early
adulthood, women tend to adapt to more traditional gender roles, accepting a higher economic dependency on their husbands.

Figure 6.7 Future Orientation: Male Respondents

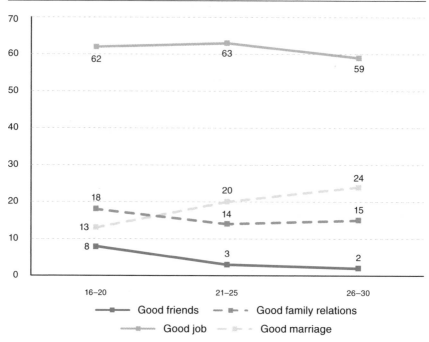

Question 127 *'What is most important for your personal future?'*

Questions 3, 4, 127.

Note Figures are given in percentages per age group. Rounding errors can occur.

In comparison, the priorities of the male respondents remain more stable across the three age groups and with a clearer priority for a 'good job'. Although a 'good marriage' gains importance with age, almost two-thirds of the males in all the age groups consider a 'good job' by far the most important aspect for their future. The qualitative interviews with males shed further light on the relation between jobs and marriage in their lives, revealing young males' concerns about the material basis of their marriage, that is, their ability to provide for their family's needs. Take for example the response of Sameh, a 29-year-old from Cairo, to the question of whether work or marriage was more important to him:

> For me, work life is more important. You know why? Because without work life, married life will not be important for me, as the married life depends on work life. If I have no ambition in my job or a good salary, my married life will fail. Most problems between

couples generally are caused by money being the issue that has the most impact on relations. (EG-6)

Precarious socio-economic conditions also come into play in the search for a marriage partner. When asked if it has become more difficult to find a partner, 63 percent of males and 61 percent of females responded yes. A look at national differences reveals that Tunisians and Jordanians (69 percent in both cases) most frequently see difficulties in this regard. Of note, the results in this line of enquiry are among the lowest in Yemen (60 percent) and Syria (59 percent), both of which are currently experiencing armed conflict.

When men and women who responded that it has become more difficult to find a partner were asked to provide the reasons behind their observation (with multiple choices possible), most women (53 percent) chose 'men are increasingly poor and cannot take care of a family'. Others also selected 'lack of trust' (33 percent) as a problem or complained that 'men's moral standards are decaying' (30 percent). This is echoed by the men, the majority of whom said the main problem is that 'women demand higher financial security' (51 percent) or that 'women have become too demanding' (42 percent). In these answers, the impact of the economic crisis of the recent years becomes obvious. There are significant class differences between the sexes, with interviewees from the lower strata emphasising economic elements, while men from the highest stratum (20 percent) asserting that 'women demand new models of partnership'.

When asked about their anxieties, however, only about one-third expressed fear of 'staying unmarried and single'. Likewise, only relatively few are anxious about a serious falling out with their parents. On the contrary, most have a rather positive outlook on the security of their family in the future, with the exception of Yemenis, with a score of 5.2 on a scale of 1 ('totally insecure') to 10 ('totally secure'), and Syrians, with a score of 3.8, thus on average expressing a good deal of scepticism about the future security of their family. Of note, Tunisians responded most positively (8.0) to the question, followed by Bahrainis (7.8) and Moroccans (7.0).

The qualitative interviews suggest that this optimism in many aspects seems rather normative in the sense that these young people feel that they are expected to be optimistic. Take the case of 17-year-old Mohammed from Jordan, who expressed serious doubts about the future. He asserted, 'For situations that take place around us, there are big question marks, for example, the refugee situation. There is hope in God, [but] for society, no one is optimistic. No one in our society is optimistic' (JO-9). Likewise, Omayma, a 17-year-old Egyptian stated,

> Things get worse on a daily basis. People can't afford food, education, healthcare, and not even jobs. For example, I want to work, but there are no vacancies. There is nothing to be optimistic about. The lack of safety . . . everything is getting more difficult, so speaking for myself, and my people, there is not a single thing to be optimistic about. (EG-5)

Older interviewees, like Sameh, a 29-year-old from Cairo, also expressed general anxiety about the future. He said,

> From my point of view, what worries the youth is the future. This generation of youths suffers from injustice and does not get a full chance, either concerning work opportunities in the government or concerning public investments for youth, and there are no possibilities to participate in political life. I see this generation of youth as very much disadvantaged in comparison to previous generations. The state doesn't look after youth. (EG-6).

Despite the sense of a generational shift in opportunities in life suggested in statements like those above, the data do not indicate any particular hostility or resentment among the young towards the older generation.

Conclusion

The family remains central in the lives and future plans of young people in MENA societies. In instances of financial difficulties, the family and kinship networks are the first entities approached for assistance. Almost all relations with the family of origin are viewed rather positively. Given the general level of insecurity in the region and the problematic state of public institutions in many of the countries surveyed, the value of reliable primary group relationships can hardly be overestimated. In these volatile environments, intergenerational conflicts seem rather unlikely to develop in the near future. Young people not only exhibit a high degree of socio-economic dependency on their families, but also a clear personal orientation towards strong family ties. The overwhelming majority of interviewees aim to form a family themselves and to assume the role of parent, if they have not already done so. In addition, most of them would change little regarding the style of upbringing they received. This does not, however, mean they would not insist on autonomy in making personal decisions, for example when it comes to the choice of a marriage partner. Likewise, their generational positioning and self-perception as youth or adult do not depend solely on the question of marriage. Young people seem to be greatly concerned, however, about the material basis of marriage. Nevertheless the realities of young people in the MENA region, and the role of the family therein, are diverse, complex, and subject to dynamic change, thus meriting further research.

PART II

ECONOMY

7

Economy and Employment

Jörg Gertel

IN THE SIX YEARS since the Arab Spring, the economic situation in the countries of the Middle East and North Africa (MENA) has deteriorated. Not only do armed conflicts dominate everyday life in Libya, Syria, Iraq, and Yemen, but the situation is extremely problematic for many other countries as well. Millions of refugees live in Jordan, Lebanon, and Turkey. Revenues from tourism, an important pillar of national economies, have collapsed in Egypt, Jordan, and Tunisia, while at the same time international investments are declining, with few exceptions, due to political instability. Unsurprisingly, the latest *Arab Human Development Report* indicates that the Human Development Index – a measure of a country's level of development – has fallen substantially since 2010; meanwhile inequality in the MENA region has increased (UNDP 2016). By no means, however, are these problems of exclusively internal origin. Internal and external causation of societal polarisation are globally articulated; they result for example from the colonial past, asymmetric exchange systems, enforced deregulation and privatisation, together with the expanding impact of the international financial system, entailing and accelerating the processes of commercialisation and commodification including its severe social consequences. Yet, how do young people themselves assess their economic situation in this destabilised context, and to what extent are they affected by economic insecurity and uncertainty?

I will argue that the situation of young people is shaped by a thorough loss of employment security, growing precariousness, and a failed promise of education as the route to upward social mobility. With few suitable jobs for qualified young people and limited mobility opportunities for the majority, the period of youth is extended for many as they lack the necessary resources to start a family; this stage is often insufficiently captured as 'waithood'. The situation entails more consequences than just 'waiting' and impacts immediately on everyday live and structurally on future prospects, with deep repercussions for the reproduction context and individual perspectives. As young adults remain part of the birth family for a longer period, they cannot liberate themselves from family bonds to become emotionally and financially independent. After decades of economic deregulation, neither publicly funded social protections nor institutionalised career tracks are available to a significant degree. In a context of expanding uncertainties, the family rather becomes the most important pillar of security, while the potential for individual frustration grows and new collective moralities, based particularly on decency and private religiosity, emerge (see Chapters 3 and 4). Arab young people, therefore, increasingly constitute a 'contained youth' (Gertel 2017), with restricted spaces of self-expression and few opportunities to develop and live their ideas.

In this chapter, the structures and dynamics underlying young people's economic situation are examined in four steps. First, as background, general economic conditions are addressed, as they shape the labour market and economic prospects. Second, an extended review of survey findings illuminates the current economic situation of young people and their parents, tracing generational dynamics and changing conditions of the labour market. Next, the continuing role of the reproduction unit 'family' and its traditional split after adolescence from the family of origin is examined. Finally, a conclusion delineates the meaning of insecurity and uncertainty in the economic life of young adults.

Background

A review of medium-term economic shifts is required before assessing the economic situation of young people and their families today. This addresses the demand for a stronger linkage between youth research and the study of larger politico-economic developments (Côté 2014; Sukarieh and Tannock 2016). Generally, post-colonial Arab countries are either oil-rich and rather wealthy, or they have a history as welfare states that aim to meet the most basic needs of the population. Two short-term historical processes had crucial effects: expanding oil revenues in Arabian Gulf countries starting in the early 1970s created temporary economic growth, while the consequent cross-national labour migration into these oil-rich countries fostered a transitory redistribution of oil-wealth. Many Egyptians, Sudanese, and Yemenis found work in the Arab Gulf states, in Libya or Iraq at the time (while Moroccans and Tunisians often migrated to Europe for work). Both, the emerging oil-rich economies and the welfare states, left their imprint: on one hand, the new petro-dollars generated economic wealth for some countries, but they also contributed to the international debt crisis of the 1980s. Emerging private banks, predominantly of Western origin working in Asia, initially provided cheap money (i.e. petro- or xeno-dollars) with low, but variable, interest rates, often for prestige projects that were barely profitable (El-Masry 1994). In the era of high interest rate policy in the mid-1980s, this lending pattern nearly led to national bankruptcies, prompting structural economic reforms of neo-liberal origin, particularly in Arab welfare states such as Egypt and Morocco. On the other hand, remittances from migrant workers – which regularly bypassed taxation in the recipient countries, often being transferred directly between relatives and social networks – enabled the formation of a new, ascending middle class in the late 1970s and early 1980s, as a result of a downstream construction boom and diverse small investments. Thus, for a short period, economic problems and resulting pressure on the labour market could successfully be cushioned, even within (now former) welfare states.

Nevertheless, the debt crisis continued to unfold and subsequent compulsory liberalisation of economies through the structural adjustment measures under the Washington Consensus was set in motion during the mid-1980s. With a growing foreign debt burden, the individual states' options for action were limited. In 1986, Egypt had to cope with about $30 billion in foreign debt. The reorganisation of national economies under the formula 'more market, less state' became mandatory and was pushed through by the International Monetary Fund (IMF) and the World Bank. A bundle of measures was applied, such as the dismantling of trade restrictions to open markets for foreign investment, exchange rate adjustments, devaluation of national currencies, privatisation of publicly held enterprises, as well as redundancies in state-owned businesses, a reduction in public expenditure, and cutbacks in subsidies (especially for foodstuffs), alongside the introduction of new taxes. This dramatic restructuring meant the end of the welfare state and a series of *Landnahme-Prozesse*, i.e. unleashing market-driven commodification processes (Dörre 2009), partly brought about macroeconomic stabilisation, but also resulting in the massive loss of secure jobs in the public sector, and increased poverty. This, in turn, provoked a series of protests and bread riots (Walton and Seddon 1994; Gertel 2014). Respondents' parents grew up during this era.

Since then, economic restructuring, commodification, and privatisation has continued apace, materialising in extraterritorial enclaves, free trade agreements and free trade zones, often structured to favour transnational corporations (Haberly 2013). In addition, the deregulation of financial transactions was enacted, particularly in the United States, and an accelerated 'technoliberalisation' (Gertel 2014) – the merging of technoscience and neoliberalism – both prepared the way for and precipitated the sub-prime mortgage and financial crisis, as well as the international food price protests of 2007–8 with huge participations in Arab countries. Further consequences were bank bailouts (financed by the public), massive losses on debt-heavy, privately owned real estate, and a sharp increase in youth unemployment in the MENA region as well as in southern European countries. Financialisation – the increasing social significance of finance capital – also impacts the Arab world, most significantly through the growing importance of sovereign wealth funds, and the expanding influence of private equity capital (Dixon 2014; Sippel 2015). Local social development has hence increasingly been subjected to greater influence from the global banking sector. At the same time, Arab states, particularly those lacking major oil revenues, suffer from shrinking economic agency; stable income sources are missing, and tax revenues are declining while liabilities are increasing. Accordingly, a retraction of the commons is taking place as water and water services have been commodified, while property rights for land, the national 'silverware', have also seen further privatisation (Gertel et al. 2014). In summary, historically moulded economic dependencies continue to have an effect, but in a globalised, polycentric world these are simultaneously articulated with and superimposed by new dynamics, entailing the expansion of both uncertainty and insecurity – to which young people are particularly vulnerable and exposed.

Economic Positioning of Youth

The economic situation of young people within society will be analysed in several steps: their assessment concerning their families' economic situation is followed by revealing their parents' education and employment context. Then, the employment situation in which they find themselves is addressed before trans-generational shifts of labour relations are investigated, and the disparities between young people's aspirations and their access to the labour market is finally scrutinised.

Economic situation of families

Young people's perspectives on the recent economic situation of their families are represented in Figure 7.1. Strikingly, more than two-thirds judge their families' economic situation to be 'very good' (11 percent) or 'good' (60 percent); only one-third perceive these to be 'bad' (19 percent) or 'very bad' (9 percent). How can these predominantly positive findings be explained despite the unambiguously difficult economic conditions six years after the Arab Spring? Three considerations are to be discussed:

1. The economic situation in individual Arab countries is not as problematic as often reported.
2. The downturn in economic conditions is serious, but the interviewees only partially perceive or describe them as problematic.
3. These unexpectedly positive assessments result from conditions caused by the interview design or data collection.

If the situation of families in individual countries is addressed comparatively, an already familiar ranking appears: empirically, in Bahrain – as the only representative of the rich Gulf states in the survey – the economic situation of the respondents' families is frequently perceived as rather good or very good. By contrast, the economic situations of Syrian refugee families in Lebanon and of families in war-torn Yemen are indicated to be particularly bad. Moreover, the situation in Palestine seems to be also problematic; more than one-quarter of families struggle with economic problems (Figure 7.1). Remarkable are the still comparatively good assessments of the economic situation in Egypt, Jordan, Lebanon, Morocco, and Tunisia – at least as perceived by the young people interviewed. With this in mind, two aspects responsible for this optimism are to be addressed immediately. First, in Egypt and Jordan, young people's perceived quality of life is largely determined by the professional activity of their fathers, many of whom work in established and socially secure public employment structures. The youth, often still living with their parents, might therefore feel safe at home, with relatively little direct exposure to economic hardship. Second, despite a balanced age distribution in the sample, the share of secondary school pupils and university students is high not only in oil-rich Bahrain, but also in Lebanon and Morocco; respondents from both of these groups generally evaluate their families' economic situation more positively than other respondents.

In these cases, do considerations apply that lead young people living in difficult economic situations not to fully perceive them as such? One could argue as follows: young people live entirely or predominantly in the context of their families, and, to a certain extent, grow up in sheltered situations and do not yet have significant responsibilities. They therefore experience their own lives – largely independent of external judgements – as 'normal' and generally as rather 'good', instead of realising it as exceptional; embedded in internal family narratives and power structures, they may also lack opportunities for comparison. Among younger groups, then, the evaluation of the family's economic situation should always be interpreted as a weighted assessment. Two aspects of data generation should also be considered: on the one hand, people living at the economic extremes had a higher probability of being excluded, because the interviews were for the most part carried out in public spaces: for example the wealthy in gated communities, and the marginalised in informal settlements or enclosed *bidonvilles*, were generally less accessible. Furthermore, easily approachable people in cities had a greater chance of being interviewed than people in remote rural areas. Moreover, it is important to consider how the question was posed. The respective question on the family's economic situation offered four options to respond: 'rather good', 'rather bad', 'very good', and 'very bad'. Intentionally, no middle option was included. Respondents were therefore compelled to choose a 'side': either 'it's going well' or 'it's going poorly'. As it is considered impolite to convey to strangers a bad image to such a question – except in situations that are evidently problematic – this context might also explain some of the weighted answers. Aspects of economic self-assessment are however not yet answered comprehensively and will be further investigated later in this chapter.

Employment among parents' generation

This section addresses parents' education, professional activity, and income situation, which are often highly correlated. A first glance of the parent generations' age structure reveals that the average age of fathers is 56 years (depending on the country it ranges between 53 and 57 years) while the average age of mothers is 50 years (ranging between 48 and 51 years, depending on the country). This cohort was thus born in the early and mid-1960s, growing up in the 1970s and during the 1980s.

Fathers: In terms of education, 16 percent of fathers in the sample are illiterate, 8 percent are able to read and write, and a further 20 percent have completed only an elementary education. These figures indicate that about one-half of fathers have only minimal or no formal education. Among those with greater levels of education, 22 percent attended secondary or intermediate-level school, 11 percent completed their school-leaving examination (baccalaureate), 4 percent possess a technical or professional diploma, 15 percent hold a university degree, and a further 1 percent hold a doctoral degree (3 percent of interviewees did not know their father's highest level

Figure 7.1 **Assessing the Economic Situation of the Family**

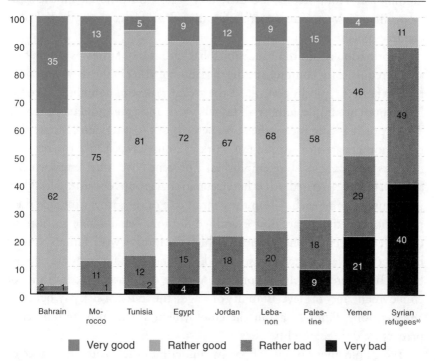

Question '*How would you assess the economic situation of your family today?*'

Questions 1, 20.

Note Figures are given in percentages. Rounding errors can occur. **a)** Syrian Refugees in Lebanon.

of education). There are, however, marked differences between individual countries: with Syrian refugees in Lebanon, the share of father with no or little formal education is 82 percent, in Yemen 70 percent, and in Morocco 62 percent. The corresponding groups are rather lower in Tunisia (45 percent), Jordan (41 percent), Lebanon (36 percent), Egypt (33 percent), and Palestine (23 percent); in Bahrain, the proportion of fathers with no or little formal education is only 6 percent.

Mothers: Education levels among mothers in the sample were in some ways similar to those of the fathers: 28 percent are illiterate, 6 percent can read and write, and a further 19 percent posses only an elementary school education. Among mothers, as well, about one-half have only minimal or no formal education. On the other hand, a sizeable proportion of mothers have attended secondary school (25 percent), 8 percent have completed a school-leaving examination (baccalaureate), 4 percent possess a technical or professional diploma, and 8 percent hold a university degree. Mothers holding a doctoral degree are extremely rare – only eleven mothers for 9,000 interviewees. This general educational profile is also reflected on a country-specific basis.

Information about the educational background of fathers is an important prerequisite for comprehending the labour market in the surveyed countries, as fathers typically contribute the greatest share of household income. In the present sample, almost all fathers work and gain monetary income. The opposite is true for mothers: 80 percent of the interviewees state that their mothers are not working or work as housewives. Only 5 percent of mothers are active as state employees, 3 percent have other employment, and 2 percent are retired. All other occupational groups constitute less than 1 percentage point each. Given the central role of the fathers' income their professional activities are now examined in more detail. Table 7.1 displays ten different occupational groups in which the interviewees' fathers were or have been active for the longest period. The individual groups are characterised by different levels of economic security, delineated by continuity of employment, income level, stability of wages, the status of sick pay, benefits, and pensions. Findings about the employment situation of respondents' parents yield three insights.

The employment profile of parents underlines the limited relevance of the European concept of 'unemployment' for Arab countries. The conventional Western concept of unemployment becomes meaningful only if in the case of previous formal work performance (including social security and tax payments) the state transfers resources to those who are now in a situation of 'unemployment'. As public transfer payments in Arab Gulf states are by no means linked to employment status, but rather to citizenship, and because other states in the MENA region rarely apply official 'unemployment benefits', the European concept of unemployment is hardly ever applicable. In the region men who are able to work but are not active in salaried jobs continuously search for work or business opportunities. Seemingly temporary unpaid activities related to seeking remuneration are thus not automatically equated with unemployment: in order to prepare situations of paid engagement, information gathering, conversations, and contact maintenance demand time and labour; it is work.

The type of employment and the mode of payment are related: daily pay often indicates job insecurity (e.g. contingent work as day labourer), fluctuating income, and the non-permanence of employment. Monthly pay, in contrast, generally represents regular income (e.g. public employee), even if the income level may fluctuate in the private sector. Of the 82 percent

Table 7.1 Employment Situation: Parent Generation – Father

	Fre-quency n=7,302 (%)	Con-tinuous Work	Stable Income	Paid Monthly (%)	Monthly income (€)	Continuation of payments in case of sickness (%)
State Employee	22	X	X	95	780	64
Employee (with insurance)	10	X	X	94	1,525	55
Retired	10	n. a.	X	93	889	n. a.
Self-employed with higher education (doctor etc)	3	(X)	(X)	71	3,054	32
Self-employed: Family Business	2	(X)	(X)	51	1,628	17
Worker (continuous employment)	5	X	(X)	63	1,015	18
Self-employed with qualification (trade, industry etc)	17	(X)		34	836	16
Self-employed: Service sector	10	(X)		27	619	10
Self-employed: Agriculture	8			12	473	7
Day labourer	11			21	424	5

Questions 31, 32, 34, 35, 36.

Note Rounding errors can occur. | This calculation is not based on a comprehensive expenditure survey and thus represents only estimations when monthly income is addressed. Be aware that knowledge about parents' income is based on children's information. Only cases where the father of respondent is still alive are included (n=7,302). The categories 'Jobless' and 'Work without income' (e. g. housewife) did not apply; the category 'Other' (2 per cent) is also not included in the table. Monthly income only relates to those who are paid per month (n=3,212). X = exists; (X) = exists partially; n. a.= not applicable. Outliers are excluded from the calculation. Bold lines represent four fields of employment security. Local currencies were converted into euros based on the average values in May 2016.

fathers who are still living, for most (89 percent of these) the survey provides information on how they are paid: monthly (61 percent); daily (15 percent); dependent on the job (11 percent); per week (5 percent); per season (3 percent); biweekly (3 percent); and some, especially very old fathers, work without payment (1 percent). The largest share of workers paid daily are found in Yemen (24 percent), and among the Syrian refugees (19 percent) and Palestinians (18 percent). In Bahrain, daily pay applies to only 2 percent and in Tunisia to 9 percent. This pattern is also reflected in the continuation of payments in the case of illness. Overall, only one-third of fathers engaging in wage labour enjoy this benefit. This relates predominantly to those who are paid per month such as public employees and pensioners, while it is rare for those with different forms of wages or income.

The family's economic stability can thus essentially be deduced from the father's occupation. Four fields of employment security can be distinguished

(Table 7.1). (a) In the first field, it becomes apparent that in the fathers' generation, one-third still work in public enterprises or as employees, thus receiving a fixed monthly wage that hardly fluctuates. Fathers who are already retired also receive a fixed income. Although the average wage level for state employees or pensioners is rather modest, these groups embody the stable economic centre of their families, as the continuously paid and hardly fluctuating income often serves to cover the families' most basic needs. (b) The second field is composed of three occupational groups, which make up about 10 percent of the sample. It encompasses workers with continuous employment, labourers in family businesses, and self-employed worker with high educational qualifications such as medical doctors and lawyers. Although their incomes may fluctuate, and work is not always guaranteed; compared to those employed in the first field, the average monthly income is significantly higher – in some cases up to four times higher. (c) A third field is composed of self-employed people without formal training, but having special qualifications for their work; they represent the transition group between the second and the fourth field. (d) The fourth field comprises people who are self-employed in agriculture, are active in the service sector, or work as day labourers. They are usually paid daily or per job, but rarely monthly, and receive the lowest income. Overall, they constitute the economically most insecure groups, and are often exposed to poverty.

Comparing the employment structure between individual countries reveals that on one hand in Bahrain, Egypt, and Jordan, at least half of the fathers have secure incomes, whereas fewer than one-sixth are in insecure employment situations (Table 7.2). On the other hand, in Palestine, Tunisia, and Yemen a rather polarised situation prevails: roughly one-third hold insecure positions versus one-third secure ones. In Lebanon and Morocco, it is the middle positions appearing clearly distinct: self-employment occupations which require qaulifications are frequent in the parents' generation, indicating that income and wealth for larger sections of the society can also be achieved via the private sector. Syrian refugees in Lebanon again occupy the bottom rank; even in the fathers' generation about two-thirds struggle with insecure employment. This structure of economic (in)security is also reflected in the disbursement of a monthly income, both concerning frequency and amount: in Bahrain almost all fathers are paid monthly, while for Syrian refugees in Lebanon less than one-third are paid monthly. The situation is also difficult in Yemen. In all of the other countries, between one-half and two-thirds of fathers are in employment situations in which they are paid on a monthly basis. Nevertheless, the amount of wages varies

Table 7.2 **Structure of Employment by Country: Father**

	Bah-rain	Jor-dan	Egypt	Tuni-sia	Pales-tine	Ye-men	Leb-anon	Mo-rocco	Syrian Ref.
State Employee	24	26	**37**	19	23	28	11	7	6
Employee (with insurance)	**23**	10	9	6	8	1	16	9	3
Retired	**27**	20	5	17	1	3	2	8	1
Secure ∑	74	56	51	42	32	32	29	24	10
Self-employed with higher education (doctor, etc)	**7**	2	**7**	1	2	1	3	1	1
Self-employed: Family Business	2	2	2	0	**5**	1	2	**5**	3
Worker (continuous employment)	3	5	5	2	6	3	**9**	7	3
Self-employed with qualification (trade, industry etc)	4	12	17	11	19	16	**29**	21	13
Medium ∑	16	21	31	14	32	21	43	34	20
Self-employed: Service sector	1	10	6	8	9	12	**18**	6	16
Self-employed: Agriculture	0	2	3	4	8	22	5	10	**23**
Day labourer	0	5	4	23	17	2	4	15	**28**
Insecure ∑	1	17	13	35	34	36	27	31	67
Other	8	6	5	9	3	**12**	3	**12**	3
Total	100	100	100	100	100	100	100	100	100
Monthly income									
Father (%)	**97**	65	68	60	53	44	55	60	31
Amount (€)	**2,590**	575	252	319	704	222	1,010	330	104

Questions 1, 31, 32.

Note Figures are given in percentages, apart from the last row. Bold figures represent the highest score per row. Rounding errors can occur. ∑ = Sum. | Figures in **blue** are subtotals and represent different fields of job security. The second and third fields have been combined. Monthly income only relates to those fathers who are paid per month. This calculation is not based on a comprehensive expenditure survey and thus represents only estimations when monthly income is addressed. Be aware that knowledge about parents' income is based on children's information. Local currencies were converted into euros based on the average values in May 2016.

markedly, ranging from a monthly average of €2,500 in Bahrain to about €100 for Syrian refugees. Even if the data allow room for interpretation with regard to the measurement accuracy of income, wages differ by a factor of 25. Sharp disparities also apply in Jordan, Lebanon, and Palestine, which differ significantly from the remaining countries – Egypt, Morocco, and Tunisia. The picture depicted by data on the frequency of monthly wages combined with average wage levels reveals that the inequality of income security is extremely serious – even if varying national purchasing powers are taken into consideration. This unequal economic framing shapes the livelihoods and everyday conditions for youth.

Economic integration of youth

This section addresses the economic integration of young people into wider society. To assess their situation, three aspects are analysed: control over a budget (spending money, labour income); access to formal credit institutions; and saving opportunities versus debt burden.

About half the young people surveyed have access to a budget, whether in the form of spending money or labour income; these are predominantly men (more than one-half) rather than women (one-third). Depending on the country, therefore, 30–70 percent of young people have own financial means at their disposal (Table 7.3). Spending money is often transfer income, usually provided by parents. Indeed, more young people have transfer income than income from their own work. On a country-specific basis, between 9 and 60 percent of the parents' households support their children with regular transfer income (Table 7.4). These are most frequent in Bahrain and Jordan, least frequent among the Syrian refugees in Lebanon. In terms of its amount, Bahrain and Lebanon lead the field, while Yemen brings up the rear. In contrast, young people who work for their money receive on average a higher income, at least when they are paid on a monthly basis. Most of the young labourers earning income that is paid on a monthly basis live in Bahrain, Jordan, and Lebanon, while in Morocco and Yemen, by contrast, regularly monthly paid incomes are more of an exception.

In order to reveal the integration of young people into the formal banking sector, access to bank accounts and credit cards are important indicators. Three insights are crucial: first, more men than women, but above all, older interviewees rather than younger ones, are those with access to banks. The highest degree of integration in the banking sector is found – as might be expected – in Bahrain: well over two-thirds of young people have a bank account and well over one-half possess a credit card. The picture for the Yemenis and the Syrian refugees in Lebanon is completely different; in these settings, almost none of the youth have access to the banking system. In all other countries, between one-sixth and one-quarter possess at least a bank account. Second, almost three-quarters (74 percent) of those who have a bank account also have control of a budget. Conversely, of the young people who do not control their own financial means, 90 percent also lack a personal bank account. Third, these findings reveal that the integration

Table 7.3 Economic Integration of Young People in the Arab World

	Own budget	(a) Monthly income	(b) Monthly transfers	Bank account	Credit card	Able to save money	Amount of savings	You have debts
	'Yes' (%)	Own work only (€)	Not own work (€)	'Yes' (%)	'Yes' (%)	'Yes' (%)	(€)	'Yes' (%)
Bahrain	70	1.377 (233)	313 (464)	79	60	24	210	1
Lebanon	70	678 (264)	171 (309)	20	17	14	109	14
Jordan	n. a.	n. a.	n. a.	18	14	16	123	21
Palestine	49	569 (152)	82 (260)	15	8	15	145	24
Morocco	30	248 (80)	126 (161)	14	17	9	74	3
Tunisia	31	210 (100)	64 (135)	25	19	14	73	15
Egypt	33	176 (151)	62 (160)	14	13	24	58	5
Yemen	35	130 (40)	30 (231)	2	1	9	31	28
Syrian Refugees	52	87 (163)	88 (86)	0	1	1	44	47
Ø	46	434	117	21	17	14	96	18

Questions 1, 63, 64, 65, 67, 70, 75, 85, 88.

Note Rounding errors can occur. | This calculation is not based on a comprehensive expenditure survey and thus represents only estimations when monthly income is addressed. Monthly income is related to those who receive money regularly on a monthly basis. The figures in brackets represent the number out of 1,000 cases per country (keep in mind: the number of the working population differs between countries). Averages (last row) are based on the nine figures per column. Figures in columns (a) and (b) are overestimated, as they represent regular and monthly paid incomes (which are higher on average). Irregular transfers and working income – paid on a daily, weekly or seasonal basis (which are lower) – are not included. The differences that emerge in the data about the availability of one's own budget in relation to the amount and frequency of the two income sources are explained by the fact that in some countries the proportion of other forms of payment – daily or job-related wages – is especially high. n. a.= not applicable.

of young people into the electronic circulation of money is asymmetrical: one-half of respondents possess neither a budget nor bank access; slightly more than one-quarter (29 percent) have their own budget, but no bank access; a small group of respondents have personal bank accounts, but do not control their own financial means (5 percent); and only about one-sixth of interviewees (15 percent) have control of both a budget and a personal bank account.

Under these conditions, who among these young people has the opportunity to save money? Only about one-seventh of young people are in a position to do so. Young men are able to save on average €130 per month, while the average monthly savings of young women amount to only €87. Opportunities to save money are also different for each country (Table 7.3). The highest savings are found in Bahrain, Jordan, Lebanon, and Palestine; smaller amounts are saved in Egypt, Morocco, and Tunisia, while the Syrian refugees in Lebanon and the Yemenis are able to save only small amounts.

In general, those who are employed are able to save more than those who are dependent on transfer income. What are the motivations to generate savings? In particular, money is reserved in preparation for potential crises (61 percent). This is followed by wanting to save money for an upcoming marriage (11 percent), for building a house (7 percent), or for the children (7 percent). Only 2 percent of those who are able to save at all, are saving for possible emigration, comprising a total of only twenty people.

Rotating savings associations are a special form of saving. They are organised privately and voluntarily and are based on social networks. The members, often between five and twenty people, agree on the amount of the deposits (usually between €10 and €100), which each person must pay in regularly – for example, weekly or monthly. These deposits are gradually paid out on a rotating basis to a different member. Even without access to formal credit institutions, this accumulation strategy offers the possibility of providing larger amounts at once. Rotating saving associations is a common form of saving in Egypt (14 percent of interviewees), Jordan (11 percent), Yemen (10 percent), Palestine (9 percent), and Bahrain (6 percent), whereas in Morocco, Lebanon, and Tunisia, and among the Syrian refugees, these networks play little or no role. The deposits in Egypt amount on average to €128 per month, in Jordan €74, in Yemen €46, in Palestine €131, and in Bahrain to €260. In some contexts these associations may actually achieve greater importance than regular savings, both monetarily and socially.

The debt situation of young people contrasts with their savings. Over one-sixth of the interviewees are in debt. The Syrian refugees in Lebanon are most affected; almost one-half of the interviewees here have liabilities. In Jordan, Palestine, and Yemen, the debt ratio among young people ranges between 20 to 30 percent, and in Tunisia and Lebanon one-sixth are in debt. In Bahrain, Egypt, and Morocco, in contrast, debt hardly plays a role. Generally, two-thirds of those with liabilities are indebted to more than one person. Spreading debts allows for enlarging the access to borrowed money, while it increases the management tasks. In order to understand the extent of indebtedness, a relational measurement was applied: 'little' refers to less than a month's budget; 'medium' equals between one and six months' budget; and 'high' corresponds to more than six months' budget. What is examined and compared in this way is the subjective importance rather than the monetary level of debt. The findings reveal that about one-half of those coping with debt see themselves in a medium debt situation, about one-quarter have little debt, and about one-third attest to being highly in debt; the last group is comprised mostly of young people in Jordan, Palestine, and Yemen.

Table 7.4 Household Relations: Transfers from and to Young People

	Bah-rain	Leba-non	Jor-dan	Pales-tine	Mo-rocco	Tuni-sia	Egypt	Ye-men	Syrian Ref.
Support from Family (%)	46	31	60	26	16	14	16	21	9
Amount (€/month)	313	171	99	82	126	64	62	30	88
Regular support to Family (%)	1	7	9	6	5	7	2	6	8
Amount (€/month)	191	308	159	231	129	92	38	58	52

Questions 1, 67, 70, 80, 81.

Note Rounding errors can occur.

Finally, the relationship between debt and savings opportunities reveals that young people from the lower strata are rarely in a position to save money, while the possibilities increase the higher the social strata is (for the delineation of social strata see Chapter 2). The reverse is true of debt, which is encountered most often in the lower strata and least in higher strata.

Occupation patterns

This section examines the occupation structure and current employment status of young people. Of course, not all are employed and work for money – many of them are pupils and students. Moreover, some young adults are currently not working (i.e. generating income) and some never work for money. Five groups can be distinguished (Table 7.5):

Pupils: Pupils are mostly male (54 percent) and the great majority (90 percent) of pupils are between 16 and 20 years old. They are almost all single (98 percent) and live with their parents (97 percent). One-third (32 percent) have their own budget, although only for very few (1 percent) is this derived from their own work. On average, pupils with a budget have control of about €80 per month, originating as transfer income from their parents.

Students: This group (52 percent male) constitutes the smallest segment of the sample. More than one-half (56 percent) are between 21 and 25 years old and another one-third are between 16 and 20 years old. The majority of them are single (91 percent) and are still living with their parents (92 percent). About one-half (49 percent) have their own budget (of about €180 per month), but only for a few (7 percent) does this derive from their own work.

Currently not working: At one-quarter, this is the largest segment. The young people in this group, for various reasons, are currently not working for money. This segment is spread almost evenly across all age groups, with the youngest being the smallest group in terms of number. Of all young people currently not working, 60 percent are men and 40 percent are women. Two-thirds are single. Only one-sixth (16 percent) have their own budget, which averages €159 per month. Income from their own work does not exist.

Never work: Almost all in this category are women (96 percent) and about one-half belong to the oldest group of young people (aged 26–30 years). A majority, more than two-thirds, are married, while nearly one-third of those who never work for money still live with their parents. Less than one-fifth have control of a budget, which is entirely based on transfer income, amounting to €94 per month.

Working: Those who are working typically belong to the oldest group of respondents: more than one-half are aged 26–30 years, although some younger people are also working and earn money. Three-quarters of this group are men. Half of those who work are single, while 40 percent are married. About one-half still live at home, although all have their own budget. For over 95 percent of them, this income is derived entirely from their own work. About 5 percent also receive additional transfer income, amounting on average to €252 per month.

The occupational status of respondents differs from country to country (Table 7.5). The sample structure in Palestine, Morocco, and Tunisia is characterised by a large number of pupils, while there are very few pupils among the Syrian refugees in Lebanon. In terms of education, a gradient, related to the overall income situation appears: of the interviewees in Bahrain, over one-half are either pupils or students. In Lebanon, Morocco, and Palestine, pupils and students account for over 40 percent of respondents. Among the Syrian refugees and Yemenis few are in school or university. But what about those who are either currently or permanently not working for money? A majority of these respondents are in fact economically active and engaging in unpaid work – for example, domestic work such as housekeeping, cooking, and child raising. Country-specific, the largest social segments of those currently not working in salaried conditions are found in Jordan and Tunisia, and the smallest group in Lebanon. The largest segment of those who never work are among the Syrian refugees in Lebanon, and are also frequent in Egypt and Yemen – particularly in the case of young married women.

Working youth
We know that uninterrupted working biographies, stable from the beginning of a professional life to its end, are increasingly disappearing, even in

Table 7.5 Occupational Situation of Young People

	School	University	Not working	Never working	Working	Total
n=9,000	18	17	25	18	22	100
Jordan	10[a]	20	**41**	16	13	100
Yemen	19	7	28	**32**	13	100
Morocco	26	19	**28**	14	14	100
Tunisia	24	15	**36**	8	17	100
Egypt	17	15	**27**	22	19	100
Palestine	**24**	18	15	20	23	100
Bahrain	21	**35**	17	5	23	100
Lebanon	20	21	14	12	**34**	100
Syrian Ref.	2	0	17	37	**44**	100

Questions 1, 25, 65, 66, 67, 68.

Note Figures are given in percentages. Rounding errors can occur. Bold figures represent the highest score per row. | Pupils in school (n=33) and students in university (n=132) who are also working were only counted for school and university and not for 'Working'. [a] Be aware that in Jordan, people under 18 years of age were not included in the sample for juridical reasons; subsequently the frequency of those going to school is obviously lower.

the rural sphere of the MENA region. Today, not only peasants and nomads are forced to change their professional activities, acquiring new skills, and to reorient themselves (Gertel and Breuer 2012). Unstable conditions apply even more to young people's (urban) professional practice. Changing employment structures reflect the sequence of social transformations and disruptions; they become visible in the empirical findings. Indeed, today's Arab youth are better formally educated than their parents, are accordingly prepared to enter a different labour market, and are in principle supposed to generate innovations in newly emerging economic and social sectors. However, given the lack of occupation opportunities requiring qualifications, they are regularly employed below their qualifications, a situation that leads to frustration, dependency on employers and parents, and often to protest and resistance (see Chapter 8). Sara, a 30-year-old married Syrian living in Lebanon exemplifies the local situation:

> The opportunities for the young are very rare. The young person studies and graduates, looks for a job but doesn't find one. The majority of college graduates work in restaurants and coffee shops. They do not find jobs suitable to their educational degree. This is one of the biggest problems that young people face. A student studies for five years at university in order

to work in a decent job and have a suitable income that allows them to do something, but this opportunity does not exist.

Travelling and working abroad is possible, but it is harmful to the country. The majority of young people travel, but it is a bad thing, because 70 percent of them leave to find jobs. But do not think that the young people who move away would find a job appropriate to their educational degree. They have to work in any available job. So we come back to the same problem. The young person studied for five years, but there are no job opportunities suitable for his/her degree, not in their country or abroad.

There are, of course, young people who find good jobs, even if it's not in the field of their degree. Do not forget about favouritism and nepotism, which means the wrong person in other people's place. There are young people who are supported by their parents in order to help them build their own business, because, certainly, the young person who studied for five years in college does not have enough capital. We can say that there are job opportunities for the young who are supported and sponsored by their parents, and they can help their friends by offering them jobs. (LB/SY-1)

Equipped with this knowledge about the social profile of working youth, we already know three features: three-quarters are male; they are predominantly from the oldest age group; and about 40 percent are married. Concerning the gender structure of employment and the role of women, two observations are crucial. First, the difference in professional activity depends on the marital status of women: The findings reveal that among unmarried women who still live with their parents only 9 percent are working in remunerated jobs, while of the unmarried women who have already established their own household, 24 percent are earning income (this is, however, a small group). The situation is different for married women: hardly any married woman who live with their parents are working to gain income (only four cases); and interestingly, likewise very few married women with their own households are working for their income. Only 12 percent of these women are actually engaged in remunerated work, 14 percent are temporarily not working for money, and 72 percent are permanently not working for money. But, of course, they all may be engaged in unpaid housework, in child caring or other reproductive activities. Accordingly, it is evident that the young women's professional activity is shaped by their marital status and way of life. Second, generational transformations in the employment status of young women are rather weak. In both generations (youth and parents), it is primarily men who are are engaged in salaried work. In the parents' generation about 20 percent of women are working and earning money, while among young women about 25 percent are employed. In both generations, these women are predominantly active in secure positions as employees. However, engaging in remunerated work today still seems to be a limited phase – one that lies between the end of education and marriage. This phase might be extended until children join the family. From a social perspective, the question arises about the extent to which traditional roles will continue (see Chapter 5) or whether married women's future professional activity will be accompanied by new opportunities to work – enabled, for example, via institutionalised child care.

Shifting generational employment patterns

Focusing on the male employment situation of young people, how can it be characterised, how does it compare with the parental occupational structure, and also in respect to employment security? It is first of all apparent that civil servants and employees no longer constitute one-third of the labour force, as in the parents' generation, but less than one-quarter. Moreover, hardly any of the young people surveyed are, of course, in paid retirement (Table 7.6). Therefore, the economically secure group of young adults, who are employed in this first field (as defined earlier in the chapter), has shrunk significantly in relation to their parents' generation – which is evident when both genders are considered together, but in particular in looking only at men in the labour force. This first field of occupations has lost a total of 20 to 24 percent of the workforce. A generational rupture in employment structure thus becomes visible. Complementing this, the second most dramatic movement is found in the fourth field, representing the most vulnerable groups of workers, which has grown considerably (with the exception of agricultural activities), with greater numbers in insecure work in the service sector and day labour in particular. If the male workers are isolated, the picture is very pronounced: today, over 40 percent of young working men are active in jobs that puts them in this fourth, most insecure, field. Meanwhile the second field – composed of self-employed people with high educational qualifications, family businesses, and also workers with secure employment – grew only slightly, while the third field experienced moderate losses. Summing up:

Table 7.6 **Employment Situation: Young People – Working**

	Frequency n=2,165 (%)	Con- tinuous work	Stable income	Paid monthly (%)	Monthly income (€)	Continuation of payments in case of sickness (%)
State Employee	9 (8)	X	X	88	593 (570)	65 (64)
Employee (with insurance)	15 (13)	X	X	87	839 (965)	55 (56)
Retired	0 (0)	n. a.	X	n. a.	n. a.	n. a.
Self-employed with higher education (doctor etc)	6 (5)	(X)	(X)	78	965 (1.009)	44 (37)
Self-employed: Family Business	4 (4)	(X)	(X)	61	424 (425)	24 (22)
Worker (continuous employment)	14 (12)	X	(X)	76	410 (422)	23 (21)
Self-employed with qualification (trade, industry etc)	14 (16)	(X)		60	447 (463)	25 (24)
Self-employed: Service sector	16 (16)	(X)		43	527 (586)	19 (16)
Self-employed: Agriculture	4 (4)			35	295 (299)	18 (16)
Day labourer	16 (19)			33	176 (181)	7 (6)

Questions 73, 75, 76.

Note Rounding errors can occur. | This calculation is not based on a comprehensive expenditure survey and thus represents only estimations when monthly income is addressed. Pupils in school (n=33) and students at university (n=132) who are also working for money are included in this calculation. The category 'Other' – amounting to 4 per cent of the youth who are working – was excluded from the table. The bold lines represent four fields of different employment security. Figures in brackets represent male respondents only (n=1,619). The calculation of the monthly income is based on 1,325 cases (395 are female with an average monthly income of 505 euros, and 930 are male with an average income of 572 euros). X = exists; (X) = exists partially; n. a. = not applicable. Local currencies were converted into euros based on their average value from May 2016.

the increasing instability of working conditions and enforced precariousness of an ever better-educated generation is striking.

This pattern of expanding uncertainty reflects the reorganisation of working society enforced by the consequences of structural adjustment programmes, including the reduction of social protections, and the privatisation of state-owned enterprises causing mass layoffs since the 1980s. When the parents' generation entered the labour market in the same decade, secure employment was still fairly accessible. Since then, with the dismantling of the former Arab welfare states, labour conditions have severely deteriorated.[1] The cross-generational shift of professional activity – the switching of

---

1. It should be borne in mind, however, that among the interviewees a cadre of first-time employ-

Table 7.7 **Generational Employment Mobility**

	N	Unchanged (%)	Upward (%)	Downward (%)
Bahrain	217	55	7	38
Lebanon	371	33	37	30
Jordan	137	47	24	29
Palestine	224	38	31	31
Morocco	125	38	30	33
Tunisia	144	40	33	27
Egypt	196	47	17	35
Yemen	134	50	18	32
Syrian Refugees	422	61	14	25
Total & Ø	**1,970**	**45**	**23**	**31**

Questions 1, 31, 32, 71, 73.

Note Rounding errors can occur. N = number of cases. ø = average. | The table compares the employment situation of fathers (Table 7.1) and sons (Table 7.6) and displays the shift in employment security by applying the four fields of employment as points of reference.

occupational fields – is a crucial indicator of social development. Overall, fewer than half of the cases (45 percent) remain unchanged (Table 7.7), with father and son working in the same field. Another 23 percent have moved into a more secure field, while 31 percent have descended into more insecure labour conditions. These findings thus provide an indication of social mobility. Looking at the individual countries, the highest proportions of those who are falling back are found in Bahrain and Egypt, while generally in all other countries about one-third of young workers are moving into more insecure positions – with the exception of Syrian refugees, who are already working predominantly in insecure labour conditions. The highest upward mobility between the generations is experienced in Lebanon, followed by Morocco, Palestine, and Tunisia. Bahrain, however, displays the least upward mobility. Generally, social mobility depends on social strata: the higher the social stratum, the higher the percentage of those who are descending: within the highest social stratum, 39 percent were descending (11 percent climbing), while in the lowest social stratum only 23 percent experienced a status of declining labour security (18 percent climbing). The generational shift within the labour structure concentrates on the higher social strata. It is here that the largest losses of secure positions are

ees are involved, who in their first years are generally offered poorer work conditions. Nevertheless, the negative shifts in wage level and wage advancement in the case of illness are obvious. However, the shift to monthly pay seems to be increasingly accepted.

occurring. Over the last generation, two mechanisms are thus simultaneously at work: the systematic abolition of the welfare state combines with the failing promise of social mobility via education.

Accessing the labour market

What kind of features characterise labour relationships and how do young people acquire their jobs? Asked about the reasons for engaging in their careers, the overwhelming majority stated that they had no other option (Table 7.8); then, with some lower frequencies, justifications follow that emphasise the importance of job security, as well as the social acceptance of work. Furthermore, it seems important that the work offers good learning opportunities, and possibilities to interact with friends and colleagues, as well as the chance to improve one's own position. Only one-quarter of respondents however, emphasise that their work is well paid.

While men often indicate the lack of other job options as a deciding factor in employment, for women, security of work is the most frequent response. However, this predicament is an issue of social stratum. On the one hand, those from the two lower social strata predominantly stress that they had no other job options (81 percent and 61 percent, respectively), while on the other hand, only one-half of those belonging to the middle and the two higher strata chose this justification. However, good pay is hardly ever decisive for the lower classes to engage in a job – they just have no choice. Subsequently, overall only about one-third of all men like their work 'a lot' or '100 percent', and this is true for only 17 percent of those from the lowest social strata. Younger men are especially sceptical. Thus, in general, not having a choice combined with weak income opportunities are shaping the labour relationships of young people.

In the MENA region, official or even public institutions advocating a transparent labour market are missing. In order to find a job the classic argument by Mark Granovetter (*The Strength of Weak Ties,* 1973) is apparent: social networks play a prominent role. On the one hand, 'weak ties' are important for learning about a vacant job position. Information about work opportunities comes primarily from friends, or in Granovetter's sense, from friends of friends. On the other hand, however, 'strong ties' also play a role in the MENA region: 'someone from the family' has often provided the important job information. Once again, the central role of families and social networks stands out. It is important to note that for about two-thirds of male youth, the wish for a good job constitutes the most important goal in life; it is far more important than a good marriage. The question then

Table 7.8 Characteristics of Professional Activity

	Total	Gender		Age		
	n=2,164	Male n=1,620	Female n=544	16–20 n=364	21–25 n=696	26–30 n=1,123
Concerning your main work: What are the reasons you are engaging in it? (Answer = 'True')						
I had no other option.	57	60	50	66	58	54
It is a secure job.	49	47	56	46	48	51
The work is socially well accepted.	46	44	50	42	47	46
I can learn a lot.	40	38	46	37	42	40
I can engage with friends and colleagues.	39	38	44	35	41	39
I have the option to upgrade my position.	38	36	42	34	38	39
It's the only work I know how to do.	31	32	26	33	28	32
It is nicely paid.	26	27	24	24	27	26
The business belongs to my family.	18	20	13	21	20	16
My boss is from the same area.	18	18	17	24	19	15
How did you get to know about this work?						
– Friends informed me.	41	41	39	49	37	40
– Somebody from the family informed me.	27	28	21	30	30	24
– Via internet.	5	5	8	1	6	6
– I was reading an advertisement.	4	4	5	1	5	5
– A public institution informed me.	4	3	5	1	3	5
– Via a private employment agency.	2	1	2	1	1	2
– Other.	18	18	19	16	19	19
Do you like this work? Answer = 'A lot' & 'One hundred percent'	39	36	46	32	40	40

Questions 3, 77, 78, 79.

Note Figures are given in percentages. Rounding errors can occur.

arises of what would constitute ideal working conditions. All of the young people, the entire sample, were asked (Table 7.9), independent of their current occupational situation – whether in school or university, not working or working – to name their most important wishes for employment; the two most frequent were a high, and a secure income. In addition, three further aspects are crucial: career advancement opportunities; engaging in an activity that makes sense; and finally, achieving something. Those who are engaged in salaried work compared to the group who never work for money display the greatest differences, reflecting, of course, also a gender gap; the first group are predominantly men, about three-quarters, whereas the second group is constituted almost exclusively of women. Starting conditions on entry into the labour market remain, however, unequal between

Table 7.9 **Imagining an Ideal Workplace**

	School	University	Not working	Never working	Working
Achieving a high income	63	61	59	57	69
Importance of secure work	65	60	62	58	64
Options to upgrade position	55	54	55	48	60
Doing something that makes sense	53	53	50	45	54
Achieving something	51	52	47	45	54
Something useful for society	48	46	44	44	52
Feeling of being accepted	48	45	44	44	51
Implement my own ideas	49	50	45	43	50
Enough leisure time	43	43	41	40	49
Having contact with others	41	44	42	39	49
Possibility to support others	45	45	42	43	48

Question *'How should an employment situation and your job look like in order for you to be satisfied?'* Answer: 'Very Important').

Questions 25, 65, 66, 67, 68, 82.

Note n=9,000 · Rounding errors can occur.

the generations, and the young people are fully aware of these changes. The 17-year-old Sara from Egypt emphasises:

> There is no doubt that the circumstances that rule our lives today are harder than in any past period. I mean that the older generations were more comfortable with their lives than us. They lived in a more calm and stable period, but our life is totally different. From the very beginning, as we opened our eyes, we experienced revolutions and unstable conditions in the streets. (EG-2)

Young People and Adults: Separation of Reproductive Units
What happens in economic terms if young people become adult? Considering marital status and gender, the following findings become apparent: among those who still live at home with their parents, comprising around two-thirds of the sample (69 percent), the larger share is male, because, on average women marry at a younger age (Table 7.10). Correspondingly, the group of young adults who have already established their own households (29 percent) includes more women than men. While the average age for men and women who still live with their parents is 21, those with their own household are 27, and they are predominantly married.

Table 7.10 **Economic Situation of Old and New Reproduction Units**

	Parents household		Own household	
	Male	**Female**	**Male**	**Female**
Frequency (%)	39	30	11	18
Age (Ø)	22	21	27	26
Married (%)	4	2	82	93
Number of People/HH (Ø)	6	6	4	5
Number of People/HH of working age (Ø)	5	5	2	3
Economic Self-Assessment: Family 2016				
Situation = 'Rather bad & Very bad'	24	20	48	38
Occupation status: Working (22 %)	23	10	58	13
Respondent: Monthly income (%)	19	10	45	10
Amount (€)	465	422	671	600
Transfer-Income from parents (%)	27	35	7	25
Amount (€)	149	115	313	138
Support to parents – irregular (%)	17	8	27	7
Support to parents – regular (%)	8	3	10	1
Amount (€)	166	123	103	154

Questions 3, 14, 15, 16, 17, 20, 25, 65, 66, 67, 68, 69, 70, 73, 75, 80, 81.

Note n=9,000 • Rounding errors can occur. ø = average. HH = Household. | Two reproduction units are juxtaposed: young people who are still living with their parents (old reproduction units), and young adults who are living in their own household (new reproduction units). In addition, there is the category 'Other', which contains 2 per cent of the cases and is not represented in the table.

The founding of a household sets a new reproduction cycle in motion: a pair moves in together and usually after a period of time have children. Reproductive activity differentiates the new households; findings show that the sizes of the households are smaller and the proportion of people able to do paid work is lower. Labour is needed for childcare and other household activities. Among the young people who work and still live with their parents, only about 10 percent of the women pursue wage labour, while about one-quarter of the men do so. In contrast, in the 'new' households of young adults, 13 percent of the women work to generate income and 58 percent of the men do. Many of them receive a fixed monthly salary. New reproduction units and a new working generation is thus established, which assume responsibilities for third parties. Here, too, however, the economic interrelationships extend beyond the young people's own households. One-quarter of all women who have already established their own households continue, for example, to receive financial support from their parents. However, it is men who remain most economically linked to their families of origin, providing irregular as well as continuous transfer payments back to their parents.

From an economic perspective, the idea of a finite, time-limited period of youth – marked by the establishment of one's own family – is blurred. Diverse economic dependencies and interrelationships continue to exist or can be reorganised. For the recent generation it is, however, evident that initial conditions for young families are very difficult. The insecure labour market situation has a clear negative effect: about half of the young men who head a household judge the economic situation in their families as 'rather bad' and 'very bad'. A completely different picture of economic conditions for young people has emerged than what seemed likely given the more optimistic assessments discussed at the beginning of the chapter.

Conclusion

How do emerging economic insecurities and social uncertainties impact on young people in the MENA region? During the last three decades, neo-liberal transformations not only dismantled the Arab welfare states and further reduced social protection mechanisms through radical market opening and massive state austerity measures, they also contributed to expand insecurities in the aftermath of the Arab Spring. New uncertainties further intensified with regime changes, escalating violence, and economic decline. A situation of precariousness now penetrates all social classes. It can in no way be linked exclusively to poverty, and it cannot simply be reduced to an outcome of internal inability or inefficiency. On the contrary, investments in energy, tourism, and land are increasingly linked to transnational corporations and international financial markets; the circulation of labour is globally articulated and highly mobile, while food prices, as for grains, are no longer decided within national borders, but, for example, via commodity futures exchanges located in New York and London.

Embedded in multiple economic articulations, two processes are crucial for Arab youth. During the past few decades, economic deterioration and social downward mobility have increased, even affecting the upper classes. Young people just establishing their own families have been particularly affected and now experience insecurity, dependency, and resignation in terms of their livelihood security and labour market conditions. Secure public jobs, often tied to the state, have largely disappeared alongside implementation of structural adjustment measures. This has far-reaching consequences for young people, who are indeed better educated than previous generations, but increasingly employed under precarious conditions.

Education is no longer a guarantor of social mobility. On the contrary, expensive private educations can contribute to family debt. The loss of secure jobs in the public sector is compounded by the loss of public assistance, which is all the more dramatic because alternative social security systems are rarely available. As a result, the importance of the family as a social and economic security system continues to grow. A break with the family is for this generation of contained youth almost unthinkable, because few other institutions exist that are able to buffer economic insecurities. The social process of insecurity becomes a permanent state; precariousness is omnipresent. The erosion of standards of normality (*Normalitätsstandards;* see Chapter 2) impacts youth and the whole of society. Young families who should be on their way to an optimistic future as well-educated double-earners are confronted with massive economic problems. This generation is exposed to a new set of social frictions.

This appears to be even more problematic as the younger segment of youths lives in a situation of borrowed security. Currently, they are still part of their families of origin and consider their situation predominantly secure, while the potential for massive uncertainty is only waiting. In different arenas – on the individual, the family, and the community levels – insecurities have expanded dramatically since the youth of their parents. Past routines and strategies no longer guarantee success, while the livelihood security of young families is threatened, and even the states of the MENA region can barely offer adequate jobs or social security for young adults and their families. An entire generation thus moves, delayed by a time lag and for the moment still almost invisible, into social marginalisation.

8

Middle Class: Precarity and Mobilisation

Jörg Gertel & Rachid Ouaissa

The income of the middle-class family is limited: it is enough for daily living, no more, no less. The threat of poverty always exists, and this is the concern of the people with limited income. Any situation where they are dismissed from their jobs, they become poor. (LB/SY-1)

> Sara, 30 years old, married, Syrian refugee living in Lebanon

The middle class is the main class in the community that builds the country. Today, because of wars the middle class has no role to play as the upper class controls everything. (YE-8)

> Rifaat, 17 years old, single, living in Taiz, Yemen

FOLLOWING THE NEO-LIBERAL REORGANISATION of Arab economies since the 1980s – including the experiences of structural adjustment measures, expansive globalisation dynamics, and opaque financialisation processes – a fundamental question has arisen as to what extent the gradual collapse of the middle classes contributed to the political mobilisation and social upheavals during and after the Arab Spring. Debates around social mobility and precarity often assume that the shrinking middle classes and the downward mobility of its members are linked to larger economic insecurities (Bayat 2011; Ouaissa 2014b), including self-perceived uncertainties and the questioning of individual positions within society (Castel and Dörre 2009; Standing 2011); which in turn can translate into social instability and political mobilisation (Lorey 2012; Marchart 2013b).

We reveal that the middle class that emerged after political independence constituted a persistent structure for decades, particularly in

Figure 8.1 **Family Class Assessment by Country**

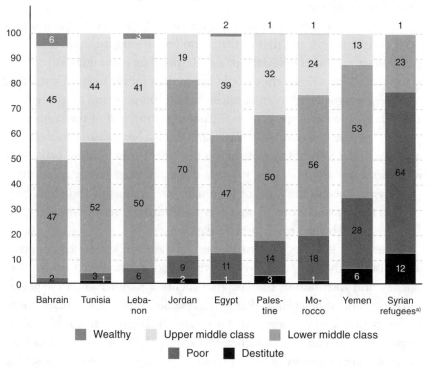

Questions 1, 47.

Note n=9,000 • Figures are given in percentages. Rounding errors can occur. **a)** Syrian Refugees in Lebanon.

middle- and low-income Arab societies, but now, indeed, is dissolving. Even though particular class positions are still perceived and experienced by young people – largely structured by the education background and labour profile of the parent generation – a series of ruptures is causing the polarisation of society. Increasing precarity not only impacts on political mobilisation, it also shapes the preference for specific political systems. The largest frequency of young people who likes to see a strong man in power is among the economic winners i.e. the upper sections of the middle classes, while a religious system based on *sharia* is most frequently favoured by the losers, i.e. by the lowest segment of the middle class and the poor. Still, a democratic system is the wish of a majority, particularly embodied by the core of the middle classes – but *Things Fall Apart*, to use the famous phrase of Chinua Achebe ([1958]2001) for capturing asymmetries of power relations that come along with the influence of new foreign forces.

How robust, we thus ask, is the situation of the middle class six years after the political upheavals?

We start our analysis with a simple question: How do young adults perceive their situation and that of their families with regard to their societal position six years after the Arab Spring? Responding to the question of what class (*tabaqa ijtimā'iyya*) they would assign their family to (see Figure 8.1), 3 per cent assigned their own families to the 'ultra-poor and destitute' (*'ala bāb Allah*), another 17 percent to the poor (*faqîra*), half of the sample (50 percent) to the 'lower middle class' (*at-tabaqa al-mutawassita ad-dunya*) and just under a third (29 percent) to the 'upper middle class' (*at-tabaqa al-mutawassita al-'ulya*). One per cent evaluated their family as 'wealthy' (*tharriyya*). Even in the wake of thoroughgoing upheavals and social ruptures in society since 2010–11 well over two-thirds therefore consider their families to still belong to the middle class.

Figure 8.1 illustrates the distribution of classes in individual countries according to the self-positioning of the respondents. Based on the frequency and distribution of class-assessments a familiar country-specific ranking results at first glance: Bahrain is revealed to be the wealthiest country containing a minute segment of poor and the largest segment of wealthy respondents. By contrast, in Yemen and among the Syrian refugees in Lebanon the largest groups of poor prevail. Generally, the middle classes are significant in all countries, but obviously vary in size. As the respondents were not given specific criteria regarding class-properties each respondent made their own assessment, which is, of course, specific to age, gender, and country background. What then can we conclude from these responses? In order to answer this question we will evaluate the empirical findings in three steps. First, we describe and characterise the middle classes according to employment- and income-situations, and in relation to consumption patterns, and leisure profiles. Second, we analyse country-specific features, identify internal class differentiations, and examine social polarisation in the wake of the Arab Spring. Finally, we will investigate the consequences of these trends with regard to political mobilisation and action.

Characteristics of the Middle Class

The Arabic term *tabaqa* is often translated as 'class' in the narrowest sense of the word, but depending on the context may also be understood as 'stratum'. The term remains ambivalent, evoking different connotations, as it might be used differently in individual countries and is seldom defined explicitly. Here, it should therefore be considered in a broad and non-theoretical

Table 8.1 Characteristics of the Middle Class: Generational Relations

	Wealthy	Upper MC	Lower MC	Poor	Desti-tute
(100 %)	1	29	50	17	3
Parents with low education					
Father	16	24	44	75	86
Mother	18	31	54	84	86
Income situation					
Father: Stable monthly income	82	72	62	33	22
Respondent: Own Budget	75	52	41	38	31
Communication profile					
Respondent: Own mobile phone	99	97	93	77	64
Expenditure/month (€)	37	20	16	8	6

Questions 30, 34, 35, 39, 47, 65, 147, 148.

Note n=9,000 • Figures are given in percentages, apart from the last row. Rounding errors can occur. | 'Low education' comprises people who are illiterate, those able to read and write, as well as those who attended primary school only. | **MC** = Middle Class.

sense. Nevertheless 'stratum' and 'class' are not used as synonyms in the following argumentation.

How meaningful is the class positioning identified by youth and what kind of properties are tied to individual class identities? Four characteristics are important: first, the class position relates to the level of formal education achieved by the parents: the lower the level of formal education of parents – both father and mother – the more frequently young people tie their families to the lower social groups (Table 8.1). Second, this corresponds to income security in the parental budget: the employment profile and a fixed monthly income of fathers indicate, for example, security (see Chapter 7). Fathers who are paid on a monthly basis are more frequently assessed as belonging to the higher classes. This is the case for about two-thirds of fathers in both middle classes. Third, the employment-profile of the father generation (Table 8.2) further reveals the internal differentiation of the two middle classes (as does the strata index; Table 8.6). In the upper middle class, half of households are economically secured by the stability of father's income, while one sixth are economically insecure. Among the lower-middle class, in contrast, only 40 per cent of households are secure and more than one-quarter are to be considered economically insecure (Table 8.2). Fourth, the pattern of education and income that shapes the parents' generation is to a large extent transferred to the current generation of youth. Two findings illustrate the linkages: on the one hand those who assign their families to be part of the higher classes are more likely to

Table 8.2 Characteristics of the Middle Class: Father's employment

	Wealthy	Upper MC	Lower MC	Poor	Destitute
State Employee	**28**	**27**	**21**	9	7
Employee (with insurance)	**16**	**14**	9	2	1
Retired	9	11	10	4	4
Secure	53	52	40	15	12
Self-employed with higher education (doctor, lawyer etc)	**19**	6	1	0	0
Self-employed: Family Business	2	2	2	3	2
Worker (continuous employment)	0	4	6	5	1
Self-employed with qualification (trade, commerce, industry etc)	12	**17**	**17**	14	11
Medium	33	29	26	22	14
Self-employed: Service sector	5	7	9	**16**	**11**
Self-employed: Agriculture	1	4	8	**18**	**25**
Day labourer	1	5	**10**	22	**26**
Insecure	7	16	27	56	62

Questions 32, 47.

Note Figures are given in percentages. Rounding errors can occur. | We ask respondent about respondent's father: *'What was his main occupation (longest period of employment)?'* For classification of the occupational groups see Chapter 7. The three highest frequencies of each class are represented in bold. Bold blue figures represent subtotals. The rows do not add up to 100 per cent because three categories are excluded from the table: 'Jobless' = 4 per cent (highest frequency among the 'Destitute' with 9 per cent); 'Work without income' = 0 per cent and 'Other' = 3 per cent. | **MC** = Middle Class.

have control over their own budget, and this budget is also comparatively higher. On the other hand, the availability of mobile phones and the level of monthly expenditure are also class-related: both increase with social status. The young people, therefore, mirror via the intensity of economic participation the class position of their parents.

To sum up: the findings gained through self-assessment of class membership are indeed plausible. Cross-checking the assessments with empirical findings did not produce any contradictions. Two insights are crucial: first, in Arab countries education and income are important features delineating class identity. Second, across generations the social structure is, to a certain extent, persistent; the social position of young people is often tied to that of their parents. Individual countries reveal these features. The wealthiest countries are Bahrain, Lebanon, and Tunisia, the poorest countries or groups, are the Syrian refugees in Lebanon, the Yemenis, and the Palestinians, and Moroccans. Depending on the criteria under review 'the' middle class appears in larger or smaller segments. In order to further

Table 8.3 Middle Class and Consumption Patterns

	All	Wealthy	Upper MC	Lower MC	Poor	Desti-tute
Food (oil, sugar)	59	21	**43**	**60**	**85**	**87**
Clothes	47	**68**	**61**	**48**	24	15
Wheat and bread	40	13	26	**40**	**56**	**78**
Water / Electricity	31	13	20	**31**	**47**	**42**
Mobile phone	27	**47**	**38**	28	10	6
Going out with friends	20	**41**	**29**	19	7	(8)
Internet	18	40	27	17	3	(6)
Housing rent	16	(4)	7	13	**38**	**34**
Local snacks	16	17	22	16	7	6
Studies	16	5	18	16	10	7
Medication	15	9	12	14	24	29
Gas bottles (cooking)	13	(2)	7	14	22	29
Transport / Travel	11	(6)	16	12	4	(4)
McDonald's, Pizza Hut, KFC	10	**44**	16	9	2	(2)
Cigarettes	10	(8)	10	10	9	14
Debts / Instalments	9	11	6	9	15	13
Cosmetics	5	(6)	7	5	1	(1)
Video / Online games	2	(9)	4	2	1	0
Music	2	(8)	3	2	2	0
Insurance	2	(3)	2	2	4	(3)
Other	5	(7)	6	5	5	9

Question 97 *'Monthly expenditures: Please identify the four items you spend most money on?'*

Note n=9,000 · Figures are given in percentages. Rounding errors can occur. | The bold figures represent the four most frequent answers per individual class. Figures in brackets indicate the number of cases, if they are low (below 10 cases). | **MC** = Middle Class.

delineate its boundaries, we select two further access points, namely, consumer behaviour and leisure choices (Table 8.3–8.5).

Class Position: Consumption and Leisure

'Tell me what you eat and I will tell you who you are.' This nineteenth-century saying carries the essence of Pierre Bourdieu's reflections when – after his years of working in Algeria on economic exchange processes – he was looking into the connection between class position and life style in France (Bourdieu [1979] 1982). Bourdieu concludes from his empirical work that cultural goods are subject to an economy, cultural needs are an outcome of socialisation, and taste thus is an identifier of class.

Two extreme positions delineate the social spectrum among the Arab youth (Table 8.3). Most of the wealthy spend their money on clothes, mobile phones, fast food and going out with friends, followed closely by expenditures on internet access. By contrast, the poor and destitute youth spend their money most frequently on food, on wheat and bread, on water and electricity, and for housing rent. Next in the ranking are medicines, and gas bottles for cooking. Between these two poles of the social spectrum, indicating utterly different consumer structures, the two middle classes are situated. Most members of the upper middle class spend money on clothes, food, mobile phones, and going out with friends. This profile shifts somewhat for the lower middle class, with most youth spending money on food, followed by clothes, wheat and bread, and water/electricity. The lower the social class the more frequent are expenditures on basic needs (Table 8.3).

How connected are class-dependent expenditure profiles to food shopping patterns among youth (Table 8.4)? In terms of products, the patterns depend on a number of factors: for example, on daily need, proximity of a supplier, and prices. Overall, grocers receive by far the highest frequency, followed by supermarkets, butchers, bakeries, and weekly markets. There are class-specific differences, however. Wealthy families are most likely to shop at a supermarket or in shopping malls, followed by hypermarkets and grocers. This is partially due to the fact that the overwhelming number of the wealthy youth surveyed live in Bahrain, which is highly urbanised, and malls and hypermarkets constitute important elements of the food supply structure. But also purchasing power and consumer desire are of key importance. Shopping at these locations is not just carried out by necessity, but is often combined with leisure. Most of the poor and destitute by contrast shop primarily in small grocers, butchers, and neighbourhood markets for their daily needs, in addition to supermarkets and weekly markets. Limited purchasing power and restricted mobility shape this pattern. The consumption behaviour of the middle classes falls between these two poles and is almost identical, following the same sequence: grocers, supermarket, butcher, baker, weekly markets, and the mall. Some minor shifts are however apparent, for example, more people from the lower middle class make primary use of grocers, while shopping less frequently in supermarkets and malls.

The importance of bread as a daily food is class dependent. While only a little over a third of the wealthy consider bread to be very important for themselves and their family, the poor and destitute see this very differently. For the vast majority of the poor, well over three-quarters, the availability of cheap bread is very important. According to their limited purchasing power they have to spend a large share of their budget on bread. Again, the middle classes are positioned within this spectrum (Table 8.4). *Halal* products are

Table 8.4 Middle Class and Food Shopping Patterns

'In order to buy food do you use ...?'	All	Wealthy	Upper MC	Lower MC	Poor	Desti-tute
Grocer	70	31	64	71	79	72
Supermarket	45	69	54	43	37	28
Butcher	45	27	44	47	43	43
Bakery	39	22	40	41	32	30
Weekly market	37	9	33	38	43	39
Mall	22	62	33	22	4	4
Neighbourhood market	16	8	13	16	21	37
Mobile hawker	16	5	9	15	27	35
Hypermarket	16	34	21	16	4	3
Street vendor	13	3	9	13	20	26
Wholesaler	13	2	11	16	11	9
Cheap bread is ...						
... 'Very important'	54	35	49	57	82	90
***Halal* products are ...**						
... 'Very important'	56	35	52	55	64	67
Buying *halal* products						
– Cosmetics	8	10	9	10	5	3
– Convenience food	32	23	30	30	42	35
– Meat	45	29	38	43	59	60

Question 98 *'How important is the availability of cheap bread for you and your family?'* 'Very important' (54 %); 'Important' (33 %); 'Not important' (13 %).
Question 109 *'Have you ever consciously bought a product – food or cosmetics – that was labelled as being* halal?' (Yes/No), 'Yes'–Information in percent.

Questions 98, 106, 108, 109.

Note n=9,000 • Figures are given in percentages. Rounding errors can occur. | Question 106; multiple answer options; Yes–answers in percentages. The bold figures represent the four most frequent answers per individual class. | **MC** = Middle Class.

also a marker of class. Unlike bread, which is particularly important as a basic staple, *halal* refers mainly to meat and to the practice of slaughtering animals according to Islamic principles. For the poor, meat is however expensive and considered as a luxury product, indeed one they can hardly afford. *Halal*-consumption thus indicates primarily a faith-based practice rather than a shopping behaviour that would provide evidence of expensive meat consumption. And in fact, we find that the frequency of purchases at butchers decreases with descending class hierarchy.

Leisure activities also provide insights into social differentiation and class positioning (Table 8.5). It is immediately notable that all young adults, across all classes, indicate 'watching television' as their most frequent activity. This is true for more women (72 percent) than men (62 percent) and the older rather than the younger groups. Beyond that, however, further differentiation between the classes is also evident. 'Surfing the internet', which comes in at second place, is most frequently the leisure pursuit of middle-class groups, particularly the upper middle class. However, in both groups it is a choice made by more men than women, and more of the younger groups than the older. For the poor and destitute, the internet hardly features in their responses. For them 'visiting neighbours and relatives' or simply 'doing something with the family' are far more important. For the wealthy, by contrast, the internet is important, but they also frequently list 'watching videos and DVDs' or 'listening to music'. This is also the group with the highest response rate for visiting the cinema and theatre (Table 8.5).

The two middle-class groups differ in how these various pursuits are weighted. Members of the upper middle class are more highly differentiated: they mainly 'listen to music', 'visit neighbours', 'go to a coffee shop', 'do something with the family', and 'practise a sport', whereas youth from the lower middle class, those who have the highest frequency of television watching also choose 'surfing the internet', 'listening to music', 'visiting neighbours' or 'doing something with family'. It is clear from these responses that the commercialisation of leisure activities increases with ascending classes. One conclusion at this point therefore is that, in addition to the predisposition of class-assignment by the parent-generation, based on education and employment status, social class positions are reproduced in the consumer and leisure patterns of youth. Both are of course not independent of access to available monetary resources. Social class is hence a social construction, one in the making. In the words of Bourdieu:

> 'Social class is not defined by a property (not even the most determinant one, such as the volume and composition of capital) nor by a collection of properties (of sex, age, social origin, ethnic origin – proportion of blacks and whites, for example, or natives and immigrants – income, educational level etc.), nor even by a chain of properties strung out from a fundamental property (position in the relations of production) in a relation of cause and effect, conditioner and conditioned; but by the structure of relations between all the pertinent properties which gives its specific value to each of them and to the effects they exert on practices' (Bourdieu [1979] 1982: 106).

Table 8.5 **Middle Class and Leisure Activities**

	All	Wealthy	Upper MC	Lower MC	Poor	Destitute
Watching TV	67	**57**	**64**	**70**	**63**	**62**
Surfing the internet	43	**44**	**57**	**45**	21	8
Visiting neighbours or relatives	27	(9)	**18**	**25**	**42**	**51**
Doing something with the family	23	9	17	23	**31**	**43**
Listening to music	23	**41**	**25**	**25**	11	11
Doing nothing, relaxing	14	16	10	13	**27**	**19**
Going to coffee shop	13	17	17	13	6	(7)
Practicing a sport	11	12	14	12	7	(8)
Just meeting people	10	(7)	7	9	20	**19**
Reading books/ magazines	9	13	13	9	5	(9)
Listening to prayers or recitations	9	(2)	7	10	10	15
Shopping	8	10	8	8	6	11
Watching Videos / DVD	6	**21**	8	7	2	0
Youth Club	4	(7)	5	4	2	(3)
Cinema or theatre	3	16	6	3	(6)	0
Playing on the computer	3	(3)	5	3	1	(1)
Other	2	(4)	2	3	3	(6)
Engaging in a project	2	(7)	2	2	2	4
Dancing / parties	2	(2)	3	2	1	(4)
Play-acting / Playing music	1	(1)	1	1	0	0

Question 164 '*What kind of leisure activities do you practice most? Please name up to three activities with the highest frequency during the week.*'

Note n=9,000 • Figures are given in percentages. Rounding errors can occur. | The bold figures represent the four most frequent answers per individual class. Figures in brackets indicate the number of cases, if they are low (below 10 cases). | **MC** = Middle Class.

Internal Differentiation and Social Mobility in the Middle Class

Starting from here, the social construction of class, the question arises, how related is the composition of the middle class to social differentiation within society? The strata index – composed of quintiles, five groups of (almost) equal size – is used to answer this question. The index is based on several variables, including the level of education of the father, a wealth ranking, home ownership, and economic self-assessment for family in 2016 (Table 8.6; see also Chapter 2). Key features of the strata index are that both gender and age structure in the five groups are equally distributed and are relatively homogeneous. With regard to marital status, however, within the group of the lowest social stratum just under half are single, while in the highest group this figure amounts to over three-quarters (78 percent) – and accordingly, many in this group still live with their parents (83 percent).

Table 8.6 Class Assessment per Strata Index

Class		Wealthy	Upper MC	Lower MC	Poor	Desti-tute
Stratum						
Lowest	(21 %)	2	2	13	67	87
Lower-middle	(21 %)	5	12	26	22	10
Middle	(24 %)	10	26	30	9	3
Higher-middle	(20 %)	18	30	21	2	0
Highest	(14 %)	65	30	10	0	0
		100	100	100	100	100

Question 47, Strata Index.

Note n=9,000 • Figures are given in percentages. Rounding errors can occur. | Black borders cluster and delineate the middle class from twelve subdivisions into six different subgroups: **UML** = Upper-middle class & Lower strata; **UMM** = Upper-middle class & Higher-middle stratum; **UMH** = Upper-middle class & Highest stratum; **LML** = Lower-middle class & Lower strata; **LMM** = Lower-middle class & Middle stratum; **LMH** = Lower-middle class & Higher stratum. | **MC** = Middle Class.

By relating the class structure to the strata-index a more precise picture of internal class structures appear: the two middle-class groups are now internally differentiated and divided into five groups each (Table 8.6). In order to simplify the analyses and better compared group properties, the ten groups have been clustered into six groups of approximately equal size. Figure 8.2 relates this high-resolution picture of class positions to the individual countries and reveals the respective patterns. In this way, two classifications are combined with one another. First, the (more subjective) self-assessment of young adults regarding the family's class structure is applied to identify 'upper' or 'lower middle class'. Second, the (more objective) strata index is calculated, in order to identify subgroups for each of the lower and upper middle classes.

If the monthly average income of the fathers and of respondent (male) for the six middle-class groups is applied as the basis for a ranking, a new order of the subgroups is achieved which breaks up the previous grouping and also the strict classification into upper and lower middle class. Now, the subgroup upper middle class with the highest stratum is followed by the subgroup, which is constituted by the lower middle class with the highest and higher-middle stratum. It is only in third and fourth places that the two other subgroups from the upper middle class are following. This implies that the young adults' self-assessment on class can be depicted more clearly, at least from this economic perspective: one

Figure 8.2 Structure of Middle Class by Country

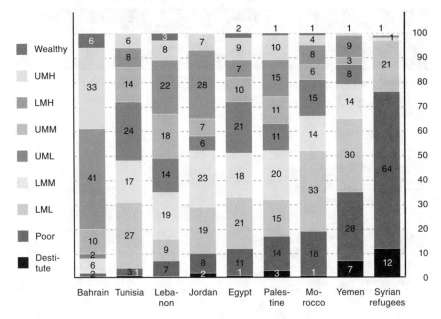

Questions 35, 47, 75, Strata Index.

Note Figures are given in percentages. Rounding errors can occur. | UML = Upper-middle class & Lowest, Lower-middle, and Middle stratum; UMM = Upper-middle class & Higher-middle stratum; UMH = Upper-middle class & Highest stratum; LML = Lower-middle class & Lowest, and Lower-middle stratum; LMM = Lower-middle class & Middle stratum; LMH = Lower-middle class & Higher-middle, and highest stratum. | **Bahrain** LML and Destitute = 0 · **Lebanon** Destitute = 0 · **Tunisia** Wealthy = 0 · **Jordan** Wealthy = 0 · **Yemen** Wealthy = 0 · **Syrian Refugees** Wealthy, UMH, LMH and UMM = 0.

Additional Table for Figure 8.2

Self-assessment – Class	Upper MC	Lower MC	Upper MC	Lower MC	Upper MC	Lower MC
Calculated Strata Index	UMH	LMH	UMM	UML	LMM	LML
Rank	1	2	3	4	5	6
Income father (€)	1,946	1,248	942	587	534	383
Income (respondent) male (€)	1,089	707	689	490	475	261
(n=7,055)	761	1,380	785	1,036	1,328	1,765

Note This table represents only the two middle classes, derived from the self-assessment of the respondents – the groups 'Wealthy', 'Poor', and 'Destitute' are not included. The internal segmentation of the two middle classes is based on the Strata Index. The order of columns reflects the amount of the average monthly income of father and son (or the male respondent). Accordingly, the groups ranking first generate the highest monthly income (Upper-middle class and Highest stratum), those ranking 6 the lowest (Lower-middle class and Lower-middle / Lowest strata). The instructions for determining the income (see Table 7.3) apply here as well. | **MC** = Middle Class.

Table 8.7 **Economic Situation of Middle Class Families in 2010 and 2016**

Class-affiliation (Self-assessment)	Upper MC	Lower MC	Upper MC	Upper MC	Lower MC	Lower MC	Poor
Groups of the middle class (n=6,274)	**UMH** 524	**LMH** 959	**UMM** 524	**UML** 774	**LMM** 969	**LML** 1,342	1,154
Economic situation							
2010 very good	39	24	22	22	15	15	10
2016	45	18	15	8	4	3	2
2010 rather good	57	62	71	72	64	59	43
2016	54	72	83	86	79	61	17
2010 rather bad	4	12	7	6	18	22	31
2016	2	9	2	5	16	32	49
2010 very bad	0	2	0	1	3	4	15
2016	0	0	0	1	1	5	33
Net mobility (% Families)	**+8**	**−1**	**−2**	**−12**	**−4**	**−19**	**−38**
– Upward mobility	16	14	12	8	14	11	10
– Downward mobility	8	15	14	20	18	30	48

Questions 20, 21, 47, Strata Index.

Note Figures are given in percentages. Rounding errors can occur. | Age groups were restricted: only those between 20 and 30 years old were included in order to select only those who are able to compare with the situation in 2010 (n=6,274). Moreover, two groups were not included: 'Wealthy' (n=83); and 'Destitute' (n=195). Bordered fields indicate higher frequencies in 2016 than in 2010 (difference above 5 per cent). **UML** = Upper-middle class & Lowest, Lower-middle, and Middle stratum; **UMM** = Upper-middle class & Higher-middle stratum; **UMH** = Upper-middle class & Highest stratum; **LML** = Lower-middle class & Lowest, and Lower-middle stratum; **LMM** = Lower-middle class & Middle stratum; **LMH** = Lower-middle class & Higher-middle, and highest stratum. | **MC** = Middle Class.

subgroup, namely the one from the lower middle class with the highest income ranking has to be repositioned. Put another way, the classification lower middle class was derived from a self-assessment; this 'class' comprises half of the total sample. If this large group is explored through the lens of the strata index three subgroups can be identified (as is the case with the upper middle class). The highest, and thus most wealthy subgroup of the lower middle class, becomes 'part' of the upper middle class, if the monthly incomes of father and son are used as classification criteria.

Based on this internal differentiation, we further juxtapose the individual class position for those aged 20 to 30 years with the economic situation of their families in 2010 and 2016 (see Table 8.7). This reveals the growth and losses that the subgroups of the middle class have experienced since the Arab Spring and demonstrates social mobility from the perspective of

Table 8.8 **Political Intentions and Actions by Young Middle Class Members**

Class-affiliation (Self-assessment)	Upper MC	Low-er MC	Upper MC	Upper MC	Low-er MC	Low-er MC	Poor
Groups of the middle class	UMH	LMH	UMM	UML	LMM	LML	
Political mobilisation							
– Political intention: 'High'	23	25	29	30	32	31	**37**
– Political action: 'High'	13	12	15	15	**18**	17	16
Preferred political system							
– Democratic system	40	37	**43**	40	41	35	37
– Strong man	**35**	33	25	23	23	24	22
– Religious state (*sharia*)	6	9	9	11	11	**13**	**13**
Role of the state							
– 'Larger role'	77	78	**80**	78	75	76	74
– 'Social security'	62	61	59	61	**66**	65	63

Question 159: *'If there is something important to you, and you want to be heard or have a political impact, which of the following possibilities would you probably or probably not consider doing? Would you …?'* (11 possible answers, e. g. 'Participate in a strike'). Out of the answering options ('Certainly not' = 1, 'Probably not' = 2, 'Maybe' = 3, 'Probably' = 4, 'Certainly' = 5) we calculated averages and classified them into three categories of political intention: 'None' (≤1) = 36 percent; 'Low' (>1–2) = 35 percent; 'High' (>2) = 30 percent.

Question 160: *'Which of these possibilities have you already used or participated in?'* We calculated the sum of 'yes' answers (e. g. 22 per cent participated in elections; 12 per cent in a demonstration; and 7 per cent boycott certain goods; someone who participated in all three of the activities thus receives 3 points) and classified them into three categories of political action: 'None' (0 points) = 65 per cent; 'Low' (1 point) = 20 per cent; 'High' (2–11 points) = 15 per cent. Just participating in an election, therefore, is considered as 'low' political action.

Question 113: *'If you look around the world, what kind of political system would you prefer?'* Possible answers: 'A democratic system' (39 per cent); 'A strong man / woman who governs the country' (26 per cent / 1 per cent); 'A combined democratic and Islamic system' (11 per cent); 'A religious state based on sharia' (11 per cent); 'A socialist system' (1 per cent); 'A combined democratic and Islamic system' (2 per cent); 'A system without nation states' (0); 'Other' (1 per cent); 'Don't know' (7 per cent).

Questions 113, 115, 116, 159, 160.

Note: Figures are given in percentages. Rounding errors can occur. | Syrian refugees in Lebanon did not answer questions 159 and 160 (n=8,000). Bold figures represent the highest percentage per row. **UML** = Upper-middle class & Lowest, Lower-middle, and Middle stratum; **UMM** = Upper-middle class & Higher-middle stratum; **UMH** = Upper-middle class & Highest stratum; **LML** = Lower-middle class & Lowest, and Lower-middle stratum; **LMM** = Lower-middle class & Middle stratum; **LMH** = Lower-middle class & Higher-middle, and highest stratum. | **MC** = Middle Class.

individual families. The result is definite: a quarter of the families experienced an economic decline (25 percent) and just under one eighth saw their fortunes improve (12 percent). The findings thus indicate a growing social polarisation: rich and poor sections of society are drifting gradually apart. The more wealthy groups are expanding, growing in wealth (more people indicate here that their economic situation in 2016 is 'very good'), while poorer groups of the middle classes are growing in despair (more people indicate here that the economic situation in 2016 is 'rather bad' or 'very bad'). A large amount of social downward mobility occurred from the lowest subgroup of the middle class to the group of the poor. This is reflected in the perception of young people. Muhammad, a 26-year-old from Zarqa, in Jordan, stressed:

> Even for people who have jobs, in both the private and the public sector, the wages aren't high enough, and people live below the poverty line. In the past, there were classes – the poor, the middle class, and the rich – but now I see only the poor and the rich. [The] middle class was abolished. All life now is just sleep and work to get money, every day. I am considered poor and live only to sustain myself. Middle class means the luxury to go out. Middle class means to live above the poverty line, but now unfortunately everyone lives below the poverty line. (JO-11)

Muataz, a 29-year-old from Cairo, shared this assessment:

> Until recently, before the revolution, the middle class existed, and its size was big. But now it is fading. In the past, there were a poor class, a middle class, and rich men. But now, from my point of view, there are only two classes left, one of them is poor, and the other one is rich. (EG-3)

This societal rupture starts at the heart of the middle class and continues into the poor sections: The number of young people in two out of three groups from the upper middle class, who assessed the economic situation of their family to be 'very good' in 2016 compared with 2010, is shrinking. This is contrasted by a small reduction in the number of people indicating the situation to be 'rather bad' or 'very bad'. The lower the social stratum overall however, the clearer are the losses in the positive areas ('very good' and 'rather good') and the growth in the negative areas ('rather bad' or 'very bad'), as is also evidenced in the more recent 'downward mobility' (Table 8.7). Indeed, dramatic social downward mobility is reflected in the expanding group of the poor. Those affected most significantly by economic decline, and this is not in the least surprising, are the Syrian refugees in Lebanon (64 percent of households), the Yemenis (59 percent), but also the Palestinians (23 percent), Egyptians (22 percent), and the Lebanese (17 percent). Those households moving up economically – not equal to even half of those on the way down – are concentrated in Palestine (25 percent), Jordan (17 percent), Morocco (15 percent), and Egypt (13 percent).

This evaluation of the economic situation corresponds to other areas of young people's everyday life: those experiencing a social decline are more likely to perceive their possibilities of living a fulfilled life as rather unstable; this instability is also true of the political situation, the trust in friends and the confidence in personal abilities. Uncertainty becomes omnipresent and inscribed into everyday life. Bushra, an 18-year-old, single, from Abyan, Yemen, emphasised,

> I have a negative outlook as I see the dark side of future. Any efforts will not have good results. For instance, in the near future I am going to graduate and then I will look for a job and I think I will not have one because all government affairs are controlled by some groups. The country conditions are bad and going from bad to worse. Society is deteriorating in all fields; economic, social, and political sides. I am afraid that deterioration will be worse especially with price increase, salaries interruption, and insecurity. (YE-1)

Jawad, a 19-year-old from Irbid, Jordan, underlined,

> Fearing poverty: I fear that I won't be able to buy a car or afford marriage or an education, or build a house. People are poor, either because their fathers are unemployed and can't afford to provide their children with an education, or they work but the salary isn't fixed and there is no insurance for them nor for their families. Their work only suffices to cover their families' most basic needs. [I] can protect myself from poverty by working. There are people who travel to another country to work rather than serve their country and live in poverty, because salaries are very low in Jordan. I am not optimistic about the future because the current economic situation in Jordan is bad and my job doesn't provide me with a good enough salary to protect myself; it doesn't meet my requirements. And there are very few employment opportunities in Jordan, which forces young graduates to travel abroad in search of work. As a young, working non-student, what would my fate there be? (JO-1)

Political Mobilisation for What Kind of Political System?

In the following we relate the downward economic mobility to the political intentions and actions of youth in the MENA region (see Table 8.8). The interest in taking political action (political intention) is most frequently seen among the groups impacted most strongly by social decline; it is most marked among the poor. The frequency of actual political activity (political action) shifts to some extent to the groups in the lower middle class, who are still affected by the socially polarising drift and the loss of economic security, but have greater resources than the poor. Intention and action are clearly correlated to one another: those who pursue keen political intentions are more frequently also politically active. However, political action is restricted to a small segment of youth: only one-third have an intention to act politically, actual action that goes beyond participation in an election, is taken only by one-sixth of the surveyed youth. Concerning the individual countries, youth in Palestine (25 percent), Yemen (21 percent), Tunisia, and Egypt (19 percent each) lie well above the average in this regard (see Chapter 13).

Is the majority of the middle class, therefore, to be considered as apolitical? Asked differently, what connections exist between class position, political mobilisation, the favoured political system, and the desired role of the state? In which class is support concentrated for the four most-preferred political systems: a combined democratic-Islamic system; a religious state based on Islamic law; democratic systems; or a strong man who governs the country? While a democratic system receives the largest support in general, there are tendencies for a segmented constituency: a strong man is more frequently supported by the wealthy; a religious system based on Islamic law is rather preferred by the poorer classes; and the centre of the middle class advocates primarily a democratic system. Three-quarters of all respondents wish for a state playing a larger role in daily life – particularly concerning the desire for social security; it is at the very top of the list for around two-thirds of youth. The longing for security and certainty, indeed, shapes the basic values of the youth and their realisation are primary targets for the future (see Chapter 3), but for the time being their implementation unfolds rather ambivalently: young people simultaneously express their deep mistrust towards politicians and institutions such as the parliament, while there is a longing for a state that can meet basic needs. Since this kind of security delivered by nation states is difficult to achieve in times of rampant globalisation, political upheaval and armed conflicts, despite the strong desire of many young people, the importance of Islam, perceived as a very private faith, moves more strongly into focus for them. Three-quarters of those in economic decline, more than in any other group, emphasise that their personal faith is stable.

Conclusion

According to the self-perception of young people the middle class makes up a large part of Arab society, but membership is not something that is freely chosen. Social classes emerge as a result of lengthy and sustained multi-generational processes and result from a nexus of social relationships. The educational and employment status of parents shape the consumer and leisure behaviours of youth in the MENA region, act as distinguishing markers, and contribute to the reproduction of class membership in the next generation. However, a series of ruptures have impacted on Arab societies and class patterns: In the long term, economic securities have been lost due to the shifts in occupational structures, linked to the dismantling of welfare states and the loss of secure public jobs (see Chapter 7); in the medium term, turbulences such as war, armed violence, revolutions, and civil strife have developed since the Arab Spring, unsettling social security even further. The middle classes are breaking into segments of varying degrees of insecurity and precarity; they are crumbling. When 'things fall apart' (Achebe [1958]2001) this is not without consequences. The young generation is particularly hit by the dynamics of social and economic polarisation, and is largely embedded into two ambivalent processes: first, political mobilisation; this is highest among those groups whose families experienced social downward mobility, but even activists are often unaware of the complexity of reasons responsible for their disenfranchisement, and thus often only address their government. Second, this generation is losing, alongside disappearing class positions, the certainty of social identities and personal perspectives. When societal structures collapse it is no longer easy to identify with a state – least of all with politics; what remains is trust in the family and the personal (religious) faith. Subsequently, the preferences of the youth for specific political systems reflect these experiences.

9

Hunger and Violence: Spaces of Insecurity

Jörg Gertel & Tamara Wyrtki

THERE ARE FEW REGIONS in the world that have been hit so frequently by recurrent protests around the price of bread, by food crises, and related political upheavals, as post-colonial North Africa and the Middle East. The so-called Arab Spring, triggered by the revolutions in Tunisia and Egypt but also the armed conflicts in Syria and Yemen, are however emblematic for many citizens of a new kind of collective experience: that of regional cross-border food insecurity. The public demands for food sovereignty expressed in the 2011 protest slogans for the right to 'bread, freedom and social justice' (*'aysh, hurriyya, 'adala ijtima'iyya*) and the desire 'to over-throw the system' (*isqat al-nizam*) symbolise the importance of bread and simultaneously the failure of respective governments to meet their people's basic needs. In no other field of everyday life are uncertainty and injustice so clearly felt than in the enormous efforts to guarantee the safety of the family and to provide enough food each day. Often food insecurity combines with violence. Particularly in situations of civil strife and hunger, structural and direct violence are highly interdependent. Galtung (1969) describes violence as the reason for the difference between the potential and the current, as rift between 'what might have been possible' and 'what is'. While direct violence encompasses direct confrontations, structural violence is inscribed into the social structure; it prevents people from meeting their basic needs and thus is closely linked to social injustice.

For many Arab families today, the danger of slipping into poverty and losing access to food is ever present. But whereas young people were often the initiators of protests in 2011, they are not per se the most vulnerable groups exposed to food insecurity and hunger. Children, pregnant women, and elderly people are more likely to suffer from insufficient nutrition and from severe consequences, particularly if food deficits combine with diseases. Youth, perhaps even more so than their parents, are some of the physically most resilient members of a household. Generally, they bear less responsibility than their parents, but of course, in times of crisis, they may be compelled to assume more tasks and have to act with higher account-ability. Subsequently, young adults respond to questions regarding security and hunger differently from their parents. We will argue that food insecu-rity and violence often combine, affecting particularly poor and vulnerable groups. Although we know that they impact severely on human situations, causing social disruption and a loss of moral standards, little is known about the causal structure of hunger, about the political economy of long chains of trade transactions and private profit. Our argument concerning spaces of insecurity unfolds in four different stages. We begin by briefly describ-ing the structure of the food system in the MENA region, and introduce explanations about the causation of food crises. We subsequently discuss the empirical findings in the regional context, and then present case studies of food insecurity and hunger, elaborating the situation of young people in each case.

Food Systems in the MENA Countries

The patterns of food provisioning in Arab nations have been increasingly connected to and determined by the global food system. Four phases are crucial. During European colonialism small-scale (subsistence) agriculture in Arab countries was restructured and selectively realigned for producing export-commodities for Europe, particularly France and England. Subse-quently, economic integration deepened in the Arab world, market pro-duction and commercialisation increased, and production-consumption linkages stretched out across ever-greater distances.

At the end of the Second World War the United States emerged to dom-inate the international food system by providing cheap grains for export – also to the newly developing Arab countries. When these young nation states became politically independent, agriculture was widely neglected while industrialisation often started with promoting the food-processing sector; investments went, for example, into sugar-, dairy- or fruit juice-fac-tories. During this period of welfare state development food subsidies were expanded, and it was ensured that the poor also benefited. At the time, large parts of the population were, thus, food secure.

Since the mid-1980s international debt crisis, economic deregulation set in and transnational food corporations benefited from 'open' markets. Indebted Arab states increasingly fell under the control of international organisations such as the World Bank and the International Monetary Fund, which in turn provided loans tied to conditions of structural adjustments, demanding among other measures the abolishment of tariffs and a reduction of government expenditures. As a result food subsidies were systematically cut and phased out. In Algeria, Egypt, Iran, Jordan, Morocco, Tunisia, and Yemen, almost all food subsidies were eliminated between 1990 and 2000 (Gertel 2005). Simultaneously the previous nature of grain deliveries as aid (predominately from the U.S.) changed into commercial relationships. Parallel to this, grain trade has been concentrated in the private sector. Companies such as Cargill, Continental Grain or ADM became the new global players governing the global food flow and international prices.

Moreover, due to asymmetrical liberalisation an arbitrary situation developed in which on the one hand trade restrictions were being dismantled and free trade demanded, while on the other hand trade blocs (EU, NAFTA) formed and operated along protectionist lines. Arab states like Morocco, Tunisia, and Egypt, who had, for example, been advised by foreign experts and hoped to expand their fruit and vegetable exports to Europe beginning in the 1980s, were often vying for limited quotas and restricted time windows. The promised advantage of free trade never materialised for them. Social polarisation increased and poverty levels rose.

With the turn of the century, the dynamic of financialisation started to penetrate global food systems (Gertel and Sippel 2016). Some economies, such as the United States, have been shifting away from industrial investments to realise higher profits with financial capital. Inter alia, supermarkets increasingly began to operate as banks. Simultaneously the importance of shareholder-value grew, and the necessity for food corporations to realise short-term profits expanded (see Dixon 2014 on Egypt). As a consequence, the financialisation of everyday life took off. Even lower- and middle-class households have progressively begun to use new financial products (e.g. derivatives as part of pension schemes). Finally, technology-based virtual price-building processes have been shaping food and future markets. Subsequently, institutional investors (such as pension funds) started to speculate in agricultural commodities triggering massive food price rises in the Arab world and elsewhere. In 2008 these led for the first time in human history essentially to over a billion people suffering from hunger. Hunger and malnutrition have since become the greatest risk to health with repercussions far more serious than those of Aids, malaria and tuberculosis combined.

To sum up: the thresholds for the development of new food crises and new social fault lines are being lowered. After 30 years of neo-liberalism, deregulation, and structural adjustment measures, the options, especially for Arab low-income countries and poor groups, to mitigate crises have been severely curtailed. Unstopped by (now abolished) government interventions, price fluctuations can directly penetrate private households, and food crises unleash their full force at the personal level. The public mass-protests of 2008 and 2010–11 reveal these vulnerabilities to globalised food crises: the Arab Spring started at the very peak of international food prices.

Explaining Food Insecurity and Hunger
Today three main causes are identified to explain food insecurity and hunger: failures of production, entitlement decline, and problems of responsibility. The supporters of the first approach argue hunger occurs when there is insufficient production of food (i.e. food availability declines). For a long time, the production problem was viewed from a Malthusian perspective and comprehended as resulting from the interaction of population increases and limited agricultural spaces. Yet, in the globally interconnected food systems, local production failures can be offset, making geographically restricted explanation attempts obsolete. Moreover, in the last few decades massive production gains have been made which also weaken purely demographic approaches. Yet, in an interconnected world, price increases resulting from production failures can be passed on to (urban) consumers across extensive distances from the agricultural producing areas to consumption areas. Problems, for instance, with wheat production in France, the United States or in Russia can therefore translate into malnutrition, hunger, and illness in Arab countries. This relates to and combines with food access problems.

The second approach scrutinises market and access problems (i.e. entitlement failures; Sen 1981). The main leverage for this approach is the asymmetrical price formation and price volatility of food within globally connected trade relationships (Prakash 2011). Even in the case when sufficient food is locally available, food insecurity and hunger may result from the lack of suitable resources and capital. In other words, individuals and groups do not have the necessary purchasing power to buy what is available. This is what Sen (1981) captures as decline in exchange entitlements. Food insecurity and hunger are thus comprehended as a problem of access. This is particularly a problem for the growing number of poor people.

The third concept stresses responsibility and intervention problems (i.e response failures; Devereux 2007). 'New' hunger crises, the ones that emerge under conditions of globalisation, are a consequence of lacking accountability and intervention failures. These problems of public action are often connected to restrictive political regimes but can also result from (aid) interventions that undermine local strategies securing livelihoods. Moreover, food crises caused by war or complex emergencies can disrupt the food chain in all its different parts: on the level of production, marketing or transfers. In such cases, food insecurity and violence are connected. Sieges like in Syria or Yemen, for example, are used in a targeted manner. Here, famines do not just 'happen', they are caused intentionally. In these cases, they should not be seen as a failure of a social or economic systems, but rather as a product of these systems. This requires studying not of just local causes, but also of external forces, and particularly those who stand to profit from hunger and violence (see Edkins 2007 on the logic of war economies).

In the following, we address four questions: How are Arab youth actually situated in the global food system? Who is particularly exposed to food insecurity? How important is the role of national governments to prevent and mitigate insecurity? What kind of problems are emerging from this context, given various group and country specificities?

Hunger and Violence in the MENA Region

When asked about important changes in their lives over the past six years since the so-called Arab Spring, respondents most frequently indicate the impact of food insecurity and violence. More than half of young adults assessed growing violence (57 percent) and food shortages (57 percent) as being 'important' and 'very important' in their lives. Among Syrian refugees in Lebanon (80 percent), in war-torn Yemen (77 percent), and unstable Egypt (71 percent) major food problems were evident, but even in Palestine and Jordan, food shortages were perceived as 'important' or even 'very important' during the past five years (Figure 9.1). Food insecurity combines in these countries with expanding social instability and violence (Figure 9.2).

Above all, the Syrian refugees in Lebanon and the Yemenis pointed to a disastrous situation when asked about their recent assessment of food provisioning (see Table 9.1). In both cases, food insecurity is directly related to violent conflicts. Exposure to violence, more generally, also prevails in Tunisia and Palestine where about one quarter of the respondents' experienced more than one encounter with violent incidents. The spectrum of incidences we were asking about includes lower intensity experiences such as being witness of violence, but also experiences such as one's house or means of production having been deliberately destroyed, experiencing expulsion or displacement, or the immediate experience of having to see

Figure 9.1 **Importance of Food Shortages**

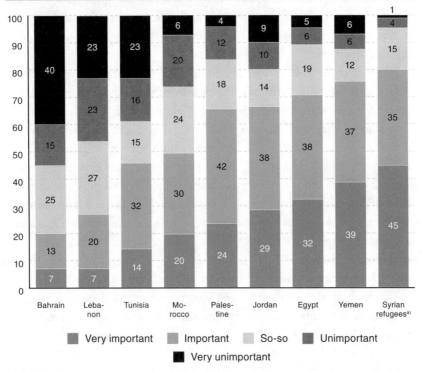

Figure 9.1 **Importance of Food Shortages**

Very important Important So-so Unimportant

Very unimportant

Question 141 *'What about changes in your life during the last five years. How important are they: Food shortages?'*

Note Figures are given in percentages. Rounding errors can occur. **a)** Syrian Refugees in Lebanon.

a doctor as a consequence of having been beaten up, having been in jail, suffered from hunger, or from torture, being injured in an armed conflict, as well as experiencing violence within the family or having experienced psychological violence, experiencing sexual harassment, joining a demonstration that turned violent or generally having experienced any form of violence. These experiences have been grouped together in the category 'Exposure to violence' (Table 9.1). If the group of the most vulnerable is analysed – those who belong both, to the lowest stratum, and simultaneously feature the highest self-assessed insecurity (see Chapter 2) – it appears that they are particularly exposed to violent experiences.

Internal group differences are particularly high in Egypt and Jordan, while in Yemen and among the Syrian refugees, and also in Palestine and Tunisia, experiences with violence cross the borders of the lower strata and concern general society. Almost two-thirds (61 percent) of those young people whose experience with growing violence is very important also state that the experience of food shortages has been very important during the last five years, revealing a high correlation between experiences of violence and food shortages.

In order to be able to identify the degree to which young people are impacted by food insecurity, we distinguish between those who assess their access to food as completely 'insecure' ('Food insecurity'; Table 9.1) and those who see themselves in danger of losing their access to food (Exposed). As well as Syrian refugees and Yemenis, young people in Lebanon, Palestine, Egypt, and Morocco also frequently indicate an exposure to food insecurity. These can often be traced back to income and purchasing power problems. A current situation of food insecurity can moreover combine with past experiences of hunger. On average 10 per cent of all respondents have already experienced hunger, though large country differences shape the picture. Again, it is the Syrian refugees and Yemenis who are affected most, but there are smaller groups also in Morocco, Palestine, Jordan, and Egypt who have already experienced hunger in their lifetime. Among them hunger was particularly felt by the most vulnerable sections (see above). In Jordan, Morocco, Palestine, and Egypt hunger experiences indeed are concentrated in these groups.

Overall, men have a higher incidence of hunger than women, the older group more frequently than the younger, and young adults responsible for their own households also suffer more frequently from hunger than youth who still live with their parents (16 percent compared to 7 percent). We are also able to say something about the temporal interconnection: over one third (36 percent) of those currently indicating insecurity in accessing food (the group of the Food Insecure) report earlier experiences of hunger. This is also the case for a little over a quarter (28 percent) of those vulnerable to food insecurity (the group of the Exposed). Other groups barely record any previous experience of hunger. These results are emblematic of the connection between hunger and poverty, as well as its persistence over time.

Another perspective can be gleaned from the government side of things. Two features are important: on the one hand, during complex emergencies, governments may disintegrate and authorities are violently contested (like in Yemen, Syria or Libya). These situations are characterised by extensive violence, loss of life and hunger, by displacements of populations, widespread damage to societies and economies, and often also by the hindrance of humanitarian assistance by political and military constraints. On the

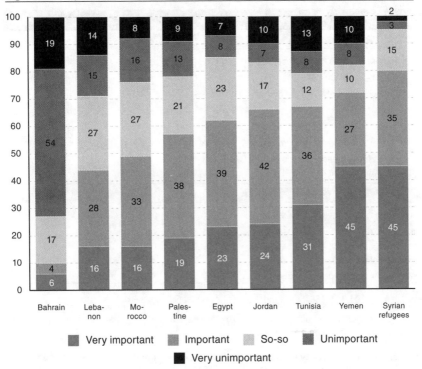

Figure 9.2 Importance of Growing Violence

Question 141 *'What about changes in your life during the last five years. How important are they: Growing violence?'*

Note Figures are given in percentages. Rounding errors can occur.

other hand, even in 'normal times', state action may be particularly restricted by import dependencies. As many poorer Arab countries are largely dependent on grain imports (like Morocco or Egypt) its uninterrupted provision at stable prices is crucial. A large proportion of the lowest classes still consume primarily bread, and this can take up the majority of a household's budget. The lowest stratum of the sample indicates that their most frequent expenditure is on food (84 percent of respondents) and particularly on wheat and bread (59 percent). This further increases for those young people among them who have already established their own household. In these cases, 94 per cent, respectively 63 per cent of the respondents state that they spend most money on food and on wheat (by selecting four out of twenty different items; see Chapter 8).

In an attempt to avoid food price protests, many countries are thus applying large subsidies. The survey results bear out the significance of this

Table 9.1 **Characteristics of Food Insecurity and Violence**

	Bahrain	Lebanon	
Food			
1. Food shortages; changes last five years (%)	20	27	
2. Food access (1–10 points) (Ø)	8.8	7.8	
3. Exposure to food insecurity (3–5 out of max. 10 points) (%)	6	17	
4. Food insecurity (1–2 out of max. 10 points) (%)	1	2	
5. Suffered hunger (%)	1	1	
6. Suffered hunger / most vulnerable group (%)	0	3	
7. Importance of cheap bread = very important (%)	21	43	
8. Possession of ration cards (%)	1	1	
Violence			
9. Growing violence; changes last five years (%)	10	44	
10. Social instability; changes last five years (%)	25	32	
11. Armed conflicts (1–10 points) (Ø)	7.0	4.9	
12. Exposure to violence (%)	0	8	
13. Exposure to violence / most vulnerable group (%)	2	10	

Questions 3, 10, 98, 104, 141, 168, Strata Index (see Chapter 2 and Appendix).

Note Bold figures represent the highest data per row (except for rows 2 and 11, where the lowest score is represented). Rounding errors can occur. ø = average

The assessment of food insecurity is based on aspects 1-8, determined by the following questions:
1. (Question 141) *'What about changes in your life over the last five years – how important are they?'* Aspect: Food shortages. Answer: 'Important' and 'Very important'.
2. (Question 10) *'Can you specify the area of security: I feel secure / insecure in the following fields.'* Aspect: My access to food. Answer: *'Please rate your situation on a scale from 1 (not at all secure) to 10 (totally secure)'*; Ø = National average.
3. & 4. The two categories refer to the same question (No. 10), but represent two independent groups: 3. 'Exposure', persons, who are exposed to food insecurity (3–5 out of 10 points); and 4. 'Food insecurity', persons, who are definitely food insecure (1–2 out of 10 points). Answers are based on the self-assessment of the respondents.
5. (Question 168) *'Have you ever … suffered from hunger?'* = Answer: 'Yes'.
6. (Question 168) 'Suffered hunger / most vulnerable group': These data represent the frequency of de facto hunger experiences of the most vulnerable group per country (those with the lowest strata profile and the highest self-assessed insecurity; see Chapter 2).

situation: with the exception of the two most wealthy countries, Bahrain and Lebanon, but also Morocco (having a fixed price for bread based on the French model) two-thirds of young adults assess the availability of cheap bread for themselves and their family to be 'very important'. Ration cards are however only available for two groups: for the Syrian refugees in Lebanon and for the Egyptians (80 percent from the lowest stratum, 55 percent from the highest stratum). They represent an important tool for public intervention, particularly to transfer resources in situations when poverty

Tunisia	Jordan	Morocco	Palestine	Egypt	Yemen	Syrian Ref.
46	68	59	66	71	77	**80**
8.8	8.0	7.1	7.5	7.3	5.8	**4.9**
5	7	16	19	12	33	**70**
1	1	3	3	4	**15**	7
2	6	6	6	5	19	**46**
3	15	11	15	15	26	**47**
64	72	40	63	65	83	**87**
2	4	1	4	**71**	0	46
66	66	48	57	62	72	**80**
47	69	52	61	59	62	**83**
6.5	6.3	6.1	4.9	6.1	**3.3**	3.9
25	17	19	27	17	42	**77**
30	32	25	36	36	42	**79**

7. (Question 98) *'How important is the availability of cheap bread for you and your family?'* = Answer: 'Very important'.

8. (Question 104) "Do you possess a ration card in order to buy or receive food?" = Answer: 'Yes'.

The assessment of experiences with violence is based on aspects 9–13, determined by the following questions:

9. & 10. (Question 141) *'What about changes in your life during the last five years. How important are they?'* Aspects = Growing violence & Social instability. Answer: 'Important' and 'Very important'.

11. (Question 10) *'Can you specify the area of security: I feel secure / insecure in the following fields:'* Aspect = The probability of armed conflict; Answer: *'Please rate your situation on a scale from 1 (not at all secure) to 10 (totally secure)'*; Ø = National average.

12. 'Exposure to violence': This information is based on a violence exposure index. It represents those who have more than one experience with violence (two or more answers with 'Yes' out of fourteen options; see Question 168; Table 3.7).

13. 'Exposure to violence': This information is based on a violence exposure index. It represents those who have more than one experience with violence (two or more answers with 'Yes' out of fourteen options; see Question 168; Table 3.7).

combines with problematic political circumstances. Demanding the right to bread is in that light a supremely political act and can even topple governments, as experienced during the Arab Spring.

Case Studies

We decided on four case studies – Egypt, Palestine, Yemen, and Syrian refugees, based on their exposure to both food insecurity and violence – to deepen the contextual understanding of hunger and the involvement of young people. Egypt is demographically not only by far the largest country in the MENA region, containing a huge segment of poor people, it is above all highly food import dependent. Palestine, in contrast, is a special case as severe poverty and social polarisation combine with a restricted spatial mobility and economic dependency on Israel. Syria and Yemen represent situations of complex emergencies. Millions of young people are exposed to hunger and death, generating different spatial mobilities. The Yemenis are predominantly internally displaced, while large segments of the Syrians crossed borders and moved as refugees, particularly into Lebanon, Jordan, and Turkey (see Chapter 10).

Egypt

Though few people suffer from acute hunger, a large number experience the structural impact of malnutrition, which, especially in the case of children, is associated with severe irreversible consequences. Egypt is highly dependent on food imports, particularly on grain and, as a result of poverty, has a per-capita consumption rate for wheat of around 180kg per annum, the highest in the world. As a consequence of turbo-charged privatisation and long-term disenfranchisement the Arab Spring was preceded by thousands of protests. Since 2011, Egypt has been unable to find political stability and has gone through several government changeovers. The Egyptian food system is currently shored up by massive subsidies, tightly monitored by the government, and increasingly transformed into a technology-based provision system. Three findings are key: the recent introduction of so-called smart cards replaces the analogue ration card system with a digital system; bread, previously available in apparently unlimited quantities, has been transformed in this process into a rationed good. This might improve public regulation and control, but not the food security situation. On the one hand, the profits of transnational corporations who trade in grains prevail; they find a robust market among the poor. On the other hand, there is little expenditure flexibility among the poor, as they have to spend a large part of their income on food, particularly on allegedly cheap grain. Moreover, by the beginning of the 1990s the threshold for moving from food security to food insecurity was already low for the overwhelming majority of low-income households. This situation has worsened severely in the past few years, primarily as a result of economic decline. Without bread subsidies and ration cards, many Egyptians would be facing a much more dramatic situation today. However, the economic costs of the subsidy system of more than one billion euros annually, has already made the Egyptian government politically dependent on the US and on Arab Gulf States. Finally, the associated costs of malnutrition, as evidenced by high spending on medication and low life expectancy, are, in contrast, hard to quantify, as is the sense of looming insecurity and uncertainty among youth. The perceived insecurity and resignation, however, relates directly to the failure of the government to provide for the basic needs. Muataz, a 29-year-old married worker from Giza, explained, 'Nowadays I think that youth have no aspirations, because [they] cannot find a job. So how can they make a family, live, eat or drink?' (EG-3). Sara, a 17-year-old woman from Bani Suef, said, 'There is no stability, every day is different from the day before, every day you are ruled by different policies, even different people, different decisions' (EG-2). Samer, a young man married with children from Cairo offered, 'I am personally very pessimistic. I also pray to find bread or beans the same price as yesterday's price' (EG-1).

Palestine
Another causal dimension of food insecurity is revealed in Palestine. Both the availability of food and insufficient purchasing power are an issue here, as they are closely linked to developments and relations with Israel. The differences between the situation in the West Bank and in the Gaza Strip are, however, still crucial, both in the extent of food insecurity as well as in the causes of food insecurity. Israel's blockade of the Gaza Strip from 2007 to 2015 contributed to an increasing uncertainty: half of all households suffered from food entitlement problems in 2014 (PCBS 2014). This situation worsened when the illegal tunnels connecting the Gaza Strip to Egypt were destroyed. High levels of unemployment, limited income-generating options, and deficient production capacity led to high food prices and deepened food insecurity. Although the volume of people and goods entering and leaving the Gaza Strip has now increased, the impact of that period is still being felt in the form of infrastructure deficits. The population of the West Bank by contrast has to contend with the restriction of economic activities as a result of restricted mobility. A complex system of physical barriers, checkpoints, and road blockades, bureaucratic obstacles, expansion of settlements, restrictions in terms of access to land and natural resources as well as the on-going displacement of the Palestinian population all lead to a weakening of the basic foundations on which livelihoods are built and thus also jeopardise food security. The agricultural sector, of particular significance in the West Bank, fulfils a dual role: it contributes to food security through subsistence farming and job creation. It is also an

important symbol of Palestinian resilience and helps to maintain and replicate Palestinian identity which is under threat in the face of on-going loss of land from occupation and Israeli settlement expansion. Hanadi, 30 years old, married with three children, describes the situation as follows:

> The occupation also leads to more poverty. High prices threaten us with poverty . . . My husband stayed unemployed for one whole year, and this destroyed us. We have debts. He could not find a job. Even our marital relationship is affected when the economic conditions are bad. Money is important. (PS-1)

Mahmoud, a self-employed 27-year-old from Birzeit whose family home was recently destroyed by the Israeli army, stated,

> The presence of the occupation is one of the main reasons for the threat of poverty. If Israel decides to close down the cities, roads, and checkpoints, people will become paralyzed and cannot work or pay their debts. [People] cannot find bread for their children. (PS-7)

Syria and Lebanon

In Syria, food security is to a massive degree determined by war. In 2016 almost 10 million people lived in circumstances of acute need, and have been classified as 'food insecure' or 'at risk of food insecurity' (FAO/WFP 2016). Several factors combine there. The flight of the rural population has brought the agricultural sector essentially to a standstill and with it domestic food production, while it also deprived this displaced population of their livelihoods. Since war broke out, the economy collapsed and sanctions took effect, food prices have soared. Prevailing import difficulties and fragmentation of markets by warring factions led to an even greater deterioration of the situation, with significant regional differences. For people in locations such as Aleppo or in the rural areas surrounding Damascus, that were in part under siege and where fighting was heavy, food was simply not available and, where it was, prices rose dramatically. In September 2016 the inhabitants of Madaya, for example, were paying four times as much for a kilo of rice as their neighbours in Damascus, and aid deliveries needed six months to enter the city, which happened only in September 2016 (WFP 2016a). With the security situation worsening by the day and the difficulty of meeting basic needs in Syria, large numbers of the population had to flee, not just to other parts of the country but also crossing the border into neighbouring countries. Ahmad, a 22-year-old, commented,

> If suppression and uprising in addition to the other circumstances remain unchanged, poverty will prevail at mass levels; famines might arise. In Syria, vegetable and bread prices are soaring in the market so people are incapable of buying them. (LB/SY-2)

Mariam, a 26-year-old, explained,

> In Syria, the prices are multiplied by ten, while people's income is still the same. There's hunger like I have never seen before. In the past, a person would never go to bed feeling hungry, I never saw this extent of fatigue and poverty before. (LB/SY-3)

In Lebanon, however, the refugees are once more faced with an uncertain food situation (see Chapter 10): over 90 per cent were considered food insecure in 2016 (WFP 2016b). Households affected often reduce spending on education and health, home owners sell their houses or land or take their children out of school to be able to leverage their labour for additional income. Although food is available in sufficient quantities in Lebanon not everyone has sufficient means to afford it. Syrian migrants in particular are exposed to a high rate of unemployment as a result of restricted access to the Lebanese labour market as well as to irregular incomes from informal sector activities; both leave them highly dependent on loans and food vouchers. The monthly gap between income and expenditure is hence growing leading to an on-going accumulation of debt in these households (see Chapter 7). Nour, 30 and married, describes her situation, stating, 'I am pessimistic. I am not able to meet my children's needs since I do not have money. [I] am not hopeful at all. I fear for my children's future. I cannot assure their basic needs' (LB/SY-5).

Yemen
Yemen experienced a war on several fronts in 2016. Armed clashes between supporters of the former president, Ali Abdallah Salih, (formerly located in Sana'a) and Shiite Houthis (from Northern Yemen) have moved gradually to the South, while frontlines are blurred by a military intervention of a Saudi-led coalition. There are also, particularly in the South, Al-Qaida and IS fighters against whom the US government is flying controversial drone

missions. Since 2015 the situation has become more acute. Over the course of the conflict several thousand people have been killed, with 2.4 million people having been displaced internally. Around half of all children under five are now chronically undernourished and 10 million people are starving. This makes Yemen currently the country with the highest rate of malnutrition anywhere in the world (Oxfam 2016). The most recent cholera outbreak has compounded the situation further and is emblematic of the drama that is playing out with the collapse of the economy, a health system in ruins and expanding food insecurity. Empirical results on Yemen show that the everyday burden of war is of crucial importance to young people. Everything else appears secondary to them. Bushra, an 18-year-old from Abyen, in the South, shared,

> My personal feeling of security decreased, because we lost security. In addition to the spread of unjustified bombings there are deliberate murders without any deterrent or punishment. All these issues are consequences of the absent state. (YE-1)

Afrah, a 28-year-old from Sana'a, emphasised, 'As a woman, I feel unsafe when I go out because of bombings, conflicts and troubles at the checkpoints' (YE-4). Ahmad, a 17-year-old from Sana'a stressed,

> Security decreased because corruption spread in all institutions, in the police and judiciary, and the country conditions became worse. The country became insecure even in the mosques, because of bombings. The economy is also bad. Factories stopped their production because of war, and also export and import activities were banned. [I] don't trust people anymore. Everything has changed for the worse since 2011 – parties, security, police, and the judiciary. (YE-5)

Young people also point to the ever-growing social disintegration and collapse of relationships of solidarity in society. Fatima, a 27-year-old, underlined, 'I don't trust anybody. These days, everyone behaves badly' (YE-7). Afrah stated,

> The threat of impoverishment is real, as our country suffers from crisis and wars. People become more selfish because of poverty and the problems they suffer today. People keep the things they have

for themselves and never think of others who are in dire need, without any solidarity because of the crisis. Wars make people less cooperative with each other and forget the social values they used to adopt. (YE-4)

Food insecurity in Yemen stands out by virtue of just how many different causes are at play: depending on location and situation there is a lack of available food, purchasing power-related access issues, combined with a failure of the international community to step in and take responsibility. These factors are further compounded by the destruction of trading routes and agricultural production, the blockade of commercial imports and a persistent and long-standing fuel crisis (Mundy 2017). The transition from subsistence farming to paid employment as the main source of income has made people in Yemen particularly vulnerable to import blockades and price rises. They cannot sufficiently provide for themselves any longer. Nonetheless, the agricultural sector is still important for the rural population. By destroying agricultural infrastructure the war therefore not only cripples production, but also leaves whole families without a livelihood and therefore access to food. People are being forced to sell their livestock well under market prices; in other words they are making rush sales which is the forerunner to local famines. In Taiz, a town on the frontline of fighting, food prices have risen dramatically. Khalid, 30 years old, married, and dependent financially on his father in Taiz, stated,

I, as father of one child and an employee without salary, suffer from the problem that we don't find friends or supporters in our time of need. They don't care about your problems at all. They run away from you to avoid giving you any help. These days the traders particularly become more selfish and egoistic, never even helping their friends because of the crisis. We are all in trouble, and the country as a whole is suffering from these problems. (YE-9).

Tahiyah, an 18-year-old woman from Aden, underlined,

People become more selfish, especially traders, as they keep increasing the prices without any consideration of people's income and salary issues. Therefore, even friends do not help each other anymore, to keep themselves away from more losses and to avoid poverty and need. (YE-12)

Conclusion

In a world of increasing uncertainties two forms of security are crucial: the provision and guarantee of basic needs; and the absence of violence. In the aftermath of the Arab Spring everyday insecurities have expanded and different forms of violence, direct and structural forms, combine, one exacerbating the other, particularly in situations of complex emergencies such as in Syria and in Yemen. Simultaneously the global food system and social developments are highly entangled. Places of security and places of insecurity are globally interlinked, shaping different spaces of food sovereignty, for instance, war and hunger in one place and profits from weapon and grain sales in other places. This also includes that retirement savings 'here' (through investment in pension funds) and food insecurity 'there' are articulated if institutional investors (such as pension funds and banks) are enabled to speculate on agricultural commodities and food prices. Insecurities thus develop within different spatialities. Spaces of hunger are locations in which food insecurity is experienced physically by individuals and groups. Causal spaces of hunger unfold in the form of globe-spanning commodity and value chains, as well as in short-term assemblages, whose (often unintended) consequences of price-building trigger malnutrition and hunger (Gertel 2015). In this sense, they are violent, as they generate irreversible social consequences. Those who are affected are, however, not able per se to identify the complex causes of war and hunger. While the consequences of fighting, displacement or poverty are obvious for everyone, mechanisms like the concentration of market power in international trading houses or globally active retail chains, economic tactics of banks or sovereign wealth funds, as well as financial speculation with food commodities or investment strategies of private equity consortia active in financial markets, are difficult to detect and sometimes are indeed actively veiled. In *Expulsions,* Saskia Sassen stresses that the 'forms of knowledge and intelligence we respect and admire are often the starting point for long chains of transactions that end in simple exclusion' (Sassen 2014, 7). Such chains of information, with fragmented and undefined responsibilities, are thus to be comprehended as forms of violence. Exclusion and hunger are (spatialised) outcomes of techno-liberal transformations that generate and enable an anonymous profit making in shareholder economies. Analogous to the debate around 'food from nowhere' versus 'food from somewhere' (Campbell 2009) we should therefore focus on sounding out the so-far unknown spaces of the complex causes of price increases and food insecurity. This will include widening our gaze beyond the on-the-ground spaces of hunger, to rather include the causal spaces manifest in global chains of transaction and price formation. It is only then that we can begin to analyse and talk about empowerment of the young generation. Sabr, a young man from Palestine, remarked,

> Everyone is preoccupied with earning income. This is what the government wants. People are tied down by loan checks and poverty. They want the people to think all the time about how to pay instalments and not to think about politics or other things. When people earn income, they start thinking about why things are difficult and start thinking about change. (PS-6)

10

Mobility, Migration, and Flight

Jörg Gertel & Ann-Christin Wagner

WE ARE LIVING IN AN AGE of 'mobilities' (Urry 2000), characterised by an accelerated movement of people, commodities, information, and images across international boarders. The MENA region represents a central node within a network of global connections. However, little is known about how young people in the region conceive of mobility, and how migration and flight affect them. The protest movements of the Arab Spring and subsequent war-driven large-scale displacements in Libya and Syria have drawn attention to population movements towards Europe. However, in contrast to migration across the Mediterranean and along the Balkan route, mobility schemes within the Arab world, including to the Gulf, as well as circular labour migration in neighbouring countries, have largely gone unreported. This has resulted in a distorted representation of migration patterns in the Middle East and North Africa in academic research and policymaking (Fargues 2017). We are thus convinced that it is crucial to give voice to youth and young adults from the region, to potential migrants and stayers.

In this chapter, we will investigate different aspects relevant to Arab youth's migration decisions. We will discuss how mobility is linked to the contextual setting of personal experiences, and how going abroad becomes part of moving on with one's life. The data reveal that only a remarkably small number of young Arabs intend to migrate, a surprising find against the backdrop of the multiple crises they are experiencing. Mobility, we find, is a much more complex project as might be expected; it depends on multiple predispositions, resource pooling strategies within kin and social networks, and often on collective selection processes aimed at identifying the most suitable migrant among potential candidates (Gertel and Sippel 2014). To situate our findings, we will start with some reflections about migration theory. Subsequently, the survey data will speak for themselves: first, about young people's flexibility to change their current situation; and second, about their reasons and determination to migrate. In the final part, we will provide a close-up on

Syrian refugees in Lebanon, taking their case as an example of how displacement affects young people in the countries under scrutiny.

Which Mobility Are We Talking About?
For a long time, despite frequent obstacles, movements between the southern and the northern shores of the Mediterranean were far from impossible. It was only after the Schengen agreement in 1995, which erected 'Fortress Europe', that young people in the Global South were hindered from moving northward. Almost simultaneously, however, the introduction of the internet led to the inception of a new social space; social interactions became increasingly decoupled from co-presence in time and space. At least temporarily, virtual emigrations suspended existing restrictions on spatial mobility (Braune 2011). By way of illustration, online chat rooms presented opportunities for communicating across gender, national, and linguistic boundaries. Virtual mobility, however, feeds back into offline reality and may fuel real-life migration aspirations. Mariam, a 25-year-old woman from Cairo, pointed out,

> Today internet is vital. Compared to the past, we now receive news online of the country, whether there is work or about other people. We can easily find information about travelling and many other things. That makes life much easier. It also comes with new opportunities for going abroad. (EG-10)

What is more, virtual spaces allow glimpses into different worlds, even to those with hardly any formal education. Ahmed, a 20-year-old electrician from Mahala, Egypt, who only attended primary school, explained what sparked his interest in finding work abroad:

> I used to go to an internet café. On the internet I meet people my age from Egypt and from other countries, like the US . . . I don't mean that I feel I am less 'worthy', but I feel that they have better opportunities than we do here. (EG-8)

In order to capture the multiple forms of spatial and social mobility and to integrate virtual mobility and flexible forms of identity formation, we suggest conceiving of *mobilities* in the plural, taking the 'mobility turn' in social sciences as a point of departure. Importantly, human mobilities are embedded into the wider circulation of goods, money, technology, and

Table 10.1 **Flexibility – Characteristics**

n=9,000	All	Gender		Age			Household	
	Aver-age	Male	Fe-male	16–20	21–25	26–30	Pa-rents	Own
Accept work in rural space, home country	49	55	43	49	51	47	50	45
Accept work in rural space, European country	35	43	27	36	37	33	38	27
Accept work in rural space, Arab country	33	40	24	33	33	31	34	29
Accept work below qualification	32	36	27	31	32	32	31	31
Leave family for qualification	39	48	30	40	43	34	43	28
Leave family even if you risk life	18	23	14	18	20	18	20	15
Marry somebody from class above	38	36	40	41	38	32	41	28
Marry somebody from class below	32	37	26	34	33	29	34	26
Marry somebody from different religion	15	20	10	15	16	14	16	12
Marry somebody older	13	14	12	11	14	14	13	12
Flexibility Index: 'High' (Ø 25 %)	25	32	18	25	27	23	27	19

Question '*In order to change your current situation, would you be ready …?*' Here: 'Agree & Rather agree'.

Five answer options Disagree; Rather disagree; Not sure; Rather Agree; Agree.

Questions 3, 4, 14, 181, Flexibility Index.

Note Figures are given in percentages. Rounding errors can occur. Household = Parents (interviewees live with their parents); Household = Own (interviewees live in their own household). ø = average. | We calculated a Flexibility Index based on scenarios that queried three categories of forced social mobility: to leave the family; to accept unknown or adverse working conditions; to marry into a different group. Between one point ('Disagree') and five points ('Agree') could be achieved per item (question). We calculated averages for each item assigning them to the three categories (family, work, marriage) and computed averages per category that were then assembled in one average value per person. Finally, we used the distribution of all individual scores to divide the whole sample into four equal groups (quartiles). The highest quartile ('High') with the highest average values (the most flexible persons) scored three points at least, matching the answers from 'Not sure' to 'Agree'.

ideas, all of which contribute to shaping uneven movements of individuals and entire populations. Much attention has been paid to the role of social difference, ethnicity, gender, and religion in determining migration. Van Hear (2014) suggests shifting the focus to the material conditions of socio-economic standing as the latter shapes not only migration outcomes, but also the migration process itself, i.e. decision-making processes, trajectories and destinations. Van Hear focuses on a specific demographic known to engage extensively in global migration: educated but underemployed youth, for whom 'migration is often seen as – and can be – a means of moving out of the precariat, but migrants often find themselves stuck in it in host countries, experiencing insecurity in life and livelihoods' (ibid.: 115). Thus, mobility is not inherently tied to poverty; rather, as the Syrian refugee crisis reveals, the most destitute are those stuck back home with no means to flee. Hence, displacement can be experienced as decoupled from actual

Table 10.2 **Flexibility – Countries**

n=9,000	Mo-rocco	Jor-dan	Tuni-sia	Egypt	Syr-ia[a)]	Bah-rain	Leba-non	Ye-men	Pales-tine
Accept work in rural space, home country	41	55	57	25	47	34	44	**63**	67
Accept work in rural space, European country	40	40	**54**	31	38	30	32	24	26
Accept work in rural space, Arab country	30	**47**	40	22	39	24	18	40	33
Accept work below qualifica-tion	31	39	35	26	40	24	16	**44**	29
Leave family for qualification	44	43	**55**	34	23	43	35	37	28
Leave family even if you risk life	**32**	19	20	18	14	24	14	17	10
Marry somebody from class above	45	42	40	36	31	34	33	**47**	30
Marry somebody from class below	36	37	36	31	23	31	24	**46**	29
Marry somebody from differ-ent religion	**29**	19	17	11	10	16	18	8	8
Marry somebody older	**24**	17	9	14	9	14	9	14	6
Flexibility Index:									
'High' (Ø 25 %)	**42**	30	26	23	22	26	20	20	15
'Relatively high' & 'High' (Ø 50 %)	**63**	56	54	51	51	49	43	40	35

Question *'In order to change your current situation, would you be ready …?'* Here: 'Agree' & 'Rather Agree'.

Five answer options Disagree; Rather disagree; Not sure; Rather Agree; Agree.

Questions 3, 181, Flexibility Index (see Table 10.1).

Note Figures are given in percentages. Rounding errors can occur. Bold figures represent the highest score per row. ø = average. [a)] Syrian Refugees in Lebanon.

movement in space, with disrupted mobility leading to 'displacement in space' and forceful immobilisation (Lubkemann 2008). In a similar vein, De Haas (2014) suggests reframing 'human mobility as people's capabil-ity (freedom) to choose where to live' (ibid.: 4). Reconsidering migratory agency as the choice between moving or staying allows to overcome arti-ficial distinctions between push and pull factors or voluntary and forced migration.

Tough Choices: Do Youth in the MENA Region Want to Live Different Lives?

Individual predisposition towards mobility is related to the preparedness to accept certain life changes. To explore young people's degree of flexibility, we scrutinise three types of potential scenarios: informants' willingness to marry into another group; leaving one's parents to receive professional trainings; and accepting unfavourable living conditions to earn money (Table 10.1). Before considering each of these categories, though, it is worth noting that migration is not the most daring endeavour youth can imagine. Rather, certain types of marital choices seem to be the hardest. In fact, respondents are even less willing to marry an older person or someone from a different religious group than putting their lives at risk during migration.

Out of group marriage

Regarding marital arrangements, who appears to be an acceptable spouse says much about the porosity, or impermeability, of social boundaries one faces when navigating social space. As outlined above, most young people rule out getting married to partners from a different religion or partners significantly older than themselves, while marriage beyond one's class boundaries appears to be more acceptable. The fact that women appear much less willing to marry a partner from a different religion in order to change their current situation might be attributed to the particular nature of interfaith marriages, making them more permissible for men. In fact, one third of all interviewees, especially men, would agree or rather agree to marrying a partner from a lower social class. However, both sexes consider marrying up more desirable. There are, however, considerable differences between individual countries, for instance, Yemen and Lebanon (Table 10.2).

Leaving home[1]

Obtaining professional qualifications appears to be an acceptable motive (at least in some countries) for leaving loved ones behind – more than one third of all informants would do so; they 'agree' or 'rather agree' to this idea. However, qualitative interviews confirm that respondents do not take migration lightly; rather, they are torn between the desire to continue their lives among family and friends and make a meaningful contribution to their home countries, and find a way out of the professional impasse they are stuck in. Hamza, a 25-year-old student from Settat, Morocco, found powerful words to express the dilemma labour migrants find themselves in:

---

1. In order to offer a more comprehensive picture in this and the following paragraph, in a few cases the perspective of those who "Disagree" and "Rather disagree" is taken, while Tables 10.1 and 10.2 represent those who "Agree" and "Rather agree". Given that the option "Not sure" is not further specified here, some trends in the text and in the figures may thus appear contradictory.

'You may not find a job in your country, and you may work abroad, then you will live abroad, far from your family and far from your friends, you will live in another world' (MA-7). By way of contrast, almost half of all respondents disagree with 'leaving home even if you risk your life', a tendency even more pronounced for young Yemenis. This might reflect their survival strategies in times of war.

Accepting unappealing work
Half of the youth surveyed would be willing ('agree' or 'rather agree') to work in rural regions of their own countries, but also, to a lesser degree, in other Arab countries and in Europe (about one-third each). High approval rates of young Moroccans and Tunisians for rural work in Europe seem to reflect longstanding menial labour migration of North Africans to the Mediterranean shores of Southern and Western Europe (Gertel and Sippel 2014). Yet, more generally, working in farming abroad does not appeal to many, with almost half of the respondents unwilling to engage in agricultural labour in other Arab countries and Europe ('disagree' or 'rather disagree'). Finally, about half of the informants are unwilling to accept employment that does not match their professional qualifications, a number slightly lower for Syrian refugees in Lebanon and young Moroccans. Note that most young Syrians are excluded from the formal labour market in Lebanon, and often pushed into exploitative and menial labour, a finding we will come back to in the final part of this chapter.

To obtain a comprehensive picture about young people's preparedness to accept life changes, we calculated a Flexibility Index, merging the three categories of social mobility: family, work, and marriage. Regarding young people's overall flexibility in accepting adverse life choices, different groups emerge, that become manifest at the national level. On average, young Moroccans and Jordanians appear to be the most flexible. No significant differences appear across age groups, but results are highly gendered, with women proving to be less flexible, indicating greater social constraints on women's life choices. Young single males with financial resources from their own labour-based income turn out to be the most flexible. However, one should ask how these predispositions relate to actual migration aspirations.

Young Arabs' Mobility Attitudes and Migration Experiences
To answer this question, we will now turn to mobility attitudes and ambitions of leaving one's country of origin. If young Arab people had had to emigrate to Europe in summer 2016 (after the closure of the Balkan route),

which countries would they have considered primary targets? Four countries stand out: Germany, France, Sweden, and the United Kingdom (Table 10.3). While Syrian refugees' preferences reflect current patterns of refugee flows (major destinations are Sweden and Germany), preferences are also linked to longstanding post-colonial and linguistic ties. For example, most young Tunisians and Moroccans would prefer to live in France. But who does this apply to – is everybody ready to leave home? In this chapter, we will investigate four aspects of migration: the number of respondents intent on migrating; linkages between personal migration aspirations and earlier experiences of living abroad; migration experiences of relatives and in one's wider social network. Finally, we will link the desire of emigration to individual predispositions, such as socioeconomic status and personal flexibility.

To start with, more than half of the surveyed youth, with the exception of Tunisians, categorically rule out the option of migration for themselves; between 48 and 71 percent, depending on the country, underline that they are 'definitely not emigrating'. While about one-third express a more or less serious interest in emigration – 13 percent 'sometimes play with the idea', and another 22 percent 'would like to emigrate' – very few are determined to go abroad (7 percent, 'I am sure that I will emigrate') (Table 10.4). How do we explain the respondents' surprisingly little interest in migration? Overall, women are more adamant about staying at home (65 percent versus 51 percent of men), whereas men are more likely to toy with the idea of emigrating (15 percent versus 11 percent for women), findings one might interpret in the light of additional obstacles to female freedom of movement. Placing migration aspirations in conversation with various other factors, including migration experiences within the family, personal predisposition for change as well as social class background, reveals a more nuanced picture.

First, few young people have experienced migration themselves, with fewer than 10 percent having lived outside their home countries throughout their lives. Moreover, previous migration experiences are circumscribed within the Arab world, with most respondents having resided in the Gulf and other Arab countries. In particular, Syrian refugees in Lebanon are much more likely to have previously lived abroad, testimony to long-standing circular labour migration of Syrian menial workers to Lebanon, Jordan, and the Gulf before the Syrian civil war (Chalcraft 2008). Nevertheless, the recent generation of young people from countries with strong historical and linguistic ties to Europe such as Lebanon, Morocco, and Tunisia, are not more likely to have spent time on the other side of the Mediterranean.

Table 10.3 Migration Experiences – Countries

n= 9,000	Mo-rocco	Tuni-sia	Egypt	Jor-dan	Pales-tine	Leba-non	Ye-men	Bah-rain	Syr-ia[a]
Emigration: Personal conviction									
– (a) Definitely not	63	40	62	56	**71**	55	**71**	**55**	48
– (b) Played with the idea	19	11	16	2	12	19	8	**22**	10
– (c) I would like to	16	**40**	19	16	15	21	19	21	32
– (d) I am sure I will	3	8	3	**27**	2	5	2	2	10
Target country (b/c/d; n=3,801)									
• Germany	24	42	15	32	41	38	15	18	**48**
• France	30	**52**	20	32	28	36	17	13	16
• Sweden	10	8	14	23	45	30	9	10	**54**
Respondent: Contact with asylum seekers	8	**19**	6	10	8	13	6	1	8
Respondent: Lived outside home country	2	5	3	10	8	9	6	1	**21**
Family member migrated	14	**41**	12	12	14	**41**	16	10	20
– Importance for you: 'yes'	41	49	43	45	56	39	**61**	27	56
Emigration & Strata (c/d; n=2,612)									
– Lowest stratum	17	**47**	21	39	17	44	18	0	44
– Lower-middle stratum	17	**46**	19	40	21	25	18	(2)	27
– Middle stratum	18	**44**	21	**44**	15	27	23	9	(13)
– Higher-middle stratum	20	**57**	29	46	17	22	33	24	(3)
– Highest stratum	28	**58**	20	42	17	32	32	25	(0)

Questions 3, 171, 173, 175, 176, 177, 178, 179, 180, Strata Index (see Chapter 2 and Appendix).

Note Figures are given in percentages. Rounding errors can occur. Bold figures represent the highest score per row. Figures in brackets represent single cases. [a] Syrian Refugees in Lebanon.

Emigration: Personal conviction (Question 179) = 'What would best describe your situation?'
    (a) Definitely not = 'I am definitely not emigrating' (58 %)
    (b) Played with the idea = 'I sometimes played with the idea of emigrating' (13 %)
    (c) I would like to = 'I would like to emigrate' (22 %)
    (d) I am sure I will = 'I am sure that I will emigrate' (7 %)
Target Country (Question 180; if Question 179 = b–d) = 'Recently, a lot of people are on their way to Europe. If you were to emigrate, what would be your preferred target countries?' (Multiple answers).
Respondent: Contact with asylum seekers (Question 177) = 'Have you been in contact (by phone, SMS, Skype) with somebody who is trying to find a job or asylum in Europe within the last three months?' (Yes = 9 %): If 'Yes' (Question 178): 'If yes, who have you been in contact with?': Family (49 %), Friends (57 %), Neighbours (5%), Others (6 %).
Respondent: Lived outside home country (Question 171) = 'Have you ever lived outside your own country?' ('Yes', n=630).
Family member migrated (Question 173) = 'Is there somebody in your family who migrated to a foreign country?' ('Yes', n=1,765). If 'Yes': Importance for you (Question 175): 'Is this emigration of any importance to you?' ('Yes', n=822).
Emigration & Strata: Two options are included: (c) 'I would like to emigrate' (22 %) & (d) 'I am sure that I will emigrate' (7 %), and their distribution in relation to social strata is analysed.

Second, respondents are more familiar with migration through relatives who have been abroad, with one fifth stating that a family member has migrated to another country in the past. Again, young people from Tunisia and Lebanon stick out in that almost half of all people surveyed report the existence of migrants among their loved ones. Regarding travel destinations of their relatives, a more diverse pattern emerges than for young people themselves. While the Gulf and other Arab countries have welcomed respondents' family members, other major destinations include Europe, the US and Canada. Again, countries like Morocco and Tunisia are noticeable in that young nationals of these countries themselves, but also their family members have overwhelmingly migrated to Europe in the past. Significantly, migration experiences within one's own family (overall, this concerns 20 percent of the respondents) appear to have resonated with young respondents, almost half of them confirm that a relative's migration has been important to them personally. However, young people from this group also have ambivalent feelings about the ways in which a loved one's migration has affected them in the past (Table 10.4). While a quarter of the respondents acknowledge having benefited from remittances sent back home (28 percent), and almost equal numbers became fascinated by the idea of living in a foreign country and their desire to emigrate grew (30 percent), still others consider a loved one's departure a personal loss (22 percent) or even express strict reservations about emigration (with 14 percent indicating that relatives' migration experiences have discouraged them from aspiring to emigration themselves). While male and female respondents have been equally affected by migration within their own families, women seem to perceive this contradiction more acutely, indicating having benefited more from money sent back (33 percent versus 24 percent for men), but also feeling the personal loss of a loved one more sharply (26 percent versus 18 percent for men).

Third, however, respondents seem to reflect on migratory movements beyond the immediate past, as 9 percent of young people have been in touch by phone or Skype with people seeking employment or asylum in Europe within the last three months (reference May/June 2016). If so, they have mostly been communicating with family members (49 percent) and friends (57 percent), which hints at the importance of experiences abroad of not only relatives, but also within wider social networks, for shaping one's own migration plans. Nevertheless, contact with refugees and asylum seekers can also have other, adverse effects. In interviews conducted with young people from Lebanon and Jordan, both among the neighbouring countries of Syria most affected by the influx of refugees, young people utter a sentiment of

Table 10.4 **Migration Experiences – Characteristics**

n=9,000	All Average	Gender Male	Gender Female	Age 16–20	Age 21–25	Age 26–30	Household Parents	Household Own
Emigration: Personal conviction								
– (a) Definitely not	**58**	51	65	57	55	62	55	66
– (b) Played with the idea	**13**	15	11	14	15	12	15	9
– (c) I would like to	**22**	26	18	24	23	20	24	18
– (d) I am sure I will	**7**	8	5	7	7	6	7	7
Respondent: Lived outside home country	**7**	8	6	5	7	10	5	11
Family member migrated (Yes = 1,765)	**20**	20	20	19	20	20	20	18
Of importance for you (Yes = 822) If 'Yes':	47	52	48	46	45	48	46	49
– Personal loss (Yes = 181)	22	18	26	13	23	25	18	27
– Profited from money	28	24	33	30	26	23	28	21
– Emigration not a goal	14	14	14	14	11	14	13	13
– Wish for emigration grew	30	35	24	33	23	27	31	20
– Feelings mixed up	21	23	19	19	20	20	18	24
Respondent: Contact with asylum seekers	**9**	11	7	8	10	9	9	8

Questions 3, 4, 14, 171, 173, 175, 176, 177, 179.

Note Figures are given in percentages. Rounding errors can occur. | Bold figures represent percentages referring to the whole sample (n=9,000). Household = Parents (interviewees live with their parents); Household = Own (interviewees live in their own household).

Emigration: Personal situation (Question 179) = 'What would best describe your situation?'
   (a) Definitely not = 'I am definitely not emigrating' (58 %).
   (b) Played with the idea = 'I sometimes played with the idea of emigrating' (13 %).
   (c) I would like to = 'I would like to emigrate' (22 %).
   (d) I am sure I will = 'I am sure that I will emigrate' (7 %).
Respondent: Lived outside home country (Question 171) = 'Have you ever lived outside your own country?' ('Yes').
Family member migrated (Question 173) = 'Is there somebody in your family who migrated to a foreign country?' ('Yes').
If 'Yes': Of importance for you (Question 175) = 'Is this emigration of any importance to you?' ('Yes').
If 'Yes' (Question 176) = 'Which of the following statements best reflects your opinion?' (Multiple answers).
– Personal loss = 'I consider it as a loss for my personal life';
– Profited from money = 'I profit from the money he/she is sending to us';
– Emigration not a goal = 'I learned from his/her experiences abroad and decided that emigration is not a goal for me';
– Wish for emigration grew = 'I am fascinated by the idea of living in a foreign country, and my wish to emigrate has grown';
– Feelings mixed up = 'My feelings about emigration started to get mixed up.'
Respondent: Contact with asylum seekers (Question 177) = 'Have you been in contact (by phone, SMS, Skype) with somebody who is trying to find a job or asylum in Europe within the last three months?' ('Yes').

being 'displaced at home', often linked to the perception of being replaced in the labour market by cheaper foreign workers, and of increasing costs of living. A 30-year-old female from Amman, herself highly educated and working in media and education, deplored,

I am a refugee and poor in my own country, and instead of supporting the youth and employing them the state only promotes
the employment of people from other nationalities. (JO-7)

Fourth, social class also plays a role in determining mobility potential.
Overall, there seems to be a tendency for young Arabs from wealthier social
strata to be more in favour of personal migration, a trend most pronounced
for respondents from Morocco, Tunisia, Yemen, and Bahrain (Table 10.3).
One might infer that, given the considerable costs that migration incurs,
better-off informants perceive themselves to be in a better position to
go abroad. In addition, while migration for employment or educational
purposes seems acceptable to many Arab youth, a complementary picture
emerges from the qualitative interviews. In fact, while finding work abroad
is certainly the main motive for many youngsters, one should not ignore
other migration motives, including wanderlust. As a 20-year-old female
university student from Casablanca put it,

I wish I could tour the world to explore the world. I have a pho-
tography hobby. I like to photograph places, I toured Morocco
with my parents from south to north. (MA-10)

Yet, the interviews also reveal that leisure travelling is reserved for certain
better-off social strata, and also highly gendered. In societies with restrictive
gender norms and limited freedom of movement, it seems to be more permissible for young men.

In sum, earlier migration experiences within one's family make one less
likely to refuse migration categorically and more likely to envision migration oneself (see Table 10.5), a tendency that holds true for both men and
women. Personal predisposition for change also moulds migration aspirations. Informants who score low on the Flexibility Index are more intent on
staying and less likely to imagine themselves as migrants, a tendency again
mediated by previous migration experiences within the family. Overall,
highly flexible respondents, mostly young men aged 20–25, who have been
exposed to migration experiences and narratives through relatives, are most
likely to consider migration for themselves.

From Way Out to Impasse: Syrian Refugees in Lebanon

In the final part of this chapter, we will provide a close-up on Syrian
youth's situation in Lebanon, illustrating the motives that steer and shape

Table 10.5 **Migration Dispositions**

Flexibility Index	Low	Low	Rather low	Rather low	Rather high	Rather high	High	High	All
n=9,000		M		M		M		M	
Emigration: Personal convition									
– (a) I am definitely not emigrating	82	67	69	42	53	28	44	22	58
– (b) I sometimes played with the idea	6	12	10	18	15	21	17	21	13
– (c) I would like to emigrate	9	16	16	30	26	38	28	47	22
– (d) I am sure that I will emigrate	2	5	4	9	7	14	11	11	7

Questions 173, 179, Flexibility Index (see Table 10.1).

Note Figures are given in percentages. Rounding errors can occur. | Bold figures are at or above the arithmetic mean.
M = Family Migration Experience. The Flexibility Index covers 98 percent of the sample and is based on four categories ('Low', 'Rather low', 'Rather high', 'High'). 'High' indicates that the respondent shows a high level of personal flexibility in terms of the three categories (family, work, marriage; see Table 10.1).

war-induced flight and onward migration. In contrast to migration in all of its different facets, flight often implies a previous threat to life, including losses of family members and property, serious cuts to the resource structure of households, and unplanned, frequently forced mobility; in short, flight has to be considered in the continuity of insecurity and vulnerability back home. In 2016, one out of five individuals in Lebanon is a Syrian, making Lebanon the country proportionally most affected by the influx of populations displaced during the Syrian civil war. Lebanon opened its borders to the displaced as early as April 2011. By January 2015, almost 1.2 million Syrian refugees had been registered with the UNHCR, the United Nation's refugee agency, in Lebanon. Notably, the UNHCR has been operating on the ground under the umbrella of a 2003 Memorandum of Understanding, as Lebanon is not a signatory to the 1951 Geneva convention on refugees, putting Syrians in the country 'in a grey area between "alien", "displaced" and "de facto refugee"' (Dionigi 2016: 23). In the absence of formal refugee camps, Syrians have self-settled in urban and rural communities. Informal tent settlements, especially in the Bekaa Valley, are abundant. However, Lebanon, a state with a fragile governance system, political and sectarian strife, and an underdeveloped infrastructure, was badly equipped to handle the massive arrival of the displaced. Only in October 2016 did the election of a new president, Michael Aoun, end a two-year political vacuum. What is more, Lebanon and Syria have historically enjoyed a rather strenuous relationship, including a 29-year military presence of Syrian troops on Lebanese territory from 1976 to 2005, and strong ties between various political factions in Lebanon and the Syrian Baathist regime. Yet, what is often overlooked is the longstanding presence of Syrian migrant workers – estimated to number between 500,000 and a million labourers – on Lebanese territory before the war. It is also noteworthy, though, that Lebanon's open border policy encouraged frequent travel and going back and forth.

Since late 2012, the Syrian civil war has increasingly threatened to spill over into the neighbouring country. Consequently, Syrian refugees in Lebanon came to be perceived as a threat to security as well as social, economic, and political stability in the country. While the Lebanese government had begun to register Syrian refugees in January 2013, two years later, it put an end to open-border policies and free movement, subjecting Syrians to new, and much tougher, visa restrictions. Shortly thereafter, in May 2015, the UNHCR had to suspend registration at the request of the Lebanese government. There are, therefore, no UNHCR statistics on the number of Syrians residing in Lebanon available for the most recent period. The multiplication of visa categories, the hardening of application criteria and the introduction of a 200USD fee for the annual renewal of residence permits put legal residency out of reach for the majority of Syrians in the country, pushing more than 70 percent of the refugee population into irregularity (Janmyr 2016). Moreover, Syrians registered with the UNHCR also had to sign a pledge not to work.

Circumstances of Syrians' flight

We will now turn to the ways in which young Syrians experience displacement to Lebanon. Given the current political situation in Lebanon and the limited nature of this dataset, the survey results should not be considered representative. They reflect the situation of 1,000 interviewees in 2016, depicting a detailed picture of a population displaced by war and having suffered considerable material losses. The data show that three-quarters of Syrian respondents left their home country during the first three years of the Syrian civil war, i.e. between 2011 and 2013. Most young people abandoned Syria in a rush, without having time to prepare (Table 10.6). Causes of Syrians' flight include fighting, poverty, material damage, and risks to one's life and the lives of loved ones: a large majority of respondents state that they left home due to violent attacks and fighting, but also when sources of income and other resources became scarce, particularly with regard to food shortage, and also when homes were destroyed. War-induced destruction and precarity as main reasons for flight resonate with Syrians' statements about the considerable material losses they incurred: more than three-quarters of the households surveyed lost property, mostly houses and machines, and, to a lesser extent, cars, valuables, and land. Moreover, although less than one-tenth of respondents lost family members during the flight, many experienced immediate threats to their lives, including fears of being kidnapped and medical emergencies. Significantly, for those who lost family members during the flight, about half of them lost a brother, testimony to the precarious situation of younger men during war time, often overlooked during emergency responses focused on displaced women and children. In particular, fear of forced recruitment drove male Syrians into exile.

Family reunifications are crucial: the large majority of respondents left Syria to follow their loved ones and reunite with family members abroad. Many household members fled together (Table 10.7). While very few Syrian youth arrived in Lebanon on their own or in the

Table 10.6 **Syrian Ref. in Lebanon: Characteristics**

	All
n=1,000	Percent
Flight: Prepared or sudden	
– Prepared	14
– Unprepared	86
Reasons for the escape	
– No income available and no resources left	87
– I had to leave with my family	85
– Fear of being kidnapped	82
– Immediate threat to life	81
– Nothing left to eat, suffering hunger	79
– Uniting with family members	77
– No prospects over there	77
– House / Apartment was destroyed	75
– Avoiding forced recruitment	68
– Medical emergency	67
Has your household lost property? If yes[a]:	85[a]
– House	91
– Machinery	41
– Car	26
– Valuables	21
– Land	20
– Animals	9
Conditions to return home	
– Ceasefire in my local region	91
– A comprehensive peace	92
– Disarmament of war parties	90
– A stable government	87
– A new political system	81
– Restoration of infrastructure	88
– Economic recovery in home country	89
– Truth commission for reconciliation	85
– Compensation for lost property	88
– Amnesty for war crimes	80

Questions 192, 193, 194, 195, 202.

Note Rounding errors can occur. | [a] About 6 per cent do not know if they lost property, these cases have been excluded from the calculation.

Reasons for the escape (Question 192) *'For yourself, what were the ultimate reasons to leave from your home?'* Five options to answer – here: 'Strongly agree' and 'Agree'.

Conditions to return home (Question 202) *'What would be the necessary conditions for returning back home?'* Five options to answer – here: 'Very important' and 'Rather important'.

Table 10.7 Syrian Refugees in Lebanon – Recent Situation

	All	Gender	
	Average	Male	Female
	n=1,000	50	50
Mobility sequence			
– Entire family left at once	67	64	70
– All are gone, but individually	7	6	7
– Some are still at home	27	30	23
Composition of the group that escaped (multiple answers)			
– Alone	9	18	1
– Husband / Wife	48	39	57
– Father	37	41	33
– Mother	41	43	39
– Brother	42	46	37
– Sister	39	41	37
– Children	44	32	56
– Other	4	3	4
Family status: recent situation			
– Family together in one place	64	63	66
– Family in one country but in different places	11	10	12
– Family lives in different countries	25	28	22
Mobility status			
– Permanently here	96	95	97
– Sometimes back	4	5	2
– Back frequently	1	1	1

Questions 3, 4, 14, 186, 187, 189, 190.

Note Figures are given in percentages. Rounding errors can occur. | Household = Parents (interviewees live with their parents); Household = Own (interviewees live in their own household).

Mobility Sequence (Question 189) *'Could you tell us something about the different steps concerning this experience?'* [Flight]. *'Please, indicate the situation that fits best.'* Entire family left at once 'The entire family (usra) left together at once'; All are gone, but individually = 'All are gone, b

company of more distant relatives or non-related others, most were accompanied by a spouse, parents, siblings, and children. However, displacement also tears families apart; about one-third left family members behind in Syria, and for two-thirds of Syrians, the entire family was reunited in exile. In one-quarter of all cases families were dispersed across different countries.

	Age			Household		
	16–20	21–25	26–30	Parents	Own	Other
	31	25	44	35	57	8
	70	67	64	76	66	37
	5	8	7	8	5	7
	25	25	29	16	29	56
	9	12	8	3	10	31
	16	45	72	8	76	21
	63	35	20	76	16	18
	71	39	22	84	18	22
	66	41	25	79	21	29
	64	42	20	77	16	38
	11	40	69	12	66	22
	5	4	3	4	3	7
	66	67	61	73	63	39
	10	12	11	10	11	10
	24	21	28	17	26	51
	98	96	94	97	95	93
	1	4	5	2	4	7
	1	0	1	0	1	0

the family members left individually in different periods'; Some are still at home = 'Some family members are still at home'.
Composition of the group that escaped (Question 187) 'Did other members of your family also come with you?'
Mobility Status (Question 186) 'Did you leave for good or are you still going back?'

Finally, imaginations of one's future also come into play, with three-quarters of young Syrians affirming that they left Syria because they could not imagine a future for themselves in their home country.

Legal limbo in Lebanon

Syrians' legal situation in Lebanese exile is ambivalent, and survey data confirm the broader picture of the precarious residency status sketched above. Only one-third of respondents claim to have proper visa, while 13 percent are not registered at all. In providing documentation, the humanitarian sector emerges as the most important factor, with 43 percent of Syrians registered with the UNHCR (and another 3 percent of Syrian Palestinians with the United Nations Works and Relief Agency for Palestine Refugees in the Near East), while only 11 percent are registered with the host country. However, legal status is of crucial importance to accessing the formal labour market. Here, survey results reflect the huge grey zone in which young Syrian workers find themselves in Lebanon. Overall, 62 percent of young Syrians surveyed, with various types of residency permits, indicate that, according to their own perception, they are allowed to work in the host country; yet, for another 26 percent, employment, while irregular, is tolerated. Twelve percent of all respondents are not allowed to work. Most respondents who have a proper

Table 10.8 Syrian Refugees in Lebanon – Scenarios

	All	Gender	
	Average	Male	Female
	n=1,000	50	50
Lebanon: To get married as you wish	50	59	39
Europe: To get married as you wish	46	55	34
Lebanon: To find a good job	69	81	57
Europe: To find a good job	66	80	51
Lebanon: To complete your studies	27	26	28
Europe: To complete your studies	37	37	37
Lebanon: To develop necessary skills	67	72	62
Europe: To develop necessary skills	70	76	63
Lebanon: To own a place to live	53	57	49
Europe: To own a place to live	59	62	56
Lebanon: To live together with your family	90	88	91
Europe: To live together with your family	80	76	84

Question *'Please estimate the chances concerning your life within the next five years for two scenarios.'*
(Options to answer: Very likely; Likely; Unlikely; Impossible).

A) *'If you stay where you are* [Lebanon]*, how likely are you ...'* Here: 'Very likely' & 'Likely'.
B) *'If you leave to Europe, how likely are you ...'* Here: 'Very likely' & 'Likely'.

work permit – all in all, approx. three-quarters of the entire sample – hold a visa (37 percent) or are registered with the UNHCR (38 percent); the chance of having a work permit decreases rapidly for young people with other types of residency status. In turn, this situation results in multiple insecurities: by way of illustration, Syrians registered with the UNHCR are legally banned from working. Legal limbo also gives rise to the disruption of educational careers, combined with informal and insecure labour, which in turn leads to lower incomes and high aid dependency, exposing refugees to poverty and hunger.

Return – under the right conditions
For the time being, there is little doubt that Syrians' current displacement has acquired a permanent nature, as the overwhelming majority of respondents do not return to Syria anymore. Yet, what emerges from the qualitative interviews is Syrians' ardent desire to return to their home country to

	Age			Household		
	16–20	21–25	26–30	Parents	Own	Other
	31	25	44	35	57	8
	66	51	33	63	31	65
	60	49	29	58	27	70
	74	70	65	69	68	78
	71	67	61	68	62	81
	29	29	25	30	25	28
	41	39	33	40	35	37
	71	72	61	69	65	71
	78	70	63	74	68	68
	53	55	52	51	54	57
	65	61	54	57	59	65
	93	87	89	88	91	88
	83	80	77	78	82	71

Questions 3, 4, 14, 203.

Note Figures are given in percentages. Rounding errors can occur. | Household = Parents (interviewees live with their parents); Household = Own (interviewees live in their own household).

reunite with loved ones. As Nabila, a 20-year-old Syrian currently residing with her husband and children in Akkar, put it,

> My biggest aim is to return to my homeland and to live there peacefully with my family. (LB/SY-6)

What is more, some respondents explicitly link return to Syria to escaping the restricted freedom of movement and frequent identity checks in Lebanon – this has to be understood in the context of exploitative labour that illegality pushes Syrians into. However, respondents do not advocate for unconditional return. Rather, they make their eventual homecoming contingent on the cessation of fighting, i.e. the establishment of a comprehensive peace, a ceasefire in their region of origin, and the disarmament of war parties, but also economic recovery, in particular restoration of infrastructure, and compensation payments for lost property. But safety and prosperity are not enough; most respondents also insist on political

Table 10.9 **Syrian Refugees in Lebanon – Imaginations about European Realities**

You need language skills in order to find work.
If you have work you will manage.
It will take years to be able to speak the language.
Integration is possible, even if it takes time.
The people over there understand us and will help us.
We always remain foreigner, only the next generation might be integrated.
Once you possess the right passport everything else is of no importance.
You just need a partner in Europe and marry him/her and you are at home.

Question *'In Europe, people might be happy or anxious about refugees. To what extent do you agree with the following statements?'* (Options to answer: 'Strongly Agree'; 'Agree'; 'So-so'; 'Disagree'; 'Strongly disagree'): Here: 'Strongly agree' & 'Agree'.

stability as a precondition for their return, albeit seeming undecided about the nature of the political regime they would like to see in place. While an overwhelming majority supports political change, e.g. in the form of a new political system, or the establishment of a truth committee for reconciliation, almost equal numbers demand amnesty for war crimes, or would be content with a stable government. Given the current state of the Syrian civil war, all of the conditions mentioned by respondents make the prospect of return recede into the distant future.

Is the grass really greener over there?

Finally, young Syrians were asked to envision their lives over the next five years for two different scenarios, remaining in Lebanon or moving to Europe. Overall, adolescents (aged 16–20) appear more optimistic than youth in their twenties, and men tend to consider various forms of social mobility more likely than women, which probably speaks to greater freedom of movement of men over women. Regarding their current situation in Lebanon, young Syrians appear cautiously optimistic. While the majority of respondents consider it unlikely (26 percent) or even impossible (47 percent) to continue their studies in Lebanese exile, a majority is confident that they can still develop necessary skills, find good jobs, and even get a place of their own in Lebanon (Table 10.8). However, young people have more reservations when it comes to marriage; about half of them think it is

All	Gender		Age			Household	
Average	Male	Female	16–20	21–25	26–30	Parents	Own
n=1,000	50	50	31	25	44	35	57
71	70	72	76	76	64	70	69
64	67	61	69	68	58	67	61
58	58	58	62	62	53	59	57
49	54	44	53	54	44	50	47
47	49	45	51	51	42	49	45
41	41	42	42	43	40	41	43
37	41	33	43	39	32	40	34
23	27	19	25	26	20	22	21

Question 3, 4, 14, 204.

Note Figures are given in percentages. Rounding errors can occur. | Household = Parents (interviewees live with their parents); Household = Own (interviewees live in their own household).

unlikely or even impossible that they might get married to a person of their choice (with high gender differences).

Interestingly, no big differences emerge when young Syrians picture their future in Europe. Surveyed youth find it slightly more likely that they would complete their studies, develop necessary skills, and find a place of their own on the other side of the Mediterranean. However, the qualitative interviews show that youth also take into consideration other, more established migration pathways, return to Syria having become increasingly unrealistic; a young construction worker concludes:

> I would like to travel to the Gulf region and work there, because I don't think about returning to Syria anymore. (LB/SY-2)

Not a surprise then that half of the young Syrians surveyed remain sceptical about onward migration to Europe. Fewer than half of all respondents agree that people in Europe might be supportive and understanding, and that integration is possible, but might take time (Table 10.9). With regard to the timeframe of integration, about half of the respondents consider that integration might be easier to accomplish for the next generation whereas they would always remain foreigners. Regarding different pathways towards integration, a majority of Syrians are confident about the positive role of employment in facilitating their new lives abroad, central to which they consider the acquisition of new language skills. Yet, more than half of them are afraid it might take years to be able to speak the language of the host country. Other routes towards getting settled in European countries, such as acquiring a new passport or getting married to a local, are considered less important (with considerable gender differences). However, it is worth noting that for all of these questions, roughly one-third of the respondents do not have a clear opinion, which might speak to respondents' heightened insecurities about the kind of lives to be found further away. On a final note, young Syrians seem to be torn between fatigue, the result of years of displacement, and a strong motivation to rebuild their lives. On the one hand, roughly one-quarter of all respondents express tiredness and the need to recover; more than one-third just hope to get to safety. On the other hand, an equal number is eager to work harder, and, to a lesser extent, learn a new language and adjust to new cultural environments – although only 16 percent agree to the last two options respectively.

Conclusion

Young people's mobility perceptions and migration aspirations in the MENA region have often been misinterpreted. Generally, only a few are determined to emigrate – much less than 10 per cent. Given the multiple crises in the region, this is a remarkably small percentage. However, the youngsters find it hard to decide between emigrating and continuing their lives back home. Many are deeply attached to their families and home countries, and are far from considering migration 'an easy way out'. Imagining leaving home triggers ambivalent feelings. Four mechanisms are shaping their decision-making and actions: in the first instance, labour migration patterns are often confined to the Arab world, but are also shaped by historical and linguistic ties with certain European countries. However, mobility aspirations cannot be reduced to finding work abroad. Young people are equally interested in travelling for leisure and broadening their horizons. Moreover, mobility attitudes are not only gendered and dependent on marital status, but also mediated by previous migration experiences of family members, personal predisposition to change, social class, and social networks. The willingness to emigrate thus ranges highest among flexible individuals with migration experiences in their social network.

Reasons for the comparatively little interest in going abroad are equally complex: heightened virtual mobility and means of communication go hand in hand with the effective hardening of EU external borders, while the costs of migration render moving more difficult, particularly for the poorest strata. Many young people have a realistic understanding of the pros and cons of going abroad, including cultural- and employment-related hurdles to integration elsewhere. They are far from considering European welfare states the 'holy land'.

In contrast, flight and asylum, often consequences of armed conflicts, are sadly part of young Arabs' everyday lives. For young Syrian refugees in Lebanon, both war-induced threats and the desire to remain or reunite with one's family are crucial causes for fleeing their home country. However, the disruption of longstanding circular migration schemes between the two countries and increased restrictions on Syrians' freedom of movement in Lebanon have transformed a situation of 'prolonged unsettlement' into 'forced settlement', turning highly mobile labour migrants into immobilised refugees. The flipside of forced displacement is forced immobility.

These findings resonate with a contemporary appreciation of migrants as the new precariat (Standing 2011). Escaping endemic unemployment in their home countries, and often endowed with higher education, they either join a low-wage and temporary labour force in industrialised countries, or move within post-colonial states in the MENA region. But in both cases the absence of opportunities for stable incomes or building careers, exposes them to yet another perpetual form of existential insecurity. Hence, restrictive immigration policies and the existence of a shadow labour reserve only apparently contradict each other. Appalling living conditions and deportation threats are a reality for many young migrants. Not a surprise then that what stands out is young people's awareness of the decoupling of movement in space from upward social mobility. While the desire to find employment or pursue an education continues to motivate some to go abroad, they seem to know all too well that migration does not necessarily come with a promise of better lives anymore.

PART III

POLITICS & SOCIETY

11

Communication

Carola Richter

'FACEBOOK REVOLUTIONS'. 'TWITTER PROTESTS'. The 'Al Jazeera effect'. Such catchphrases to convey the allegedly immense effects of media on political and social change in the Middle East and North Africa (MENA) have proliferated in the past decade. Indeed, the spread of media technology among Arab youth is very high as revealed in the data analysed here from a survey of 9,000 Arab youth. The survey revealed that 75 percent of all Arab youth interviewed access the internet and spend an average of 5.2 hours per day online. On average, more than three-quarters possess a smartphone (78 percent), and 86 percent of all households own a TV set. In 2008, the political scientist Marc Lynch had warned that even scholars tend to overemphasise the role of media in political change in non-Western countries (Lynch 2008: 18). After 2011 he argued that scholars and activists alike were trapped in a 'Tahrir bubble', in which those involved in protests and their academic observers alike repeated the opinion that social media had played an exceptional role in the political mobilisation of Arab societies (Lynch 2013). Beyond activists' circles, the question, therefore, arises about what role media play in the everyday lives of ordinary young people in the MENA region. Which kind of media do they prefer? What do their communication habits look like? How does that relate to societal transformations?

It will be argued here that media usage habits are globally converging as similar technologies and formats become available, including in the MENA region. Mistrust in media and political disengagement, however, are causing a thorough shift in social media use; media now increasingly serve as private communication and to sustain existing social networks. Mediatised communication is thus both a trigger and a coping mechanism to deal with uncertainty in the everyday lives of young Arab people. The argument unfolds in three steps. First, the ways in which media technologies and certain platforms and services are integrated into quotidian communication patterns of young people will be analysed. Second, the issue will be

Table 11.1 **Use of Social Media in the MENA Countries**

Country		WhatsApp	Viber	Skype	Facebook	Twitter	Instagram
Bahrain	(100)	92	11	15	20	41	88
Egypt	(75)	85	44	22	99	35	38
Jordan	(92)	84	26	22	82	14	31
Lebanon	(94)	97	44	19	85	24	43
Morocco	(72)	89	19	25	95	18	17
Palestine	(70)	60	39	15	92	14	33
Tunisia	(88)	25	42	36	98	15	33
Yemen	(31)	93	19	7	66	15	18
Syrian Refugees[a]	(55)	98	12	2	25	4	3
Overall		80	30	20	75	22	38

Questions 1, 149, 154.

Question *'Do you use ... (name of platform)?'* (Multiple answers possible).

Note Figures are given in percentages. Rounding errors can occur. | Answers refer to respondents who use the internet; details are given in brackets after the country name. [a] Syrian Refugees in Lebanon.

addressed of whether there is an Arab exceptionalism or specific characteristics with regard to political information seeking and sharing through media. To what extent does media have a particular political place in society, and, in terms of evaluating statements about the so-called Facebook revolutions and Al Jazeera effects, how much do young people trust media? Third, the problem of an often-assumed homogeneity of media use patterns in the MENA region will be discussed. While the empirical findings suggest a wide distribution of media for communication, the country breakdowns show remarkable differences. Obviously, the digital divide is not only a concern between northern and southern countries, but exists also within the MENA region. Communication patterns, therefore, have to be interpreted in light of an Arab digital divide.

Staying Connected: Arab Youth in the Age of Mediatisation

Today, communication for young people is increasingly mediated communication. This is as true for MENA youth as it is for their European counterparts (Feierabend et al. 2016). In recent years, rapid developments in media technology have significantly changed communication practices, and indeed, are changing them still. Just as the generations before them, young people today continue to take actions similar to those back then – connecting with friends, consuming news, sharing their thoughts with their acquaintances – but they connect in a different way, influenced by new technologies. This process is what communication scholars have termed 'mediatisation', referring to the incorporation of all kinds of new media technologies into quotidian practices (Hepp and Krotz 2014). Accordingly, boundaries between online and offline communication are increasingly blurred, which is also true for the distinction between private and public communication. Most likely, circles of friends that frequently meet at 'offline' places, such as schools, universities, and coffee shops, are consolidated by the use of social media, in particular through instant messaging services such as WhatsApp. Mediated communication is thus an essential part of young people's lives in the MENA region and helps them to stay connected.

Instant messaging: staying in contact with family and friends

Instant messaging services such as WhatsApp, Viber, and Skype are at least as important as social networking and sharing services like Facebook, Twitter, and Instagram. While WhatsApp and Facebook are the most-used services throughout the region, some local preferences are worth mentioning (Table 11.1). Facebook is most often used in the two countries typically referred to as the birthplaces of the Arab Spring – Egypt and Tunisia – as well as in Morocco and Palestine. Nearly all young people who use the internet in these countries are also on Facebook.

Facebook services also include instant messaging, so it can be assumed that those using Facebook heavily also use it for private conversations with family and friends. Bahraini youth and Syrian refugees, however, almost neglect Facebook by comparison to other groups. WhatsApp is the most commonly used instant messaging service region-wide, with only Tunisians preferring Viber over it. Bahraini youth can be distinguished from the rest by their preference for Instagram and Twitter. Among young people in other Arab countries, Twitter plays only a minor role. Although Twitter has lately added a private communication feature, it is still seen as a rather public communication channel with a more political character that does not seem as appealing as other platforms.

A must-have: personalised smartphones

The dominance of instant messaging correlates with the extremely high convergence of mobile telephony and internet access. The internet is almost exclusively accessed via smartphones. Although the internet is used most in homes, other larger or stationary devices, such as laptops, personal computers, and tablets, play a limited role. Often users seek out Wi-Fi

Table 11.2 **Internet Devices and Internet Access Points**

Country	Internet devices				Internet access points					
	Smart-phone	Lap-top	Desk-top PC	Tab-let	At home	Every-where	Internet café	Work-place	School / Uni-versity	Shops / Restau-rants
Bahrain	100	1	0	0	99	2	3	4	1	1
Egypt	91	17	25	20	78	53	27	16	14	25
Jordan	90	16	9	10	84	37	18	32	11	19
Lebanon	98	27	6	12	89	50	24	32	22	18
Morocco	92	28	20	11	72	42	43	13	26	27
Palestine	81	31	27	9	88	42	13	14	20	8
Tunisia	82	35	27	12	83	43	27	11	16	8
Yemen	95	13	22	5	63	26	23	9	7	4
Syrian Ref.	99	1	1	0	84	41	1	24	1	1
Total	**92**	**19**	**14**	**9**	**85**	**37**	**20**	**18**	**14**	**13**

Questions 1, 149, 151, 152.

Question 152 *'Which devices do you usually use to connect to the internet?'*
Question 151 *'And where do you use it?'* (multiple answers).

Note Figures are given in percentages. Rounding errors can occur. Answers refer to respondents who use the internet.

hotspots in stores and coffee shops and at universities and schools to stay connected (Table 11.2).

Indeed, the data also show that on average across the Arab world, everyone aged 16–30 possesses a smartphone (Figure 11.5b). With the exception of Tunisia, this age group prefers smartphones over basic mobile phones that only allow phone calls and text messages. The smartphone has become the key asset for merging available communicative functions. It can be personalised and allows them to stay connected almost everywhere they go.

Communication purposes: the private beats the political

Contrary to the assumption of overtly political use of social media inspired by the myth of the Facebook revolution, young Arabs principally use social media for non-political purposes (Figure 11.1).

For all the respondents in all of the countries examined and across gender boundaries and education levels, 'keeping in contact with family and friends' is the most important purpose for using social media. Sharing pictures, music, and videos and organising meetings with their friends are also ranked as important. Thus, particular new technological features that enable the quick-and-easy sharing of digital media products are indeed one catalyst for using social media. Looking for work opportunities seems to be

Figure 11.1 **Use Purposes of Social Media in the MENA Countries**

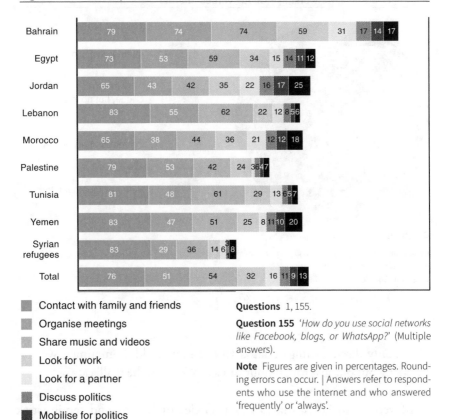

Contact with family and friends

Organise meetings

Share music and videos

Look for work

Look for a partner

Discuss politics

Mobilise for politics

Mobilise for religion

Questions 1, 155.

Question 155 *'How do you use social networks like Facebook, blogs, or WhatsApp?'* (Multiple answers).

Note Figures are given in percentages. Rounding errors can occur. | Answers refer to respondents who use the internet and who answered 'frequently' or 'always'.

another feature that increasingly draws young people to social media, while looking for a partner online is not yet a common practice among MENA youth. Online matchmaking only seems to be of more interest to Bahrainis.

Yet, the main purpose of social media use is to consolidate bonds with existing networks, thus substituting older mediation channels, such as letters and the telephone, and easily overcoming physical boundaries, such as distance. Zeinab, a 26-year-old woman from Morocco, stated:

'My friends and my relationship with neighbours is normal. We meet once in a while. We learn from each other about various things related to cooking. Now, I spend my free time on Facebook, chat with friends, telling what happened during the day. We

Figure 11.2 **Social Networking – Clique versus Internet**

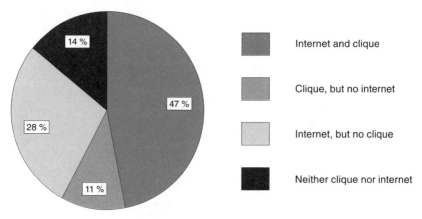

Questions 129, 149.

Question 129 *'Are you part of a fixed group of friends – a 'clique' – that is meeting frequently and where everybody knows one another very well?'*
Question 149 *'Do you use the internet?'*

Note Figures are given in percentages. Rounding errors can occur.

mainly discuss things related to the household. Sometimes, we hang out but just for an hour or two. We go to the mall' (MA-4).

Moreover, social media can help circles of friends and family stick together despite security issues and the economic hardships that many complain about. Samir, a 30-year-old man from Egypt, said:

'Now, I stopped doing many things [such as going out]. Security and money are the most important things. How can you be happy if you have no money? Even if you have money, it's better to save it' (EG-1).

Along the same lines, Bob, a 22-year-old Lebanese, said:

'We can no longer camp anywhere because of the fear of strangers and foreigners and as a result of the various thefts and violations. New opportunities are found on Facebook through groups and pages debating the subject and criticising and opposing the entry of refugees into Lebanon' (LB-2).

Friendships strengthened online
Young people were also asked whether they are part of a clique, i.e. a fixed group of friends. The results of this question were combined with internet usage (Figure 11.2). About half of the respondents are both part of a clique and internet users. Again, this indicates that friendships are also maintained online.

Fatima, a 30-year-old Bahraini woman working in the education sector, stated about her friends offline, 'We talk, laugh, play cards or PS [PlaySta-tion], walk, go to clubs, go shopping, it depends, we do things we like, [and online] we talk, chat on WhatsApp or Snapchat' (BH-1). Only 11 percent of the respondents belong to a clique but claim to have no access to the inter-net. A much larger group of 28 percent use the internet but is not part of a particular clique. Those who are not attending school, university or going to work are generally less likely to belong to a clique. These two results indicate that while online communication might function as a substitute for non-existing or difficult-to-establish offline bonds, offline-only clique building is rarely found in the MENA region. Still, 14 percent of respondents neither belong to a clique nor use the internet and thus seem to be rather disconnected from (mediatised) friendships. These are significantly more often female interviewees, who tend to be older and are usually married and not so well off (Figure 11.2). Nawal, a married 20-year-old female Syrian ref-ugee of the neither-clique-nor-internet type, simply stated, 'My only inter-est is my home and my children. I do not have time to waste' (LB/SY-6).

Despite this latter statement, one can conclude that mediatised com-munication is part of the daily routine of Arab youth. Friendships are maintained with a smartphone in hand, writing WhatsApp messages, and sharing photos. Digitally mediated communication is also a means to overcome uncertainties by staying connected and sustaining existing famil-ial bonds and friendships that might otherwise perish because of security issues, geographical distances, or economic hardships.

Between Mistrust and Disillusionment:
Media Use and Political Information
While private purposes of communication are more frequent and obvi-ously outweigh political communication purposes, media are still the most important gateway to political information. Despite having lived their formative years in the midst of the Arab Spring, however, the majority of the young people interviewed shows little interest in (formal) politics. Still, for some respondents, social media was seen as a means of political

participation at some times. During the Arab uprisings, they considered using social media a political act, but this seems not to have been the case in 2016, at the time of this research. The interviews reveal a broad political disillusionment after the Arab uprisings that made some respondents abstain from social media use for political purposes.

Hikmat, a 22-year-old student from Palestine, explained:

'What happened to me is that I stopped using Facebook as much as before, and I stopped using social media networks in general and now I don't use them at all. I only watch news and I don't participate in anything' (PS-2).

Sara, a 17-year-old schoolgirl from Egypt, remarked:

'I used to share, but not anymore, as I believe that if I share something untrue I will be a part of the lie. So I share what I'm 100% sure of, or something funny that doesn't relate to politics' (EG-2).

The political scientist Marc Lynch (2013) also diagnosed a 'Twitter devolution' across the region because a plethora of actors share their content online which 'contributed to a dangerous polarization' that is even affecting families. A 25-year-old Egyptian university graduate acknowledged, 'In the beginning we used to share opinions but no one was interested in listening or agreeing with others. Everyone only wanted to assert their opinion, and I saw people fighting over their opinions and people offending each other, and it's in vain at the end, as no one listens. I just listen to the news to know what's happening and what's new and so on' (EG-10). Most likely, with regard to political debate, social media for a lot of respondents has become nothing more than a one-way channel of receiving news. The scepticism as to the political liberating role of social media is further elaborated by the public intellectual Evgeny Morozov (2011), who argues that digital media helped primarily authoritarian institutions like regime elites to find new and more effective ways of controlling and repressing their people.

Media credibility and political interest

Half a decade after the Arab Spring, in 2016, social media has lost its high political credibility and is now frequently accessed on a similar level as traditional mass media such as TV, radio and newspapers are. Actually, the various forms of media are not seen as trustworthy because they were the

Figure 11.3 **Trust in Media and Government in the MENA Countries**

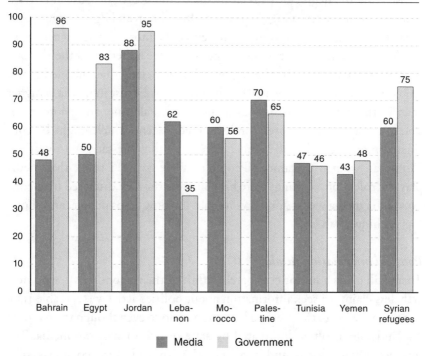

Questions 1, 114.

Question 114 *'What about your trust in different institutions?'* Here: 'Limited trust' and 'Trust'.

Note Figures are given in percentages. Rounding errors can occur.

regimes' rubber stamp for so many decades. Although privatisation of print and audio-visual media has led to professional presentation and production styles, political loyalty to the regime or partisanship with certain political actors often prevents the media from being independent (Richter and El Difraoui 2015). Frequently, the respondents blamed the media for bias towards a political faction, of producing fake news, or reporting unethically and exaggerating in order to produce scandals. The degree of trust in the media in contrast to that in the government is displayed in Figure 11.3.

A major problem here is limited media literacy within society. It seems difficult to build independent opinions from a multitude of sources if based on the assumption that the media should display the 'truth'. Iman, a 23-year-old Bahraini woman, complained, 'They have 100 faces. I don't trust them. When there is an issue you can find a lot of different comments and opinions about the same issue. And you get lost, you don't know who to believe. It's incredible' (BH-10).

Relating the degree of trust in media to the degree of trust in government can be quite revealing (Figure 11.3). In Bahrain and Egypt, young people strongly trust the government but tend to be more sceptical with regard to media. Potentially, the young respondents are adhering to the rhetoric of stability guaranteed by the regime while believing that the media may jeopardise this stability. When, on the other hand, trust in media is higher than in the government, such as in Lebanon, Palestine, and Morocco, it speaks in favour of a more pluralistic media scene which might be considered more credible and is indeed seen as a fourth estate. A 30-year-old Moroccan woman explained, 'People now are aware. I think that media plays its role. Lots of things were hidden, now they are disclosed by media. To me the media works and plays its role. TV now helps people, and shows lots of things' (MA-9).

Political information through TV
There still exists a minority – barely a fifth of the respondents – who nevertheless claims to seek information about politics actively (see Table 11.3). For them TV is still the preferred medium to do so even though the national TV landscape is often dominated by state-owned or partisan media. The internet follows closely, and in Bahrain, Jordan, and Morocco, it even outweighs television as the number one information source, possibly due to its greater plurality. Oday, 22 years old and from Jordan, mentioned this side effect of using online media, stating, 'I don't follow the news or anything, but I learn of some things through Facebook' (JO-13). On the other hand, through satellite transmission and a common language, TV channels also acquire pan-Arab audiences; the news channels Al Jazeera and Al Arabiya in particular are clearly targeting broadly regional instead of national audiences. A 30-year-old house painter from Morocco mentioned, 'I was sitting with friends in the café; everybody gave his opinion; we were watching Al Jazeera and Al Arabiya; they were giving the news' (MA-3).

Informational preferences, however, vary strongly from country to country. Yemenis rely mostly on non-mediated, face-to-face communication while for Jordanians this does not seem to be an important source. Bahrainis tend to use a variety of sources, probably to compare and judge, whereas Syrian refugees watch TV almost exclusively to stay informed, most likely because access to other channels of information is difficult. Only in Yemen – and to a lesser degree in Bahrain and Palestine – do a significant amount of people still obtain information from the radio. Newspapers also seem to be an outdated information channel for the youth. Only Bahrain

Table 11.3 **Active Information Gathering in the MENA Countries, by Type of Media**

Country	Active information gathering	TV	Inter-net	Face-to-face conversation	Mobile	News-paper	Radio
Yemen	32	53	18	83	17	7	43
Palestine	23	75	66	32	21	10	23
Lebanon	21	67	45	36	23	6	5
Tunisia	21	80	69	25	3	14	15
Morocco	17	69	71	42	24	29	16
Syrian Ref.	17	89	7	19	7	1	4
Egypt	14	76	66	53	26	26	6
Bahrain	12	75	91	81	82	65	28
Jordan	8	62	67	16	19	14	4
Total	**18**	**71**	**51**	**46**	**22**	**16**	**19**

Questions 1, 157, 158.

Question 157 'Do you inform yourself actively about politics?' ('Yes').
Question 158 'What sources and means of information do you use?' (Multiple answers).
Note Figures are given in percentages. Rounding errors can occur.

stands out here, with 65 percent answering that they get information from newspapers, albeit this accounts for only 12 percent of active information seekers. These ambivalent results can be related to the availability of media and to the level of media freedom and plurality in a given country. For example, Bahrainis tend to diversify their news sources and include newspapers, radio, and internet because they have the financial means to do so and because the infrastructure enables one to counter state-owned television.

In Yemen and Palestine, the radio infrastructure is decentralised so people can get local news that is often neglected by TV and national newspapers. Morocco and Egypt have a rather lively newspaper sector with several private and oppositional quality newspapers available. Young Tunisians seem to value their TV as a good information source, probably because of its professionalisation after 2011. In summary, mistrust in media is widespread. Those who search for political information nevertheless use media to get the news but are very doubtful about its credibility. Interestingly, people then tend to diversify their sources of information and rely on a range of media to get different views, but also on face-to-face communication to verify the news.

The Internet Versus TV: The New Digital Divide

Communication patterns differ in the MENA countries. While for the most part age, education, rural or urban location, and even gender are not

Figure 11.4 Use of Internet and Media Availability in MENA households

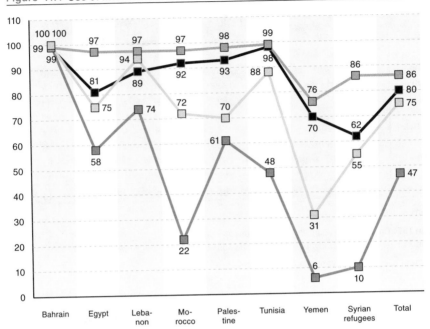

—□— Television available in household

—■— Satellite antenna available in household

⋯□⋯ Use of internet

—□— Internet access available in household

Questions 1, 55, 149, 151.

Question 55 *'Which of the following items do you have available in your household?'* (Multiple answers).

Question 149 *'Do you use the internet?'*

Note Figures are given in percentages. Rounding errors can occur.

significant for explaining differences in media use, the country is. In particular, looking at the number of young people who have internet access at all, have internet at home, and the number of hours spent on the internet by country clearly indicate a digital divide across the MENA region.

Internet and smartphones

In the sample, Bahrain represents the extremely rich Gulf countries with a well-developed digital infrastructure, state care, and a high living standard. On the other side of the spectrum are Yemenis and Syrian refugees along with Palestinians, who are all exposed to violent conflicts and often face

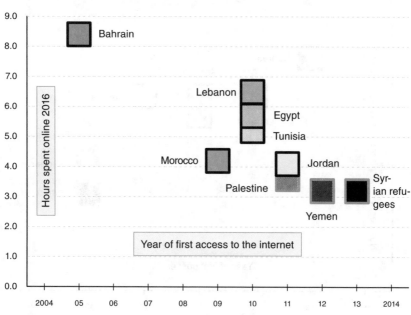

Figure 11.5a Digital Divide: First Use of the Internet and Time Spent Online in the MENA Countries

Questions 1, 150, 153.

Question 150 *'In what year did you start using [the internet]?'*
Question 153 *'How many hours do you use the internet per day?'*

Note Information is given as an arithmetic mean.

economic difficulty in places that are not able to supply sufficient infrastructure to support their basic needs. The latter groups also have the least access to the internet, adopted the internet and smartphones later, and on average possess fewer such devices than their Arab counterparts. While all of the Bahraini youth in our sample use the internet and have an internet connection at home, only 31 percent of the Yemenis and 55 percent of the Syrian refugees in Lebanon have access to the online world. Being badly equipped, only 6 percent of Yemenis and 10 percent of Syrian refugees have internet access at home (Figure 11.4). The middle position is occupied by poorer countries, such as Morocco, Egypt, and Tunisia, but during the 2000s these states strongly developed their internet infrastructure, promoted the availability of computers, and liberalised the telephone industry to allow for market competition (Abdulla 2007).

What further adds to the digital divide is that the youth in many Arab countries were rather late adopters of digital media and smartphones in

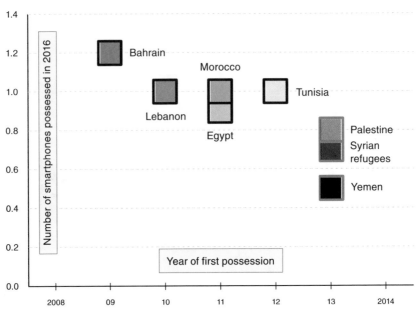

Figure 11.5b **Digital Divide: First Possession of a Smartphone –**
Number of Own Devices

Questions 1, 145, 146.

Question 145 *'When (year) did you get your first mobile phone/smartphone?'*
Question 146 *'How many mobile phones / smartphones do you currently possess?'*

Note Information is given as an arithmetic mean. Data for Jordan are not available.

particular. While in Bahrain the average young person started using the internet in 2005 and switched to smartphones in 2009, Palestinians, Yemenis, and Syrian refugees did not go online before 2011 and only possessed their first smartphones in 2013. The digital divide is also reflected in the time young people spend on the internet per day: it ranges from 8.4 hours per day in Bahrain to 3.2 hours for Yemenis and Syrian refugees (Figures 11.5a and 11.5b). Ghadir, a 23-year-old unemployed Bahraini graduate, stated, 'I spend about three quarters of the day on the internet' (BH-7). With regard to gender differences in internet use, there is no gap across the MENA countries. In Tunisia, Egypt, and Palestine, young women even spend a few minutes more online than men.

Expenditure on communication varies
Following up on the diagnosed digital divide, as expected Yemenis, Syrian refugees, as well as Palestinians rank expenditures for mobile phones and

**Figure 11.6 Ranking of Spendings on Communication Activities in the
MENA Countries**

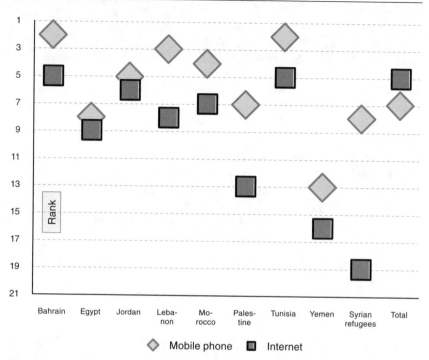

Mobile phone ◇   Internet ■

Questions 1, 97.

Question 97 *'Please identify the 4 items you spend the most money on.'* (Multiple answers: 4 out of 21 options).

internet as less important than do their counterparts in the other MENA countries (Figure 11.6). For them, basic necessities, such as food, gas, electricity, and clothing, need to be prioritised. For Bahrainis, on the other hand, mobile phones occupy the second highest position of monthly spending, while the internet comes in fifth place. Bahrainis also spend a significant amount of money on videos and gaming, which are not important in the other countries. Gassem, a 25-year-old Bahraini, said, 'Youth in my country are only busy with football and PlayStation, nothing else' (BH-2). Except Bahrain, in all other MENA countries the majority of young people use prepaid cards instead of phone contracts. Houssam, a 26-year-old worker from Lebanon, explained, 'I should be realistic and accept the fact that my total income is $100. I use most of this amount to recharge my phone for work purposes, and the rest of the money goes to covering the household expenses' (LB-7). This indicates that staying connected is very important but prepaid cards allow one to quickly

Table 11.4 **The Most Common Leisure Activities in the MENA Countries, by Gender**

Country	TV		Surfing the internet		Doing something with the family		Visiting neighbours or relatives		Doing nothing, just relaxing		Coffee shop	Shopping
	m	**f**	**m**	**f**	**m**	**f**	**m**	**f**	**m**	**f**	**m**	**f**
Bahrain	63	67	49	50	9	8	5	10	22	24	12	14
Egypt	64	73	53	46	18	25	16	25	6	8	28	17
Jordan	74	85	57	46	26	26	30	33	16	9	13	15
Lebanon	59	74	55	50	15	16	11	30	10	9	23	11
Morocco	76	87	38	34	9	21	7	25	3	3	37	12
Palestine	58	73	57	49	32	42	31	39	8	6	15	7
Tunisia	66	84	60	63	6	23	3	11	3	6	62	5
Yemen	37	39	31	9	27	44	39	68	21	23	1	7
Syrian Ref.	63	62	20	11	27	36	44	53	39	36	1	2
Total	**67**		**43**		**23**		**26**		**14**		**13**	**8**

Questions 1, 3, 164.

Question 164 *'What kind of leisure activities do you engage in most? Please identify up to 3 activities in which you engage the most during the week.'*

Note Figures are given in percentages. Rounding errors can occur. **m** = Male interviewees; **f** = Female interviewees.

limit monthly expenses in times of scarcity. Even if no money is charged on the phone, Wi-Fi connections and the phone itself still allow for reachability.

The amount of money spent varies greatly from country to country in terms of monthly expenditures for mobile phones, ranging from the equivalent of €6 per month in Yemen to €33 in Bahrain. In relation to the countries' average gross domestic product, telephony is most expensive in Tunisia and least expensive in Bahrain. Women and those with a low level of education in general tend to spend slightly less money on mobile phones and internet than their male or higher-educated counterparts. With regard to gender differences, only in Tunisia do women spend more money on their phone.

Bridging the Digital Divide: Television Still Important
Despite the scientific focus on the internet and mobile phones as means of communication, television is still the most popular medium among the youth across the MENA region. When asked about favourite leisure activities, sitting in front of the TV was the favourite of 67 percent of the respondents in all countries except Yemen. Almost everywhere, it is more important than surfing the internet and outweighs all other activities such as meeting friends, doing sports or shopping. TV reaches 86 percent of Arab

households; it is easily available and cheap, with satellite connection (available in 80 percent of the surveyed households) being the most convenient form of receiving a multitude of pan-Arab and international channels. One also does not have to leave the house and can watch alone or with friends.

Alternatives to TV, such as cinemas, theatres, and discos, are not yet common in most Arab countries but are perhaps desperately needed. Hamza, a 25-year-old high school graduate from Morocco, expressed a common complaint, when he said:

'[The state] should create areas and spaces where the young can spend their time rather than spend it at coffee shops doing nothing. They should do something. They should do some activities. They should keep themselves busy, not only watching TV or connecting to the internet' (MA-7).

The lack of accessibility to other activities might be the reasons for the pervasiveness of television as a leisure activity, which is even more favoured by women than by men.

Indeed, there is a remarkable gender difference with regard to some of the activities. Table 11.4 shows a selection of the most popular leisure activities according to gender. Women consistently watch more TV than men. On the other hand, more men surf the internet in their spare time than women. Going to a coffee shop is also a typical male activity and is particularly practised in Tunisia and Morocco. In Tunisia, more men even tend to go to the coffee shop in their spare time than surf the internet.

Most likely due to the bad financial situation and weak technological infrastructure, Yemen is the low outlier, where visiting neighbours and relatives is the favourite activity – even before watching TV. Young Yemeni women do not spend their leisure time on the internet either but instead visit neighbours and relatives or do something with the family. In general, it is interesting that family activities and visiting neighbours are more frequently done by those groups that are on the losing side of the digital divide, namely Yemenis, Palestinians, and Syrian refugees. Women especially tend to spend their time with a network of relatives. Bahrainis are again an exception. Among them, visits paid to family and relatives play a rather minor role. Instead, 'doing nothing, relaxing' is more common, with out-of-home activities not extending much beyond going to malls and fast food restaurants. 'Doing nothing' also seems to be an inexpensive alternative to kill time among young Syrian refugees and Yemenis. Marwan, a 30-year-old married man from Yemen, said, 'I don't have a TV. As I told you it is the bad conditions; I have nothing to do' (YE-13).

In summary, the digital divide is a clear reflection of economic gaps within the MENA region when the availability of devices and the priority given to mediated communication is considered. During the past decade, however, some states invested in upgrading the communication infrastructure while some did not, as can be observed for example in the comparison of Egypt and Yemen. Meanwhile, TV seems to be the device still available to most people and that allows for broad national and transnational communication, albeit on a one-to-many instead of a many-to-many basis.

Conclusion

Obviously, global media use is converging because similar technologies and formats are available. Youth in the MENA region are no exception to this. The survey's main results indicate that smartphones are the main device to access the internet and the dominant purposes of internet use are connecting to friends and sharing digital products. Interestingly, traditional mass media is still present in the bouquet of media use, despite a strongly controlled or polarised media landscape in most countries. Due to economic hardships and insufficient infrastructure, however, quite a lot of young people have limited or no access to digital media, particularly in Yemen and among Syrian refugees.

Another interesting aspect of convergence is that typical markers of difference, such as gender and education, do not play out as strongly with regard to media usage patterns as one might have expected. That women in Tunisia and Bahrain spend slightly more time on the internet and their mobile phones than men may also point to an upcoming trend of women adopting new communication technology as early as men. With regard to still prevailing social restrictions for women's physical movement in public spaces, social media might also have a compensatory function.

Political participation on social media, as could have been expected as a result of the perceived importance of media after the Arab uprisings, only plays a minor role. Frustration with polarisation and unethical reporting seems to have led to mistrust of all kinds of media and political disengagement in relation to media. Instead, social media are particularly used to mediate private communication and sustain existing social networks. This can be seen as an indicator that mediated communication is both a trigger and a coping mechanism for uncertainty in the everyday lives of young Arab people.

12

Politics

Mathias Albert & Sonja Hegasy

YOUNG PEOPLE IN THE ARAB WORLD are regarded as the prime movers behind the protests that shook the Middle East and North Africa (MENA) in 2010–11. On average, young people in the region today are better educated compared to their parents' generation, yet their chances for upward social mobility are much lower, partly because job creation has not kept up with population growth. In addition, their freedom of movement to Europe and the United States has been restricted after the al-Qaida attacks in September 2001. It has become more difficult for them to move abroad for purposes of education (or merely for tourism), even when they have the financial means to do so (see Chapter 10). It may sound banal, but popular global holiday options like Airbnb or Homeexchange are out of reach for Arab youths. To put it succinctly, young people's chances of realising their professional and personal aspirations have decreased considerably in the 2000s, and many have experienced far-reaching changes themselves. The upheavals in the region, often described as the Arab Spring, reflected the politicisation of young adults with restricted means of expressing themselves politically.

This chapter traces how close to, or how alienated from, politics young people in the Arab world feel. 'Politicisation' here primarily pertains to a high level of sensibility regarding political issues marking the 'end of post-colonialism' (Dabashi 2012). At the same time, a large number of young people claim not to be interested in politics, which they often associate with pure party politics. The findings show that a political system ruled by a 'strong man' at the top is relatively unpopular among young people in the region, except for the case of Palestine.

The rapid pace of political shifts in the region has more often than not invited only summary analysis and observations on the macro-scale of international politics. Often, the assessments of and attitudes towards these developments by the people most affected, i.e. the populations of the countries in the MENA region, remain overlooked. These populations are, however, important subjects as well as agents of political and social change. The present study presents a unique opportunity to inquire about the views that young people living in the region have on a range of political matters six years after the uprisings began in the region. It can only be a snapshot of the situation in 2016, but it does provide insight into the self-perception of those aged 16–30.

This chapter not only presents and analyses the range of attitudes and opinions held by young people in the region, it also seeks to assess the degree to which political issues matter to them, and then looks into how interested young people are in politics. A general interest in politics can be seen to form the basis for any kind of productive engagement in the political process, although political interest does usually not fully translate into civic engagement or political mobilisation. The trust that young women and men in MENA countries have in various institutions, most notably the state, is also examined. Here, an essential question is to what degree do young people want the state to play a role in their respective societies. Connected to but somewhat separate from issues of trust in the state are youth attitudes towards the political system in general. The issue here is not only satisfaction with the form of the political system they live under, but also preferences regarding possible alternatives.

The views that young people have on Arab Spring events in the MENA region are also addressed. The issue here is not primarily whether they welcomed specific developments, but in particular their views of their effects on political and social change. It is noteworthy that, in retrospect, respondents to the qualitative survey see the popular uprisings that have swept the region since 2010–11 negatively, in light of the wars in Yemen, Syria, Libya, and the unstable situations in Lebanon, Iraq, and Egypt. As a 25-year-old female respondent from rural Morocco said, 'I have never taken part in any demonstration and do not intend to do so. These uprisings were fruitless. They still live with the political and economic problems, and the country is witnessing total destruction' (MA-6).

Themes and Issues

Political interest
Generally, young people's statements and claims about politics and their interest in it need to be treated with caution. The country survey indicates that on average only 18 percent of young people are 'interested' or 'very

Figure 12.1 **Political Interest**

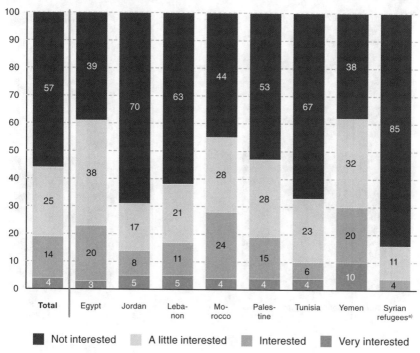

Not interested   A little interested   Interested   Very interested

Question 156 *'Are you interested in politics?'*

Note Figures are given in percentages. Rounding errors can occur. **a)** Syrian Refugees in Lebanon.

interested' in politics. While, most notably, 23 percent of young people in Egypt say they are interested or very interested, and 28 percent say so in Morocco, only 19 percent do so in Palestine, 16 percent in Lebanon, 13 percent in Jordan, and 10 percent in Tunisia (Figure 12.1).

This level of interest in politics may appear rather low (and it is, if compared, for example, with the case of Germany, in Chapter 15). It is also necessary, however, to read these numbers with some additional qualifications, as they tend to hide sometimes vastly different understandings of what politics – and accordingly political interest – actually is. Thus, for example, in some of the qualitative interviews, when asked about 'politics', interviewees understood the term only in the sense of pure party politics or as purely national politics of the country they live in, and it was these kinds of politics in which they said they had no interest. In these cases, the lack of interest in politics often reflected distrust in and frustration with politicians. A 30-year-old woman from Marrakesh, Morocco, who had only

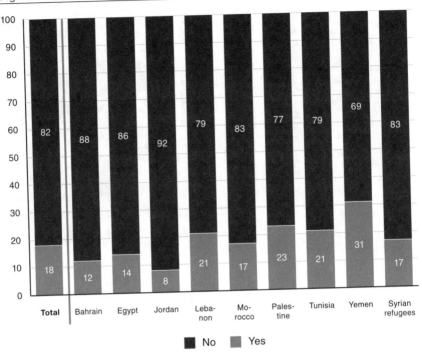

Figure 12.2 **Political Information**

Question 157 *'Do you inform yourself actively about politics?'*

Note Figures are given in percentages. Rounding errors can occur.

attended primary school, said, 'As I told you, I am not interested in politics ... It does not work as well as it should ... There are many problems, in politics, in education, they keep talking about fighting illiteracy, leaving school early, and we hear about this in the media. But they just keep talking and do not act' (MA-9).

Other respondents made it clear, however, that beyond party politics, politics was very important for them in many other aspects of their daily life. In Yemen, an 18-year-old female participant responded, 'I am not interested in politics since it is frustrating and wasteful. Politics is only for individual advantage, and it is all insincere. Politics plays a role in everything in our life' (YE-122). Nonetheless, some participants who also said they were not interested in politics went on to mention the shortcomings and corruption of the national healthcare system as a major problem that needs reform and an area the 'Minister of Health should work on' (MA-9). Others denied any 'interest in politics', as they took the question to mean

Figure 12.3 **Preferred Political System**

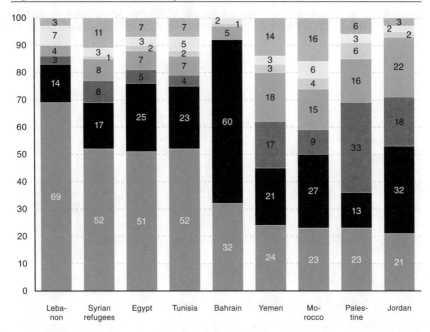

Don't know

Other

A combined socialist and Islamic system

A combined democratic and Islamic system

A religious state based on *sharia*

A strong man who governs the country

A democratic system

Question 113 *'If you look around the world, what kind of political system would you prefer?'*

Note Figures are given in percentages. Rounding errors can occur. | Political systems that achieve less than 2 percent in total are not represented (A socialist system; A strong woman who governs the country; A system without nation states).

their active involvement in politics. However, other respondents initially claimed no interest in politics, but continued to exhibit quite an intense interest in international political issues when asked about their priorities regarding national and foreign politics. Just weeks before Donald Trump's swearing in as US president, many respondents were well informed about his political agenda. Many pointed to his policies of deporting Muslims from the United States and shutting down mosques, and noted his rejection of the idea of climate change. In this pattern, a female student from Casablanca said that she was not interested in politics, but continued to answer the question directly following the one on an interest in politics. She stated,

Table 12.1 **Political Intentions (Actions Considered)**

	Total	Bahrain	Egypt
Participate in a demonstration	11	9	15
Participate in a strike	11	8	10
Join a political party	8	8	8
Participate in elections	30	12	40
Inform via internet/Twitter about joining group	8	3	10
Mobilise others via internet in order to act	8	2	10
Boycott certain goods	15	4	22
Distribute flyers	7	1	7
Sign an online petition	5	2	8
Engage in an association	11	2	8
Act as a sprayer	4	1	6

Question 159 *'If there is something important to you, and you want to be heard or have a political impact, which of the following possibilities would you probably or probably not consider doing? Would you ...?'*

Table 12.2 **Political Participation (Actions Applied)**

	Total	Bahrain	Egypt
Participate in a demonstration	12	8	19
Participate in a strike	6	3	3
Join a political party	4	3	3
Participate in elections	22	9	36
Inform via internet/Twitter about joining group	2	0	2
Mobilise others via internet in order to act	2	0	1
Boycott certain goods	7	1	13
Distribute flyers	2	0	1
Sign an online petition	1	0	2
Engage in an association	5	0	1
Act as a sprayer	1	0	1

Question 160 *'Which of these possibilities have you already used or participated in?'*

'We are more interested in foreign policy, for instance, American policy. I don't tend to follow politics generally. I don't believe we have real politics here in Morocco that would make me want to follow it. The parliamentarians make too many promises that they do not put into action when they become minister' (MA-10). She also seemed well informed about the US presidential race and pointed to UNICEF and the United Nations Mission for the Referendum in Western Sahara, MINURSO, as two organisations

Jordan	Lebanon	Morocco	Palestine	Tunisia	Yemen
3	13	5	8	18	16
3	14	13	10	16	12
2	10	8	7	8	13
16	35	21	27	39	47
5	9	9	7	13	6
7	8	13	6	15	8
11	10	15	18	15	23
7	6	11	5	5	11
4	7	9	4	6	3
5	13	16	13	15	17
3	3	9	3	4	4

Note Figures are given in percentages for 'Probably' and 'Certainly'. Rounding errors can occur. Syrian Refugees in Lebanon did not participate in this question (n=8,000).

Jordan	Lebanon	Morocco	Palestine	Tunisia	Yemen
2	15	5	11	23	12
2	10	2	11	9	5
1	8	2	6	2	7
14	21	15	22	24	2
3	2	1	3	3	2
2	3	3	3	2	3
6	4	3	15	4	9
2	2		3	2	3
1	2	1	1	1	
2	6	6	10	8	6
1	1	1	2	2	2

Note Figures are given in percentages for 'Yes' (multiple answers possible). Rounding errors can occur. | Syrian Refugees in Lebanon did not participate in this question (n=8,000).

where the United States plays a role in Morocco. The 30-year-old interviewee from Marrakesh who first elaborated that she was 'not at all' interested in politics, continued by saying, 'What is important to me is domestic politics. We are living in this country. There should be some justice first . . . I think healthcare is the priority, because people always live with these problems' (MA-9). A 17-year-old female respondent from Alexandria who also said she wasn't interested in politics, stated, 'Foreign politics affects Egypt more, because we are dependent on aid and imports' (EG-5).

The qualitative part of the survey showed that in contrast to their self-perception, respondents in fact debated political issues quite actively, and frequently. While, as illustrated, the lack of interest in politics might only pertain to specific kinds or aspects of politics, a number of respondents had obviously been turned away from politics through distrust in the political system, political parties, parliament or politicians. Others, quite simply, indicated that they had other things to worry about. Of note, only 4 percent of Syrian refugees say they are interested or very interested in politics.

Without exception, although to varying degrees, political interest in all countries studied is higher among young men than young women, and, almost without exception, the level of political interest relates to the level of education (the more education, the more interested). There is also a strong tendency among young people who have a budget of their own to be more interested than those without financial means at their disposal, although the relationship is not a linear one. Marital status across different countries does not seem to make a big difference.

The differences between countries regarding the level of political interest are not necessarily mirrored in the intensity with which young people seek information about politics. Thus, for example, only 14 percent in Egypt say they actively seek such information, while 23 percent say they are 'interested' or 'very interested' in politics, whereas in both Lebanon and Tunisia more claim to be seeking information than are interested in politics (21 percent versus 16 percent in the case of Lebanon, 21 percent versus 10 percent in the case of Tunisia). While some of these differences can be explained by those who claim to be 'a little' interested in politics still actively seeking information about it, the differences could also reflect that, at least to some degree, knowledge about politics might actually induce a turning away from it.

Regarding the sources of information used by those who actively inform themselves about politics, it is interesting to note that in most countries, television remains the most important source, although, unsurprisingly, it is closely followed by the internet (see Table 11.3). In the case of Jordan, Morocco, and Bahrain, the internet has already surpassed TV in this respect. In most countries face-to-face conversation remains the third most important source of information, after TV and the internet.

Being interested in politics of course is something different from somehow being active in the political realm. Regarding the latter, it is also necessary to distinguish between the consideration of different means of political action on the one hand and actual activity on the other. Regarding the latter, participating in elections as a 'regular' form of participation allegedly stands out in all the countries,[1] followed by boycotting certain goods for political reasons. Even though it is not unusual that interviewees tick off 'boycott' as a form of political action in any country, as it requires the least commitment in terms of resources, it is still noteworthy that boycotting goods is a prominent form of political action in the Middle East, with Yemen and Egypt even surpassing Palestine in this respect. This can partly be seen in the context of widespread debates on boycotting goods from Denmark and from Israel and growth of the Boycott, Divestment, Sanctions (BDS) movement over the last decades.

On average, the next most important activities considered beyond boycott and elections are 'engaging in an association', 'participating in a demonstration', and in 'strikes', but differences between countries are relatively significant. Contrary to widespread assumptions, when asked about political actions considered, mobilisation via the internet is low, at 8 percent ('probably' or 'certainly'). It even falls to 2 percent when asked 'Which of these possibilities have you already used or participated in?' Thus, for example, only 7 percent of young people in Jordan would 'probably' or 'certainly' consider mobilising others via the internet and 5 percent would engage in an association. Fifteen percent of those in Tunisia would mobilise others via the internet, and 13 percent of those in Morocco. In Yemen, the third most frequent political action considered is 'engaging in an association'.

In all countries, there is a stronger inclination among young men to become politically active than among young women. The difference is pronounced, 34 percent of males versus 25 percent of females show a high degree of willingness to be politically active (registering 2.1 points on a scale of 1–3, where 1.0 is 'no willingness'; see Table 8.8, cf. Table 12.1). On the other hand, the situation is reversed when it comes to a low, but still existent degree of willingness to be politically active: here 37 percent of females are engaged versus 33 percent of males (representing 1.1–2.0 points). When asked about political actions undertaken, most people had already taken part in an election. This group, however, represents only one-fifth of respondents. Twelve percent had participated in a demonstration, with Tunisians scoring the highest, with 23 percent. Other forms of political action, such as going on strike, or joining a political party scored far lower, at 2–6 percent.

1. This could, however, reflect a research bias of international surveys carried out in the region.

While at first glance one might expect that differences in social characteristics with regard to considering or executing political action would mirror the relevant differences regarding political interest in general, the picture is mixed when looking at individual countries and individual aspects of political participation. Thus, for example, Tunisia registers more young women than men who have considered participating in or have actually participated in an election. In many other countries, a gender difference, skewed toward young males, exists but is not strongly pronounced.

From a list of 28 aspects of personal life important to the interviewee, 'being politically active' scored lowest, which again reflects the frustration with political developments in recent years. With the exception of Yemen, the lack of importance of engaging in politics was consistent across the countries. In other words, from the Syrian refugees to Moroccan and Bahraini youths, being politically active ranked lowest in all countries, and in Yemen it ranked second lowest. As argued above, however, this lack of interest may not pertain to politics in a broad sense, but mainly to formal politics and corrupt elite politics.

When asked about their preferred political system (Figure 12.3), a religious state based on Sharia was not among the first or second preferences in any of the countries studied, save for Palestine, where 33 percent preferred such a political system, followed by 23 percent who opted for a democratic system. A democratic system received most support in Lebanon (69 percent), Tunisia (52 percent), Egypt (51 percent), and among Syrian refugees (52 percent). Only 25 percent of the young people in Egypt stated that they wanted a 'strong man' to govern the country. A preference for strong-man rule received most support in the monarchies, that is in Jordan (32 percent) and Morocco (27 percent), as well as in Bahrain (60 percent).

A state in demand?

There are a number of crucial consistent patterns across most countries in the region when it comes to views regarding the role the state should play in society and on the role that it actually does play. The study finds that the state is valued highly among young people: almost all respondents either would prefer a larger role for the state in daily life or think it is 'good as it is'. Only a very small faction (2–6 percent) of young people would prefer the state to play a smaller role in daily life. This is an important finding regarding both the legitimacy as well as the desired role of the state in the MENA region. It helps to understand why the divestiture of the state and its institutions in Iraq, Syria, Yemen, and Libya, as well as the wish for regime change

Figure 12.4 **Role of State in Daily Life**

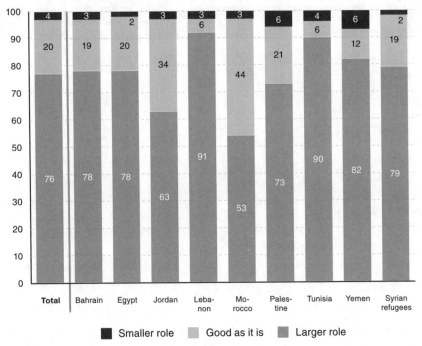

Question 115 '*Should the state play a larger or a smaller role in daily life or is it good as it is at the moment?*'

Note Figures are given in percentages. Rounding errors can occur.

in other countries (as in Egypt and Palestine, and possibly Morocco) are often viewed quite sceptically, even if state institutions do not deliver on their promises to their citizens.

In almost all countries studied, the three rights that young people deem most important are the absence of violence, security of basic needs, and freedom of opinion and speech.[1] The choice of these rights gives the first clue as to why demands as well as hopes connected to the state are high. Increasing instability affects every aspect of youths' lives. Social and physical security as classical responsibilities of the state are most important among those surveyed, no matter their age. Differences are more pronounced among the other rights, reflecting the particular situation in the respective countries. Thus, for example, respondents in Egypt value freedom of movement

---

1. Respondents were given a list of seven rights and asked to identify the three most important to them (Question 111).

Table 12.3 **Three Most Important Rights**

	Total	Bah-rain	Egypt	Jor-dan	Leba-non	Mo-rocco	Pales-tine	Tuni-sia	Ye-men	Syrian Ref.
Absence of violence	85	99	76	79	88	81	82	86	78	94
Security of basic needs	83	95	81	76	75	59	86	76	94	93
Basic rights for minorities	28	82	19	32	19	33	6	23	17	20
Freedom of opin-ion and speech	48	22	37	45	63	56	64	63	44	35
Freedom of assembly	11	0	10	19	9	22	7	16	5	7
Freedom to elect political leaders	14	0	24	18	16	17	12	11	17	8
Freedom of movement	29	0	31	19	30	24	43	25	44	42

Question 111 '*Please rank the three most important rights for you.*'

Note Figures are given in percentages. Rounding errors can occur. | Indicated are the frequencies of the three most important ranks.

slightly higher (31 percent) than the freedom to elect political leaders (24 percent) or minority rights (19 percent). In spite of this ranking, the valuation of the freedom to elect political leaders was higher in Egypt than in any other country. In Palestine, basic rights for minorities play only a minor role (6 percent), whereas freedom of movement is highly valued (43 percent).

The picture changes markedly when it comes to the question of whether the state can actually provide the respective rights that young people deem as most important to them. Whereas 89 percent in both Egypt and Jordan, as well as 87 percent in Morocco, say that the state can ensure an absence of violence, only 50 percent of young people in Palestine believe it can and even fewer in Lebanon (42 percent) and Yemen (41 percent). The perception is similar regarding security of basic needs, where again the opinion that the state can secure this right is highest in Egypt (89 percent), Jordan (88 percent), and Morocco (80 percent) and lowest in Palestine (46 percent), Yemen (43 percent), and Lebanon (35 percent).[1] In Yemen, where war is being waged without much international attention or efforts at resolution, youth are especially hopeless about their security and their ability to find work. An 18-year-old single woman from the governorate of

---

1. The figures for Syrian refugees have been excluded here, where numbers in relation to the capacity of the state to provide valued rights are lowest.

Table 12.4 **Trust in Institutions**

	Total	Bah-rain	Egypt	Jor-dan	Leba-non	Mo-rocco	Pales-tine	Tuni-sia	Ye-men	Syrian Ref.
Family	91	94	92	71	94	88	97	96	96	95
Educational system	78	97	64	86	82	73	87	67	73	74
Military	77	95	85	75	93	n. a.	52	87	59	74
Public health system	73	98	64	n. a.	66	66	79	66	68	72
Police	68	96	77	39	73	n. a.	72	63	50	71
Legal system and courts	64	94	73	52	58	53	70	65	51	57
Government	63	95	80	91	34	51	62	43	46	65
Religious organisations	58	89	52	59	49	56	61	42	59	51
Media	57	48	49	87	61	58	68	46	40	55
Trade unions	53	89	44	79	55	45	54	36	26	47
Human rights NGOs	53	86	39	46	53	49	57	35	44	64
Tribe	51	86	25	50	33	48	71	17	66	61
Parliament	46	89	44	54	34	41	41	36	28	49
United Nations	44	16	36	96	45	41	31	33	23	79
Neighbourhood associations	40	87	34	28	13	55	49	27	43	20
Parties	38	86	33	47	33	40	39	20	23	23
Zawiya (religious school)	28	83	26	n. a.	13	47	20	10	6	18
Militas (armed groups)	24	12	25	90	9	n. a.	23	6	16	8

Question 114 *'What about your trust in different institutions?'* 'Trust' & 'Limited Trust'.
Note Figures are given in percentages. Rounding errors can occur. n. a. = not applicable.

Abyan said, 'We lost security with the spread of unjustified bombings and deliberate murders without any deterrent or punishment. All these issues are consequences of the absence of the state' (YE-122).

Across a range of rights, Palestine, Yemen, and Lebanon stand out with respect to young people's perception of the state's limited ability to provide the basic rights most valued, largely reflecting the degree of fragility of statehood in these places compared to other countries in the region. This situation is only partly mirrored in attitudes towards the question of whether the state should play a larger role in daily life: whereas 91 percent of young Lebanese – more than in any other country – think the state should play a larger role, the values for Palestine (73 percent) and Yemen (82 percent) are somewhat lower. Tunisia is similar to Lebanon in that most young people prefer a larger role for the state in daily life (90 percent). Although in Jordan and Morocco the numbers are lowest in this respect, there is still a majority in both countries that would like to see a larger role for the state (63 percent in Jordan and 53 percent in Morocco).

Those who wish to see a larger role of the state in daily life were asked whether that larger role should pertain to the issues of social security, surveillance, transparency, or other issues. In most cases, social security was valued higher than surveillance, and surveillance higher than transparency, and 'other' invariably ranking fourth. The only two countries in which surveillance, expressing the wish for physical security, was valued significantly higher than social security were Jordan (28 percent social security versus 48 percent surveillance) and Lebanon (51 percent social security versus 65 percent surveillance). This is less surprising for Lebanon, where the absence of the state is widely deplored, as well as in Jordan, which (like Egypt) sees itself as a frontline state with joint borders with Israel. In Yemen, these two sectors were equally important (61 percent surveillance, 60 percent social security).

These different preferences highlight that the demand for a larger role of the state in daily life does not necessarily pertain to a wish for the state to have more power, but often accompanies a desire for a more effective, efficient, and legitimate performance by state institutions. Thus, for example, while 48 percent of young people in Jordan who want a larger role for the state would prefer more activity in the area of surveillance, Jordan in comparison to other countries in the region also has the lowest trust in the police as an institution (39 percent). In general, trust in various institutions, state as well as non-state, varies widely across countries. The family remains the most trusted institution. The three other institutions in which trust is consistently high – above 50 percent in all countries studied – are the education system, the military, and the legal system/courts.

Trust in the educational system on the one hand mainly means trust in individual teachers, who are also cited as role models in some of the qualitative answers. On the other hand, sharp criticism of the educational system – particularly the on-going privatisation of education from kindergarten to university – is expressed throughout the qualitative interviews. By now, most families, from household helper to university professor, will save their money in order to enrol their children in private institutions of learning (see Mazawi and Sultana 2010). Nonetheless, in relation to other institutions, trust in the educational system remains rather high, ranging from 64 percent in Egypt to 87 percent in Palestine.

Regarding other institutions, variations in the level of trust are wide among those that do not consistently rank above 50 percent. One consistent pattern, confirmed in the qualitative interviews as well, is that trust in government is usually always higher than trust in parliament or in political parties, and that religious organisations command a high level of trust. In Lebanon and Tunisia, however, trust in religious organisations is below 50 percent.

Events since 2011

Asef Bayat (2013) has pointed to widespread feelings of despair and disappointment following the MENA region uprisings. He shows how revolutions were increasingly regarded negatively in the context of failed post-colonialism in the second half of the twentieth century. In the post-Fanonian, post-Aflaq, and post-Banna world,[1] the revolutionaries became bureaucrats and dictators, and the ideal of revolution largely disappeared from the region. Instead, reform became the main ideal for achieving change. Thus, Bayat argues, the demands of 2011 were for reform, not about reversals of the social orders and political systems. The protesters did not adopt methods or means for a takeover or prepare themselves for such. Thus, the uprisings failed and brought about an outcome regarded as negative and destructive by both supporters and opponents.

In Egypt, Lebanon, Palestine, and Tunisia, the number of those who say they have already participated in a demonstration is actually higher than for those who say they are considering doing so to have a political impact.[2] There are different possible, not mutually exclusive reasons for this remarkable difference. In the events during and following 2011, many young people might have spontaneously participated in a demonstration without having previously considering doing so. Others may have participated in the past, and a lack of consideration to do so in the future reflected disillusionment with the impact of political action. A 29-year-old male from Egypt who had never participated in demonstrations, and was not inclined to do so in the future either, still saw the events of 2011 as the turning point in the politicisation of youths. He said,

---

1. The influential political voices of Frantz Fanon, Michael Aflaq, and Hassan al-Banna offered different political visions for the post-colonial Arab world.

2. There is one aspect to bear in mind in this context: the case of young people under voting age who might consider participating in an election in the future, yet obviously have not had an opportunity to actually do so.

Of course, before the January 25 Revolution, politics was not important for me, as for a lot of people. We did not begin to know or understand politics and were not even interested except after the revolution. Then one started to follow the news and understand the world – what is right and things like that – because of course, we were far away, or let's say there was a barrier between us and these things. I think that there is no one in Egypt now who is not politically attuned. At least he will have a political opinion . . . Since the revolution, there is no one in Egypt who is not concerned with politics [*ihtimam*]. (EG-6)

To shed light on how the participants in the survey look at the events of 2011 more than five years on, it is helpful to take a closer look at the terms used to refer to these events as well as statements invoking these references. Whereas the 'Arab Spring' is a term often used by observers outside the MENA region, according to the present survey, on average only 16 percent use this term (multiple answers were possible). The term conveys an idea of break-up and departure from outdated and dysfunctional governors and systems of government. Many also regard the Arab Spring as an element of foreign intervention (see Hegasy 2016). Eighty to ninety percent of all survey participants did not definitely disagree with the following two statements (answering 'agree' or 'so-so'): 'External actors instigated these events' and 'International actors have long worked for Arab regimes to fall'. From such a perspective, the preferred terms for describing the mobilisations since 2011 are rather 'insurgency', 'riot', 'rebellion', 'civil war', 'coup', or 'anarchy'. Seventy-four percent of interviewees used one of these six terms. Syrian refugees do not use the term 'Arab Spring', which for them reflects the fact that the protest movement turned into a civil war. They describe the protests primarily as 'chaos' and 'anarchy' (54 percent), and secondarily as foreign intervention (26 percent). Fifty-nine percent of all respondents used more positive terms like 'Arab Spring', 'revolution', 'uprising', or 'popular movement'. Respondents in countries that did not directly experience the protest movements, such as Lebanon, Palestine, and, to a lesser degree, Jordan, also tend to regard them as foreign interventions and chaos.

Nearly one-third of respondents preferred the term 'revolution'. In Tunisia, it was more prominent among those aged 16–20. In Egypt, 65 percent of respondents selected 'revolution', with no strong variation between age groups. Male and female responded alike in this instance, and the numbers are basically the same across all social strata. Although in the eyes of

Figure 12.5 'With the events, we are better off today'

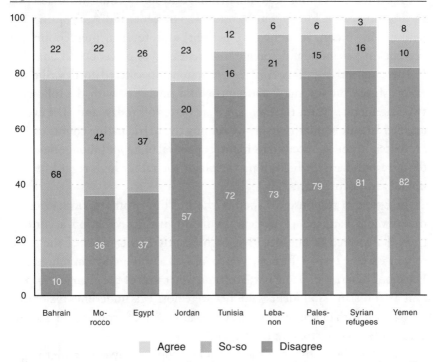

Note Figures are given in percentages. Rounding errors can occur.

foreign observers little might have changed in Egypt, as the head of state is still a former military general – like the deposed Hosni Mubarak – two reasons for the use of 'revolution' need to be taken into consideration. First, 'revolution' is the official, state-sponsored term used by all national media for developments since January 2011. Second, the fall of Mubarak is still regarded as unprecedented in Egypt's post-colonial history and counts as an example of self-empowerment unthinkable during the preceding forty years. It is an event that citizens regard as a complete turnaround, i.e. a revolutionary situation. Most young people in the region – when asked whether related events continue today, and whether the revolution remains on-going – answered in the positive, with responses ranging from 43 percent in Egypt to 76 percent in Tunisia. All regimes in the Middle East have, obviously successfully, adopted the term 'revolution' and present themselves as the solution to the grievances voiced in 2011.

The three expressions preferred in non-Arab Spring countries to describe the uprisings were 'foreign intervention' (20 percent) and 'Arab Spring' (19 percent) in Jordan; 'anarchy' (42 percent) and 'foreign intervention' (33 percent) in Lebanon; and 'foreign intervention' (39 percent) and 'anarchy' (33 percent) in Palestine. Among the statements offered to describe the events since 2010–11, most participants did not agree with the following two statements: 'With the events, we are better off today' and 'The events enabled Islamic solidarity to grow'. Among the participating countries, 'we are better off today' received its highest approval in Egypt (about one-quarter of respondents), which in part explains the rather high regard for the military in Egypt (Figure 12.5).

In Egypt in response to whether the Muslim Brotherhood had made these events happen, 42 percent (with no distinct variation according to age) answered in the negative. Significantly higher rates of the same response were given in Tunisia, Yemen, as well as among Syrian refugees in Lebanon. In terms of being better off today because of the changes, 72 percent of Tunisian respondents said they were not. This underlines major dissatisfaction with developments in Tunisia although the country is regarded as the only 'success story' in the region.

As stated above, the majority of young people today have rather negative impressions of the uprisings. A 26-year-old Moroccan woman with a secondary school education from a developed town (in terms of infrastructure), said:

'I did not like them, because so many innocents lost their lives. If the problem is political, the politicians should solve this problem with opposition politicians. Why do innocent people have to pay for this? I do not want society to be the scapegoat, but now everywhere we see kids becoming orphans, homeless and exiled . . . What I associate with the Arab Spring is that, if someone is faced with social injustice, he might commit suicide. This gave rise to the youth revolution, because they felt this injustice. Too much oppression gives birth to an explosion. So, I associate the Arab Spring with this. This is how it started. It started because of injustice and false promises' (MA-4).

Some respondents mentioned activities they participated in due to the mobilisation triggered in 2011 – like protests against water and electricity shortages and training for healthcare services – but overall they expressed feeling deceived. As a 19-year-old Yemeni respondent with no income stated, 'I first thought that these uprisings were aiming to defeat the corruption in these countries to achieve development. However, we found that they only made things worse' (YE-2).

Youth and Politics: The Road Ahead

Two important findings from the survey data on politics merit particular emphasis: the high degree of reliance on the state for social security (which is regarded as its main priority) and the high degree of references to foreign involvement in regard to the events of 2010/11 (which should not necessarily be interpreted as adhering to conspiracy theories). The high level of dissatisfaction of young people in Tunisia with their situation in 2016 compared to pre-2011 is also noteworthy. One of the most important insights to be gained from this study is that despite a high degree of disillusionment and feelings of insecurity, young people have not completely lost interest in or turned away from politics. The level of interest and of political activity is low, but the qualitative interviews suggest that survey questions about politics need to be taken with a grain of salt. The interest in politics (or lack thereof) indicated by young people often pertains only to 'high' formal, institutional, or party politics. There remains a broader understanding of, and a higher degree of engagement with, everyday politics. Youth are not totally discouraged by or turning away from institutional politics. As this survey shows, their views of politics rather go hand in hand with demands addressed to state institutions (and not, most notably, supplementary non-state organisations). There remains, in other words, significant potential among young people for constructively changing the political order of the future.

13

Mobilisation

Nadine Sika & Isabelle Werenfels[1]

THE 2010–11 ARAB UPRISINGS marked a peak of youth mobilisation in the Middle East and North Africa (MENA) region, with young people assuming the role and showing the capacity to develop and alter state-society relations. In the aftermath of the Arab uprisings and the toppling of long-standing Arab rulers, the focus of researchers and policymakers on youth (mass) mobilisation abated. Attention instead shifted to the role of youth as agents for change in the MENA polities as well as to what was increasingly seen as disillusionment with formal political processes, even in politically pluralist or democratising contexts, such as Lebanon, Morocco, Tunisia, and, until 2013, Egypt. This does not, however, imply that youth in the post-Arab uprising era have not been mobilising for political or social causes and change. On the contrary, the findings point to the fact that despite increased socio-economic problems in the aftermath of the so-called Arab Spring, and despite the crackdown of incumbent regimes against activists, a large number of young people continue to mobilise. They engage more actively, however, to attain socio-economic goals than political change. Also, mobilisation has taken more diverse shapes.

In the first two years following the Arab uprisings, youth political mobilisation was very high across the region. Strong protest movements emerged from Bahrain to Morocco, calling for various political reforms, good governance, and political accountability. Reactions of incumbent Arab regimes varied from using excessive coercion of some young political activists to co-opting others under the regime's umbrella, to employing a few political reforms, like altering some provisions in the constitution, changing the government, or calling for new elections. These so-called authoritarian upgrading measures have led to the waning of political activism and a return to old and new forms of civic activism. This activism does not directly threaten

---

1. The authors would like to thank Barbara Heckl for her excellent and precise comments.

or challenge the existence of MENA regimes, but it is rather centred upon incremental social, political, and economic change. Hence, mobilisation and participation may not necessarily be directed against a regime per se, but may well include collective action within the confines or even in support of these regimes (Albrecht 2008).

Community and grassroots activism are important types of youth mobilisation, where youth who face the same challenges mobilise others to their cause. For instance, they could mobilise to find secure housing or access to healthcare. An example of such single-issue protest movements was the 2015 #YouStink movement in Lebanon, in which activists, first in the virtual sphere and later physically, mobilised against the ineptness of the government to pick up and dispose of garbage in Beirut.

New forms of mobilisation and participation across the region include establishing youth initiatives and business start-ups. These reach out to other young people through training sessions for those lacking access to good education or business opportunities. Mobilisation could also be triggered by simple information. For instance, in Tunisia a watchdog organisation, Al Bawsala, tweeted 'live' from the Constituent Assembly's debates on women's rights in the new constitution and sparked immediate protests by activists in front of the parliament. In Egypt, the sexual harassment debate on Twitter following rapes in Tahrir Square in summer 2014 mobilised anti-sexual harassment activists trans-regionally. Mobilisation beyond the national arena is similarly taking place across social media with regard to human rights issues in the MENA region (Transfeld and Werenfels 2016). The growing role of social media in Arab youth mobilisation has been reflected in the notion (even if exaggerated) of the Facebook and Twitter 'revolutions', as dubbed in Western media when referring to the 2008 demonstrations in Egypt. Here two young Egyptians were the driving force in mobilising for demonstrations via the internet, and in doing so, laid the foundation for what was later to become the April 6 Movement (Herrera 2012).

Youth are active in different types of organisations ranging from parties and unions to non-governmental organisations (NGOs) and religious associations that work for the eradication of poverty, enhancement of education, and promotion of gender equality as well as improvement of the environment. These young people might not necessarily mobilise against the regime, but could be working with governmental institutions to promote their causes. Some young activists also choose to mobilise openly in favour of existing systems or rulers, for instance, the youth-based Mustaqbal Watan, a political party in Egypt whose members advocate and mobilise people to support social and political decisions of President Abdel Fattah al-Sisi's regime.

The data confirms and further nuances this diffuse and broad picture of mobilisation, as it provides the basis for profound understanding of mobilised youths. We define mobilised youth as those who are prepared to engage in (organised) political action, that is, a demonstration or a strike, to make their voices heard and have a political impact. They are those who display higher political and civic participation levels than the rest of the youth populations in the Arab countries analysed in this study.[1]

This chapter seeks to understand four sets of questions with regard to mobilised youth, irrespective of whether they are in favour of or in opposition to their ruling regime: Who mobilises? Where and how do they mobilise? Why do they take to political or civic action? What is their relationship to the state and for which visions of society or the political order do they mobilise?

Levels of Mobilisation: Egypt in the Lead

This study by the Friedrich-Ebert-Stiftung (FES) analyses the degree of Arab young people's intent to mobilise through a political intention index, which is based on the inclination of young people to engage in specific political activities, such as elections, demonstrations, strikes, boycotts, and membership in civic or political organisations. Despite a generally low interest in politics (see Chapter 12), the survey results show that almost one-third of all youth (30 percent) can be considered mobilised, based on a high degree of political intention. Slightly more than one-third engage to a low degree (34 percent), and a similar number is not active at all (36 percent) (see Table 13.1).

Across countries, however, the inclination to politically mobilise varies widely. Egypt is at the top end of the spectrum, with the largest percentage of mobilised youths (41 percent). This could, at least in part, be explained by a highly polarised and ideological landscape in which each camp strongly mobilises against its 'foe'. In addition, since the 2011 uprising until 2014, prior to Sisi's inauguration, there has been a surge in the level of youth political participation. That there have been two parliamentary elections (in 2011 and 2016), two presidential elections (in 2012 and 2014), and two constitutional referendums (in 2011 and 2014) has provided young people with venues for participation more so than in other countries in the

---

1. This chapter does not include Syrian refugees in Lebanon, as their situation with regard to mobilisation fundamentally differs from that of youth living in their countries of origin.

Table 13.1 **Political Mobilisation by Country**

	Morocco	Tunisia	Egypt	Jordan	Palestine	Lebanon	Yemen	Bahrain	Total
None	31	25	21	52	34	35	19	69	36
Low	30	40	38	31	36	37	46	18	34
High	39	35	41	17	30	28	35	13	30

Questions 1, 159 & Political Intentions Index (cf. Table 8.8).

Note Figures are given in percentages. Rounding errors can occur. | For the definition of the categories see Table 8.8.

region, even Tunisia, where fewer elections have taken place. In Morocco (39 percent) and Tunisia (35 percent) as well, more than one-third of young people can be considered mobilised.

These results are not surprising, as Tunisia has the most open political system and political mobilisation bears few risks. Morocco, while not democratic, has a pluralist and relatively competitive political system – elections were upcoming during the period interviews were conducted for this study – and with it a strong civil society, by regional comparison. Yemen, with more than one-third of youth engaged in a high level of political action (35 percent), can be explained by the political turmoil and polarisation between Houthis and the pro-Saudi camp against a backdrop of an uprising in 2011, an initial transition process, as well as a political history of a certain degree of pluralism.

At the low end of the regional spectrum is Bahrain followed by Jordan. For Bahrain, these results may be taken with a grain of salt, as the repression following the local uprising in 2011 may have made representatives of the oppressed Shi'i majority population more hesitant to commit to political action or to even consider it. One 26-year-old Bahraini, who said that he was concerned about politics, put it this way, stating, 'I am trying not to get too involved in politics, because involvement in politics is not good.' The low degree of inclination to mobilise in Jordan can partly be explained by fear of repression, which was often cited in the qualitative interviews, but this low level of mobilisation also coincides with a high rate of satisfaction with the government and a strong sense of security as well. These factors can explain a desire not to rock the boat, especially against the backdrop of a neighbourhood witnessing violent domestic conflicts.

These findings correspond with the relation found between mobilisation and insecurity: the less secure a young person feels, the more likely he or she is to mobilise. Of those feeling insecure, more than one-third tend to

	Lowest stratum	Lower-middle stratum	Middle stratum	Higher-middle stratum	Highest stratum	Total
Distribution in %	14	21	27	22	16	100
No engagement	12	17	23	**24**	**24**	100
Low engagement	14	**23**	**30**	21	12	100
High engagement	**15**	**24**	**28**	21	12	100

Questions Strata Index (see Chapter 2 and Appendix) & Political Intentions Index (see Chapter 8; Table 8.8).

Note Figures are given in percentages. Rounding errors can occur. Bold figures indicate values that are above the respective average.

highly engage in political action, while among those feeling secure, it is less than a quarter. Moreover, there are indications that where youth have been directly touched by violence, they are more likely to mobilise than where they have not. There is indeed a relation between repeated experiences with violence and a high degree of political activism. Of those who are highly politically active, about one-third (30 percent) experienced violence in more than one form. Of respondents with repeated exposure to violence, almost half were highly politically active.

Finally, pessimism appears to be a stronger driver of mobilisation than optimism. Overall, youth in the region tend to be optimistic about both their personal and their society's future. Like the non-mobilised Arab youth, the majority of mobilised youth (59 percent) is optimistic. Among pessimists, however, a higher percentage is mobilised than among optimists (37 versus 29 percent), indicating that pessimism does not lead to political inaction. On the contrary, pessimists tend to be the more mobilised.

Mobilised Ideal Type: Middle Strata, Male, Unmarried
Across the MENA region, young people from the socio-economic middle strata are more mobilised than those from the highest stratum (see Chapter 8) (Table 13.2). Yet the numbers differ strongly across countries. In Yemen, for instance, those from the lowest social stratum are the largest group among those with a high degree of political activism (30 percent). Morocco is the only other country in which the lowest stratum is represented fairly strongly (22 percent) among mobilised youths, with the largest group from the lower middle class (40 percent).

Within the highest stratum, the upper class, far more young people are politically inactive (53 percent) than active (22 percent). In the lower strata,

Table 13.3 **Distribution of Non-Active, Rather-Active and Very-Active Youths within Different Strata**

	Lowest stratum	Lower-middle stratum	Middle stratum	Higher-middle stratum	Highest stratum	Ø
No engagement	32	29	30	39	53	36
Low engagement	35	38	38	33	26	34
High engagement	33	33	32	28	22	30

Note Figures are given in percentages. Rounding errors can occur. ø = average.

Table 13.4 **Political Action and Social Background**

Political mobilisation	Number of cases	Gender		Age	Marital status		Living situation	Own budget	
		M	F	Years	Single	Married	With parents	Yes	No
None	2,863	47	53	22.7	70	25	74	46	54
Low	2,759	48	52	23.1	65	28	71	41	59
High	2,378	59	41	22.8	72	22	77	40	60
Total	8,000	51	49	22.9	69	25	74	43	57

the lower class and the lower middle class, the percentage of mobilised and non-mobilised youth is fairly equal (about one-third each) (Table 13.3).

Another characteristic of mobilised youth is that a large majority is male (Table 13.4). Among those highly politically active, 59 percent are male and 41 percent female. The gender gap with regard to mobilisation is highest in Yemen, 70 percent male compared to 30 percent female, followed by Bahrain. Several female interviewees in Yemen said they would like to be politically active, but hesitate due to the place traditionally ascribed to them by their family, society, and the state. On the other hand, the gender gap is lowest in Tunisia, with 53 percent of mobilised youths being male compared to 47 percent female.

A further difference between those who are highly politically active to further political or social cause(s) and those who are not is their marital status. Seventy-two percent of the mobilised youth are single, while 22 percent are married (Table 13.4). These numbers, however, need to be interpreted against the backdrop of two-thirds of those interviewed not being married. Even so, the degree of mobilisation among singles is higher than among the married.

In rural areas, the percentage of mobilised youth is slightly higher than in cities. Thirty-three percent of youth in rural areas are very active, compared to 28 percent in small cities and 30 percent in cities with more than 100,000 residents. In Egypt and Tunisia, mobilised youth tend to be more urban, whereas in Morocco and Yemen, the majority live in small cities.

Interestingly, with regard to age and occupational status, patterns between those not active at all and those mobilised barely differed. The two younger age cohorts (16–20 and 21–25) were slightly stronger represented among the mobilised than the group aged 26–30. The average age across the region of those displaying a high degree of political action (22.8 years old) and those not mobilised at all (22.7 years old) was virtually identical (Table 13.4).

Finally, mobilised youth tend to be less religious than the non-mobilised youth population. While among the non-mobilised, 72 percent are quite or very religious, less than two-thirds among those with a high degree of political intent characterised themselves as such (62 percent). Yet, among the mobilised, a minority of 37 percent fall into the category of having a low or rather low degree of religiosity. In Tunisia, almost two-thirds of those with a high degree of political intent said they have a low or rather low degree of religiosity. While this is an exception to the regional pattern, it is in line with overall degrees of religiosity in Tunisia.

The data furthermore reveals that among very religious Arab youths, a large majority show no or limited political intentions. Generally, political intent is higher amongst the less religious than amongst religious youths. In two countries, it is particularly high: Yemen and Morocco. In Yemen, half (50 percent) of young people who declared a low degree of religiosity are mobilised, while in Morocco it is an astonishing 90 percent. Yet, it is not possible to draw the general conclusion from these two cases that the (more) secular are mobilising strongly where they are a tiny minority in very religious societies. For instance, in Jordan the percentage of somewhat religious youth is equally low, as in Morocco (8 percent), yet only 18 percent of those somewhat religious show a high degree of political intent, the lowest figure among the eight countries. Mobilisation of the non-religious thus can be better explained with the national political context and political conjunctures, such as upcoming elections in Morocco and political turmoil in Yemen, in which the stakes of the non-religious are particularly high, as religious actors tend to dominate the political or military arenas.

Figure 13.1 **Types of Youth's Civic and Political Engagement**

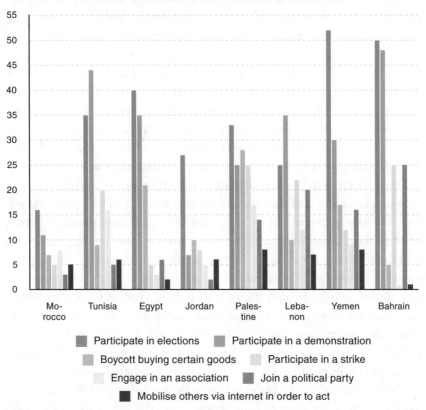

Participate in elections ■ Participate in a demonstration
■ Boycott buying certain goods   Participate in a strike
   Engage in an association ■ Join a political party
■ Mobilise others via internet in order to act

Question 1, 160, Political Intentions Index (see Table 8.8).

Note Figures are given in percentages. Rounding errors can occur. | Shown are the actual actions of those who are politically highly mobilised.

Venues of Activism: Demonstrations Over Party Engagement

The most common type of political engagement amongst civically and politically active youth is participating in elections (34 percent) followed by demonstrations (29 percent). Participation in civic associations and political parties is rather low amongst mobilised youth. Only 9 percent participate in civic associations, while participation in political parties stands at 10 percent. Though a rather modest number, it is far higher than the 4 percent of overall youth engagement in parties. Mobilised youth are particularly interested in civic and political engagement in their respective schools and universities. These results are not surprising, as the public sphere has largely been closed to street politics in the MENA since the Arab uprisings.

The preferred channel of political or civic engagement again displays substantial variety across and within countries. In Tunisia, for example, demonstrations are more popular than elections with certain groups of youths (males, the middle classes, the unmarried, the rural). In contrast, Jordanian mobilised youth tend mainly to participate in elections, while almost never participating in demonstrations (Figure 13.1). Palestinian youths have the highest levels of participation in schools and universities, reflecting both their above average degree of political action and the curbing of general mobilisation and of the public sphere in the Occupied Palestinian Territories by both the Palestinian Authority and the Israeli military.

The main reason youth gave in most countries for not mobilising is the absence of initiatives in their immediate surroundings. This was closely followed by the feeling that the struggle to make ends meet does not permit additional engagement. Perceptions of initiatives only serving those who lead them or not providing any income are further reasons for non-engagement. Forty-two percent of non-mobilised youth say they do not engage civically because their family does not wish them to do so. Interestingly with regard to this reason for non-engagement, differences across the region are particularly large. Lebanon takes the lead, followed by Yemen. In contrast, in Bahrain, Egypt, Jordan, and Tunisia, this real or perceived family constraint plays a minor role for non-engagement compared to other reasons.

In the context of the Arab uprisings, there was much debate concerning the relation between mobilised youth and the use of social networking sites, specifically in Tunisia, Egypt, and Yemen, where mobilisation resulted in regime breakdown. The FES survey reveals that there is indeed a notable correlation between mobilisation and social networking sites. Mobilised youths' average use of Facebook is 88 percent compared to 73 percent of the rest of young people. Even though Twitter is used much less than Facebook, mobilised youth tend to use it more often than weakly or non-mobilised youth (26 percent versus 21 percent). Social networking sites are important venues for political mobilisation amongst activists. Fifteen percent mobilise their friends, family, and others against certain political positions (Table 13.5).

Online mobilisation is closely related to the medium for receiving news and political information. The survey shows that the internet is the second most important medium for receiving political information and news (64 percent) amongst highly mobilised youth, after TV (68 percent), while the print press (newspapers) is the least important source (20 percent). The link between increasing use of internet communication technologies and

Table 13.5 **Use of Social Networks**

	Mobilised youth	Weakly and non-mobilised youth
Share music/videos/pictures	56	56
Discuss politics	18	8
Mobilise for politics	15	7
Oppose specific political positions	15	7
Discuss religious affairs	20	12
Mobilise for religion	20	11
Oppose religious positions	15	8

Question 155 *'How do you use social networks like Facebook, blogs, or WhatsApp?'* (Respondents who answered 'Always' or 'Frequently').

Note Figures are given in percentages. Rounding errors can occur.

the degree of political intent as well as ensuing venues of actual engagement require further analysis by scholars and policymakers, since the internet is becoming the main source of both political knowledge and mobilisation, replacing 'traditional' sources of information.

Priorities: Socio-economic Over Political
When asked the main reason behind their civic and political participation, the majority of mobilised youth said they are interested in helping the poor (26 percent), followed by helping other young people (24 percent). Interest in gender equality and in helping to integrate migrants and refugees tend to be of low interest to mobilised youth (Table 13.6). These results clearly show that mobilised youth are more interested in socio-economic change, than in political change per se. They also tend to reflect the general social and religious discourse in these countries, where policymakers and religious leaders tend to prioritise economic reforms over socio-political reforms. The low interest in gender equality is also a reflection of the patriarchal Arab societies in which these young mobilised people live. One might expect interest in refugee issues to be higher amongst mobilised youth compared to the rest, especially in Lebanon and Jordan, who host a high number of Syrian and Palestinian refugees, but this was not the case, again showing this population's inclination to conform with the rest of the society and to the political discourse in their countries. Generally, however, interest in politics is related to mobilisation. Two-thirds of young activists have an interest in politics, compared to one-third of the rest of the youth population.

When asked about their most important concerns, activists tend to believe that security of basic needs is most important, followed by the

Table 13.6 **Main Reasons for Civic and Political Engagement**

	Mo-rocco	Tuni-sia	Egypt	Jor-dan	Pales-tine	Leb-anon	Ye-men	Bah-rain	To-tal
For helping poor and vulnerable people	21	29	23	19	29	35	27	31	26
For the interest of the young people	21	15	37	22	26	30	25	5	24
For a better and cleaner environment	21	20	24	16	27	42	23	6	24
For improving living together in my area of residence	17	18	31	14	25	33	25	9	23
For elderly people who depend on help and support	19	28	16	15	27	37	19	27	23
For organising useful activities in the leisure time of young people	20	16	32	17	24	33	21	5	23
For the culture and traditions of my country	16	20	17	20	22	28	19	13	19
For improving the situation of disabled people	17	23	17	16	22	39	13	12	20
For guaranteeing safety and order in my area of residence	20	21	16	15	27	33	25	23	22
For my religious conviction	17	22	20	20	30	29	23	11	22
For equal rights of men and women	16	19	14	16	24	33	18	6	19
For social and political changes in my country	16	13	19	14	15	27	10	28	17
For better provisions for and integration of foreign migrants/refugees	17	16	11	11	9	16	5	9	12
For those who are coming from situations of armed conflicts	16	13	11	12	9	14	18	5	13
For other goals and groups	11	13	11	19	13	14	5	3	11

Question 161 *'Do you engage for social or political goals or commit yourself for the benefit of other people for the following issues?'*

Note Figures are given in percentages. Here: Percentage of those responding 'Frequently' among mobilised youth. Rounding errors can occur.

absence of violence. Freedom of expression is only third on their list of priorities. In Bahrain and Egypt, freedom of expression ranked even lower. In Bahrain, the third priority was to provide basic rights for minorities, while in Egypt freedom of movement was the third most important issue of concern (Tables 13.7). These results confirm that mobilised youth in the region tend to be more concerned with economic and security issues than with political issues. Though freedoms are important, mobilised youth tend to believe that a good standard of living with security is more important than freedom of expression. In Bahrain, it is understandable that for mobilised youth, minority rights are amongst the three most important issues: the majority of Bahrain's population is Shiʻi, while the ruling family is Sunni.

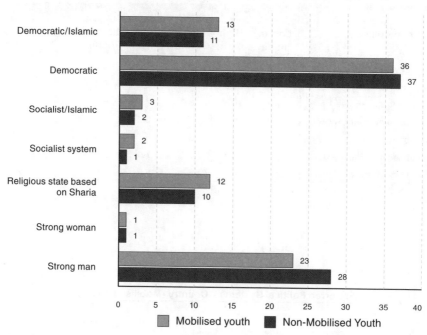

Question 113 *'If you look around the world, what kind of political system would you prefer?'*

Note Figures are given in percentages. Rounding errors can occur. | Other information was not considered here, therefore 100 per cent was not achieved (n=8,000).

Despite freedom of expression coming in third as a priority for mobilised youth, their first choice for a political system is a democratic system (36 percent). In this they do not differ from the average youth population, amongst whom 37 percent also prefer a democratic system. The second preferred political system amongst mobilised youths is one led by a 'strong man' (23 percent), followed by a combined democratic and Islamic state (13 percent) (Figure 13.2). It is interesting to note that amongst the eight countries surveyed, youth activists living in the three monarchies – Jordan, Morocco, and Bahrain – tended to prefer living in states headed by strong men. Overall, only 12 percent of youth activists are interested in living in a religious state based on Sharia law. Interestingly, the highest percentage of youth activists interested in a religious state are in the Palestinian territories, with 30 percent preferring a purely Islamic state compared to 25 percent in favour of a democratic state. Activists in Lebanon and Bahrain on the other hand are the least interested in a religious state, registering 3 percent and 0 percent, respectively (Figure 13.3). The paradox that Bahrain contains the

Table 13.7 **Importance of Fundamental Rights**

Degree of mobilisation	Morocco		Tunisia		Egypt		Jordan	
	Low or none	High	Low or none	High	Low or none	High	Low or none	Hi
Absence of violence	8.3	6.6	9.4	9.4	8.4	7.6	8.4	8
Security of basic needs	8.0	6.9	9.5	9.6	8.2	8.0	8.5	8
Basic rights for minorities	7.3	6.3	8.0	7.6	6.0	6.7	6.7	6
Freedom of opinion and speech	7.9	6.9	9.1	8.7	7.3	7.2	8.0	7
Freedom of assembly	7.5	6.7	8.7	8.4	6.8	6.7	7.3	7
Freedom to elect political leaders	6.8	6.4	7.7	7.5	6.9	7.1	5.9	5
Freedom of movement	7.5	6.7	8.8	8.5	7.4	7.4	7.3	6

Questions 1, 110, 159.

Figure 13.3 **Preferred Political System by Country (Mobilised Youth)**

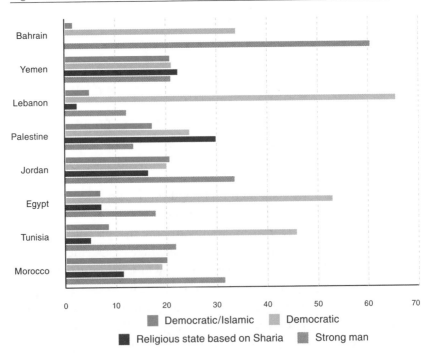

Questions 1, 113, 159.

Note Figures are given in percentages. Rounding errors can occur.

Palestine		Lebanon		Yemen		Bahrain		Total	
Low or none	High	Low or none	High	Low or none	High	Low or none	High	Low or none	High
9.1	9.0	9.0	8.9	8.7	8.9	9.3	9.3	8.9	8.4
9.2	9.1	9.2	9.0	9.3	9.6	9.1	9.3	8.9	8.6
7.0	7.5	8.1	8.1	7.5	7.7	8.7	9.0	7.5	7.3
8.3	8.5	8.7	8.7	7.7	8.4	6.7	7.0	7.9	7.9
7.3	7.9	8.5	8.5	4.6	6.2	6.1	6.2	7.1	7.3
6.3	7.1	7.6	8.0	6.1	7.6	5.4	5.8	6.5	7.1
8.1	8.4	8.6	8.4	7.6	8.4	6.1	6.3	7.6	7.7

Note Data represented as an arithmetic mean of question 110 on a scale from 1 ('Not at all important') to 10 ('Totally important').

highest number of very religious among the mobilised could be related to Bahrainis' above average satisfaction with the status quo as reflected in their levels of trust in institutions.

Trust in Institutions: Military First

Levels of trust are low with regard to state and non-state institutions amongst young Arabs as a whole. Nevertheless, mobilised youth tend to have lower levels of trust in state institutions than the rest of the survey population, but more trust in political parties and human rights organisations (Figures 13.4 and 13.5).

The highest level of trust amongst young people in general is in the military. This also holds for mobilised youth, with an average of 54 percent saying that they have total trust in it. Tunisian and Lebanese activists have the highest trust levels in the military, at 79 percent, while the lowest levels are found amongst Palestinian activists, at 24 percent (Table 13.8). These results are not surprising, as the military in Tunisia did not side with long-time president Zine al-Abidine Ben Ali during the uprisings, and in the new era, it has been vital in the fight against terrorism.[1] In contrast to the police, the military has little corruption and no history of repression. On the other hand, in the Palestinian territories, there is no functioning military, only the National Security Forces, a police force

---

1. One 30-year-old Tunisian reflecting this sentiment, simply remarked, 'The army protects the Tunisian citizen against terrorists.'

Figure 13.4 **Trust in Institutions (Mobilised Youth)**

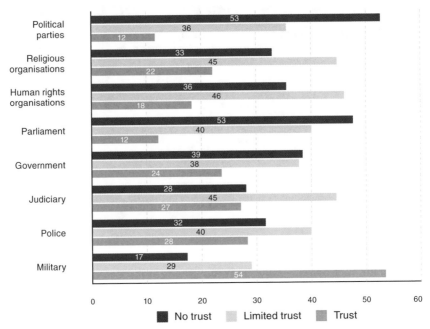

Question 114 *'What about your trust in different institutions?'* (Without answer option Unknown). Family (as an institution) is not represented here.

Note Figures are given in percentages. Rounding errors can occur.

with paramilitary capabilities. With the rift between Hamas and the Palestinian Authority after the 2006 parliamentary elections, the National Security Forces came into direct confrontation with Hamas, further enhancing violence and divisions amongst Palestinians. These developments help to explain the low levels of trust amongst Palestinian youth towards their military.

By contrast, trust in the police force is rather low among mobilised Arab youth, with only 28 percent saying that they have total trust in it. While the remaining youth population also has low levels of trust in the police, it still has more trust (42 percent) than mobilised youth (Figure 13.5). Trust in the judicial system is also very low at 27 percent among activists. The highest levels are amongst Egyptian activists, with 43 percent trusting the judicial system. These same activists, however, have less trust than the remaining Egyptian youth population, at 54 percent (Tables 13.8). The Egyptian judiciary is known for its semi-impartiality and independence from the regime in some aspects.

Figure 13.5 **Trust in Institutions (Non-mobilised Youth)**

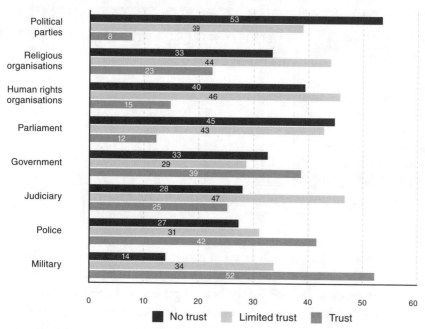

Questions 1, 114, 159.

Note Figures are given in percentages. Rounding errors can occur. | Family (as an institution) is not represented here.

Trust towards the government is at 24 percent among mobilised respondents. Lebanese activists have the lowest levels of trust in their government, with 63 percent not trusting it at all. Conversely, Jordanian and Bahraini activists display very high trust levels in their governments, 65 percent and 80 percent respectively (Table 13.8). It remains unknown whether these findings are related to a better perceived performance by the governments of these two countries or to greater fear of criticising them.

The least-trusted state institution amongst mobilised MENA youth is the parliament. Only 12 percent of young activists trust their respective parliaments (Figure 13.4). There is no variance vis-à-vis the general youth population, whose trust levels towards the parliament are the same. This mirrors the awareness of young people in the region towards rigged elections and of the executive branch's power over the legislature, thus further weakening parliament, essentially making it a mouthpiece of the rulers rather than the citizens' representation. It is rather ironic to find Tunisian activists at the low end (10 percent) in level of trust of the parliament, along

Table 13.8 Trust in Institutions by Country

Mobilised?	Morocco		Tunisia		Egypt	
	[Highly] Yes	Weakly / No	[Highly] Yes	Weakly / No	[Highly] Yes	Weakl No
Military	n. a.	n. a.	79	72	61	70
Police	n. a.	n. a.	25	30	25	41
Judiciary	21	7	27	34	43	54
Government	17	4	10	16	26	45
Parliament	14	3	10	8	14	18
Human rights organisations	20	11	20	13	18	17
Religious organisations	25	14	14	11	25	35
Political parties	19	3	3	3	14	9

Question 114 *'What about your trust in different institutions?'* Here: 'Trust'.

with Bahrain (8 percent), Yemen (10 percent), and Palestine (10 percent) (Table 13.8). Tunisia is the only state in the region engaged in a democratisation process, and the youth there in general and mobilised youth in particular had high expectations in their first legitimate parliament and little patience for drawn-out political processes. One 25-year-old Tunisian stated, 'The members of parliament make fake promises. They don't achieve these promises. They are not credible. They don't assume their responsibilities towards the citizen.' Other Tunisian youths speak of politicians as liars, engaged in squabbling, and working only for their personal interest. Basically, they expressed disappointment with the status quo and the lack of socio-economic change since 2011. This can also be discerned in Tunisian youths being the least satisfied with their opportunities in life, as the survey revealed.

Remarkably, trust in parliament is lower than trust in human rights organisations amongst mobilised and non-mobilised youth (Figures 13.4 and 13.5). Political parties enjoy the least trust amongst youth, with 9 percent. Youth activists have a little more trust than the rest of the youth, with 12 percent. Activists in Bahrain and Tunisia tend to have the lowest trust in political parties, at 2 percent and 3 percent, respectively (Table 13.8). Like parliaments, political parties in the region tend to be perceived as mere window dressing, instruments for co-opting the opposition and for legitimating the rulers in the eyes of the international community. Political parties rarely have a true say in political debates. Egypt is an interesting case in point. Since Sisi came to power, the number of political parties has surpassed those active during the Mubarak regime, but the majority

Jordan		Palestine		Lebanon		Yemen		Bahrain	
[Highly] Yes	Weakly / No	[Highly] Yes	Weakly / No	[Highly] Yes	Weakly / No	[Highly] Yes	Weakly / No	[Highly] Yes	Weakly / No
48	61	24	28	79	85	36	33	26	20
17	26	30	37	28	35	20	20	80	86
32	35	26	31	22	17	22	23	24	11
65	82	22	27	9	9	16	16	80	83
25	35	10	12	11	9	10	11	8	5
19	25	19	19	16	12	22	24	3	4
39	51	24	24	19	15	26	37	4	4
27	31	11	8	19	6	4	5	2	3

Note Figures are given in percentages. Rounding errors can occur.

of these parties have established a coalition called 'For the Love of Egypt' (Fi Huub Misr). The coalition's main role in parliament is to legitimise the regime.

Trust towards religious organisations stands at 22 percent amongst activists. Bahrainis have the least (4 percent), followed by Tunisians (14 percent) and Lebanese (19 percent). Both Tunisian and Lebanese activists, however, have higher levels of trust in religious organisations than the rest of youth populations in their countries.

Trust in human rights organisations stands at 18 percent amongst activists in the countries analysed, compared to 15 percent amongst non-activists. Trust is lowest in Bahrain, at 3 percent. Bahrain, Jordan, and Yemen are the only countries under analysis in which trust in human rights organisations is lower amongst mobilised youths than in the rest of the youth population (Table13.8).

Conclusion

This chapter has identified main characteristics and priorities of mobilised youth in the MENA region and noted similarities and differences between the mobilised and the rest of the Arab youth populations. The mobilised youth tend to live in rural areas, be less religious, come from middle-income strata, and be more interested in politics and more inclined to use the internet and social networking sites than the average population of young people. In addition, mobilised youth tend to be bachelors. They are also more likely to have experienced violence, and more likely to be pessimistic than the rest of the youth population.

The trust levels of mobilised youth in both state and non-state institutions tend to be in line with those of the general population. Nevertheless, on average their trust levels in formal state institutions are lower than among the rest of young people, with parliaments receiving particularly low ratings. Mobilised youth, however, exhibit higher levels of trust in non-governmental institutions than do non-activists. When it comes to the anxieties they face and the types of political order they prefer, mobilised youth tend to follow the trends within their respective countries more so than trends in other countries.

The national political and social contexts and recent history of a country have a strong impact on patterns of mobilisation. Young people living in republics who experienced regime breakdown after the Arab uprisings tend to be more mobilised than youth living in Arab monarchies. At the same time, the degree of pluralism and political freedoms as well as specific political conjunctures and characteristics (e.g. frequency of elections) may override the republic versus monarchy pattern and have an important impact on mobilisation levels across the region.

Yet, mobilised youth are not primarily concerned with political issues, such as freedom of speech. Rather, security of basic needs and an absence of violence are their top concerns. Overall, those mobilised are not more concerned with political freedoms and civic rights, including minority rights, than non-activist Arab youth. Their focus is primarily on socio-economic rights and social issues. This explains, last but not least, why youth mobilisation patterns in the only Arab country rated 'free' by Freedom House, Tunisia, barely differ from those in the rest of the MENA region (Puddington and Roylance 2017).

14

Civic Engagement

Friederike Stolleis

STUDIES ON THE ROLE AND NATURE of civil society in the Middle East and North Africa (MENA) have come to different conclusions over time. Until the early 1990s, European and US-American academics described MENA societies as being largely apathetic and passive, and dominated by tribal and religious ties, leaving little room for Western-style civil society and even less for young people. This picture was challenged in the mid-1990s by a new approach, which held that civil society in the region could represent a decisive element for democratic transformation processes (Norton 1995, 1996). Supporting civil society subsequently made its way into Western development cooperation with MENA countries. As democratic transitions failed to materialise, however, the enthusiasm for civil society started to fade. Only with the Arab Spring did the interest of analysts as well as practitioners return to civil society. As the recent uprisings were in large part initiated or supported by youth, young people in the MENA region shifted into focus as potential mediators of positive change. On the basis of empirical results, this chapter analyses the motivations of young men and women for civic engagement as well as their commitment to civil society organisations.

Civil Society Organisations and the Arab Spring

Religious charities, guilds, and educational institutions represent age-old forms of non-governmental organisation in the MENA region, dating back centuries. Civil society organisations (CSOs) in today's understanding, such as trade unions, professional associations, and student committees, only emerged during the colonial era and played a prominent role in the struggle for independence. In the post-colonial era, MENA civil societies were shaped by the political contexts in which they evolved. With most regimes in the region being authoritarian and restrictive, they sought to maintain a firm grip on civil society through co-optation or other means of control.

Since the late 1980s, due to economic reforms and outside pressure in many MENA countries, CSOs were able to emerge at a relatively basic level. Often, the engagement of its members was to fill holes in public infrastructure. The increasing inability of many MENA states to provide basic services for their growing populations has led to a proliferation of CSOs over the past two decades. These associations as well as many informal initiatives have come to provide a large array of services and thus represent a stabilising element for the societies and states.

In many countries of the MENA region, CSOs have to work as so-called governmental non-governmental organisations (GONGOs).[1] Not all do so out of conviction; in many cases this is the only possibility of engaging at all. The relationship of the organisations towards the government is therefore ambivalent. MENA governments use a considerable number of tactics to control, co-opt, or discredit civil society.[2] As a result, CSOs tend to be weak and fragile. Many of them face internal challenges in identifying clear missions and strategies and – due to the lack of financial autonomy, being mostly donor-driven in their choices – they often implement sporadic, ad hoc programmes and projects. Weak internal governance and democratic procedures often lead to a lack of efficiency, transparency, credibility, and accountability on the ground (Halaseh 2012).

Arab Spring has provided a sudden boost to civic engagement across the MENA region. Even in those countries that did not experience mass protests and revolutions, restrictions were at least temporarily loosened as leaders tried to assuage their restless populations. In general, institutionalised CSOs played only a minor role in the uprisings. Even if trade unions participated in the Tunisian and Egyptian revolutions, non-governmental organisations rushed to stabilise new governments in Libya and Yemen, and members of political parties and trade unions protested in the streets of Morocco, none of these institutions can be labelled as the driving force behind the Arab Spring. In many cases they were as surprised by developments as the ruling regimes (Yom 2015). Instead, the social movements that led to protests in many of the MENA countries were sparked primarily by young people informally mobilising one another. These engaged young people, often not only marginalised by the state, but also by the CSOs themselves, formed their

---

1. Or as FLANGOs (first lady non-governmental organisations), when placed under the patronage of a first lady – a common feature in many MENA countries.

2. This is especially true for human rights organisations (Carothers and Brechenmacher 2014; with a focus on Egypt, Brechenmacher 2017).

own groups and movements and took action to voice their demands (see Chapter 13).

How has the Arab Spring affected civic engagement by young people? An evaluation of civil society in the MENA region through its formal CSOs would find it relatively unchanged by the uprisings. With few exceptions – such as Tunisia and Libya and Syrian CSOs in opposition-held areas or in exile – CSOs have generally been weakened by shrinking spaces due to new NGO regulations and anti-terror laws in many of the countries. As illustrated by the wave of non-institutionalised activism witnessed during the Arab Spring, however, focusing on CSOs obviously does not capture the full scope of political and non-political civic engagement in the MENA region.

This is especially true when looking at young people. To get beyond the issue of membership in formal CSOs in the survey conducted for this study, young people were questioned about the cause of their engagement before being asked in which institutional framework their activities take place. Their answers illustrate that young people are, in general, willing to engage for the benefit of other people or certain goals and issues, but they are much less willing to adhere to formal CSOs in doing so.

The results show a clear relation to social standing: while civic engagement is higher among those in the higher socio-economic strata, membership in CSOs is lower among them, meaning that engagement in the framework of a formalised institution is mostly the domain of youth belonging to the lower and middle strata of society. Among the latter youth, widespread feelings of insecurity and pessimism are found, driving, at least in part, their motivation to actively adhere to a CSO in order to engage for a cause.

Youth Civic Engagement

In general, civic engagement is important for young people in the MENA region. The majority of those interviewed (64 percent) stated that they engage frequently or occasionally for social or political goals or are committing themselves for the benefit of other people. Slightly more than one-third (36 percent) of interviewees declared that they never engage for any of the mentioned goals or topics.

Among those who do engage, helping poor and vulnerable people and protection of the environment were most commonly cited (Figure 14.1). These are followed by a variety of volunteer activities that can broadly be labelled as charity or rather apolitical. Engaging for social and political change comes in last among the civic activities relevant for all countries. (Less frequently mentioned is engagement for migrants and refugees as

Figure 14.1 **Goals and Themes of Civic Engagement in General**

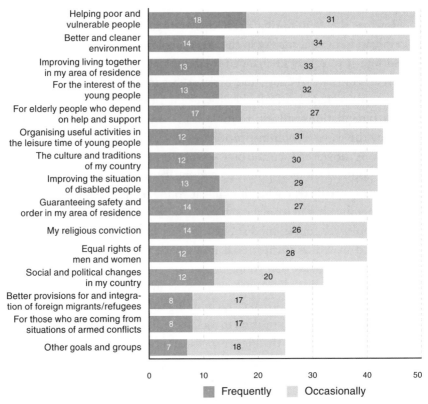

Note Figures are given in percentages. Rounding errors can occur.

well as victims of armed conflict, issues which are not necessarily relevant across all countries.) This is unsurprising given the difficult circumstances for politically motivated civic engagement in most of the countries under study. Where civic engagement is under tight control, engaging for a certain cause is already a political act in itself.

Many of those who are actively engaged try to improve the situation in their immediate surroundings through awareness campaigns on health, social, or environmental issues, while distancing themselves from 'politics'. Hanadi, a 31-year-old teacher in Palestine, described her activity as follows:

> I joined the Palestinian Red Crescent as a volunteer, but this has nothing to do with politics. We conduct activities for schools and

kindergartens, and we organise open days for them. We organise summer camps. These are nice things. We take courses to raise health awareness because diabetes is widespread. We need to raise awareness and reduce threats to the lives of people. We need to teach them how to take medication. These are social issues and have nothing to do with politics. (PS-1)

Others see their engagement as a form of charity, helping the poor. In cases where there is an acute humanitarian crisis, such as among Syrian refugees in Lebanon and in Yemen, this is often combined with volunteer work for international or national relief organisations in the distribution of goods. Ranim, a 22-year-old student in Tyre, Lebanon, remarked,

My friends and I decided on New Year's to help poor people and go on the streets, because small children do not know the meaning of Christmas and New Year's. The parents' situation is bad, and children need toys and clothes and heaters, so we did our best to help them. Some time ago my school friends and I did a cleaning campaign, where we cleaned the park, and the teacher also suggested that we help a family in need (LB-9).

Fatima, a 21-year-old student and herself a Syrian refugee, lives today in Baalbek, Lebanon, where she helps Syrian families:

I volunteered with Save the Children. We have helped Syrian refugees through awareness and by spreading optimism among them. . . . I have enrolled with the Red Cross too, where I got a health certificate. I used to assess the requirements and needs of refugees. I stopped my activities when the camp moved from the region. I have also contributed in the distribution of water as well as bathrooms, wood, tents, and sometimes food. This experience was very successful. I was very happy to have participated in these jobs, because I have contributed to spreading joy in kids' hearts through the things we have offered them, like school bags and other stuff. (LB/SY-11)

Esraa, a 21-year-old housewife in Taiz, Yemen, said,

I belong to a youth group, so I have friends with whom I conducted seminars in our district on culture and awareness. We were from

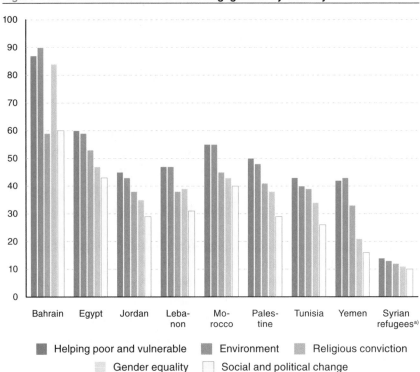

Figure 14.2 **Goals and Themes of Civic Engagement by Country**

■ Helping poor and vulnerable   ■ Environment   Religious conviction
Gender equality   ☐ Social and political change

Question 161 *'Do you engage for social or political goals or commit yourself for the benefit of other people for the following issues?'* ('Frequently' and 'Occasionally'; Multiple answers possible).

Note Figures are given in percentages. **a)** Syrian Refugees in Lebanon.

different areas. We had awareness sessions discussing social issues, such as early marriage . . . [After the Arab Spring] I didn't join any group officially, but I participated in relief activities. We worked for several relief organisations as distribution representatives. Our duties were ensuring equal distribution to poor families. (YE-6)

How far civic engagement is driven by one's religious conviction is difficult to determine, as it can be one among other underlying motivations. Even when young people organise religious festivities, these events usually have both a social and charitable dimension as a statement by Ahmad, a 17-year-old worker in Sanaa, Yemen, illustrates:

I'm involved in some activities with a group of friends in my neighbourhood, coordinated by the neighbourhood supervisor.

Figure 14.3 **Goals and Themes of Civic Engagement by Social Strata**

Figure 14.3 **Goals and Themes of Civic Engagement by Social Strata**

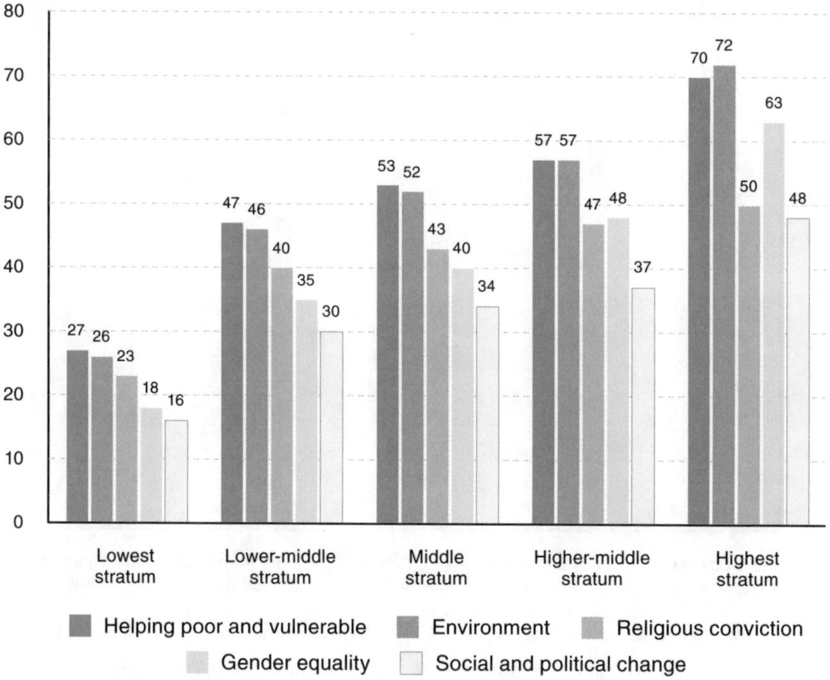

Question 161 *'Do you engage for social or political goals or commit yourself for the benefit of other people for the following issues?'* ('Frequently' and 'Occasionally'; Multiple answers possible).

Note Figures are given in percentages. Rounding errors can occur.

This group helps organise activities and checkpoints during the celebrations of Prophet Muhammad's birthday. We were one of the controlling committees that arranged for the people to enter the square and helped the old and disabled. (YE-5)

The general preference for certain causes does not vary much when answers are analysed on a national level. When looking, for example, at five different issues for civic engagement across different national groups, the similarities in ranking are striking (Figure 14.2). In general, civic engagement notably increases with economic well-being, with Bahrain displaying the highest percentages of young people engaged and Syrian refugees in Lebanon the lowest. The only major exception is a lower percentage engaging for religious beliefs in Bahrain, which is to be understood in the context of the obvious political delicacy of Sunni–Shi'i frictions in the country.

Figure 14.4 **Institutions of Civic Engagement by Social Strata**

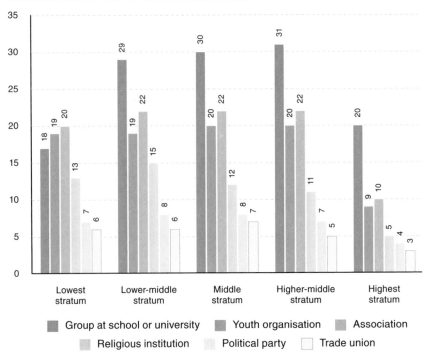

Question 162 *'Where and how do you engage?'*

Basis Interviewees who responded 'Frequently' or 'Occasionally' to Question 161.

Note Figures are given in percentages. Rounding errors can occur.

When it comes to social standing, there is a clear correlation between civic engagement and socio-economic strata: the higher the social stratum, the more likely young people are to engage in civic activities (Figure 14.3). This is valid for all five exemplary fields of civic engagement. The overlap between higher socio-economic strata and active civic engagement is most visible when it comes to engaging over equal rights for men and women and is less so but still present when it is on behalf of religious convictions. This confirms other findings of this study indicating that contrary to what is commonly assumed, religiosity does not decrease with higher social standing (see Chapter 4).

While civic engagement is clearly related to social strata, with the highest stratum being the most involved, this does not apply to activities through csos (Figure 14.4). Here, participation of the highest stratum is clearly the lowest, whereas the middle strata are the most likely to engage within the framework of a CSO. An exception is membership in school or university groups, which might be automatic or even sometimes compulsory, and with students often too young to make independent decisions. Even here, the middle strata have a higher presence than the highest or the lowest strata, although the higher strata certainly provide for more high school and university students.

The discrepancy between the relatively high level of at least occasional engagement for a variety of causes and the rather low membership in CSOs confirms the need for more comprehensive and in-depth analysis of civil engagement than simply focusing on formal institutions. As has been shown, young people in the MENA region are willing to engage for certain causes, while keeping their distance from matters associated with politics. They are much less willing, however, to adhere to formalised institutions. This contrast becomes even more striking when looked at through the lens of social standing: while young people belonging to the highest stratum of society are the most likely to engage in civic activities, they are the most unlikely to do this within the framework of a CSO. Much of youth civic engagement in the MENA region hence takes place within the field of informal civic activism, such as through public education and consciousness raising, volunteerism, and community services.

Civil Society Organisations and Engaged Youth
In most countries covered by this survey, young people who seek the framework of formalised CSOs for their activism have the choice between joining youth organisations at school or university, religious institutions, or becoming a member of one of the traditional institutions of political action (political parties, trade unions). In general, the degree of association with CSOs is relatively low among youth in the MENA region. It is important to note that the data presented here only reflects the answers of two-thirds of the youths interviewed, i.e., those who stated that they engage occasionally or frequently in pursuing social or political goals or commit themselves for the benefit of others (Figure 14.5). While young people often join a group at school or university (thus totalling 36 percent of all engaged youths), the decision to join a political organisation, such as a political party or a trade union, is taken by only 10 percent and 7 percent of them, respectively.

Joining a university group or a youth organisation usually offers access to a variety of activities aimed at improving discussion skills and raising intellectual awareness among young people, as examples from Palestine and

Figure 14.5 **Institutions of Civic Engagement in General**

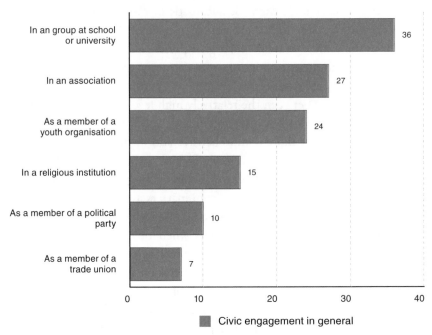

Question 162 *'Where and how do you engage?'* (Multiple answers possible).

Basis Interviewees who responded 'Frequently' or 'Occasionally' to Question 161.

Note Figures are given in percentages. Rounding errors can occur.

Lebanon illustrate. Hikmat, an 18-year-old student from al-Bireh, Palestine, shared information on her activities:

I am active in the cultural committee at the university. I express my ideas freely there . . . On every occasion, we organise a small party and raise awareness among students, have discussions on many issues and discuss books. We have a group specialised in books, and through this group we get ideas about books. We have activities inside and outside the university. We organised a book fair at the al-Bireh Cultural Club. (ps-2)

Mahmoud, a 27-year-old divorced supermarket owner from Birzeit, Palestine, would prefer more action on the ground:

I joined leftist organisations. They . . . organise camps and activi-

Figure 14.6 **Institutions of Civic Engagement by Country**

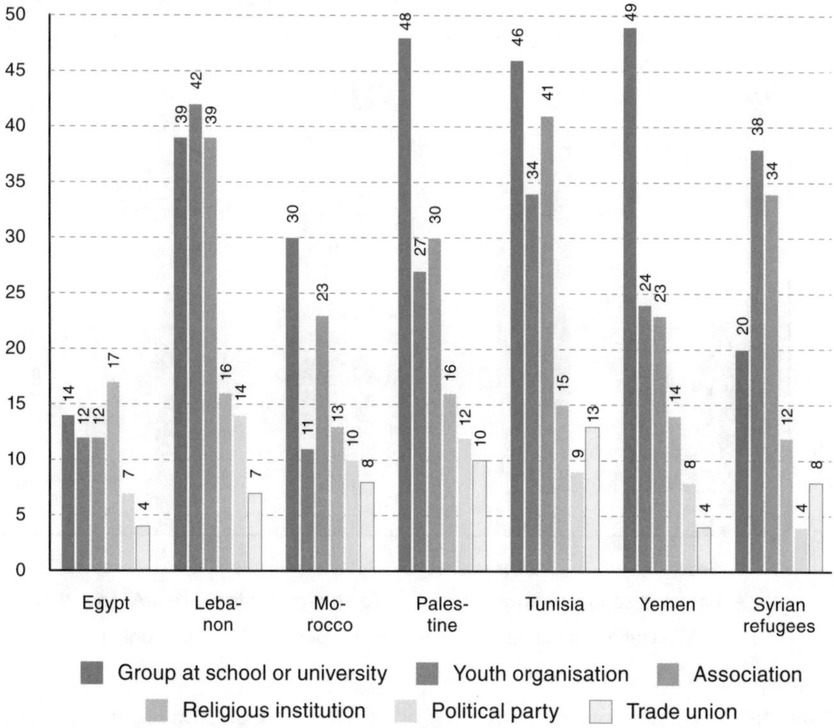

Question 162 *'Where and how do you engage?'*

Basis Interviewees who responded 'Frequently' or 'Occasionally' to Question 161.

Note Figures are given in percentages. Rounding errors can occur.

ties for young people, but it is not sufficient. There are circles for discussion and self-criticism. It is a sharing of ideas and experiences more than discussions. It widens the perspective and the horizon. We discuss the internal situation in Palestine and our role in society, but action on the ground is not very strong. In Palestine, people talk a lot but do not take action on the ground. (PS-7)

Bob, a 22-year-old student from Byblos, Lebanon, explained,

I participated in Chekka's Lebanese Scouts, and I carried out activities such as helping children with special needs during the holidays and the major events. The scout members and friends,

Figure 14.7 Institutions of Civic Engagement – Security / Insecurity

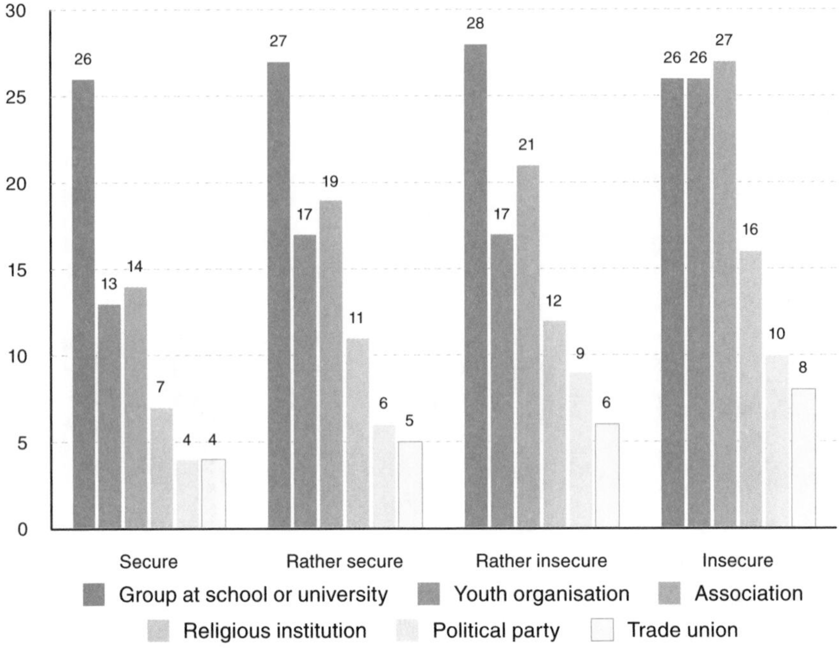

Question 162 *'Where and how do you engage?'*

Basis Interviewees who responded 'Frequently' or 'Occasionally' to Question 161. The categories 'Secure', 'Rather secure', 'Rather insecure', 'Insecure' relate to the young people's self-assessment (Question 10). For calculation see Figure 2.1.

Note Figures are given in percentages. Rounding errors can occur.

we spend our free time in the coffee shops playing billiards in addition to having political debates and participating in festivals. (LB-2)

When looking at CSO membership at a national level, the results reflect the broader legal structures and political circumstances that surround them (Figure 14.6). Engaged youths' membership in school or university groups is highest in Yemen, Palestine, and Tunisia, where these structures are well integrated into the educational system. Youth groups outside educational facilities are most popular among Lebanese youths as well as with Syrian refugees, who lost their former state-run youth organisations at school and university after leaving their home country.

Associations are most active in Lebanon and Tunisia, where NGO laws allow relatively unrestricted activities, as well as among Syrian refugees,

Figure 14.8 **Institutions of Civic Engagement – Optimism / Pessimism**

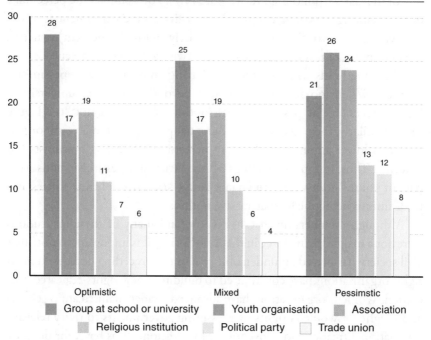

Question 162 *'Where and how do you engage?'*

Basis Interviewees who responded 'Frequently' or 'Occasionally' to Question 161. The categories 'Optimistic' and 'Pessimistic' relate to the young people's assessment (Question 165).

Note Figures are given in percentages. Rounding errors can occur.

providing support for the lack of state services. Only in Egypt are religious institutions more popular than other organisations among engaged youth.

Membership in political parties is generally low across the MENA region, but by comparison slightly higher in Lebanon, where political affiliations are relatively unrestricted and often overlap with the sectarian divisions among the population. Membership is lowest among Syrian refugees. The interest in trade unions is also low among engaged youth, but highest in Tunisia, where trade unions played a significant role in the 2011 revolution and still do in the political transformation process.

What characterises engaged youth who decide to join an institutionalised CSO? What is their outlook on the world around them? Whereas engagement within the framework of a group at school or university, whether voluntary or compulsory, does not point to any specific characteristics among those youth, engagement in other CSOs does reveal a clear tendency: the more insecure the respondents feel, the more likely they are to engage in one of the CSOs from the survey (Figure 14.7). For example, the percentage of those among the young people who perceive their environment as secure who engage in a youth organisation is relatively low (13 percent), whereas the percentage of those feeling insecure is twice as high (26 percent).

The same holds when it comes to having an optimistic or pessimistic attitude. When looking at engagement beyond school and university, a higher percentage of 'pessimists' than 'optimists' are active in CSOs (Figure 14.8). Similarly, the percentage of young people engaged in a youth organisation is lower among optimists (17 percent) that among pessimists (26 percent). Thus, it appears, feelings of insecurity and pessimism constitute part of youths' motivation to engage in a CSO, with political parties and trade unions being the least attractive options.

Although membership in CSOs is low, and many of these institutions were not a major driving force in the Arab Spring, it is important to note that civil society has played an undeniable role in the preceding decades: human rights organisations have contributed to building a new rights-educated generation. Women's organisations have advanced gender-mainstreaming efforts and fought for women's rights by pressuring governments to ratify relevant international treaties and conventions. In addition, CSOs have, for decades, lobbied for better quality and access to education, which in turn has produced a generation of young people with an outlook on life different from those before it (Halaseh 2012). They have thus, directly and indirectly, contributed to the political and social changes the MENA region is currently experiencing. Many young people might not be aware of the importance of these achievements for their lives or, due to their proximity to states' positions – as many governments have subscribed to gender equality and education as well – do not perceive them as civil society achievements. In any case, they apparently do not motivate young people to increase their engagement in CSOs.

Reasons for Non-Engagement

Obviously, not every young person engages beyond pursuing his or her own benefit. But only slightly more than one-third (36 percent) of the surveyed youth said they never engage in pursuit of social or political goals or commit themselves for the benefit of other people. When asked the reasons for their non-engagement, the answers were manifold (Figure 14.9). Some simply stated that there was no civic engagement initiative they could possibly join, because they live in the countryside or some other area with no CSOs or informally organised activities. Among them is Ghizian, a 30-year-old food seller from Tasaltante, rural Marrakech, Morocco:

Figure 14.9 **Reasons for Non-engagement in General**

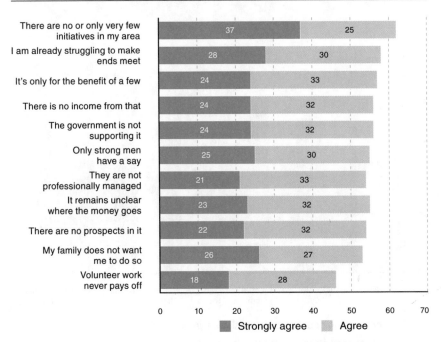

Question 163 *'What are practical reasons for why you are NOT engaging in social projects?'*

Basis Interviewees who responded 'Never' to any option of Question 161 ('I don't know' was not regarded).

Note Figures are given in percentages. Rounding errors can occur.

I did not join any group because people here do not have qualifications. You find here illiterate people, uncultured, and they do not follow what is going on. There are no awareness campaigns; no association comes to talk to people. We are isolated and that's all. There may be an impact in other places, and people talk about this, but here we know only what we see on TV. (MA-9)

Others do not engage because they do not see any prospect in it, because they do not trust the CSOs, such as 24-year-old Ayham, who works as a mechanical engineer in Irbid, Jordan:

I am not a member of any organisations or associations because I don't trust these groups. They rely on brainwashing youth and try to change their way of thinking. They plant ideas in their heads and exploit their needs. (JO-3)

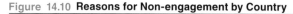

Figure 14.10 Reasons for Non-engagement by Country

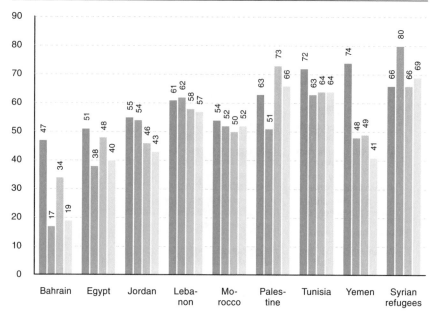

■ There are no or only very few initiatives in my area
■ I am already struggling to make ends meet
■ The government is not supporting it
□ There are no prospects in it

Question 163 *'What are practical reasons for why you are NOT engaging in social projects?'*

Basis Interviewees who responded 'Never' to any option of Question 161 ('I don't know' was not regarded).

Note Figures are given in percentages. Rounding errors can occur.

Others are convinced that the government will not take the concerns of civil society into consideration. One of them is Ranim, a 22-year-old student from Tyre, Lebanon:

Right now my only concern is to finish my education. I do not think of anything else, and I have never joined groups or organisations. In other countries, similar associations and organisations help people to express their opinion, and they succeed. But in our country the government does not take our opinion into consideration, and most of the time it ignores it. (LB-9)

Also among those forgoing civil engagement are those who are struggling to make ends meet and therefore do not have the capacity to engage as they go about their work to provide for the family. This is the case for many young people living through crises caused by war. Marwan, a 31-year-old married taxi driver in Taiz, Yemen, remarked,

> I have not joined any group so far in spite of many invitations from different organisations. I rejected all of them . . . All I care about is my family – how I can provide food for them and good living conditions, especially when I see beggars and homeless in the streets. All I want is to protect my family with all my might. (YE-10)

Ahmad, a 22-year-old single construction worker and Syrian refugee in Beirut, Lebanon, said,

> The situation has changed a lot and the events are escalating. We are now forced to work more than one shift in order to support our families during this miserable and expensive way of life. I left school, and I am no longer able to see my friends frequently. I don't have enough time to join any movements or organisations because of the current circumstances (LB/SY-2).

When reasons for non-engagement on a national level are analysed, the answers are almost as equally distributed as in the regional sample, with few exceptions (Figure 14.10). Young people in Yemen and Bahrain cite the absence or scarcity of initiatives near their place of residence as their reason. The answer 'I am already struggling to make ends meet' is, not surprisingly, the reason mentioned most often by Syrian refugees. In Palestine, youths cite the lack of government support as important in their refraining from civic engagement. NGO laws are strict there, as they are in Bahrain and Egypt, where restrictions on CSOs dramatically increased after the Arab Spring.

Conclusion

This survey reveals an overall openness to civic engagement among young people in the MENA region, with about two-thirds of the interviewees stating that they engage for social or political goals or volunteer for the benefit of others. Issues such as helping poor and vulnerable people and protecting the environment were most popular, followed by a variety of volunteer activities in domains that can broadly be labelled charitable or apolitical. Engaging for social and political change came in last among civic activities given the difficult circumstances for politically motivated civic engagement in most of the countries under study. This comes as no surprise. Where civic engagement is under tight control, engaging for a cause is already a political act in itself.

While young people are in general willing to engage in certain causes, they are more reluctant to do so within an institutionalised framework. Among those who do engage, only one-third do so through a CSO. This tendency becomes even more pronounced when considering the respondents' social standing: Young people belonging to a high stratum of society are more likely to engage on a voluntary basis, but less likely to become a member of a formal CSO, while the opposite holds true for young people from lower social strata. The latter are also more likely to feel insecure and pessimistic.

In this, today's young people in the MENA region certainly differ from previous generations. For the older generations, civic engagement within the framework of a formal CSO, such as a trade union or a political party, was part of the anti-colonial struggle. At that time, these organisations were run by upper-class residents of larger cities. With the political and social changes in the region, values and aims of young people have changed as well. In addition, with authoritarian regimes in the MENA region maintaining a firm grip on CSOs and with the compromises the latter accepted, these institutions obviously lost much of their attractiveness to young people wanting to engage in certain causes.

To understand young people's role in civic engagement, it is important to broaden the definition of civil society by recognising that it is not solely about formal hierarchical structures and organisations. Civil society activism is more than non-governmental organisations or CSOs. Youths in authoritarian and closed systems find ways to mobilise on their own to become involved in social or political issues. While classic civil society activism can easily be studied and supported, it will not bring about positive change by itself. More promising might be to look at civil society using the notion of 'activated or activist citizenship', which goes beyond the examination of civic engagement as the product of formal organisations and structures (see Durac and Cavatorta 2015: 178ff.).

On a practical level, in order to bridge this gap between the willingness of young people to engage and their reluctance to commit to an organisation, national CSOs should consider how to reach out and cooperate with those who are active in the informal space of civic society. The same holds for Western strategies for civil society support, typically directed towards formal CSOs. Where the local legislative framework permits, it is certainly worth trying to support popular, widespread, and established social currents. Such an approach would not only allow the support to reach a larger and more representative part of society and thus put the respective project on safer ground; it would also enable and encourage the participation of young people who are, as has been shown, more than willing to engage for a variety of causes, but very often lack access or are not convinced of the idea of membership in the available civil society organisations.

PART IV

COMPARING YOUTH

15

The FES MENA Youth Study and the German Shell Youth Study

Mathias Albert & Jörg Gertel

THE PRESENT STUDY ASCERTAINS the living situation and attitudes of young people in the MENA region. It provides a rich reservoir of data and paints a nuanced picture of the region's young generation. Although it is not easy to compare situations and attitudes between countries, much less across a region, or among countries within a region and others outside of it, it is nonetheless a comparison worth examining. A comparison of the present results and design aspects with those from the German Shell Youth Study allows for reflection on these projects individually, as well as in respect to each other.[1] Such an exercise might help, for example, to gain more insights from certain data. What does it mean, for example, if 25 percent of young people in one country say they are interested in politics? Is that a lot or a little? It pays to assess and compare such numbers not only intra-regionally, but also in light of results from other areas. Direct comparisons, where warranted and methodologically sound, could also be instructive as well. What does it mean, for example, that levels of optimism among young people in many Arab countries are consistently higher than among young people in Germany, when the latter have fewer problems regarding their future in economic terms? Comparing the picture of a region (i.e. the MENA region) with that of a single country (i.e. Germany) is not a futile exercise of comparing entities of different geographical and political orders. Rather, it helps to shed additional light on differences within the MENA region, as it highlights a range of issues where differences between some

---

1. The Shell Youth Survey (*Shell Jugendstudie*) has been commissioned by the German subsidiary of the oil and gas company Shell. It is an independent, comprehensive study of the living situations and attitudes of young people in Germany. The latest survey was published as *Jugend 2015: 17. Shell Jugendstudie* (Shell 2015).

Table 15.1 Germany and Arab Countries: Family

	Germany	Bahrein	Tunisia	Jordan
Persons per household				
One	**13**	1	1	1
Two	**24**	3	3	7
Three to five	60	42	63	29
Six and more	4	54	33	63
Housing situation				
With parents	60	92	90	86
With partner	16	7	6	12
Alone	**13**	1	1	1
Shared apartment with friends	**9**	0	1	0
Importance of a family				
One needs a family	62	81	**96**	92
One can live alone	**22**	10	3	7
Definitely happier alone	1	**4**	1	0
Don't know	14	6	1	1
Children				
One needs own children	41	58	82	87
One can live happily without children	**36**	27	13	8
One is definitely happier without children	**4**	**4**	1	1
Not sure	**18**	12	4	4
Children's education				
In exactly the same way	14	21	46	45
About the same	**59**	38	24	24
Differently	19	**39**	23	21
In a very different way	6	2	7	**10**
Relations between generations:				
Now: In harmony	54	**70**	28	45
Future: Deterioration	**34**	11	10	12

Questions 3, 15, 16, 133, 138, 139, 142, 143.

countries in the region are in fact more pronounced than between some individual Arab countries and Germany.

We deliberately opted for a comparative analysis with the German Shell Youth Study. Since starting in 1953 it has inspired a range of youth surveys in a number of countries, not least because of its comprehensiveness but also because of the intensity of public debate it evokes. More narrowly, some aspects and questions used in the Shell survey have found

Lebanon	Palestine	Egypt	Morocco	Yemen	Syrian Ref.[a]
1	0	1	1	1	5
1	5	3	1	2	9
71	30	**80**	63	16	41
27	65	16	35	**81**	45
93	85	91	**93**	80	54
5	14	8	5	19	**30**
1	0	1	1	1	5
0	0	0	1	0	4
90	93	89	93	90	95
5	4	6	7	6	2
1	1	1	0	2	2
4	2	3	0	2	2
84	89	83	86	88	**93**
7	4	8	11	8	4
1	1	1	1	1	1
8	6	8	2	3	3
38	37	30	27	35	**55**
39	35	28	48	26	32
20	22	34	20	30	10
3	7	9	5	8	3
39	45	39	65	33	50
12	15	6	8	9	12

Note Figures are given in percentages. Rounding errors can occur. | The data cover the age group of 16 to 25 years. Bold figures represent the highest score per row. [a] Syrian Refugees in Lebanon.

their way into the MENA survey, thus providing a sound basis for comparison. This chapter briefly outlines similarities and differences between the two surveys (referring particularly to the latest, the 2015 German Shell Youth Study), and continues to discuss their insights, focussing on five themes: characteristics of 'youth'; families and generations; economic situations; politics and the state; and pessimism or confidence.

Table 15.2 German and Arab Youths: Ideas and Visions About Personal Life

	Arab countries (Rank)	Germany (Rank)	Arab countries (%)	Germany: muslims (%)	Germany: total (%)
Believing in God	1	18	65	46	10
Respecting law and order	2	5	56	52	31
Having a partner whom I can trust	3	1	54	69	66
Achieving a high standard of living	4	17	51	28	12
Engaging in a good family life	5	3	49	48	41
Aiming for more security	5	12	49	28	20
Living a consciously healthy life	7	11	46	28	21
Having good friends who appreciate and accept me	8	1	44	66	66
Being proud of the history of my country	8	20	44	5	6
Acting always in an environmentally conscious way	10	14	42	17	15
Being diligent, hardworking, and ambitious	10	8	42	37	26
Enjoying life as much as possible	10	6	42	42	30
Being financially independent from others	10		42		
Being independent from others		6		38	30
Being connected to others	14	10	39	27	22
Developing my imagination and creativity	15	8	35	25	26
Tolerating opinions that I do not agree with	16	15	30	21	13
Acting independently of the advice of others	17		29		
Living and acting autonomously		4		40	36
Supporting socially excluded and marginalised people	18	15	24	21	13
Allowing my decisions to be guided by my emotions	19	13	25	24	16
Doing what others do	20	23	15	11	2
Having power and exerting influence	20	22	15	14	4
Pursuing my own agenda, even if against the interest of others	22	19	12	17	9
Being politically active	23	21	10	8	5

Question 131 *'As individuals, we have ideas and visions about our personal life, our attitudes, and behaviour. If you reflect about possible achievements in your life, how important are the following points for you, on a scale from 1 = absolutely unimportant to 10 = absolutely important?'* Arab countries = 'Absolutely important' / Germany = 'Extremely important'.

Note The data cover the age group from 16 to 25 years. Rounding errors can occur. Not all of the questions mentioned relate to the German or the Arab questionnaire in the same way. Two pairs of almost similar questions are represented in italics in the table above. The second of each pair is the German version. Also, the options for answering in the two questionnaires differ. The German respondents were offered seven possible answers. The lowest value (1) stands for 'Not important', and the highest value (7) stands for 'Extremely important'. Respondents in the countries of the MENA region, on the other hand, had to choose between ten variants, with the lowest value (1) standing for 'Absolutely unimportant', and the highest value (10) standing for 'Absolutely important'. Accordingly, no direct comparison of the assessments can be made. However, given that the respondent's maximum differentiation opportunity is already achieved with seven options on one scale, and given that the linguistic connotations of the two benchmarks in both questionnaires are comparable ('Absolutely important' and 'Extremely important'), a comparison by ranking the items/response options based on the frequency of the corresponding scale values of 10 or 7 seems possible and useful.

Conceptual Basis

The present study uses a range of instruments and a mix of quantitative and qualitative methods inspired by, and akin to, the Shell youth survey. The latter, due to its long tradition, has recorded and analysed changes over time, whereas the MENA study is a first-time survey, making its results a snapshot of the present. It shares some topics with the German study (e.g. attitudes towards politics, optimism and pessimism about the future), but it also has its own independent structure and includes sections specific to the MENA region (e.g. attitudes towards the Arab Spring). The basic study designs are, however, similar enough that a comparative analysis seems to be warranted and promising in terms of generating knowledge that allows contextualising the results of each study in light of the other. The 2015 Shell survey captures insights from 2,558 young people aged 12–25, based on face-to-face interviews conducted as computer-assisted personal interviewing (CAPI). Fieldwork and interviews took place in early 2015. The FES survey in contrast involved 9,000 young people, aged 16–30, who were interviewed in early summer 2016 (Appendix 1: Methodology). In order to allow comparison of the two samples, the age structure was adjusted and restricted to youths aged 16–25. The weighted sub-samples thus capture 1,893 young Germans and 6,133 young people from the MENA region. Subsequently, the results here are slightly different from those published in the Shell study and the findings presented in the previous chapters.

Who Are the 'Youth'

'Youth' may be comprehended differently in various regions of the world. Its common denominator everywhere, however, is that it marks the life span between childhood on one side and adulthood on the other. Although these phases in themselves are not easy to identify in substantive terms, the notion of 'adolescence' emphasises that youth is often thought of in processual terms, as the journey towards becoming an adult. While the transitions from childhood to adolescence and from adolescence to adulthood in many cases are still subject to traditional and religious rites of passages, in modern societies the transition from youth to adulthood is marked by the combination of concrete steps, such as exiting the educational system, entering the labour market, establishing a relationship with a life partner, and starting a family.

Distinctions between European and post-colonial countries may be traced back to a different sequence or composition of these steps, and to the fact that some steps may temporally be delayed and pulled away from each other in the life course of young people; single periods are increasingly experienced in isolation from each other, such as exiting the education system (especially if concerning degrees in higher education), the entry into the labour market, and developing a solid partnership. Starting a family of one's own in industrialised societies now often drags on well beyond the age of 30. These transition points between adolescence and adulthood are increasingly blurred: growing numbers of young people do not accomplish this transition in all of its steps (e.g. one-person households are on the rise; cf. Table 15.1), while youthfulness simultaneously has manifested itself as an ideal in everyday culture to be aspired to even in older age. Although the findings might be similar for Germany and the Arab countries in terms of the transition to adulthood occurring later in life, there seems to be one marked difference: whereas in Germany the transition is blurred, in MENA countries it has been deferred.[1] In the case of Germany, the transition might occur later in life than it previously did, but a major reason for this is the increasing diversity in the form and timing of the transition. In MENA countries, however, there has been no such increase in variety. To the contrary, because of difficult economic situations resulting in dreary prospects for employment, and subsequently to difficulties in establishing a family, young people often find themselves to be adults-in-waiting. We designate their situation as a form of 'contained youth' (cf. Chapter 7). That is, these young adults not only find themselves in a state of waiting (or 'waithood'), they are at the same time more dependent on their parents and families than ever before and find it increasingly difficult to emancipate themselves not only economically, but also emotionally and in terms of values.

A closer look at values reveals a rather complementary structure of different groups of youth (see Table 15.2). For MENA youth, belief in God is by far the most important aspect and potential achievement of one's personal

---

1. The notion of a deferred adolescence is not to hide the fact that for a significant number of youth in the MENA region, particularly young women, adolescence does not take place at all. Rather, it is 'skipped' because of direct active involvement in managing household affairs after the end of childhood.

life. For a large majority, faith is however considered to be a private matter.[1] In terms of importance, belief in God is followed by a desire for an absence of violence and for economic security. The latter are expressed in the importance of respecting law and order, in achieving a high standard of living, and in striving for more security. The social dimension of security is crucial as well, such as having a trusted partner, a good family life, and good friends (cf. Chapter 3). For German youth, social aspects are of most importance, that is having a trusted partner, good friends, and a good family life. These aspects are followed by the ambition to take responsibility for one's own life and actions and to live an independent life. Doing what others do is, thus, of least importance. This, combined with the personal goals of being diligent and hard working on the one hand, and developing one's imagination and creativity on the other, allows for less reliance on family ties, creates room for personal experiences, and helps preparing for the next step – entering the competitive labour market. The values held by adolescent German Muslims are of note in that it reveals that they oscillate between those of MENA and German youth. They display, for example, high accordance with other German youth in the most important, top-ranking aspects of having a trusted partner and good friends. They also bridge positions, meaning they fall somewhere in the middle, between MENA youth and non-Muslim Germans on the importance of achieving a high standard of living and tolerating the opinions of others. In turn, belief in God and respecting law and order are as important for German Muslims as for young people in the Arab world.

Family and Generations

The family structures of Germany and the MENA countries are quite different. Among German youth, more than one-third lives in one- and two-person households, while such small households are an exception in the MENA countries (see Table 15.1). This relates directly to the housing situation. With the exception of Syrian refugees, more than 80 percent of MENA youth live with their parents, and almost no one lives alone or in a shared-housing arrangement. The role of the family obviously differs among societies, while the dramatic impact of recent transformations further complicates the situation. The countries of the MENA region, particularly those

---

1. Being religious does not necessarily correlate with being less tolerant. Thus, while young people in Germany are far less religious than young people in the MENA countries, a considerably smaller group of young Germans emphasises that it is absolutely important to 'tolerate opinions that they do not agree with' (see Table 15.2).

Table 15.3 Germany and Arab Countries: Economy and Social Strata

	Germany	Bahrein	Tunisia	Jordan	
Economic situation					
Very good	11	**25**	4	9	
Rather good	69	67	62	63	
Rather bad	16	6	25	22	
Very bad	4	2	9	6	
Social strata					
Lowest stratum	11	0	30	20	
Lower-middle stratum	22	2	**29**	23	
Middle stratum	30	13	25	26	
Higher-middle stratum	25	**36**	14	22	
Highest stratum	12	**50**	3	10	
Respondent employed: 'Yes'	**33**	**8**	**8**	**11**	
Mode of employment		Ø Arab countries			
State Employee	3	**5**			
Employee (with insurance)	**70**	10			
Worker (continuous employment)	**21**	15			
Family Business	0	**5**			
Self-employed with higher education	0	**3**			
Self-employed: Trade etc	3	**14**			
Self-employed: Agriculture	0	**5**			
Day labourer	/	**37**			
Imagining an ideal workplace: 'Very important'					
A secure job	69	51	**84**	61	
Earning a high income	32	58	**78**	60	
Options to upgrade my position	38	45	**74**	58	
Possibility of doing something that makes sense to me	52	45	68	52	
Feeling of achieving something	24	37	65	56	
Feeling of being accepted	45	30	**60**	53	
Doing something useful for society	46	37	**63**	46	
Possibility of implementing own ideas	58	41	59	51	
A job that allows for enough leisure time	49	44	49	45	
Having a lot of contacts with other people	32	25	53	52	
Possibility to support others	29	37	49	48	
Confidence about implementing job aspirations 'Totally confident'/'Very confident'	18/19	34	25	32	

Questions 3, 25, 62, 65, 66, 67, 68, 72, 82, 83, Strata index.

Lebanon	Palestine	Egypt	Morocco	Yemen	Syrian Ref.
8	9	10	6	3	0
63	51	62	**76**	32	11
25	27	23	16	38	**44**
4	13	5	3	27	**45**
9	20	26	50	56	**94**
18	28	**29**	23	23	5
36	27	25	12	15	1
29	17	13	12	5	0
8	7	8	3	1	0
21	**17**	**13**	**9**	**10**	**41**
		Ø Arab countries			
72	67	50	42	73	58
75	59	54	48	65	61
72	52	37	37	64	55
69	51	36	42	56	49
68	50	35	35	56	47
60	48	34	37	53	48
62	45	32	33	53	46
69	49	32	34	54	45
60	38	32	28	44	45
60	39	29	35	51	43
60	42	35	36	52	48
32	22	11	11	27	10

Note Figures are given in percentages. Rounding errors can occur. ø = average. | The data cover the age group from 16 to 25 years. Bold figures represent the highest score per row.

Economic situation (Question 62) *'How do you assess your personal economic situation today?'* In order to be able to compare this question with the sample from Germany, we ignored those answers in the German sample that answered the question with 'don't know' (742 cases, 39 percent), and we calculated the distribution on a total of 1,135 cases (16 cases without response).

Social strata For this table, the calculation of the Strata Index for the countries of the Mena region has been adapted to the Shell Youth Study (Shell 2015, p. 430). For the index calculation a maximum of 14 points can be achieved: 3–6 points = 'Lowest stratum'; 7–8 points = 'Lower-middle stratum'; 9–10 points = 'Middle stratum'; 11–12 points = 'Higher-middle stratum'; 13–14 points = 'Highest stratum'. The calculation of index points rests on four pillars, which are almost identical for the two studies: (1) Father's education (up to 6 points); (2) personal economic situation (up to 3 points; for calculating the Strata Index all other chapters of this study used the assessment about the economic situation of the family; here, the assessment of the personal economic situation was applied); (3) home ownership (up to 2 points); (4) wealth ranking (up to 3 points). The Shell Youth Study relates the wealth ranking to personal estimation about the number of books available in the household, and awards a maximum of 3 points for 'very many' and 0 points for 'just a few' books. In contrast, the present study applies three other indicators: internet access, (1 point), air conditioning (2 points), own car (3 points). A comparison is therefore possible, but there are deviations in 3 of the 14 points because they have been adjusted to a different context.

Respondent employed This statement refers to the employment status: 'Working' in the Arab countries (n=984); 'Erwerbstätig' in Germany (n=620) (see Chapter 7).

Mode of employment (Question 72) The categories 'Day labourer' and 'Self-employed: Service sector' do not exist in the sample of the Shell Youth Study. The number of cases from the Arab countries is too small to generate sensible mean values for the individual employment categories.

Imagining an ideal workplace (Question 82) *'How should an employment situation and your job be in order for you to be satisfied?'* We consider the indication 'Very important'.

Confidence about implementing job aspirations (Question 83) *'How confident are you about the possibility of realising your wishes concerning your job?'* The statement 'Totally confident', the highest value, was included in the calculation. The Shell Youth Study uses four predefined response options. We also show the highest value here 'Very confident'. The first number in the Germany column stands for pupils, apprentices and university students. The second number represents all others.

lacking oil wealth, have to struggle with severe economic difficulties. Public welfare systems have been depleted over the course of decades by policies of economic restructuring and the privatisation of almost everything. During crises and in contexts of widespread uncertainty, the family – traditionally a crucial institution in Arab societies – has remained trusted, and is relied upon more than ever as the single institution that young people overwhelmingly trust, offering them security and assistance in everyday struggles as well as in emergencies.

Ninety percent of young Arabs, with the exception of Bahrainis, believe that one needs a family to live a happy life (see Table 15.1). In Germany, this figure does not rise to two-thirds of respondents. More than 20 percent of German youths believe that one can live alone and be happy. A considerable number of them are also uncertain as to whether starting a family or having children are requirements for happiness. In this respect, the role of children for living a happy life is less pronounced among more young Germans than their peers in Arab countries. Bahrainis, with high levels of income, education, and urbanisation, hold a position in between. To get a sense of the relationship between generations, an important indicator can be derived from asking whether young people would raise their children the same way they were raised by their own parents. In Germany and the Arab countries, the majority of young people would raise their children in about the same way or exactly the same way they were raised. The picture differs somewhat in Bahrain, Egypt, and Yemen, where about 40 percent disagree and would raise their children somewhat differently or completely differently from their parents. Nevertheless, these findings reinforce the special role of the family in Arab societies as ascribed by the recent generation of young people. Generational perspectives beyond the family are viewed more critically. Relations between the older and the younger generations are perceived as in a state of tension. Generational relations that are more frequently in harmony are only found in Bahrain, Morocco, Germany, and among Syrian refugees. About one-third of young Germans are however sceptical about inter-generational relations, feeling certain that they will deteriorate in the future.

Economic Situations

At first glance, young people generally assess their economic situation as positive, connoting a high degree of satisfaction. About two-thirds in Germany and in the Arab countries describe their personal financial situation as rather good (Table 15.3). The two exceptions are Syrian refugees in Lebanon and Yemenis. Their countries are both experiencing on-going warfare with its severe human and economic impacts. Moreover, young people's judgement of their economic situation is often based on a rather subjective reasoning, particularly shaped by the sheltered situations of living together with their parents and depending on their income. Young adults who are already married assess their economic situation completely differently, that is predominately as rather bad or very bad (see Chapter 7). A closer look reveals the profound socio-economic stratifications within Germany and the Arab countries. In Germany, the percentage of people occupying the highest and lowest strata is relatively small, as most people belong to the middle strata. In contrast, the situation in the Arab world is characterised by polarisation; the extremes being the case of Bahrain – where half of families belong to the highest stratum and few belong to the lowest stratum – versus

Table 15.4 Germany and Arab Countries: Politics and Future

	Germany	Bahrein	Tunisia	Jordan	
Interest in politics					
Very interested	8	1	3	5	
Interested	**39**	6	6	8	
A little interested	**38**	21	25	15	
Not interested	15	72	67	72	
Do you inform yourself about politics? 'Yes'	**42**	10	20	8	
Using the internet? 'Yes'	92	**100**	90	93	
(hours/day)[a]	3[a]	**9**	6	4	
Personal future					
Rather pessimistically	4	8	8	8	
Rather optimistically	61	36	71	**78**	
Mixed, both ways	**35**	57	22	14	
Society's future					
Rather pessimistically	44	29	29	17	
Rather optimistically	51	71	71	83	

Questions 3, 149, 153, 156, 157, 165, 166.

Note Figures are given in percentages. Rounding errors can occur. | The data cover the age group from 16 to 25 years. Bold figures represent the highest score per row.
[a] When calculating the duration of surfing the internet the figures are not unproblematically ready for comparison: For Arab countries, assessments are rather over-represented, as the daily time spent on

the cases of Morocco, Yemen, and the Syrian refugees, among whom half to almost all families belong to the lowest social stratum, and almost no one belongs to the highest group. In Tunisia, Jordan, Palestine, and Egypt, the size of the lowest stratum is double that in Germany. Only Lebanon exhibits distributions similar to Germany.

The occupational and employment status of young people reinforces the impression of Lebanon being a MENA outlier in terms of economy. While in Germany one-third of young people aged 16–25 work, among the Arab countries only Lebanon comes close to this figure, with slightly over 20 percent of young people being employed. In all other countries the share of young people working is well below that level. Something of an exception in this regard are the Syrian refugees, where young people are heavily dependent on their own work to make a living. Moreover, the structures of employment in Germany and the MENA countries are also completely

Lebanon	Palestine	Egypt	Morocco	Yemen	Syrian Ref.
5	3	2	4	**9**	0
10	13	19	24	20	3
20	27	**38**	28	32	10
65	57	40	45	38	**87**
20	20	12	16	32	15
96	72	79	76	31	52
7	4	6	4	3	3
17	11	8	8	10	**36**
72	60	68	**78**	76	49
11	29	24	14	15	15
43	45	19	16	22	**46**
57	55	81	**84**	78	54

internet was asked for, while for Germany, the assessment is rather under-represented, as the weekly use was inquired.

When asked about the future of society, about 6 percent did not answer this question in the German sample.

different: almost all of the Germans active in the labour market are employees or workers with guaranteed monthly salaries that do not fluctuate and whose benefits include payment in case of sickness. Only about one-third of youth in Arab countries have similar working conditions. The majority are self-employed in trades, in the service sector, or in agriculture or work as day labourers, in other words, earning money under often insecure conditions. Young Germans at an earlier stage are thus more frequently in a position to live independently of their families, enabled by economic integration via institutionalised paths bridging national education systems and globalising labour markets.

For German and MENA youth, the features of an imagined ideal employment situation are however quite similar. Having a 'secure job' ranks highest in terms of a satisfying employment situation among both groups (see Table 15.3). In the MENA region, earning a high income is second, and the option to upgrade one's position is found to also be important for most Arab youths. In general the level of ambition concerning the feeling of achieving something is higher among young people in the MENA region than among young people in Germany, while the latter more frequently identify being able to implement one's own ideas and do something that 'makes sense' as being important. When asked about degrees of confidence in realising their desires pertaining to a job, depending on the country between 10 percent and one-third of the young people claim they were very or totally confident in this respect. The more sceptical groups live in Egypt and Morocco, and, as one might expect, the Syrian refugees are also rather sceptical. Structural forces, such as the position of one's family within society, play a role in this respect. In Arab countries only 14 percent of the lowest stratum are 'totally confident', whereas 45 percent of the highest stratum are. In Germany this applies to 7 percent of the lowest and to 27 percent of highest stratum, indicating more equal access to the labour market.

Politics and the State

Young people in Germany and in the MENA region reveal marked differences in their interest in politics (Table 15.4). In Germany, almost one-half of young people claim they are interested or very interested in politics, while only about one-sixth say the same in the MENA region. While there are crucial disparities between individual Arab states (see Chapter 12), interest does not exceed 30 percent in any of them. With the exceptions of Egypt, Morocco, and Yemen, about two-thirds of young people decisively indicated that they have no interest in politics. A complex setting of individual factors is responsible for these differences, but generally speaking the problematic economic situation in Arab countries and increasing insecurity because of terror attacks and armed conflicts since 2010–11 have contributed to an erosion of trust in politics and politicians. This is also reflected in young people having very low confidence in parliaments.[1] Despite the above views, the level of trust is relatively high in regard to state institutions seen, by and large, as independent of party bickering, such as the legal system and the military. In many MENA countries, young people on a rather broad scale actually favour an increased role for the state in organising daily affairs and providing social security (see Chapter 12). This suggests a shared relative distrust in party politics that is not mirrored in a distrust of the state itself

---

1. Young people, who in principle would otherwise be willing to engage in politics, frequently mention this low level of trust, combined with experiences of repression and limitations on freedom of expression, as an obstacle to political involvement.

as long as it is seen to play the role of an honest broker and organiser of societal affairs.

Since the events of 2010–11 internet use and politics in the MENA region seem to have become enmeshed. Internet use, however, varies from country to country. Internet access, for example, ranges from almost complete access for young people in Bahrain, to about only one-third for young people in Yemen. Moreover, the intensity correlates with social status. In the MENA region, youth in the lowest stratum use the internet for about four hours a day, whereas those in the highest stratum have an average use of seven hours per day. Young Germans from the lowest stratum in contrast use the internet for about two hours a day, while those from the highest stratum access it for about three hours daily. The intensity of internet use does however not correlate with interest in politics. Social media use in Arab countries instead increasingly serves for private communication and to sustain existing social networks (see Chapter 11).

Pessimism or Confidence?

One could claim confidence to be the privilege of youth. After all, young people have their lives ahead of them. Of course, not every society, let alone every individual's personal situation, offers the same opportunities in life. In many cases, however, this does not seem to have an effect on a person's degree of optimism. Thus, for example, in the case of Germany, in 2015 about 61 percent of young women and men said they were 'rather optimistic' regarding their own future, up from only 50 percent in 2006. While some viewed their future as mixed, sometimes optimistically and sometimes pessimistically, in 2015 only 4 percent took a decidedly negative view (down from 10 percent in 2006). Of importance, the degree of optimism strongly correlates with social status. Thus, while almost three-quarters of young people from the highest social stratum had a rather optimistic view of their future, the same held true for only one-third of those from the lowest social stratum. While, for technical reasons, the absolute numbers between the Shell and MENA studies cannot be compared, it is possible to assess relative levels of optimism in this respect. In general, in regard to their own future and personal lives, young people across the MENA region have an equally pronounced optimism, with almost two-thirds saying they are rather optimistic. The main difference compared to the German case is the independence of this optimism from social status, if not to say the slightly negative correlation. In the lowest stratum about 60 percent are rather optimistic while in the highest stratum 'only' 53 percent have a rather optimistic view of their own future and personal life. The differences among individual Arab countries are more pronounced than between different strata of the entire MENA region. Unsurprisingly, Syrian refugees living in Lebanon are less optimistic than others, but young people in Bahrain, a wealthy country, are even less optimistic and frequently have mixed feelings about their future. Perhaps they feel they have something to lose. Another remarkable difference between young people in Germany and in the MENA region pertains to the relative level of assessment of the future of their societies. In the case of Germany, the number of those with an optimistic view about their society's future has increased over recent years, from 41 percent in 2006, to more than 44 percent in 2010, to 51 percent in 2015. Nonetheless, the level of optimism over the years has remained well below the degree of optimism about their personal future.[1] This contrasts with the MENA region, where almost 70 percent of young people have an optimistic view of their society's future, a figure that exceeds the level of how young people assess their own future.

Conclusion

Young people are part of the societies in which they live. It therefore should come as little surprise that in many respects attitudes and life situations differ between the young women and men in the Arab countries studied here and those in Germany. The comparisons in this chapter also show, however, that there is a range of characteristics and attributes that in the end are not so different as well. In the context of the present study, the most important one is that young people in Germany and the MENA countries highly value security. This pertains in particular to security in regard to their future personal plans, that is, the security associated with entering the job market, such as finding a good position with secure terms of employment and social security. It is in this realm that young people in the MENA states face structural disadvantages. Amidst political and economic uncertainty, and due to the lack of institutionalised career options, they have become a contained youth, more than ever dependent on their families to provide security. It remains an open question as to what extent unemployment,

---

1. Of note, the question about youths' personal future offers three answering options ('rather pessimistic', 'rather optimistic', 'so-so'), while the question about the future of their society offers only two options ('rather pessimistic' and 'rather optimistic'). As a consequence, these percentages cannot easily be compared, as it is more likely to achieve high numbers concerning the future of society. E.g. concerning personal futures, about 40% opted in 2006 for 'so-so', while 35% did so in 2015).

non-competitiveness, and precarity result from a globalising labour market that produces too few qualified jobs, and to what extent they are consequences of young people's thorough entanglement and dependence on their families, turning adolescence into a trap that precludes timely experiences of self-responsibility and empowerment.

In terms of comparing the actual MENA survey and the Shell survey, it is safe to say that despite many differences in the details, the biggest difference between them is rooted in Shell's long tradition. Repeatedly conducting and publishing a comprehensive survey over a long period of time not only has the scientific advantages of monitoring changes over time, rather than offering snapshots of the situation at a given moment, but it also allows for a refinement of methodological tools. In addition, it has the potential to increase the impact of the survey in public debates, raising awareness about the situation of young people and keeping the issue on the agenda. It is in this sense that one hopes the present survey is the first in a long line of successors.

APPENDICES

Appendix I: Methodology

Thorsten Spengler, Helmut Dietrich,
David Kreuer, & Jörg Gertel

Survey Objective

Coping with Uncertainty: Youth in the Middle East and North Africa is the result of an outstanding joint effort by the Friedrich-Ebert-Stiftung (FES), the University of Leipzig, Kantar Public (formerly TNS Infratest Politikforschung), and TNS Maroc and several other research centres and polling institutes from the Middle East and North Africa (MENA). Ultimately, twenty-one entities and fifty-six co-organisers took part in this cooperative survey, combining their expertise in providing technical, organisational, and content-related know-how. While the Scientific Advisory Board was responsible for scientific guidance (see the preface), the project leader, based in Rabat, Morocco, managed and coordinated the field survey.

The primary objective of the survey was to better understand the situation of young people in the MENA region six years after the onset of the Arab Spring. Specifically, the study focuses on the uncertainties and insecurities that have since unfolded there. One key question drove the research methodology: How to produce scientifically validated information about young people in Arab countries whose everyday situations have, in many respects, only been poorly explored?

Based on the possibilities of being able to conduct on-site field research and extensive face-to-face interviews, eight countries were selected – Bahrain, Egypt, Jordan, Lebanon, Morocco, Palestine, Tunisia, and Yemen – in addition to Syrian refugees living in Lebanon, for a total of nine survey groups. During summer 2016, about 450 trained individuals conducted hour-long interviews with more than 9,000 young people. A total of 1,000 interviews (net) was targeted for each country or survey group. This sample size is considered sufficient to generate an adequate representation of the target group as well as of socio-demographic and regional subgroups (e.g. age, gender, level of education). The universe of the survey comprises population aged 16–30 (in Jordan aged 18–30) who are residents in private households. With the exception of the Syrian refugees in Lebanon, only nationals of the respective countries were interviewed.

The preferred survey method was face-to-face interviews conducted with computer-aided personal interviewing (CAPI) technology.[1] Since not all participating institutions were able to fulfil the technical requirements for a CAPI

Table A.1 **Survey Groups and Methods**

Country / Survey group	Survey method
Egypt	CAPI
Bahrein	PAPI
Yemen	CAPI
Jordan	CAPI
Lebanon	PAPI + CAPI
Morocco	CAPI
Palestine	PAPI
Syrian Refugees in Lebanon	PAPI + CATI
Tunisia	PAPI

survey, face-to-face surveys also consisted of paper and pencil interviewing (PAPI). In the case of the Syrian refugees, some computer-aided telephone interviewing (CATI) was carried out in addition to PAPI. Table A.1 provides an overview of the survey methods used for the different survey groups.

Sampling

An important quality aspect for a survey is the sampling method and the sample's representativeness. The strength of the sampling method depends on the extent to which the sample is representative of the population, or in other words, by how similar the sample and the population of interest are in all relevant aspects. The major goals of the survey in the MENA region were to ensure the comparability of the different national samplings and that each of the samplings reflected the country's composition with respect to the survey universe as accurately as possible.

For reasons of feasibility, a nationwide quota sampling method was chosen. Truly random sampling was not possible for practical, legal, and budgetary reasons. Total population, population distribution, and addresses were not known or accessible to the public in every country. Thus, detailed

---

1. This interview method guarantees a high quality of data collection and allows for a complex questionnaire structure. Inconsistent or inadmissible responses by the interviewees or data entries by the interviewers can easily be detected and avoided by the software via immediate checks. This also ensures that the interviewer does not miss any questions or ask a wrong question.

Table A.2 Regions and Sampling Points

Country / Survey group	Survey areas and regions taken into account for sampling and weighting	Number of sampling points
Egypt	Cairo, Giza, Helwan, Asyut, Minya, Beni Suef, Qalyubia, Gharbia (Tanta, Mahalla), Dakahlia, Alexandria.	46
Bahrain	Muharraq, Manama (capital), Al-Tijari (Manama commercial area), Riffa (south).	13
Yemen	Ibb, Abyan, Sana'a City, Sana'a, Al-Bayda, Taiz, Al-Jawf, Hajjah, Al-Hudaydah, Hadramaut, Dhamar, Shabwah, Aden, Lahij, Ma'rib, 'Amran, Dhale, Raymah, Al-Mahwit. (Al-Mahrah, Sa'ada, and parts of other northern and southern governorates were excluded).	103
Jordan	Irbid, Ajloun, Jerash, Mafraq, Balqa, Madaba, Amman, Zarqa, Karak, Tafila, Ma'an, Aqaba.	100
Lebanon	Beirut, Beqaa, Mount Lebanon, Nabatieh, North, South.	100
Morocco	Casablanca, Rabat, Fès, Marrakech, Drâa, Tanger, Souss, Béni Mellal, Oriental.	73
Palestine	Hebron, Jenin, Tubas, Bethlehem, Ramallah, Jericho, Jerusalem, Nablus, Salfit, Tulkarm, Qalqiliya, Gaza, Khan Yunis, Rafah, Northern Gaza, Deir al-Balah.	107
Syrian Refugees in Lebanon	One formal and about 4,000 informal refugee camps across six (pre-reform) governorates: Beirut, Beqaa, Mount Lebanon, Nabatieh, North, South.	100
Tunisia	Ariana, Béja, Ben Arous, Bizerte, Gabès, Gafsa, Jendouba, Kairouan, Kasserine, Kebili, Kef, Mahdia, Manouba, Medenine, Monastir, Nabeul, Sfax, Sidi Bouzid, Siliana, Sousse, Tataouine, Tozeur, Tunis, Zaghouan.	80

information about the population universe, a precondition of random sampling, does not exist. Moreover, the respective governments in most countries required permits to conduct interviews in private homes, and these would have been difficult to obtain in eight countries simultaneously, particularly given the current political situation. The local institutes, responsible for fieldwork and sampling, have however an established set of methods for selecting sampling points and identifying eligible households to survey, with the aim of randomising the selection process as much as possible. To standardise the selection process, all interviewers were provided with detailed instruction manuals, which they had to carefully follow in order to find eligible respondents. We aimed to ensure to the closest extent possible a geographic spread of respondents according to the distribution of the survey universe in the respective country (except in the case of Syrian refugees in Lebanon). Some sparsely populated, remote areas, such as the desert regions of Morocco and Egypt, were however excluded from the samples. For each geographic area, the institutes provided a list of sampling points. The regions covered and the number of sampling points per country are displayed in Table A.2.

Questionnaire Development

The Scientific Advisory Board developed the questionnaire in collaboration with the University of Leipzig (Institute of Geography and Oriental Institute) and Kantar Public. It was divided into ten sections: social profile of the respondents, income and occupation, consumption and expenditure, identity formation, communication and use of internet, role of the state, religion, participation, experience with violence, and mobility. The University of Leipzig developed the questions for the sections by combining insights from the German Shell Youth studies with the university's expertise on the MENA region. Based on several rounds of discussion among the members of the Scientific Advisory Board, Kantar Public, and representatives of local FES offices, a preliminary English master version of the questionnaire was drafted by the University of Leipzig in autumn 2015.

This early master version consisted of about 200 closed-ended questions, some with extensive item or statement batteries. It did not contain any open-ended questions (see Appendix II: Questionnaire). The English questionnaire served as the basis for all Arabic, country-specific questionnaires. The translation entailed the following steps:

1. Development of the master questionnaire in English, including the programming of the CAPI version.
2. After several rounds of quality control reviews by the project group (which was composed of the authors of this text, changing members of Scientific Advisory Board, and representatives from local research institutes), the final English master version was translated into Modern Standard Arabic.
3. The Arabic master version and the English master were forwarded to the national institutes for adjusting translations into the respective Arabic dialects. This concerns Morocco, Tunisia, Lebanon, and Palestine while institutes in the other countries used the Modern Standard Arabic version.
4. The University of Leipzig then double-checked the national translations together with the requested questionnaire changes and retranslated them into English.
5. Finally, all questionnaire changes were discussed and either accepted or rejected by the project group.

The final Arabic master version and the adjusted national questionnaires were handed over to TNS Maroc and a subcontractor for programming. The

CAPI master script was tested and (after some changes) verified by the project group. After approval of the master script, the national versions of the questionnaire (CAPI and PAPI) were generated, delivered to the local field institutes, and tested by their research teams. The estimated average interview duration for all countries ranged between sixty to seventy minutes.

Interviewer Training and Fieldwork

In each country, a trained staff of approximately fifty people recruited by social research institutes conducted the interviews. Recruitment criteria included age (aged circa 25–35), gender (circa 60 percent female, 40 percent male), and professional experience as interviewers. The aim of having a mix of interviewers in terms of geography, local dialects, and religion was also factored into the selection process.

To ensure comparable data generation across all countries, it was essential that all interviewers receive the same training programme and materials to be well prepared. Written interviewer guidelines were developed by the University of Leipzig and TNS Maroc in cooperation with Kantar Public and provided to the national field institutes. The interviewers of all national field institutes received a three-day training conducted by local fieldwork managers and supervisors from the institutes. Either a project manager of TNS Maroc or the FES project director accompanied all training sessions. The main focus of the training was to provide local field managers and interviewers with information on the background and central objectives of the survey, schedule of the survey, content of the questionnaire, how to ask certain questions, and how to conduct the interview (e.g. how to select potential interviewees, how to approach them, and how to ask them to take part in the survey). During the training, all participating interviewers had to conduct test interviews to familiarise themselves with the questionnaire, the wording of questions, and filter questions.

Each national institute conducted a minimum of twenty pilot interviews to test the research tools (survey method and questionnaire). The main objective of these interviews was to check the comprehensibility of the questionnaire; its language, translations, and interview instructions; the completeness of answer categories for each question; and the functionality of filters. Furthermore, the pilot served to train the interviewers, highlight potential problems (e.g. poor response to specific questions), and test the CAPI questionnaire application as well as the social acceptance of the use of CAPI tablets in rural and peripheral urban areas. All pilot interviews were conducted during the interviewers' training in March 2016.

During the following weeks, the results of the pilot phase were analysed and the questionnaire adjusted where necessary. Experiences and suggestions for enhancements were collected in a standardised template and provided to the project group. All comments and recommendations made by the different institutes were reviewed and discussed by the team. Ultimately, only a few minor amendments resulted from pre-testing, the exception being extra questions for the Syrian refugees in Lebanon, for whom some questions were deleted while others were developed. All changes in wording and expressions were translated once again, double-checked by the University of Leipzig, and finally approved by the project group.

The fieldwork for the main phase was conducted in the first three weeks of May 2016, with the exception of Tunisia (May–June 2016) and Morocco (June–July 2016). All interviews were carried out in the local Arabic dia-

Table A.3 **Distribution of Interviews**

Country / Survey group	Number of interviews realised (gross)	Number of interviews approved (net)
Egypt	1,139	1,130
Bahrain	1,039	1,038
Yemen	811	808
Jordan	1,000	1,000
Lebanon	1,000	1,000
Morocco	1,069	1,065
Palestine	1,002	1,001
Syrian Refugees in Lebanon	999	999
Tunisia	998	998
Total	**9,057**	**9,039**

lect. Interviews were held at respondents' homes or in such public places as cafés, community centres, and the like. It was of major importance that the respondents felt comfortable, so the interview location was chosen accordingly. The number of interviews conducted, the base for the survey findings, is given in Table A.3. All in all, data for 9,057 interviews (gross) were delivered for the main survey groups. Out of these, eighteen interviews were deleted due to incoherencies or missing data. Thus, the net number of interviews totalled 9,039. Overall, the target of 1,000 net interviews could be achieved for most of the countries or survey groups. For Tunisia and the target group of Syrian refugees in Lebanon, the planned number of interviews was only missed by one and two interviews, respectively. Due to the escalating situation of armed conflicts and war in Yemen, only 808 net interviews could be completed there.

Data Collection, Checks, and Weighting

The data collected was stored in a central CAPI database at TNS Maroc and its subcontractor. Survey data collected through PAPI and CATI techniques had to be entered into the CAPI system manually by the local field institutes.

The ability of the CAPI technique to include automated plausibility checks wherever appropriate cannot substitute for a thorough ex-post data check and cleaning. This is because not all theoretically possible checks for consistency and plausibility can reasonably be implemented through CAPI, because overloading the interview must be avoided. Also, increased complexity of the questionnaire would have increased the risk of errors in the CAPI survey. Since CAPI was not used to conduct the interviews in some countries, thorough data checks became even more necessary. During fieldwork, Kantar Public carried out data validation with sets of interim data via Excel and SPSS (statistical software program) syntaxes. In parallel, Kantar Public and the University of Leipzig conducted the final comprehensive data check.

Kantar Public was responsible for data amendments. As the final dataset comprised all data, the checking syntax was implemented in the same way for all countries. A set or range of acceptable values was established for each variable, and the validity of each recorded value was checked in isolation from the rest of the data. A check for missing values was also included. Furthermore, checks were carried out with regard to filters (i.e. whether a certain question had to be answered according to the structure and sequencing of the questionnaire).

Structural differences among the results are common in random samplings. To ensure that the final structure of the sampling conveyed the structure of the survey universe, differences were cleared by factorial weighting. To correct these structural differences, the weighting factors must be based on comparisons of the sample structure to the structure of the target population (i.e. the demographic structure of the countries in question). The survey data was weighted for all target groups with respect to the structural variables of age (three groups, aged 16–20, 21–25, and 26–30), gender, and region, based on statistics available (UN 2015; CIO 2015). The weighting procedure was executed in an iterative process, by which the weights were iteratively developed by comparing the actual distribution with regard to the target structure of the sample. This process was continued until an approximate ideal distribution for the three structural variables was achieved and no further improvements were possible. The iterative process ensures that deviations caused in a previous step are corrected in subsequent steps. It yields weighting factors for each single respondent. The weighting steps were conducted on a country-by-country basis. In contrast to the national surveys, the survey data for Syrian refugees was only weighted with respect to gender, because no other statistics for this universe were available. The weighting process is described here using Egypt as an example, with a total of 1,130 interviews. In the first step, the actual distribution of the age groups was compared with the target distribution of the groups:

- group 1, aged 16–20: actual 34.9 percent, target 32.6 percent
- group 2, aged 21–25: actual 36.7 percent, target 34.7 percent
- group 3, aged 26–30: actual 28.4 percent, target 32.7 percent

As a result, respondents of group 1 received a weight of 0.94, group 2 of 0.95, and group 3 of 1.15. Because the interview number was 'reduced' to 1,000 for each survey, the three groups received the following reduced starting weights: 0.83, 0.84, and 1.02, respectively.

In the second step, the structure variable 'gender' was examined:

- group 1, men: actual 47.1 percent, target 51.1 percent
- group 2, women: actual 52.9 percent, target 48.9 percent[1]

In the final step, the distribution for the regions was adjusted. For Egypt, there were a total of 11 regions (see Table A.2).

By adjusting one structural variable, the distribution of the other structural variables changes as well, which causes a deterioration of their target distributions. It is due to this effect that the iteration process is carried out until the target figures are achieved. The number of iterative cycles conducted strongly depends on the quality of the sample. In the example here, only three iteration cycles were needed, which speaks favourably of the quality of the sampling data. Case weights for the different surveys range between 0.349 and 2.500. The case weight details for each survey country are listed in Table A.4.

In a final weighting step, all national samples were adjusted to net samples of 1,000 interviews. Thus, for overall results that include all nine target

---

1. Without the starting weights for age, the weights for gender would have been 47.3 percent versus 52.7 percent.

Table A.4 Survey Groups and Weighting

Country / Survey group	Weighting (min.–max.)
Egypt	0.571–2.080
Bahrain	0.700–1.210
Yemen	0.400–2.500
Jordan	0.349–2.500
Lebanon	0.707–1.397
Morocco	0.517–2.379
Palestine	0.763–1.596
Syrian Refugees in Lebanon	1.001–1.001
Tunisia	0.474–1.803
Total	**0.349–2.500**

groups, each group has the same weight, independent of the country's size of population or other factors. For all countries (but not for Syrian refugees in Lebanon), the data sources used for weighting gender and age were United Nations statistics (UN 2015) and official figures for Bahrain (CIO 2015). The statistics for the regional distribution of national populations provided by the national institutes, together with their sample information, were used as the basis for the calculation of regional weighting.

Qualitative Interviews

As important as the insights from quantitative surveys are, not all aspects of everyday life can be captured numerically. Additional depth and contextual explanations can often be obtained through qualitative research, which was therefore included early on in the project design. The questionnaire for these interviews was aligned to the themes of the quantitative survey:

- youth opportunities and politics
- family, trust, and intergenerational justice
- the Arab Spring
- international politics.

All interviewees had already participated in the quantitative survey. The following quotas were established for interviewee selection among those who agreed to in-depth interviews:

- male/female: 50/50
- large city/small town/rural: 33/33/33
- basic/secondary/higher education: 30/40/30.

For each country or survey group, at least ten qualitative interviews were carried out in late 2016 and early 2017 (see Table A.5). The same institutions that had been responsible for carrying out the quantitative surveys recruited the male and female interviewers. The complete interviews were provided as audio files, with full Arabic transcriptions and English translations, and then shared with the authors of the volume.

Table A.5 **Qualitative Interviews**

Country / Survey group	Qualitative interview dates
Egypt	22–26 December 2016
Bahrain	21 December 2016 to 7 January 2017
Yemen	20 December 2016 to 12 January 2017
Jordan	17 December 2016 to 11 January 2017
Lebanon	17 December 2016 to 10 January 2017
Morocco	8–16 December 2016
Palestine	8–21 December 2016
Syrian Refugees in Lebanon	23 December 2016 to 10 January 2017
Tunisia	1–10 January 2017

Appendix II: Questionnaire

GIVEN THE INTERNATIONAL CONSTITUTION of the Scientific Advisory Board, the questionnaire for this study of the youth in the Middle East and North Africa was developed in English. The English master version was then translated into Modern Standard Arabic, and for some countries, further adjusted to the respective Arabic dialect. Thus, the English version presented here was not applied during field research. This version also does not indicate filters applied for individual questions, instructions, and multiple-answer options.

In the chapters, some authors might in a few cases use slightly different English when referencing the questionnaire. For example, if they worked from the Arabic master version, they may have adopted or preferred slightly different translations or phrasing. Hence, this English version of the questionnaire only serves to better orientate readers.

1	Please select fi eldwork country (to be completed by interviewer)					
☐	Morocco	☐	Jordan	☐	Yemen
☐	Tunisia	☐	Palestine	☐	Bahrain
☐	Egypt	☐	Lebanon	☐	Syrian Refugees (in Lebanon)

2	Please tell me your nationality							
☐	Moroccan	☐	Jordanian	☐	Yemeni	☐	Stateless
☐	Tunisian	☐	Palestinian	☐	Bahraini	☐	Other
☐	Egyptian	☐	Lebanese	☐	Syrian		

3	Record gender		
☐	Male	☐	Female

4	Can you please tell me your year of birth?

5	Identify milieu of residence (to be completed by interviewer)		
☐	Refugee camp	☐	Small city 20,001–100,000
☐	Hamlet < 50	☐	Medium-sized city 100.001–500,000
☐	Village 50–1,000	☐	Large city > 500,000
☐	Rural centre 1,001–20,000		

6	Please select the fi eldwork region (to be completed by interviewer)

7	Please select the fi eldwork area (to be completed by interviewer)		
☐	Urban	☐	Rural

8	Please select the sampling point (to be completed by interviewer)

9 | If you consider your personal situation in all its parts and aspects today (school / job, family, economic situation, political transformations, future developments, etc.), all in all, do you feel rather secure or rather insecure?
Please rate your situation on a scale from 1 (not at all secure) to 10 (totally secure)

		1 Not at all secure	2	3	4	5	6	7	8	9	10 Totally secure
	Personal situation	☐	☐	☐	☐	☐	☐	☐	☐	☐	☐

10 | Can you specify the area of security? I feel secure / insecure in the following fields:
Please rate your situation on a scale from 1 (not at all secure) to 10 (totally secure)

		1 Not at all secure	2	3	4	5	6	7	8	9	10 Totally secure
	My economic situation	☐	☐	☐	☐	☐	☐	☐	☐	☐	☐
	My health status	☐	☐	☐	☐	☐	☐	☐	☐	☐	☐
	My emotions	☐	☐	☐	☐	☐	☐	☐	☐	☐	☐
	My exposure to violence	☐	☐	☐	☐	☐	☐	☐	☐	☐	☐
	My access to food	☐	☐	☐	☐	☐	☐	☐	☐	☐	☐
	The future of my family	☐	☐	☐	☐	☐	☐	☐	☐	☐	☐
	The probability of armed conflict	☐	☐	☐	☐	☐	☐	☐	☐	☐	☐
	My future professional career	☐	☐	☐	☐	☐	☐	☐	☐	☐	☐

11 | Would you consider yourself to belong to the youths or to the group of adults?

	☐	Youths		☐	Adults

PERSONAL SITUATION

12 | Please tell me your country of birth

	☐	Morocco	☐	Lebanon	☐	Libya
	☐	Tunisia	☐	Yemen	☐	Iraq
	☐	Egypt	☐	Bahrain	☐	Other
	☐	Jordan	☐	Saudi Arabia		
	☐	Palestine	☐	Syria		

13 | Birth sequence: Are you ...?

	☐	Single child	☐	Oldest child	☐	Middle child	☐	Youngest child

14 | Marital status: Are you ...?

	☐	Single	☐	Divorced
	☐	Engaged	☐	Widowed
	☐	Married		

15 | What is your current living situation?

	☐	Living with parents (within same household)	☐	Living alone
	☐	Living together with parents in one house (but own household)	☐	Living in a shared apartment with friends

	□	Living with my own family / partner (without parents)		□	Other

16	**Including yourself: how many people live in your household?**
	—

17	**Among those: how many people are between 16 and 65 years old including yourself?**
	—

18	**Who is the head of household among the people you are living with?**		
	□	Myself	□	My mother
	□	My husband / wife	□	Nobody
	□	My father	□	Somebody else

19	**Who manages everyday affairs for your household?**		
	□	Myself	□	My mother
	□	My husband / wife	□	Nobody
	□	My father	□	Somebody else

20	**How would you assess the economic situation of your family today?**						
	□	Very good	□	Rather good	□	Rather bad	□	Very bad

21	**How would you assess the economic situation of your family in 2010?**						
	□	Very good	□	Rather good	□	Rather bad	□	Very bad
	□	Do not know						

22	**What is your mother language(s)?**				
	□ Colloquial Arabic ('amiya, darija)	□ Spanish	□ Syriac (*siryaniya*)
	□ Amazigh	□ English	□ Nobiin (*nubiyya*)
	□ Kurdish	□ German	□ Other
	□ French	□ Armenian	

23	**What other languages do you speak fluently?**				
	□ Colloquial Arabic ('amiya, Darija)	□ Spanish	□ Nobiin (Nubiyya)
	□ Standard Arabic	□ English	□ Other
	□ Amazigh	□ German	□ No other language
	□ Kurdish	□ Armenian	
	□ French	□ Syriac (Siryaniya)	

24	**Are you a student?**		
	□	Yes	□	No

25	**Are you going to…?**						
	□	School	□	University	□	Vocational training	□	Disrupted (Refugee, etc.)

26	How many years did you go to school (excluding pre-school and university)? Please, calculate total years (maximum: up until baccalaureate).
	___

27	Highest degree achieved		
	☐ Illiterate	☐	Baccalaureate / A-levels / *tawjihi*
	☐ Read and write but no formal education	☐	Technical / vocational diploma
	☐ Primary school	☐	University degree (bachelor's, master's)
	☐ Secondary / intermediate school	☐	PhD

PARENTS

Father

28	Please, tell us something about your father: Is your father still alive?		
	☐ Yes	☐ No	☐ Don't know

29	How old is your father? (Age)
	___
	☐ Don't know

30	What is / was his level of education (highest degree):		
	☐ Illiterate	☐	Technical / vocational diploma
	☐ Read and write but no formal education	☐	University degree (bachelor's, master's)
	☐ Primary school	☐	PhD
	☐ Secondary / intermediate school	☐	Don't know
	☐ Baccalaureate / A-levels / *tawjihi*		

31	And what is / was his main occupation? (Job held the longest)
	☐ State employee
	☐ Employee (with insurance)
	☐ Worker (no insurance, but continuous employment)
	☐ Remunerated labourer as part of a family business
	☐ Self-employed with higher education (medical doctor, lawyer, etc.)
	☐ Self-employed without higher education, but qualification (trade, commerce, industry, etc.)
	☐ Self-employed in agriculture
	☐ Self-employed in service sector (continuous work, unstable income)
	☐ Day labourer (unstable employment, unstable income)
	☐ Jobless
	☐ Work without income
	☐ Retired
	☐ Other

32	And what is / was his main occupation? (Job held the longest)
	☐ State employee

	☐	Employee (with insurance)
	☐	Worker (no insurance, but continuous employment)
	☐	Remunerated labourer as part of a family business
	☐	Self-employed with higher education (medical doctor, lawyer, etc.)
	☐	Self-employed without higher education, but qualification (trade, commerce, industry, etc.)
	☐	Self-employed in agriculture
	☐	Self-employed in service sector (continuous work, unstable income)
	☐	Day labourer (unstable employment, unstable income)
	☐	Jobless
	☐	Work without income
	☐	Retired
	☐	Other

33	Concerning his main occupation, please tell me ...			
	The number of hours per day he is working	___	☐	Don't know
	How many days during the week	___	☐	Don't know
	How many weeks during the month	___	☐	Don't know
	How many months during the year	___	☐	Don't know

34	What about his income? In his main occupation, is he ...?							
	☐	Paid per day	☐	Paid every fort-night	☐	Paid per season	☐	Don't know
	☐	Paid per week	☐	Paid per month	☐	Paid per job/task	☐	Not paid

35	Can you please tell me how much he earns? Per day / week / month / season / job		
	Per day	Per month	
	Per week	Per season (total for last year)	
	Per fortnight	Per job / task (total for last year)	

36	Does he receive continuous payment in case of sickness?				
	☐	Yes	☐ No	☐	Don't know

Mother

37	Please, tell us something about your mother: Is your mother still alive?				
	☐	Yes	☐ No	☐	Don't know
38	How old is your mother (age)?				
	___				
	☐	Don't know			

39	What is / was her level of education (highest degree):			
	☐	Illiterate	☐	*Technical / vocational diploma*
	☐	Read & write but no formal education	☐	University degree (bachelor's, master's)
	☐	Primary school	☐	PhD
	☐	Secondary / intermediate school	☐	Don't know
	☐	Baccalaureate / A-levels / *tawjihi*		

40		What kind of different tasks / jobs did or does your mother do? Please tick.
	☐	State employee
	☐	Employee (with insurance)
	☐	Worker (no insurance, but continuous employment)
	☐	Remunerated labourer as part of a family business
	☐	Self-employed with higher education (medical doctor, lawyer, etc.)
	☐	Self-employed without higher education, but qualification (trade, commerce, industry, etc.)
	☐	Self-employed in agriculture
	☐	Self-employed in service sector (continuous work, unstable income)
	☐	Day labourer (unstable employment, unstable income)
	☐	Jobless
	☐	Work without income (e. g. housewife)
	☐	Retired
	☐	Other

41		And what is / was her main occupation? (Job held the longest)
	☐	State employee
	☐	Employee (with insurance)
	☐	Worker (no insurance, but continuous employment)
	☐	Remunerated labourer as part of a family business
	☐	Self-employed with higher education (medical doctor, lawyer, etc.)
	☐	Self-employed without higher education, but qualification (trade, commerce, industry, etc.)
	☐	Self-employed in agriculture
	☐	Self-employed in service sector (continuous work, unstable income)
	☐	Day labourer (unstable employment, unstable income)
	☐	Jobless
	☐	Work without income (e. g. housewife)
	☐	Retired
	☐	Other

42	Concerning her main occupation, please tell me ...			
	The number of hours per day she is working	__	☐	Don't know
	How many days during the week	__	☐	Don't know
	How many weeks during the month	__	☐	Don't know
	How many months during the year	__	☐	Don't know

43	What about her income? In her main occupation, is she ...?							
	☐	Paid per day	☐	Paid every fort-night	☐	Paid per season	☐	Don't know
	☐	Paid per week	☐	Paid per month	☐	Paid per job / task	☐	Not paid

44	Can you please tell me how much she earns? Per day / week / month / season / job			
	Per day	_____	Per month	_____
	Per week	_____	Per season (total for last year)	_____
	Per fortnight	_____	Per job / task (total for last year)	_____

45	Does she receive continuous payment in case of sickness?				
	☐	Yes	☐	No	☐	Don't know

46	Would you consider yourself as being part of the working class?						
	☐	Yes	☐	No	☐	Does not apply	☐	Don't know

47	Class assessment: How would you describe your family?
	☐	Wealthy
	☐	Upper middle class
	☐	Lower middle class
	☐	Poor
	☐	Destitute ('ala bab Allah, etc.)

HOUSING

48	What kind of neighbourhood do you live in?						
	☐	Public housing	☐	Informal housing	☐	Private housing	☐	Refugee camp

49	Informal housing type				
	☐	Informal land	☐	Illegal construction	☐	Provisional/deteriorated house

50	What kind of housing / building are you living in today?		
	☐	Mansion	☐	Informal/provisional housing
	☐	Single house	☐	Tent
	☐	Terraced house	☐	Room
	☐	Apartment	☐	Other

51	How many years have you personally been living in this housing situation?
	____

52	Are you/ Is your head of household ...?
	☐	Tenant
	☐	Owner of the place you live in
	☐	Living in accommodation provided free of charge by a company, institution, or individual
	☐	Other

53	Did you ...?				
	☐	Inherit	☐	Buy the house/apartment	☐	Build the home

54	Do you have a room for yourself?				
	☐	Yes	☐	No	☐	No reply

55	Which of the following items do you have available in your household?					
	☐	Tap water	☐	Television	☐	Air conditioning
	☐	Electricity	☐	Satellite antenna	☐	Moped, motorcycle
	☐	WC	☐	Refrigerator	☐	Car/pick-up/lorry/tractor
	☐	Separate kitchen	☐	Computer/laptop/tablet		
	☐	Stove	☐	Internet access		

56	Does your household own livestock?		
	☐ Yes	☐	No

57 Can you please tell me how many animals you own?

Sheep	_____	Mules	_____
Goats	_____	Dromedary, camel	_____
Chicken	_____	Water buffalo	_____
Cows	_____	Rabbits	_____
Horses	_____	Pigeons	_____
Donkeys	_____	Other	_____

58	Does your household own agricultural land?		
	☐ Yes	☐	No

59 Can you please tell me how much agricultural land you own?

Irrigated land (m²)	_____	☐	Don't know
Rainfed land (*bour*, etc.) (m²)	_____	☐	Don't know

60	Does your household currently produce food for its own consumption?		
	☐ Yes	☐	No

61 How large is its share, if you consider the total food expenditure? Please give a rough estimate.

In per cent (%)	1	5	10	15	20	25	30	35	40	45	50	60	70	80	90	100	Don't know
Food expenditure	☐	☐	☐	☐	☐	☐	☐	☐	☐	☐	☐	☐	☐	☐	☐	☐	☐

ECONOMY

62	How do you assess your personal economic situation today?			
	☐ Very good	☐ Rather good	☐ Rather bad	☐ Very bad

63	Do you possess a private bank or postal account?		
	☐ Yes	☐	No

64	Do you possess a private credit card?		
	☐ Yes	☐	No

65	Do you personally have some money available, either from working, from your family, or from other sources?		
	☐ Yes	☐	No

66 If you do not have any money at your disposal, can you please indicate your situation?

☐	Student
☐	Vocational training or internship
☐	Temporary without work (less than three months)
☐	Long-term unemployed (more than three months)

		Permanently not working (e. g. young spouses who are not permitted to work)
	☐	Retired / sick

67	**What are the different sources of your budget?**							
	☐	From family	☐	From own work	☐	From scholarship	☐	Other

68	**If the only source for your budget is your family or transfers from other persons/ institutions, could you please describe your situation?**
	☐	Student
	☐	Vocational training or internship
	☐	Temporary without work (less than three months)
	☐	Long-term unemployed (more than three months)
	☐	Permanently not working (e. g. young spouses who are not permitted to work)
	☐	Retired with transfer income from government support (e. g. handicapped)
	☐	Retired, no income (e. g. sickness)
	☐	Does not apply

69	**You said you receive money from the family or from other sources (excluding income from your own work). Do you …?**			
	☐	Receive it on a regular basis	☐	Receive it on an irregular basis

70	**If you have to guess, how much money do you receive on average per month from your family or other sources (excluding income from your own work)?**
	_____

71	**If you work for money: how many jobs do you have today?**
	_____

72	**What kind of different tasks/jobs are you doing?**
	☐	State employee
	☐	Employee (with insurance)
	☐	Worker (no insurance, but continuous employment)
	☐	Remunerated labourer as part of a family business
	☐	Self-employed with higher education (medical doctor, lawyer etc.)
	☐	Self-employed without higher education (trade, commerce, industry, etc.)
	☐	Self-employed in agriculture
	☐	Self-employed in service sector (continuous work, unstable income)
	☐	Day labourer (unstable employment, unstable income)
	☐	Retired
	☐	Other

73	**Please rank these jobs concerning your income from most important (1) to least important (3).**			
		1	**2**	**3**
State employee		☐	☐	☐
Employee (with insurance)		☐	☐	☐
Worker (no insurance, but continuous employment)		☐	☐	☐

Remunerated labourer as part of a family business	☐	☐	☐
Self-employed with higher education (medical doctor, lawyer etc.)	☐	☐	☐
Self-employed without higher education (trade, commerce, industry, etc.)	☐	☐	☐
Self-employed in agriculture	☐	☐	☐
Self-employed in service sector (continuous work, unstable income)	☐	☐	☐
Day labourer (unstable employment, unstable income)	☐	☐	☐
Retired	☐	☐	☐
Other	☐	☐	☐

74 What about Jobs: Please tell me …

What about … Job 1: Please tell me …

How many hours per day you are working	_____
How many days during the week you are working	_____
How many weeks during the month you are working	_____
How many months during the year you are working	_____

What about … Job 2: Please tell me …

How many hours per day you are working	_____
How many days during the week you are working	_____
How many weeks during the month you are working	_____
How many months during the year you are working	_____

What about … Job 3: Please tell me …

How many hours per day you are working	_____
How many days during the week you are working	_____
How many weeks during the month you are working	_____
How many months during the year you are working	_____

75 And how much are you paid per job? Job 1:

Day	_____	Month	_____
Week	_____	Job / task	_____
Fortnight	_____		

And how much are you paid per job? Job 2:

Day	_____	Month	_____
Week	_____	Job / task	_____
Fortnight	_____		

And how much are you paid per job? Job 3:

Day	_____	Month	_____
Week	_____	Job / task	_____
Fortnight	_____		

76	Do you receive continuous payment in case of sickness? (Answer for each job)			
		Yes	No	
	Job 1	☐	☐	
	Job 2	☐	☐	
	Job 3	☐	☐	

77	How did you find out about your most important job?		
☐	Friends informed me about the job	☐	Via a private employment agency
☐	Via Internet	☐	A public institution (e. g. employment office) informed me
☐	Somebody from my family informed me	☐	Other
☐	I read an advertisement		

Job 1

78	Concerning this work, what are the reasons you are engaging in it?	True	Partly true	Not true
	I had no other option	☐	☐	☐
	It is the only work I know how to do	☐	☐	☐
	It is a secure job	☐	☐	☐
	The business belongs to my family	☐	☐	☐
	My boss is from the same area	☐	☐	☐
	It's nicely paid	☐	☐	☐
	It's work that is socially well accepted	☐	☐	☐
	I can engage with friends and colleagues	☐	☐	☐
	I can learn a lot	☐	☐	☐
	I have the option to upgrade my position	☐	☐	☐

79	Do you like this work?
☐	Not at all
☐	A little
☐	So-so
☐	A lot
☐	100 percent

80	Do you support your parents financially? If yes, is that on an irregular or regular basis?
☐	I do not support my parents financially
☐	I support my parents financially on an irregular basis
☐	I support my parents financially on a regular basis

81	How much money per month do you support your parents with?
	_____

82	How should an employment situation and your job be in order for you to be satisfied?	1 Not important at all	2 Rather not important	3 So-so	4 Rather important	5 Very important	Don't know
	Earning a high income	☐	☐	☐	☐	☐	☐

Options to upgrade my position	☐	☐	☐	☐	☐	☐
A secure job	☐	☐	☐	☐	☐	☐
Having a lot of contacts with other people	☐	☐	☐	☐	☐	☐
Feeling of achieving something	☐	☐	☐	☐	☐	☐
Feeling of being accepted	☐	☐	☐	☐	☐	☐
Possibility to support others	☐	☐	☐	☐	☐	☐
Possibility of implementing own ideas	☐	☐	☐	☐	☐	☐
Doing something useful for society	☐	☐	☐	☐	☐	☐
Possibility of doing something that makes sense to me	☐	☐	☐	☐	☐	☐
A job that allows for enough leisure time	☐	☐	☐	☐	☐	☐

83	How confident are you about the possibility of realising your wishes concerning your job?
☐	Not confident at all
☐	Rather not confident
☐	Rather confident
☐	Totally confident
☐	Does not apply

84	Are you already at the maximum of your performance concerning your studies, your work, or your daily affairs? What describes your situation best?
☐	I am consistently not using my full potential and I am ill
☐	I am consistently not using my full potential
☐	I am not using my full potential
☐	I live a good balance between work and leisure
☐	I feel stressed
☐	I am permanently stressed
☐	I am permanently stressed and I am ill
☐	No reply

85	Are you in a position to save money?		
☐	Yes	☐	No

86	How much money do you save per month on average?
	————

87	For what purpose do you save money primarily?		
☐	For security reasons, in case of emergency	☐	For my retirement
☐	As dowry for my marriage	☐	Migration
☐	For building or buying a house	☐	Other
☐	For my children		

88	Do you have debts, either with institutions (e. g. banks) or individuals?		
☐	Yes	☐	No

89	To how many institutions (e. g. banks) or persons do you have debts?				
	Institutions (e. g. banks)	__	Persons		__

90	How high are your debts?
	☐ Few (less than one monthly budget)
	☐ Medium (between one and six monthly budgets)
	☐ High (more than six monthly budgets)

91	Have you ever been a member of a rotating savings association?		
	☐ Yes	☐	No

92	When (year) did you last participate in a rotating savings association?
	_____

93	How many members took part, including yourself?
	__

94	What amount did you personally invest per month?
	_____

95	Do you have health insurance?				
	☐ Yes	☐	No	☐	Don't know / No answer

96	Is this insurance …?				
	☐ Private	☐	Public	☐	Don't know

97	Please identify the 4 items you spend the most money on.						
	☐ Wheat and bread	☐	Internet	☐	Music	☐	Studies
	☐ Food (oil, sugar, etc.)	☐	Video and online games	☐	Going out with friends	☐	Cosmetics
	☐ Local snacks	☐	Paying debts/ instalments	☐	Water/electricity	☐	Other
	☐ McDonald's, Pizza Hut, KFC	☐	Transport/travelling	☐	Housing rent		
	☐ Clothes	☐	Cigarettes	☐	Gas cylinders (cooking)		
	☐ Mobile phone	☐	Medication, drugs	☐	Insurance		

98	How important is the availability of cheap bread for you and your family?				
	☐ Very important	☐	Important	☐	Not important

99	Do you buy or bake bread in your household?				
	☐ Buy	☐	Bake	☐	Buy and bake

100	Have you ever made the experience of having to wait for being supplied with bread (except during Ramadan)?		
	☐ Yes	☐	No

101	Is that ...?						
	☐	Before 2010	☐	After 2010	☐	Both before and after 2010	

102	Did that happen ...?							
	☐	Consistently	☐	Frequently	☐	From time to time	☐	Rarely

103	Can you please indicate the average hours of waiting per week?
	_____

104	Do you possess a ration card in order to buy or receive food?		
	☐	Yes	☐	No

105	How important is the ration card for you and your family?					
	☐	Very important	☐	Important	☐	Not important

106	In order to buy food, do you use ...?			
	☐	Weekly market	☐	Bakery
	☐	Street vendor (sitting on the ground)	☐	Supermarket (self-service)
	☐	Mobile hawker with carriage	☐	Hypermarket
	☐	Stall at the neighbourhood market	☐	Wholesaler
	☐	Grocer	☐	Malls
	☐	Butcher	☐	Other

107	Can you please tell me the frequency of use of each selected outlet to buy food items?					
		Daily	Every second day	Twice a week	Weekly	Monthly	Less frequently than once a month
	Weekly market	☐	☐	☐	☐	☐	☐
	Street vendor (sitting on the ground)	☐	☐	☐	☐	☐	☐
	Mobile hawker with carriage	☐	☐	☐	☐	☐	☐
	Stall at neighbourhood market	☐	☐	☐	☐	☐	☐
	Grocer	☐	☐	☐	☐	☐	☐
	Butcher	☐	☐	☐	☐	☐	☐
	Bakery	☐	☐	☐	☐	☐	☐
	Supermarket (self-service)	☐	☐	☐	☐	☐	☐
	Hypermarket	☐	☐	☐	☐	☐	☐
	Wholesaler	☐	☐	☐	☐	☐	☐
	Malls	☐	☐	☐	☐	☐	☐

108	A lot of food products we consume are produced outside the Arab World. How important is it for you that all of them are halal products?					
	☐	Very important	☐	Important	☐	Not important

109	Have you ever consciously bought a product – food or cosmetics – that was labelled as being halal? Which type?					
	☐	Cosmetics	☐	Meat	☐	None
	☐	Convenience food	☐	Other	☐	Don't know

110 How important for your life is the ...?

	1 Not at all important	2	3	4	5	6	7	8	9	10 Totally important
Absence of violence	☐	☐	☐	☐	☐	☐	☐	☐	☐	☐
Security of basic needs	☐	☐	☐	☐	☐	☐	☐	☐	☐	☐
Basic rights for minorities	☐	☐	☐	☐	☐	☐	☐	☐	☐	☐
Freedom of opinion and speech	☐	☐	☐	☐	☐	☐	☐	☐	☐	☐
Freedom of assembly	☐	☐	☐	☐	☐	☐	☐	☐	☐	☐
Freedom to elect political leaders	☐	☐	☐	☐	☐	☐	☐	☐	☐	☐
Freedom of movement	☐	☐	☐	☐	☐	☐	☐	☐	☐	☐

111 Please rank the three most important rights FOR YOU (1 = most important).

	1	2	3
Absence of violence	☐	☐	☐
Security of basic needs	☐	☐	☐
Basic rights for minorities	☐	☐	☐
Freedom of opinion and speech	☐	☐	☐
Freedom of assembly	☐	☐	☐
Freedom to elect political leaders	☐	☐	☐
Freedom of movement	☐	☐	☐

112 Related to these three rights, can the state provide what you need?

	Yes	No
Absence of violence	☐	☐
Security of basic needs	☐	☐
Basic rights for minorities	☐	☐
Freedom of opinion and speech	☐	☐
Freedom of assembly	☐	☐
Freedom to elect political leaders	☐	☐
Freedom of movement	☐	☐

113 If you look around the world, what kind of political system would you prefer?

☐	A strong man who governs the country	☐	A democratic system
☐	A strong woman who governs the country	☐	A combined democratic and Islamic system
☐	A religious state based on *sharia*	☐	A system without nation states
☐	A socialist system	☐	Other
☐	A combined socialist and Islamic system	☐	Don't know

114 What about your trust in different institutions?

	No trust	Limited trust	Trust	Unknown
Public health system	☐	☐	☐	☐
Educational system	☐	☐	☐	☐
Media	☐	☐	☐	☐
Family	☐	☐	☐	☐

United Nations	☐	☐	☐	☐
Police	☐	☐	☐	☐
Government	☐	☐	☐	☐
Trade unions	☐	☐	☐	☐
Parliament	☐	☐	☐	☐
Zawiya (religious school, Sufi orders)	☐	☐	☐	☐
Human rights NGOs	☐	☐	☐	☐
Neighbourhood associations	☐	☐	☐	☐
Tribe	☐	☐	☐	☐
Parties	☐	☐	☐	☐
Religious organisations	☐	☐	☐	☐
Legal system and courts	☐	☐	☐	☐
Military	☐	☐	☐	☐
Militias (armed groups)	☐	☐	☐	☐

115 | **Should the state play a larger or a smaller role in daily life or is it good as it is at the moment?**

☐	Larger role	☐	Good as it is	☐	Smaller role

116 | **If larger: Can you please specify the area where the state should be more present?**

☐	Social Security	☐	Surveillance	☐	Transparency	☐	Other

117 | **If smaller: Can you please specify the area where the state should be less present?**

☐	Social Security	☐	Surveillance	☐	Transparency	☐	Other

118 | **How do you term the events that have been taking place in the MENA region since late 2010 / early 2011?**

☐	Arab Spring	☐	Uprising	☐	Popular movement (haraka sha'biyya)
☐	Revolution	☐	Civil war	☐	Other
☐	Insurgency	☐	Foreign intervention	☐	No answer
☐	Riot	☐	Coup d'état (inqilab)		
☐	Rebellion	☐	Anarchy (fawda)		

119 | **Now, talking about these events, how would you judge the following statements?**

	Disagree	So-so	Agree	Don't know
The events did not change anything	☐	☐	☐	☐
The events are continuing	☐	☐	☐	☐
The events were started by the youth and then hijacked by others	☐	☐	☐	☐
The events united the youth globally	☐	☐	☐	☐
The events were of great importance for myself	☐	☐	☐	☐
The events were enabled by the secular youth	☐	☐	☐	☐
The Muslim Brotherhood made the events happen	☐	☐	☐	☐
The Islamists are strengthened by the events	☐	☐	☐	☐
The events changed my life	☐	☐	☐	☐
With the events, we are better off today	☐	☐	☐	☐

The events enabled Islamic solidarity to grow	☐	☐	☐	☐
The events enabled the secular forces to grow	☐	☐	☐	☐
The events brought the Arab people closer to each other	☐	☐	☐	☐
The events are responsible for widespread violence	☐	☐	☐	☐
International actors have supported Arab regimes too long	☐	☐	☐	☐
External actors instigated the events	☐	☐	☐	☐
International actors have long worked for Arab regimes to fall	☐	☐	☐	☐
The US wanted to stir up the whole region	☐	☐	☐	☐

120	Please, consider the following statements. Do you rather disagree or agree?										
		1 Completely disagree	2	3	4	5	6	7	8	9	10 Completely agree
	I perceive myself as a citizen with the same rights as all other citizens	☐	☐	☐	☐	☐	☐	☐	☐	☐	☐
	In this society not everybody has the same rights	☐	☐	☐	☐	☐	☐	☐	☐	☐	☐
	I feel excluded from society	☐	☐	☐	☐	☐	☐	☐	☐	☐	☐
	I am part of a minority	☐	☐	☐	☐	☐	☐	☐	☐	☐	☐

SOCIETY AND IDENTITY

121	How religious are you, on a scale of 1 (not religious) to 10 (very religious)?											
		1	2	3	4	5	6	7	8	9	10	Answer rejected
	Today	☐	☐	☐	☐	☐	☐	☐	☐	☐	☐	☐
	Five years ago	☐	☐	☐	☐	☐	☐	☐	☐	☐	☐	☐

122	Would you tell me your religious conviction?					
	☐	Muslim	☐	Jewish	☐	None
	☐	Christian	☐	Other	☐	No answer

123	Which visible signs of your religious orientation are you wearing/using? (Interviewer: Observe, don't ask).		
	☐ Prayer bump	☐	Cross
	☐ Headscarf	☐	Short djellaba (for men only)
	☐ Niqâb (for women only)	☐	None
	☐ Tattoo	☐	Other

124	What do you think? 'Religion is a private matter and nobody should interfere.'				
	☐ Yes	☐	No	☐	I do not care

125	Should Islam play a larger or a smaller role in daily life, or is it good as it is at the moment? (Auto-code 'does not apply' for non-Muslims)
	☐ Larger role
	☐ Good as it is
	☐ Smaller role

	□	Answer rejected
	□	Does not apply

126 What about your attachments to different groups. Do you feel attached to ...?

	1 Not at all	2	3	4	5	6	7	8	9	10 To- tally	Don't know
Your national community	□	□	□	□	□	□	□	□	□	□	□
Your religious community	□	□	□	□	□	□	□	□	□	□	□
The Arab nation	□	□	□	□	□	□	□	□	□	□	□
Your tribal community	□	□	□	□	□	□	□	□	□	□	□
People of your region	□	□	□	□	□	□	□	□	□	□	□
Your family	□	□	□	□	□	□	□	□	□	□	□
Young people around the world	□	□	□	□	□	□	□	□	□	□	□

127 What is most important for your personal future?

□	Good marriage	□	Good job	□	Good friends	□	Good family relations

128 Do you feel connected to young people in other countries who share the same interests?

	Yes	No
Music scene	□	□
Soccer	□	□
Other sports	□	□
Human rights movements	□	□
Fashion	□	□
Gaming	□	□
Travel	□	□
Religious groups	□	□
Other	□	□

129 Are you part of a fixed group of friends – a clique – that is meeting frequently and where everybody knows one another very well?

□	Yes	□	No

130 How satisfied are you with your circle of friends?

□	Very satisfied
□	Satisfied
□	So-so
□	Unsatisfied
□	Very unsatisfied

131 As individuals, we have ideas and visions about our personal life, our attitudes, and behaviour. If you reflect about possible achievements in your life, how important are the following points for you, on a scale from 1 = absolutely unimportant to 10 = absolutely important?

	1	2	3	4	5	6	7	8	9	10	No reply
Respecting law and order	□	□	□	□	□	□	□	□	□	□	□
Achieving a high standard of living	□	□	□	□	□	□	□	□	□	□	□

Paying attention to the codes of honour and shame	☐	☐	☐	☐	☐	☐	☐	☐	☐	☐	☐
Having power and exerting influence	☐	☐	☐	☐	☐	☐	☐	☐	☐	☐	☐
Developing my imagination and creativity	☐	☐	☐	☐	☐	☐	☐	☐	☐	☐	☐
Aiming for more security	☐	☐	☐	☐	☐	☐	☐	☐	☐	☐	☐
Acting independently of the advice of others	☐	☐	☐	☐	☐	☐	☐	☐	☐	☐	☐
Supporting socially excluded and marginalised people	☐	☐	☐	☐	☐	☐	☐	☐	☐	☐	☐
Pursuing my own agenda, even if against the interest of others	☐	☐	☐	☐	☐	☐	☐	☐	☐	☐	☐
Being diligent, hardworking, and ambitious	☐	☐	☐	☐	☐	☐	☐	☐	☐	☐	☐
Tolerating opinions that I do not agree with	☐	☐	☐	☐	☐	☐	☐	☐	☐	☐	☐
Being politically active	☐	☐	☐	☐	☐	☐	☐	☐	☐	☐	☐
Being able to select my partner	☐	☐	☐	☐	☐	☐	☐	☐	☐	☐	☐
Enjoying life as much as possible	☐	☐	☐	☐	☐	☐	☐	☐	☐	☐	☐
Doing what others are doing	☐	☐	☐	☐	☐	☐	☐	☐	☐	☐	☐
Safeguarding the traditions of my home country	☐	☐	☐	☐	☐	☐	☐	☐	☐	☐	☐
Engaging in a good family life	☐	☐	☐	☐	☐	☐	☐	☐	☐	☐	☐
Being proud of the history of my country	☐	☐	☐	☐	☐	☐	☐	☐	☐	☐	☐
Avoiding Westernisation	☐	☐	☐	☐	☐	☐	☐	☐	☐	☐	☐
Having a partner whom I can trust	☐	☐	☐	☐	☐	☐	☐	☐	☐	☐	☐
Having good friends who appreciate and accept me	☐	☐	☐	☐	☐	☐	☐	☐	☐	☐	☐
Being connected to others	☐	☐	☐	☐	☐	☐	☐	☐	☐	☐	☐
Living a consciously healthy life	☐	☐	☐	☐	☐	☐	☐	☐	☐	☐	☐
Allowing my decisions to be guided by my emotions	☐	☐	☐	☐	☐	☐	☐	☐	☐	☐	☐
Being financially independent from others	☐	☐	☐	☐	☐	☐	☐	☐	☐	☐	☐
Acting always in an environmentally conscious way	☐	☐	☐	☐	☐	☐	☐	☐	☐	☐	☐
Believing in God	☐	☐	☐	☐	☐	☐	☐	☐	☐	☐	☐
Spreading the message of Islam	☐	☐	☐	☐	☐	☐	☐	☐	☐	☐	☐

132 Whom do you approach …?

	My partner	Family	Friends	Neighbours	*Awlâd bled*	Internet platforms	Religious scholars	Public institutions	Private initiatives	Nobody	Don't know	Other
In case you need money?	☐	☐	☐	☐	☐	☐	☐	☐	☐	☐	☐	☐

In case you are looking for work?	☐	☐	☐	☐	☐	☐	☐	☐	☐	☐	☐	☐	
In case you are sick?	☐	☐	☐	☐	☐	☐	☐	☐	☐	☐	☐	☐	
In case of personal problems?	☐	☐	☐	☐	☐	☐	☐	☐	☐	☐	☐	☐	

133   **Do you believe that one needs a family to live a happy life, or can one be as happy or even happier living alone?**

☐	One needs a family	☐	One can live alone and be happy	☐	Alone, one definitely is happier	☐	Not sure

134   **How would you describe the relations between men and women ...?**

	In harmony	In tension	Don't know
... In your country	☐	☐	☐
... In your neighbourhood	☐	☐	☐
... In your family	☐	☐	☐

135   **Has it become more difficult to find a partner in recent years?**

☐	Yes	☐	No	☐	Don't know

136   **Why has it become more difficult to find a partner in recent years? Men:**

☐	Women demand higher financial security
☐	Women no longer accept traditional rules
☐	Women demand new models of partnership
☐	Women have become too demanding
☐	Lack of trust
☐	Other

137   **Why it has become more difficult to find a partner in recent years? Women:**

☐	Men are increasingly poor and cannot take care of a family
☐	Men are not ready to accept an educated woman
☐	Men's moral standards are decaying.
☐	Men have become too demanding
☐	Lack of trust
☐	Other

138   **What about children. Does one need children in order to live a happy life, or can one be as happy or even happier without children?**

☐	One needs own children	☐	One can live happily without children	☐	Without children, one definitely is happier	☐	Not sure

139   **Would you (or do you) raise your children the same way as your parents raised you?**

☐	In exactly the same way	☐	About the same	☐	Differently	☐	In a very different way

140 | Let us now talk about your anxieties concerning the future. Are you anxious about ...?

	Very much	Fairly	A little	Not at all	Cannot happen	No reply
Losing your work	☐	☐	☐	☐	☐	☐
Becoming poor	☐	☐	☐	☐	☐	☐
Becoming seriously sick	☐	☐	☐	☐	☐	☐
Not having friends	☐	☐	☐	☐	☐	☐
Being forced to leave your country for political reasons	☐	☐	☐	☐	☐	☐
Staying unmarried and single	☐	☐	☐	☐	☐	☐
Falling out seriously with your parents	☐	☐	☐	☐	☐	☐
Not being as successful in life as you wish	☐	☐	☐	☐	☐	☐
Becoming a victim of a terror attack	☐	☐	☐	☐	☐	☐
Becoming dependent on drugs	☐	☐	☐	☐	☐	☐
Being forced to leave your country for economic reasons	☐	☐	☐	☐	☐	☐
Increasing insecurity	☐	☐	☐	☐	☐	☐
Armed conflicts threatening your family	☐	☐	☐	☐	☐	☐

141 | What about changes in your life during the last 5 years. How important are they?

	Very unimportant	Unimportant	So-so	Important	Very important	Do not apply
Changes within the family	☐	☐	☐	☐	☐	☐
Social instability	☐	☐	☐	☐	☐	☐
Job losses	☐	☐	☐	☐	☐	☐
Food shortage	☐	☐	☐	☐	☐	☐
Sectarian divisions	☐	☐	☐	☐	☐	☐
Increasing separation from the outside world	☐	☐	☐	☐	☐	☐
Growing violence	☐	☐	☐	☐	☐	☐
Climate change	☐	☐	☐	☐	☐	☐

142 | How would you describe the relations between the younger and older generations ...?

	In harmony	In tension	Don't know
... In your country	☐	☐	☐
... In your neighbourhood	☐	☐	☐
... In your family	☐	☐	☐

143 | How will these generational relations develop in the future ...?

	Will improve	Will remain as they are	Will deteriorate	Don't know
... In your country	☐	☐	☐	☐
... In your neighbourhood	☐	☐	☐	☐
... In your family	☐	☐	☐	☐

144 | What about the distribution of wealth between the generations? Which of the following statements corresponds most with your opinion?

☐	Wealth is equitably distributed between the younger and the older generation
☐	The younger generation should reduce their demands in favour of the older generation

		The older generation should reduce their demands in favour of the younger generation
	☐	Don't know

COMMUNICATION

145	When (year) did you get your first mobile phone / smartphone?					
145a	Regular	_____	☐	Don't remember	☐	Never
145b	Smartphone	_____	☐	Don't remember	☐	Never

146	How many mobile phones / smartphones do you currently possess?			
	Regular	_	Smartphone	_

147	Do you currently possess a contract or do you use prepaid?				
	☐ Contract		☐ Prepaid	☐	Both

148	How much money do you spend for your mobile per month?		
	_____	☐	Don't know

149	Do you use the Internet?		
	☐ Yes	☐	No

150	In what year did you start using it?		
	_____	☐	Don't remember

151	And where do you use it?			
	☐	At home	☐	In shops, cafés, restaurants, etc.
	☐	At your workplace	☐	Everywhere where I have access to the net
	☐	Internet café (cyber)	☐	Other
	☐	In school / university		

152	Which devices do you usually use to connect to the Internet?	
	☐	Phone / Smartphone
	☐	Tablet /iPad
	☐	Desktop PC
	☐	Laptop
	☐	Smart TV

153	How many hours do you use the Internet per day?
	_____

154	Do you use ... ?							
	☐	Facebook	☐	Blogs	☐	WhatsApp	☐	Instagram
	☐	Skype	☐	Twitter	☐	Viber	☐	None

155	How do you use social networks like Facebook, blogs, or WhatsApp?				
		Never	Rarely	Frequently	Always
	Share music / videos/ pictures	☐	☐	☐	☐

	Look for work opportunities	☐	☐	☐	☐
	Organise meetings with my friends	☐	☐	☐	☐
	Keep in contact with friends and family	☐	☐	☐	☐
	Look for a possible partner	☐	☐	☐	☐
	Discuss politics	☐	☐	☐	☐
	Mobilise friends and other people for politics	☐	☐	☐	☐
	Actively oppose specific political positions	☐	☐	☐	☐
	Discuss religious affairs	☐	☐	☐	☐
	Mobilise friends and other people for religious affairs	☐	☐	☐	☐
	Actively oppose specific religious positions	☐	☐	☐	☐

PARTICIPATION

156	Are you interested in politics?						
	☐	Very interested	☐	Interested	☐	A little interested	☐ Not interested

157	Do you inform yourself actively about politics?		
	☐ Yes		☐ No

158	What sources and means of information do you use?							
	☐	Face-to-face conversation	☐	Internet	☐	Newspaper	☐	Other
	☐	Mobile	☐	TV	☐	Radio		

159 If there is something important to you, and you want to be heard or have a political impact, which of the following possibilities would you probably or probably not consider doing? Would you ...?

	Certainly not	Probably not	Maybe	Probably	Certainly	No answer
Participate in a demonstration	☐	☐	☐	☐	☐	☐
Participate in a strike	☐	☐	☐	☐	☐	☐
Join a political party	☐	☐	☐	☐	☐	☐
Participate in elections	☐	☐	☐	☐	☐	☐
Inform yourself via Internet or Twitter about joining an existing group	☐	☐	☐	☐	☐	☐
Mobilise others via Internet in order to act	☐	☐	☐	☐	☐	☐
Boycott buying certain goods	☐	☐	☐	☐	☐	☐
Distribute flyers	☐	☐	☐	☐	☐	☐
Sign an online petition	☐	☐	☐	☐	☐	☐
Engage in an association	☐	☐	☐	☐	☐	☐
Act as a sprayer	☐	☐	☐	☐	☐	☐

160	Which of these possibilities have you already used or participated in?			
	☐ Participate in a demonstration		☐	Distribute flyers
	☐ Participate in a strike		☐	Sign an online petition
	☐ Join a political party		☐	Engage in an association
	☐ Participate in elections		☐	Act as a sprayer

☐	Inform yourself via Internet or Twitter about joining an existing group	☐	None of the above
☐	Mobilise others via Internet in order to act	☐	No reply
☐	Boycott buying certain goods		

161 Do you engage for social or political goals or commit yourself for the benefit of other people for the following issues?

	Frequently	Occasionally	Never
For the interest of the young people	☐	☐	☐
For improving living together in my area of residence	☐	☐	☐
For organising useful activities in the leisure time of young people	☐	☐	☐
For a better and cleaner environment	☐	☐	☐
For improving the situation of disabled people	☐	☐	☐
For better provisions for and integration of foreign migrants/refugees	☐	☐	☐
For guaranteeing safety and order in my area of residence	☐	☐	☐
For helping poor and vulnerable people	☐	☐	☐
For social and political changes in my country	☐	☐	☐
For elderly people who depend on help and support	☐	☐	☐
For those who are coming from situations of armed conflicts	☐	☐	☐
For the culture and traditions of my country	☐	☐	☐
For my religious conviction	☐	☐	☐
For equal rights of men and women	☐	☐	☐
For other goals and groups	☐	☐	☐

162 Where and how do you engage?

	Yes	No
In a group at school or university	☐	☐
In an association	☐	☐
In a religious institution	☐	☐
As a member of a political party	☐	☐
As a member of a syndicate	☐	☐
As a member of a youth organisation	☐	☐

163 What are practical reasons for why you are NOT engaging in social projects?

	Strongly disagree	Disagree	So-so	Agree	Strongly agree	Don't know
There are no or only very few initiatives in my area	☐	☐	☐	☐	☐	☐
They are not professionally managed	☐	☐	☐	☐	☐	☐
It remains unclear where the money goes	☐	☐	☐	☐	☐	☐
It's only for the benefit of a few	☐	☐	☐	☐	☐	☐
Only strong men have a say	☐	☐	☐	☐	☐	☐
Volunteer work never pays off	☐	☐	☐	☐	☐	☐
The government is not supporting it	☐	☐	☐	☐	☐	☐
There is no income from that	☐	☐	☐	☐	☐	☐
There are no prospects in it	☐	☐	☐	☐	☐	☐
My family does not want me to do so	☐	☐	☐	☐	☐	☐
I am already struggling to make ends meet	☐	☐	☐	☐	☐	☐

164	What kind of leisure activities do you engage in most? Please identify up to 3 activities in which you engage the most during the week.		
	☐	TV	☐ Visiting a youth club
	☐	Listening to music	☐ Practising sport
	☐	Watching videos/DVDs	☐ Visiting neighbours or relatives
	☐	Surfing the Internet	☐ Just meeting people
	☐	Doing nothing, just relaxing, hanging out	☐ Engaging in a project
	☐	Reading books or magazines	☐ Doing something with the family
	☐	Going to the coffee shop	☐ Shopping
	☐	Going to the cinema or theatre	☐ Engaging with playing music or play-acting
	☐	Dancing, going to parties	☐ Listening to prayers and recitations
	☐	Computer gaming	☐ Other

165	How do you perceive your own future and personal life?		
	☐ Rather pessimistically	☐ Rather optimistically	☐ Mixed, both ways

166	And what about the future of our society? Do you perceive it ...?	
	☐ Rather pessimistically	☐ Rather optimistically

STABILITY AND MOBILITY

167	In life, some things continuously change; others rather remain as they are. To what extent is there stability in the different areas of your life?						
		Unstable	Rather unstable	So-so	Rather stable	Stable	Do not apply
	My economic situation	☐	☐	☐	☐	☐	☐
	Trust in my friends	☐	☐	☐	☐	☐	☐
	Personal belief in my skills	☐	☐	☐	☐	☐	☐
	Relations with my family	☐	☐	☐	☐	☐	☐
	Personal faith in my religion	☐	☐	☐	☐	☐	☐
	Political situation	☐	☐	☐	☐	☐	☐
	Prospects to live a fulfilled live	☐	☐	☐	☐	☐	☐
	Relationship with my partner	☐	☐	☐	☐	☐	☐

168	Have you ever ...?			
		Yes	No	No reply
	Witnessed violence	☐	☐	☐
	Experienced your house or your means of production being deliberately destroyed	☐	☐	☐
	Needed to see a doctor as you have been beaten up	☐	☐	☐
	Been in jail	☐	☐	☐
	Suffered from hunger	☐	☐	☐
	Suffered from torture	☐	☐	☐
	Been injured in an armed conflict	☐	☐	☐
	Experienced violence within the family	☐	☐	☐
	Experienced expulsion or displacement	☐	☐	☐

Experienced psychological violence	☐	☐	☐
Been beaten up several times	☐	☐	☐
Experienced sexual harassment (verbally, physically)	☐	☐	☐
Joined a demonstration that turned violent	☐	☐	☐
Experienced any form of violence	☐	☐	☐

169 Would you consider yourself a refugee?

☐	Yes	☐	No

170 Do you rather agree or rather disagree with the following statements?

	Strongly disagree	Disa-gree	So-so	Agree	Strongly agree	Does not apply
If I consider all the violence presented in the media, I get sad and depressed	☐	☐	☐	☐	☐	☐
In the public space, the situation is becoming increasingly tense	☐	☐	☐	☐	☐	☐
In order to be able to defend myself, I practise a self-defence sport (karate, etc.).	☐	☐	☐	☐	☐	☐
Others continuously threaten me	☐	☐	☐	☐	☐	☐
I am afraid that armed conflicts will threaten my livelihood and my family	☐	☐	☐	☐	☐	☐
I believe that the use of violence will only cause further violence	☐	☐	☐	☐	☐	☐
I hate violence. I cannot stand it when people suffer from it	☐	☐	☐	☐	☐	☐
In order to defend myself, or my family, the use of violence is legitimate	☐	☐	☐	☐	☐	☐
In case of severe conflicts, there is no other solution: we have to demonstrate strength, even with violence	☐	☐	☐	☐	☐	☐
Women dressing inappropriately should not complain about sexual harassment	☐	☐	☐	☐	☐	☐

171 Have you ever lived outside your own country?

☐	Yes	☐	No

172 Where exactly did you live?

☐	Gulf	☐	Europe	☐	Australia	☐	Latin America
☐	Other Arab country	☐	USA / Canada	☐	Asia	☐	Sub-Saharan Africa

173 Is there somebody in your family who migrated to a foreign country?

☐	Yes	☐	No

174 Where to exactly?

☐	Gulf	☐	Europe	☐	Australia	☐	Latin America
☐	Other Arab country	☐	USA / Canada	☐	Asia	☐	Sub-Saharan Africa

175 Is this emigration of any importance to you?

☐	Yes	☐	No

176	**Which of the following statements best reflects your opinion?**
☐	I consider it as a loss for my personal life
☐	I profit from the money he/she is sending to us
☐	I learned from his/her experiences abroad and decided that emigration is not a goal for me
☐	I am fascinated by the idea of living in a foreign country, and my wish to emigrate has grown
☐	My feelings about emigration started to get mixed up

177	**Have you been in contact (by phone, SMS, Skype) with somebody who is trying to find a job or asylum in Europe within the last three months?**		
☐	Yes	☐	No

178	**If yes, who have you been in contact with?**						
☐	Family	☐	Friends	☐	Neighbours	☐	Others

179	**What would best describe your situation?**		
☐	I am definitely not emigrating	☐	I would like to emigrate
☐	I sometimes played with the idea of emigrating	☐	I am sure that I will emigrate

180	**Recently, a lot of people are on their way to Europe. If you were to emigrate, what would be your preferred target countries?**							
☐	Sweden	☐	Finland	☐	Luxembourg	☐	Switzerland
☐	Spain	☐	France	☐	Netherlands	☐	Other
☐	Belgium	☐	Germany	☐	Portugal	☐	None
☐	Bulgaria	☐	Greece	☐	United Kingdom		
☐	Denmark	☐	Italy	☐	Austria		

181	**In order to change your current situation, would you be ready …?**						
		Disagree	Rather disagree	Not sure	Rather agree	Agree	Does not apply / Don't know
	To leave your family in order to obtain good professional qualifications	☐	☐	☐	☐	☐	☐
	To leave your family even if you risk your life	☐	☐	☐	☐	☐	☐
	To accept work that is very much below your qualification	☐	☐	☐	☐	☐	☐
	To marry somebody from a class that is way above your personal background	☐	☐	☐	☐	☐	☐
	To marry somebody from a class that is way below your personal background	☐	☐	☐	☐	☐	☐
	To accept work in a rural region of your country	☐	☐	☐	☐	☐	☐
	To accept work in a rural region in an Arab country	☐	☐	☐	☐	☐	☐
	To accept work in a rural region in Europe	☐	☐	☐	☐	☐	☐
	To marry somebody with a different religion	☐	☐	☐	☐	☐	☐
	To marry somebody who is significantly older than you	☐	☐	☐	☐	☐	☐

182–184	**[Technical information]**

185	When did you leave Syria (last departure)?			
	Month __		Year _____	

186	Did you leave for good or are you going back?		
	☐ Permanently here	☐ Sometimes go back	☐ Going back frequently

187	Did other members of your family come with you?						
	☐ Alone	☐ Father	☐ Brother	☐ Children
	☐ Husband/wife	☐ Mother	☐ Sister	☐ Other

188	How many members of your household (*usra*) have fled to this day?
	__

Could you tell us something about the different steps concerning this experience?

189	Please, indicate the situation that fits best.
	☐ The entire family (*usra*) left together at once
	☐ All are gone now, but the family members left individually in different periods
	☐ Some family members are still at home

190	What is your situation today?
	☐ Today the family (*usra*) is together in one country and in one place
	☐ Today the family is together in one country, but in different places
	☐ Today the family lives in different countries

191	Please, identify the countries.
	Country 1 _____
	Country 2 _____
	Country 3 _____

192	For yourself, what were the ultimate reasons to leave your home?	Strongly agree	Agree	So-so	Disagree	Strongly disagree	Does not apply
	I had to leave with my family	☐	☐	☐	☐	☐	☐
	Immediate threat to life	☐	☐	☐	☐	☐	☐
	House / apartment was destroyed	☐	☐	☐	☐	☐	☐
	No income available and no resources left	☐	☐	☐	☐	☐	☐
	Nothing left to eat, suffering hunger	☐	☐	☐	☐	☐	☐
	Fear of being kidnapped	☐	☐	☐	☐	☐	☐
	Uniting with family members	☐	☐	☐	☐	☐	☐
	Avoiding forced recruitment	☐	☐	☐	☐	☐	☐
	No prospects over there	☐	☐	☐	☐	☐	☐
	Medical emergency	☐	☐	☐	☐	☐	☐

193	Had you been able to prepare yourself to leave or was it a sudden decision?	
	☐ Prepared	☐ Unprepared

194	**Has your household lost property?**				
	☐ Yes		☐ No		☐ Don't know

195	**What is ultimately lost?**			
	☐ House	☐ Car		☐ Animals
	☐ Machinery	☐ Land		☐ Valuables

196	**Did anyone in your family lose their life during the flight?**	
	☐ Yes	☐ No

197	**How many persons?**
	_____

198	**Who from your family lost their life during the flight?**						
	☐ Husband	☐ Children		☐ Mother		☐ Sister
	☐ Wife	☐ Father		☐ Brother		☐ Other

199	**What are the main reasons?**	
	☐ Violent attacks and fighting	☐ Stress in situations of insecurity
	☐ Insufficient medical supply	☐ An age-related death
	☐ Infectious disease	☐ Other
	☐ Hunger	☐ Don't know
	☐ Drowning	

200	**What is your current legal status?**	
	☐ Visa	☐ Registered by UNHCR
	☐ Not registered (visiting, etc.)	☐ Registered by UNRWA
	☐ Registered by host state	

201	**Are you allowed to work?**
	☐ Not allowed and not tolerated
	☐ Not allowed but tolerated
	☐ Allowed

202	**What would be the necessary conditions for returning home?**	Very unimportant	Rather unimportant	So-so	Rather important	Very important	Does not apply
	Ceasefire in my local region	☐	☐	☐	☐	☐	☐
	A comprehensive peace	☐	☐	☐	☐	☐	☐
	Disarmament of the war parties	☐	☐	☐	☐	☐	☐
	A stable government	☐	☐	☐	☐	☐	☐
	A new political system	☐	☐	☐	☐	☐	☐
	Restoration of infrastructure	☐	☐	☐	☐	☐	☐
	Economic recovery in my home country	☐	☐	☐	☐	☐	☐
	Establishment of a truth committee for reconciliation	☐	☐	☐	☐	☐	☐
	Compensation payments for lost property	☐	☐	☐	☐	☐	☐
	Amnesty for war crimes	☐	☐	☐	☐	☐	☐

Compensation payments for lost property	☐	☐	☐	☐	☐	☐
Amnesty for war crimes	☐	☐	☐	☐	☐	☐

Please estimate the chances concerning your life within the next five years for two scenarios.

203 A: If you stay where you are, how likely are you …?

	Very likely	Likely	Unlikely	Impossible	Does not apply
To get married as you wish	☐	☐	☐	☐	☐
To find a good job	☐	☐	☐	☐	☐
To complete your studies	☐	☐	☐	☐	☐
To develop necessary skills	☐	☐	☐	☐	☐
To own a place to live	☐	☐	☐	☐	☐
To live together with your family	☐	☐	☐	☐	☐

B: If you leave for Europe, how likely are you …?

	Very likely	Likely	Unlikely	Impossible	Does not apply
To get married as you wish	☐	☐	☐	☐	☐
To find a good job	☐	☐	☐	☐	☐
To complete your studies	☐	☐	☐	☐	☐
To develop necessary skills	☐	☐	☐	☐	☐
To own a place to live	☐	☐	☐	☐	☐
To live together with your family	☐	☐	☐	☐	☐

204 In Europe, people might be happy or anxious about refugees. To what extent do you agree with the following statements?

	Strongly Agree	Agree	So-so	Disagree	Strongly disagree	No reply
The people over there understand us and will help us	☐	☐	☐	☐	☐	☐
Integration is possible, even if it takes time	☐	☐	☐	☐	☐	☐
We always remain foreigners. Only the next generation might be integrated	☐	☐	☐	☐	☐	☐
You just need a partner in Europe and marry him/her and you are at home	☐	☐	☐	☐	☐	☐
Once you possess the right passport, everything else is of no importance	☐	☐	☐	☐	☐	☐
If you have work, you will manage	☐	☐	☐	☐	☐	☐
You need language skills in order to find work	☐	☐	☐	☐	☐	☐
It will take years to be able to speak the language	☐	☐	☐	☐	☐	☐

205 If you would have to assess your remaining energy for the tasks of the next three months, what would describe your situation?

☐	I am tired	☐	I am ready to learn a new language
☐	I need to recover	☐	I am ready to adjust to a new cultural environment
☐	I am just hoping for a safe situation	☐	No answer
☐	I am ready to work even harder		

Appendix III: Strata Index

Table A.6 **Strata Index: Variables, Scores and Shares**

	Score	Percentage
Father's level of education (highest degree)		
– Primary school	2	44
– Secondary / intermediate school	4	37
– University	6	15
– Unknown	2	3
Assessment of the economic situation of the family in 2016		
– Very good	3	11
– Rather good	2	60
– Rather bad	1	19
– Very bad	0	9
Housing situation		
– Tenant	1	30
– Owner	2	68
– No Answer	1	3
Wealth ranking (highest score counts)		
– Air conditioning	2	32
– Own vehicle	3	39
– Internet access	1	47
– None of the above	0	42

Questions 20, 30, 52, 55.

Note (n=9,000). The calculation of the Strata Index is based on four aspects: Father's level of education, family's economic situation, housing ownership, and wealth indicators (see Chapter 2). Given the 15 different aspects to score, between 3 and 14 points could be achieved. We classified the 9,000 single sums into quintiles – five groups, ideally of the same size (see Figure 2.2). The 'Lowest stratum' scored 5 points and less, the 'Lower-middle stratum' between 6 and 7 points, the 'Middle stratum' between 8 and 9 points, the 'Higher-middle stratum' between 10 and 11 points, and the 'Highest stratum' scored 12 points and more. The 'Percentage' reveals the distribution throughout the whole sample.

THE CALCULATION OF THE STRATA INDEX is based on four variables: father's level of education, family's economic situation, home ownership, and wealth indicators (see Chapter 2). Given the fifteen different response options – with between 0 and 6 points assignable to each variable – a total of 3 to 14 points could be accumulated. The 9,000 individual totals were then classified according to five quintiles, that is, five groups ideally of the same size (see Figure 2.2): the 'lowest stratum' scored 5 points or less, the 'lower-middle stratum' 6 or 7 points, the 'middle stratum' 8 or 9 points, the 'higher-middle stratum' 10 or 11 points, and the 'highest stratum' scored 12 points or more. The percentage reveals distribution for the entire sample.

Bibliography

Abdulla, Rasha (2007): *The Internet in the Arab World: Egypt and Beyond,* New York: Peter Lang.

Achebe, Chinua ([1958] 2001): *Things Fall Apart,* London: Penguin.

AHDR (*Arab Human Development Report*) (2006): *Arab Human Development Report 2005: Towards the Rise of Women in the Arab World,* New York: United Nations Development Programme.

AHDR (*Arab Human Development Report*) (2005, published 2006): *Arab Human Development Report 2016: Youth and the Prospects for Human Development in a Changing Reality,* New York: United Nations Development Programme.

Albert, Mathias, Hurrelmann, Klaus, Quenzel, Gudrun, and TNS Infratest Social Research (2015): *Jugend 2015: 17. Shell Jugendstudie* (17th Shell Youth Study), Frankfurt am Main: Fischer Taschenbuch Verlag.

Albrecht, Holger (2008): 'The Nature of Political Participation', in Ellen Lust-Okar and Saloua Zerhouni, eds, *Political Participation in the Middle East and North Africa,* Boulder: Lynne Rienner, pp. 15–32.

Al-Ali, Naje, Ali, Zahra, and Marler, Isabel (2016): 'Reflections on Authoring the Chapter on Young Women for the 2016 Arab Human Development Report', in *Jadaliyya,* 9 December 2016, http://www.jadaliyya.com/pages/index/25627/reflections-on-authoring-the-chapter-on-young-women.

Alhassen, M. and Shihab-Eldin, A., eds, (2012): *Demanding Dignity: Young Voices from the Front Lines of the Arab Revolutions,* Ashland, Oregon: White Cloud Press.

Alsharekh, Alanoud, ed., (2007): *The Gulf Family: Kinship Policies and Modernity,* London: Saqi Books.

Atkinson, Anthony B. (2015): *Inequality: What Can Be Done?,* Cambridge, Massachusetts: Harvard University Press.

El Ayadi, Mohammed, Tozy, Hassan and Rachik, Mohamed (2013): *L'Islam au Quotidien: Enquête sur les valeurs et les pratiques religieuses au Maroc,* Casablanca: Editions prologues.

Barakat, H. (1993): *The Arab World: Society, Culture, and State,* Berkeley: University of California Press.

Bauman, Zygmunt (2007): *Liquid Times: Living in an Age of Uncertainty*, Cambridge: Polity Press.

Bayat, Asef (2007): *Making Islam Democratic: Social Movements and the Post-Islamist Turn*, Palo Alto, California: Stanford University Press.

——— (2010a): *Life as Politics: How Ordinary People Change the Middle East*, Amsterdam: Amsterdam University Press.

——— (2010b): 'Muslim Youth and Claimfor Youthfulness' in Linda Herrera and Asef Bayat, eds, *Being Young and Muslim: New Cultural Politics in the Global South and North*, Oxford: Oxford University Press, pp. 27–47

——— (2011): 'Reclaiming Youthfulness', in Samir Khalaf and Roseanne Saad Khalaf, eds, *Arab Youth: Social Mobilization in Times of Risk*, London: Saqi Books, pp. 47–66.

——— (2013): 'Revolution in Bad Times', in *New Left Review,* no. 80, March, pp. 47–60.

——— (2017): *Revolution without Revolutionaries: Making Sense of the Arab Spring*, Stanford: Stanford University Press.

Bayat, Asef, and Herrera, Linda eds, (2010): 'Introduction: Being Young and Muslim in Neoliberal Times' in Linda Herrera and Asef Bayat, eds, *Being Young and Muslim: New Cultural Politics in the Global South and North,* Oxford: Oxford University Press, pp. 3–24.

Beckert, Jens (2016): *Imagined Futures: Fictional Expectations and Capitalist Dynamic,* London: Harvard University Press.

Bennani-Chraïbi, Mounia (1994): *Soumis et rebelles: Les jeunes au Maroc,* Paris: CNRS Éditions.

Bonnefoy, Laurent, and Catusse, Myriam, eds, (2013): *Jeunesses Arabes: Du Maroc au Yémen. Loisirs, cultures et politiques,* Paris: La découverte.

Boubekeur, Amel, and Olivier, Roy (2009): *Whatever Happened to the Islamists? Salafism, Heavy Metal Muslims and the Lure of Consumerist Islam,* London: Hurst.

Bourdieu, Pierre (1979 [1982]): *Die feinen Unterschiede: Kritik der gesellschaftlichen Urteilskraft,* Frankfurt: Suhrkamp.

——— (1980): *La jeunesse n'est qu'un mot: Questions de sociologie,* Paris: Minuit.

————(1983): 'Ökonomisches Kapital, Soziales Kapital, Kulturelles Kapital', in R. Kreckel, ed., *Soziale Ungleichheiten,* Göttingen: Schwartz, pp. 183–98.

Braune, Ines (2008): *Aneignungen des Globalen: Internet-Alltag in der arabischen Welt: Eine Fallstudie in Marokko,* Bielefeld, transcript Verlag.

————(2011): 'Internet(forschung) in der arabischen Welt: Laute Hoffnungen, leiser Wandel', in *Global Media Journal,* vol. 1, no. 1, pp. 1–13.

Brechenmacher, Saskia (2017): *Civil Society under Assault: Repression and Responses in Russia, Egypt, and Ethiopia,* Washington, DC: Carnegie Endowment for International Peace.

Burson-Marsteller (2015): 7th Annual ASDA'A Burson-Marsteller Arab Youth Survey 2015, available online, http://www.burson-marsteller.swiss/was-wir-tun/unser-denken/7th-annual-asdaa-burson-marsteller-arab-youth-survey-2015/

Calkins, Sandra (2016): *Who Knows Tomorrow? Uncertainty in North Eastern Sudan,* New York–Oxford: Berghahn.

Campbell, Hugh (2009): '*Breaking New Ground in Food Regime Theory: Corporate Environmentalism, Ecological Feedbacks and the "Food from Somewhere" Regime?',* in *Agriculture and Human Values,* vol. 26, no. 4, pp. 309–19.

Carothers, Thomas, and Brechenmacher, Saskia (2014): *Closing Space: Democracy and Human Rights Support under Fire,* Washington, DC: Carnegie Endowment for International Peace.

Carvatorta, Francesco (2012): 'Arab Spring: The Awakening of Civil Society. A General Overview', in *IEMed Mediterranean Yearbook,* pp. 75–81.

Castel, Robert, (2009): 'Die Wiederkehr der sozialen Unsicherheit', in Robert Castel and Klaus Dörre, eds, *Prekarität, Abstieg, Ausgrenzung: Die soziale Frage am Beginn des 21. Jahrhunderts,* Frankfurt: Campus, pp. 21–34.

Castel, Robert, and Dörre, Klaus, eds, (2009): *Prekarität, Abstieg, Ausgrenzung: Die soziale Frage am Beginn des 21. Jahrhunderts,* Frankfurt: Campus.

Catusse, Myriam, and Destremau, Blandine (2016): 'Governing Youth, Managing Society: A Comparative Overview of Six Country Case Studies', Power2Youth, Working Paper 14, June. available

online, https://halshs.archives-ouvertes.fr/halshs-01574738/
document

Chalcraft, John (2008): *The Invisible Cage: Syrian Migrant Workers in Lebanon.* Stanford: Stanford University Press.

Chambers, Robert (1989): 'Vulnerability, Coping and Policy', IDS Bulletin, vol. 20, no. 2, pp. 1–7.

Chambers, Robert, and Conway G. R. (1987): 'Sustainable Rural Livelihoods: Practical Concepts for the 21st Century', IDS Discussion Paper 296, available online, https://www.ids.ac.uk/publication/sustainable-rural-livelihoods-practical-concepts-for-the-21st-century

CIO (Central Informatics Organization) (2015): Population of Bahrain 2014: http://www.data.gov.bh/en/ResourceCenter/DownloadFile?id=1453

Côté, J. (2014): 'Towards a New Political Economy of Youth', in *Journal of Youth Studies,* vol. 17, no. 4, pp. 527–43.

Credit Suisse (2016): *Global Wealth Report 2016,* available online, https://www.credit-suisse.com/corporate/en/articles/news-and-expertise/the-global-wealth-report-2016-201611.html

Crush, Jonathan , ed., (1995): *Power of Development,* London–New York: Routledge.

Dabashi, Hamid (2012): *The Arab Spring: The End of Postcolonialism,* London: Zed Books.

Davis, Susan S., and Davis, Douglas A. (1989): *Adolescence in a Moroccan Town: Making Social Sense,* New Brunswick: Rutgers University Press.

De Haas, Hein (2014): 'Migration Theory: Quo Vadis?' DEMIG project paper 24, International Migration Institute, University of Oxford, https://www.imi.ox.ac.uk/publications/wp-100-14

Dekmejian, R. H. (1988): 'Islamic Revival: Catalysts, Categories, and Consequences, in S. T. Hunter, ed., *The Politics of Islamic Revivalism: Diversity and Unity,* Washington, DC: Center for Strategic and International Studies, pp. 3–19.

Devereux, Stephen (2007): Introduction for 'Old Famines to New Famines', in S. Devereux, ed., *The New Famines: Why Famines Persist in an Era of Globalization,* London: Routledge, pp. 1–26.

Dhillon, Navtej (2008): '*Middle East Youth Bulge: Challenge or Opportunity?',* Washington, DC: Brookings Institution Press.

Dhillon, Navtej, and Yousef, Tarik, eds, (2009): *Generation in Waiting: The Unfulfilled Promise of Young People in the Middle East*, Washington, DC: Brookings Institution Press.

Dionigi, Filippo (2016): 'The Syrian Refugee Crisis in Lebanon: State Fragility and Social Resilience', *LSE Middle East Centre Paper Series 15*, http://eprints.lse.ac.uk/65565/1/Dionigi_Syrian_Refugees%20in%20Lebanon_Author_2016.pdf

Dixon, Marion (2014): 'The Land Grab, Finance Capital, and Food Regime Restructuring: The Case of Egypt', in *Review of African Political Economy*, vol. 41, no. 140, pp. 232–48.

Dörre, Klaus (2009): 'Prekarität im Finanzmarkt-Kapitalismus', in Robert Castel and Klaus Dörre, eds, *Prekarität, Abstieg, Ausgrenzung: Die soziale Frage am Beginn des 21. Jahrhunderts,* Frankfurt: Campus, pp. 35–64.

Durac, Vincent, and Cavatorta, Francesco (2015): *Politics and Governance in the Middle East*, London: Palgrave.

Durham, D. (2000): 'Youth and the Social Imagination in Africa: Introduction to Parts 1 and 2', in *Anthropological Quarterly,* vol. 73, no. 3, pp. 113–20.

Edkins, Jenny (2007): 'The Criminalization of Mass Starvations: From Natural Disaster to Crime against Humanity', in S. Devereux, ed., *The New Famines: Why Famines Persist in an Era of Globalization,* London: Routledge.

Ellis, Frank (2000): *Rural Livelihoods and Diversity in Developing Countries*, Oxford: Oxford University Press.

El-Masry, Gamal Zaki (1994): *Die afrikanische Auslandsverschuldung,* Berlin: Haupt Verlag.

Elwert, Georg Hans-Dieter Evers, and Wilkens, Werner (1983): 'Die Suche nach Sicherheit: Kombinierte Produktionsformen im sogenannten Informellen Sektor', in *Zeitschrift für Soziologie*, vol. 12, no. 4, pp. 281–96.

Emperador Badimón, Montserrat (2009): 'The Unemployed Graduate's Movement in Morocco: Challenging the Unlikelihood of a Collective Action', in *Revista Internacional de Sociología*, vol. 67, no. 1, pp. 29–58, DOI: 10.3989/ris.2009.i1.121.

Escobar, Arturo (1995): *Encountering Development: The Making and Unmaking of the Third World,* Princeton: Princeton University Press.

Esposito, J. L. (1999): *The Islamic Threat: Myth or Reality?*, Oxford: Oxford University Press.

Evers, H.-D., F. Betke, and S. Pitomo (1983): Die Komplexität der Grundbedürfnisse: Eine Untersuchung über städtische Haushalte der untersten Einkommensschichten in Jakarta, Bielefeld: Universität Bielefeld, Fakultät für Soziologie, Forschungsschwerpunkt Entwicklungssoziologie.

FAO/WFP (Food and Agriculture Organization/World Food Programme) (2016): Special Report: FAO/WFP Crop and Food Security Assessment Mission to the Syrian Arab Republic, Rome, FAO/WFP.

Fargues, Philippe (2017): 'Mass Migration and Uprisings in Arab Countries: An Analytical Framework', in *International Development Policy*, vol. 7, pp. 170–83.

Feierabend, Sabine, Plankenborn, Theresa, and Rathgeb, Thomas (2016): 'Jugend, Information, Multimedia: Ergebnisse der JIM-Studie 2016', in *Media Perspektiven*, vol 12, pp. 586–97.

El Feki, Shereen, Heilman, Brian, and Barker, Gary, eds., (2017): *Understanding Masculinities: Results from the International Men and Gender Equality Survey (IMAGES): Middle East and North Africa.* Cairo and Washington, DC: UN Women and Promundo-US.

Fritzsche, Yvonne (2000): 'Modernes Leben: gewandelt, vernetzt und verkabelt', in A. Fischer, Yvonne Fritzsche and Werner Fuchs-Heinritzl, eds, *Jugend 2000: 13th Shell Jugendstudie*, Opladen: Leske und Budrich, pp. 181–220.

Fuller, Gary (1995): 'The Demographic Backdrop to Ethnic Conflict: A Geographic Overview', in Central Intelligence Agency, ed., *The Challenge of Ethnic Conflict to National and International Order in the 1990s*, Washington, DC, pp. 151–54.

Galtung, Johan (1969): 'Violence, Peace, and Peace Research', in *Journal of Peace Research*, vol. 6, no. 3, pp. 167–91.

Gebel, Michael, and Heyne, Stefanie (2014): *Transitions to adulthood in the Middle East and North Africa: Young women's rising?*, New York: Palgrave.

Gellner, Ernest (1969): *Saints of the Atlas*, Chicago: University of Chicago Press.

Gertel, Jörg (2005): 'Food Security and Nutrition: The Impact of Globalization and Urbanization: Middle East/North Africa', in Uwe Kracht and Manfred Schulz, eds, *Food and Nutrition Security in the Process of Globalization*, Münster: Lit Verlag, pp. 183–97.

———— (2007): 'Theorien über Entwicklung und Unterentwicklung: Grundlegungen und fachwissenschaftliche Leitlinien', in Dieter Böhn and Eberhard Rothfuß, eds, *Entwicklungsräume: Handbuch des Geographieunterrichtes*, vol. 8.1, Köln: Aulis Verlag, pp. 52–72.

———— (2010): *Globalisierte Nahrungskrisen: Bruchzone Kairo,* Bielefeld: transcript Verlag.

———— (2014): 'Krise und Widerstand', in Jörg Gertel and Rachid Ouaissa, eds, *Jugendbewegungen: Städtischer Widerstand und Umbrüche in der Arabischen Welt,* Bielefeld: transcript Verlag, pp. 32–75.

———— (2015): 'Spatialities of Hunger: Postnational Spaces, Assemblages and Fragmenting Liabilities', in *Middle East: Topics and Arguments,* vol. 5, pp. 25–35.

———— (2017): 'Arab Youth: A Contained Youth?', in *Middle East: Topics and Arguments*, vol. 9, pp. 25–33, http://meta-journal.net/article/view/7218.

Gertel, Jörg, and Breuer, Ingo, eds, (2012) Alltagsmobilitäten: Aufbruch marokkanischer Lebenswelten. Bielefeld: transcript Verlag.

Gertel, Jörg, and Ouaissa, Rachid, eds, (2014): *Jugendbewegungen: Städtischer Widerstand und Umbrüche in der Arabischen Welt,* Bielefeld: transcript Verlag.

Gertel, Jörg, and Sippel, Sarah Ruth, eds, (2014): *Seasonal Workers in Mediterranean Agriculture: The Social Costs of Eating Fresh* Milton Park/New York: Routledge.

———— (2016): 'The Financialisation of Agriculture and Food', in Mark Shucksmith and David L. Brown, eds, *Routledge International Handbook of Rural Studies,* London – New York: Routledge, pp. 215–26.

Gertel, Jörg, Rottenburg, Richard, and Calkins, Sandra, eds (2014): *Disrupting Territories: Land, Commodification and Conflict in Sudan*, Woodbridge: James Currey.

Giddens, Anthony (1992): *Die Konstitution der Gesellschaft: Grundzüge einer Theorie der Strukturierung,* Frankfurt: Campus.

Granovetter, Mark (1973): 'The Strength of Weak Ties', in *American Journal of Sociology,* vol. 78, no. 6, pp. 1360–80.

Haberly, Daniel (2013): 'White Knights from the Gulf: Sovereign Wealth Fund Investment and the Evolution of German Industrial Finance', in *Economic Geography,* vol. 90, no. 3), pp. 293–320.

Haenni, Patrick (2005): *L'islam de marché: L'autre révolution conservatrice*, Paris: Seuil.

Halaseh, Rama (2012): 'Civil Society, Youth and the Arab Spring', in Stephen Calleya and Monika Wohlfeld, eds, *Change and Opportunities in the Emerging Mediterranean*, Malta: Mediterranean Academy of Diplomatic Studies, University of Malta.

Hamdi, Samiha, and Weipert-Fenner, Irene (2017): 'Mobilization of the Marginalized: Unemployed Activism in Tunisia', Working Paper, American University in Beirut, https://www.aub.edu.lb/ifi/publications/Documents/working_papers/20171026_tunisia_working_paper.pdf, accessed 27.10.2017.

Harvey, David (2005): *A Brief History of Neoliberalism*, Oxford: Oxford University Press.

Hasso, Frances S. (2011): *Consuming desires: Family crisis and the state in the Middle East*, Stanford, California: Stanford University Press.

Hecker, Pierre (2012): *Turkish Metal: Music, Meaning, and Morality in a Muslim Society*, London: Ashgate.

Hecker, Pierre (2014): "A Clash of Lifestyles?' – Jugendliche Lebensstile im politischen Diskurs der Türkei', in Jörg Gertel and Rachid Ouiassa, eds, *Jugendbewegungen*, Bielefeld: transcript, pp. 326-352.

Hegasy, Sonja (2016): 'Gesellschaftspolitik in der Grauzone: Die Arbeit der Friedrich-Ebert-Stiftung in Ägypten von 1994 bis 2014', in Sigrid Faath, Sonja Hegasy, Volker Vinnai, and Achim Vogt, eds, *Herausforderungen in arabischen Staaten: Die Friedrich-Ebert-Stiftung im Nahen Osten und in Nordafrika, Reihe Geschichte der internationalen Arbeit der Friedrich-Ebert-Stiftung*, vol. 13, Bonn: Verlag J. H. W. Dietz Nachf., pp. 327–84.

Hegasy, Sonja, and Kaschl, Elke (2007): *Changing Values among Youth: Examples from the Arab World and Germany*, Berlin: Klaus Schwarz-Verlag.

Hepp, Andreas, and Krotz, Friedrich, eds, (2014): *Mediatized Worlds*, Houndsmills: Palgrave.

Herrera, Linda (2012) 'Youth and Citizenship in the Digital Age: A View from Egypt', *Harvard Educational Review*, vol. 82, no. 3, pp. 333–52.

———— (2017a): 'It's Time to Talk about Youth in the Middle East as the Precariat', in *Middle East: Topics and Arguments*, vol. 9, pp. 35–44, DOI: 10.17192/meta.2017.9.7061.

———— (2017b): 'The Precarity of Youth: Entrepreneurship Is Not the Solution', in *Mada masr*, 17 February, https://www.madamasr.com/en/2017/02/11/opinion/society/the-precarity-of-youth-entrepreneurship-is-not-the-solution/.

Herrera, Linda, and Bayat, Asef, eds, (2010): *Being Young and Muslim: New Cultural Politics in the Global South and North*, Oxford – New York: Oxford University Press.

Honwana, Alcinda (2012): *The Time of Youth. Work, Social Change and Politics in Africa*. Sterling: Kumarian Press

Honwana, Alcinda (2013): *Youth and Revolution in Tunisia*, London: Zed Books.

Honwana, Alcinda, and De Boeck, Filip, eds, (2005): *Makers and Breakers: Children and Youth in Postcolonial Africa*, Oxford: James Currey.

Hopkins, Nicholas S., ed., (2003): *The New Arab Family*, Cairo: American University in Cairo Press.

Janmyr, Maja (2016): 'Precarity in Exile: The Legal Status of Syrian Refugees in Lebanon', in *Refugee Survey Quarterly*, vol. 35, pp. 58–78.

Joseph, Suad, (2008): 'Familism and critical Arab family studies' in Katherine M. Yount and Hoda Rashad, eds, *Family in the Middle East: Ideational change in Egypt, Iran, and Tunisia*, New York: Routledge, pp. 25–39.

Kepel, Gilles (2000): *Jihad: Expansion et Déclin de l'Islamisme*, Paris: Gallimard.

Khalaf, Samir and Khalaf, Roseanne S., eds, (2012): *Arab Youth: Social Mobilisation in Times of Risk*, London: Saqi.

Labidi, Lilia (2017): 'Celibate Women, the Construction of Identity, Karama (Dignity), and the "Arab Spring"', in *Gender*, vol. 9, no. 1, pp. 11–29, DOI: 10.3224/gender.v9i1.02.

Lamloum, Olfa, and Ben Zina, Mohamed Ali (2015): *Les jeunes de Douar Hicher et d'Ettadhamen: une enquête sociologique*, Tunis: International Alert.

Larzillière, Pénélope, (2004): *Être jeune en Palestine*, Paris: Voix et regards, Balland.

Lorey, Isabell (2012): *Die Regierung der Prekären*, Wien – Berlin: Verlag Turia and Kant.

Lubkemann, Stephen C. (2008): Involuntary Immobility: 'On a Theoretical Invisibility in Forced Migration Studies', in *Journal of Refugee Studies*, vol. 21, no. 4, pp. 454–75.

Lynch, Marc (2008): 'Political Opportunity Structures: Effects of Arab Media', in Kai Hafez, ed., *Arab Media: Power and Weakness*, New York: Continuum, pp. 17–32.

———— (2013): 'Twitter Devolutions: How Social Media Is Hurting the Arab Spring', in *Foreign Policy*, 7 February, http://foreignpolicy.com/2013/02/07/twitter-devolutions/

MacKenzie, Donald (2014): 'A Sociology of Algorithms: High-Frequency Trading and the Shaping of Markets', February, http://www.maxpo.eu/Downloads/Paper_DonaldMacKenzie.pdf.

Mannheim, Karl (1928/29): 'Das Problem der Generationen', in *Kölner Vierteljahreshefte für Soziologie*, vol. 7, 157–84.

Marchart, Oliver (2013a): 'Auf dem Weg in die Prekarisierungs-gesellschaft', in Oliver Marchart, ed., *Facetten der Prekari-sierungsgesellschaft: Prekäre Verhältnisse. Sozialwissenschaftliche Perspektiven auf die Prekarisierung von Arbeit und Leben*, Biele-feld: transcript Verlag, pp. 7–20.

———— (2013b): *Die Prekarisierungsgesellschaft: Prekäre Proteste. Politik und Ökonomie im Zeichen der Prekarisierung*, Bielefeld: transcript Verlag.

Mazawi, André E., and Sultana, Ronald G. (2010): *World Yearbook of Education 2010: Education and the Arab 'World'. Political Projects, Struggles, and Geometries of Power*, London: Routledge.

Meijer, Roel, ed., (2000): *Alienation or Integration of Arab Youth: Between Family, State and Street*, Richmond: Curzon.

Milanović, Branko (2016): *Global Inequality: A New Approach for the Age of Globalization*, London: Harvard University Press.

Mitchell, Timothy (1999): 'Dreamland: The Neoliberalism of Your Desires', in *Middle East Report*, vol. 29, Spring, pp. 28–33, http://www.merip.org/mer/mer210/dreamland-neoliberalism-your-desires

Morozov, Evgeny (2011): *The Net Delusion: The Dark Side of Internet Free-dom*, New York: Public Affairs.

Müller, Herta (2002): *Marktwirtschaft und Islam: Ökonomische Entwick-lungskonzepte in der islamischen Welt unter besonderer Berücksich-tigung Algeriens und Ägyptens*, Baden-Baden: Nomos.

Mundy, Martha (2017): 'The War on Yemen and Its Agricultural Sector', Paper 50, *The Future of Food and Challenges for Agriculture in the 21st Century*, 24–26 April, http://elikadura21.eus/wp-content/uploads/2017/04/50-Mundy.pdf.

Murphy, Emma C. (2012): 'Problematizing Arab Youth: Generational Narratives of Systemic Failure', in *Mediterranean Politics,* vol. 17, pp. 5–22.

Norton, Augustus Richard, ed., (1995 and 1996): *Civil Society in the Middle East,* vols. 1 and 2, Leiden: Brill.

Offe, Claus (1984): *Contradictions of the Welfare State,* London: Hutchinson.

Ouaissa, Rachid (2012): 'Arabische Revolution und Rente', in Werner Ruf, ed., *Periplus-Jahrbuch für außereuropäische Geschichte,* Berlin:Lit Verlag. 57-77 pp. 57–77.

———— (2014a): 'Jugend Macht Revolution: Die Genealogie der Jugendproteste in Algerien', in Jörg Gertel and Rachid Ouiassa, eds, *Jugendbewegungen: Städtischer Widerstand und Umbrüche in der Arabischen Welt,* Bielefeld: transcript Verlag, pp. 114–28.

———— (2014b): *Die Rolle der Mittelschichten im Arabischen Frühling: Ein Überblick,* Wiesbaden: Springer VS.

Oxfam (2016): *Yemen's Invisible Food Crisis,* Oxford: Oxfam.

Pascon, Paul, and Bentahar, Mekki (1969): 'Ce que disent 296 ruraux', in *Bulletin Economique et Social du Maroc,* no. 11–12, pp. 1–44.

PCBS (Palestinian Central Bureau of Statistics) (2014): *Socio-Economic & Food Security Survey 2014,* State of Palestine, http://fscluster.org/state-of-palestine/document/sefsec-2014.

Pieterse, Jan Nederveen (2001): *Development Theory: Deconstructions/Reconstructions,* London: Sage.

Piketty, Thomas & Goldhammer, Arthur (2014): *Capital in the Twenty-First Century.* Cambridge Massachusetts : The Belknap Press of Harvard University Press.

Prakash, Adam, ed., (2011): *Safeguarding Food Security in Volatile Global Markets,* Rome: FAO.

Puddington, Arch, and Roylance, Tyler (2017): 'Populists and Autocrats: The Dual Threat to Global Democracy', https://freedomhouse.org/report/freedom-world/freedom-world-2017

Reckwitz, Andreas (1999): 'Anthony Giddens', in Dirk Kaesler, ed., *Klassiker der Soziologie,* vol. 2, *Von Talcott Parsons bis Anthony Giddens,* München: C. H. Beck, pp. 311–37.

Richter, Carola (2011): 'Revolutionen 2.0? Zur Rolle der Medien beim politischen Wandel in der arabischen Welt 2011', in Margret Johannsen, Bruno Schoch, Corinna Hauswedell, Tobias Debiel,

Christiane Fröhlich, eds, *Friedensgutachten 2011,* Münster: LIT, 2011, pp. 48–60.

Richter, Carola and El Difraoui, Asiem, eds, (2015): *Arabische Medien,* Konstanz: UVK.

Rooke, Tetz. (2000): 'Escape from the Family: A Theme in Arabic Autobiography', in Roel Meijer, ed., *Alienation or Integration of Arab Youth: Between Family State and Street,* Richmond: Curzon, pp. 207–23.

Sachs, Wolfgang (1992): *The Development Dictionary: A Guide to Knowledge as Power,* London – New York: Zed Books.

Salehi-Isfahani, Djavad (2008): 'Stalled Youth Transitions in the Middle East: A Framework for Policy Reform', Middle East Youth Initiative Working Paper 8.

Sassen, Saskia (2014): *Expulsions: Brutality and Complexity in the Global Economy,* Cambridge, Mass.: Belknap Press/Harvard University Press.

Schaeffer Davis, Susan, and Davis, Douglas (1989): *Adolescence in a Moroccan Town,* New Brunswick – London: Rutgers University Press.

Schulze, Reinhard (2012): 'Die Passage von politischerer Normenordnung zu lebensweltlicher Werteordnung: Erkenntnisse aus dem arabischen Frühling', in *Periplus: Jahrbuch für außereuropäische Geschichte,* Berlin: Lit Verlag, pp. 32–56.

Schwarz, Christoph H. (2017): 'Generation in Waiting" or "Precarious Generation"'? Conceptual Reflections on the Biographical Trajectories of Unemployed Graduates Activists in Morocco', in Peter Kelly and Jo Pike, eds, *Neoliberalism and Austerity: The Moral Economies of Young People's Health and Well-being,* London: Palgrave Macmillan, pp. 313–32.

Schwarz, Christoph H. and Oettler, Anika (2017): 'Editorial: Political Temporalities of Youth', in *Middle East: Topics and Arguments,* vol. 9, pp. 5–14, DOI: 10.17192/meta.2017.9.7634.

Scoones, Ian (2015): *Sustainable Livelihoods and Rural Development,* Rugby: Fernwood Publishing.

Scott, Joan W. (1991): 'The Evidence of Experience', in *Critical Inquiry,* vol. 17, no. 4, pp. 773–97.

Scott, James C. (1998): *Seeing Like a State: How Certain Schemes to Improve the Human Condition Have Failed,* New Haven and London: Yale University Press.

Sen, Amartya (1981): *Poverty and Famines: An Essay on Entitlement and Deprivation,* Oxford: Claredon Press

Sharabi, Hisham (1988): *Neopatriarchy: A Theory of Distorted Change in Arab Society,* New York: Oxford University Press.

Shell (2015): *Jugend 2015: 17. Shell Jugendstudie* (17th Shell Youth Study), Frankfurt am Main: Fischer Taschenbuch Verlag.

Simon, David, ed. (2006): *Fifty Key Thinkers on Development,* London/ New York: Routledge.

Singerman, Diane (2007): 'The Economic Imperatives of Marriage: Emerging Practices and Identities among Youth in the Middle East', Middle East Youth Initiative Working Paper 6, Wolfensohn Center for Development at Brookings/Dubai School of Government, September.

Sippel, Sarah Ruth (2015): 'Food Security or Commercial Business? Gulf State Investments in Australian Agriculture', in *Journal of Peasant Studies,* vol. 42, no. 5, 981–1001.

Stack, Carol B. (2003): 'Frameworks for Studying Families in the 21st Century', in Nicholas S. Hopkins, ed., *The New Arab Family,* Cairo: American University in Cairo Press, pp. 5–19.

Standing, Guy (2011): *The Precariat: The New Dangerous Class,* London– New York: Bloomsbury.

Sukarieh, Mayssoun (2017): 'The Rise of the Arab Youth Paradigm: A Critical Analysis of the *Arab Human Development Report 2016*', in *Middle East: Topics and Arguments,* vol. 9, pp. 70–83, DOI: 10.17192/meta.2017.9.6896.

Sukarieh, Mayssoun, and Tannock, Stuart (2016): 'On the Political Economy of Youth: A Comment', in *Journal of Youth Studies,* vol. 19, no. 9, 1281–89.

Swedenburg, Ted (2012): 'Egypt's Music of Protest: From Sayyid Darwish to DJ Haha', in *Middle East Report: Egypt: The Uprising Two Years On,* no. 265, pp. 39–43.

Taylor, Charles (2009): *Ein säkulares Zeitalter,* tr. Joachim Schulte, Frankfurt: Suhrkamp.

Tobin, Sarah (2016): *Everyday Piety: Islam and Economy in Jordan,* Ithaca: Cornell University Press.

Transfeld, Mareike, and Werenfels, Isabelle (2016): '#HashtagSolidarities: Twitter Debates and Networks in the MENA Region', *SWP Research Paper, RP5,* Berlin, https://www.swp-berlin.org/

en/publication/hashtagsolidarities-twitter-debates-and-networks-in-the-mena-region/.

UN (United Nations) (2015): *Demographic Yearbook 2014*, New York, tables 6 and 7: http://unstats.un.org/unsd/demographic/products/dyb/dyb2014.htm.

UNDP (United Nations Development Programme) (2002): *Arab Human Development Report: Creating Opportunities for Future Generations*, Amman: United Nations Publications.

———— (2009): *Development Challenges for the Arab Region: A Human Development Approach*, New York: UNDP.

———— (2016): *Arab Human Development Report 2016: Youth and the Prospects for Human Development in a Changing Reality*, Beirut: UNDP.

Urry, John (2000): *Sociology Beyond Societies: Mobilities for the Twenty-First-Century*, London: Routledge.

Van Hear, Nicholas (2014): 'Reconsidering Migration and Class', in *International Migration Review*, vol. 48, pp. 100–21.

Van Leeuwen, R. (2000): 'The Lost Heritage: Generation Conflicts in Four Arab Novels', in R. Meijer (ed.), *Alienation or Integration of Arab Youth: Between Family State and Street*, Richmond: Curzon, pp. 189–205.

Walton, John, and Seddon, David (1994): *Free Markets and Food Riots: The Politics of Global Adjustment*, Oxford: Blackwell.

WFP (World Food Programme) (2016a): *Market Price Watch Bulletin*, September, http://documents.wfp.org/stellent/groups/public/documents/ena/wfp287851.pdf?_ga=1.105505034.844806155.1479134593.

———— (2016b): *Vulnerability Assessment of Syrian refugees in Lebanon: Food Security Findings*, http://reliefweb.int/report/lebanon/wfp-lebanon-vasyr-2016-food-security-findings.

Winckler, Onn (2005): *Arab Political Demography*, vol. 1, *Population Growth and Natalist Policies*, Brighton, Portland: Sussex Academic Press.

Yom, Sean (2015): 'Arab Civil Society after the Arab Spring: Weaker but Deeper', Middle East Institute, Washington, DC, http://www.mei.edu/content/map/arab-civil-society-after-arab-spring-weaker-deeper

Acknowledgements

We would like to thank all the young people and young adults who agreed to participate in this study and to answer our questions. Their responses form the basis of our findings. In addition, we would like to thank everyone involved in preparing, organising, conducting, and evaluating the survey. Transposing the spoken word into various analogue and digital writing systems plays an important role in knowledge generation. We are particularly grateful to the authors of the study. They made it possible to present the empirical findings in a format that makes these insights into the situation of young people from the MENA region accessible to a broader audience. We would like to thank Erena Le Heron for her proofreading work, and Gerd Kempken for the graphic design and layout – both were highly committed in reviewing linguistic consistency and preparing the illustrations for this publication.

Jörg Gertel would like to thank Leipzig University, which enabled him to provide systematic support to the research project over a two-year period and to help drive it forward. He is particularly grateful to David Kreuer, whose work has made a valuable contribution to this study from its inception. His role encompassed devising the questionnaire, extensive translation, preparation of the data, calculation of analytic variables, as well as systematic data validation in the individual chapters.

Finally, he would also like to thank Christel Eißner, Johannes Frische, Tom Heyne, Gudrun Mayer and Tamara Wyrtki from Leipzig University for their assistance in testing various questions and for fascinating discussions on interpretation of the empirical findings.

The editors, June 2018

About the Authors

MATHIAS ALBERT is professor of political science at the University of Bielefeld and a coordinator of the Shell Youth Study. In addition to youth studies, his research interests include world society theory, sociology of international relations, global conflict studies, and the geopolitics of the Polar Regions.

INES BRAUNE is assistant professor at the Center for Near and Middle Eastern Studies at the University of Marburg. She also has a background in media studies. Her research interests include youth, media practices, and everyday life and cultural studies. She is co-editor of the open access journal *Middle East Topics and Arguments*.

HELMUT DIETRICH was programme director for the Friedrich-Ebert-Stiftung in Rabat, Morocco. In this capacity he coordinated the field survey of the study and also the cooperation with local partner organisations. He has researched and published in the field of migration studies, with a focus on the Mediterranean, and has lectured at the Universities of La Manouba (Tunisia) and Oran (Algeria).

JÖRG GERTEL is professor for Arabic studies and for economic geography at the University of Leipzig. He has been associated with the Universities of Freiburg, Damascus, Cairo, Khartoum, Seattle, and Auckland, and specialises in the field of global studies with a focus on insecurity and uncertainty. His research interests include youth, food, and urban studies. He developed the questionnaire and coordinated the academic debate for *Coping with Uncertainty: Youth in the Middle East and North Africa*.

SONJA HEGASY is deputy director of the Leibniz-Zentrum Moderner Orient in Berlin. She received her MA in Middle Eastern studies and languages from Columbia University, New York, and her PhD from the Free University Berlin. Her research interests include civil society and youth movements, politics of memory, world society, and cultural globalisation.

RALF HEXEL is director of the Department for the Near/Middle East and North Africa at the Friedrich-Ebert-Stiftung. He has worked at the Foundation since 1993, holding various leading positions for projects in Europe, Africa, and the Middle East and North Africa. After receiving his PhD in Latin American literature from the University of Rostock, he worked as a consultant for German and Austrian NGOs in Africa.

DAVID KREUER is a PhD candidate at the University of Leipzig's Department of Middle East Studies and the Helmholtz Centre for Environmental Research – UFZ. His research interests include youth studies, pastoralism, and rural social change. He was involved in verifying and calculating the survey data for *Coping with Uncertainty: Youth in the Middle East and North Africa*.

RACHID OUAISSA is professor of politics at the Center for Near and Middle Eastern Studies at the University of Marburg. His main areas of research are political, economic, and societal developments in the Middle East and North Africa, the rise of Islamist movements in the region, and the role of the Arab middle class in transformation processes.

CAROLA RICHTER is professor of international communication at the Institute for Media and Communication Studies at the Free University of Berlin. She investigates media systems and communication cultures in non-Western countries, focusing on the Middle East and North Africa. She is a founding member of the Arab-European Association for Media and Communication Researchers as well as a member of the Arab-German Young Academy of Sciences and Humanities.

CHRISTOPH H. SCHWARZ is a sociologist at the Center for Near and Middle Eastern Studies (CNMS) at the University of Marburg. As a post-doctoral research fellow at that university's Research Network Reconfigurations, he is currently working on intergenerational relations in social movements in Morocco and Spain. His research interests include youth and social change, migration, gender, education, and methodology.

NADINE SIKA is an assistant professor of comparative politics at the American University in Cairo. She has been a Humboldt Foundation visiting fellow at the German Institute of International and Security Affairs in Berlin and a guest scholar at the Political Science Institute at University of Tübingen. Her latest book is *Youth Activism and Contentious Politics in Egypt: Dynamics of Continuity and Change* (2017).

THORSTEN SPENGLER is a senior consultant at Kantar Public (formerly TNS Infratest Political Research) in Berlin. He was involved in questionnaire development and data consolidation, control, and evaluation for *Coping with Uncertainty: Youth in the Middle East and North Africa*. He earned his diploma in social geography from the Technical University of Munich and an MBA in European management at London South Bank University.

FRIEDERIKE STOLLEIS is desk officer at the Department for the Near/Middle East and North Africa of the Friedrich-Ebert-Stiftung in Berlin. She holds a PhD in Near and Middle Eastern studies from the University of Bamberg and an MA in social anthropology from the University of Cologne. Her research interests include civil society, sectarianism, and conflict transformation with a focus on Syria and Lebanon.

ANN-CHRISTIN WAGNER is a PhD candidate in international development at the University of Edinburgh and is associated with the Institut Français du Proche-Orient in Amman and the Refugee Studies Centre, University of Oxford. Prior to her doctoral studies, she worked with the International Organization for Migration in Geneva. She recently conducted a year of ethnographic fieldwork with urban Syrian refugees along the Jordanian-Syrian border.

ISABELLE WERENFELS heads the Middle East and Africa Research Division at the German Institute of International and Security Affairs in Berlin. She holds a PhD in political science from Humboldt University of Berlin and an MSc in development studies from SOAS University of London. Her research interests include transformation and authoritarian resilience, social media networks, and migration policies.

TAMARA WYRTKI holds a Masters Degree in Arabic Studies and another Masters in Geography; she is a PhD candidate in the Department of Geography and also a research fellow at the Collaborative Research Centre (SFB 1199) at the University of Leipzig. Her research interests include food insecurity, migration, and globalisation. She conducted background research on the countries surveyed and assisted in the pre-testing of the questionnaire for *Coping with Uncertainty – Youth in the Middle East and North Africa*.